WHAT OPERA MEANS

Elisabeth Höngen as Lucretia
(Milein Cosman, 1950)

Defining Opera

WHAT OPERA MEANS
Categories and Case-studies

Christopher Wintle

edited by
Kate Hopkins

Plumbago Books
2018

Plumbago Books and Arts
26 Iveley Road,
London SW4 OEW

plumbago@btinternet.com
www. plumbago.co.uk

Distribution and Sales:
Boydell & Brewer Ltd.
PO Box 9
Woodbridge
Suffolk IP12 3DF
UK

Boydell and Brewer Inc.
668 Mount Hope Avenue
Rochester
NY 14620
USA

What Opera Means. Categories and Case-studies
Christopher Wintle (1945-)
Edited by Kate Hopkins (1978-)
'Defining Opera', general editor Christopher Wintle

First published 2018

Logo by Mary Fedden, RA, OBE © Plumbago Books and Arts 2001

ISBN: 978-0-9931983-4-2 (hardback), 978-0-9931983-5-9 (softback)

Typeset in Adobe Minion Pro by Julian Littlewood
Musical examples typeset by Matthew Rye

Printed and bound in the United Kingdom

Contents

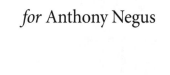

for Anthony Negus

Hans Hotter as Wotan
(Milein Cosman, 1948)

Author's Preface

This book was born of crisis. In October 1986 I read a paper to an opera conference at Cornell University. The conference went well, and yielded a book that is still read.[1] Yet as I listened to speaker after speaker, I sensed a problem. For all their merits, the papers seemed to lack a ground-plan for the understanding of opera. True, the conference was devoted to 'opera libretti of the later nineteenth century', so if there was a problem it was mine – and true too, I had been brought there to talk about words *and* music. Yet, I thought, if 'libretto' is just one in a complex of elements that make up opera, it ought not to stand alone. It should be 'dialectically engaged' with the other elements; it should be part of a holistic ground-plan. But what would a model of dialectic engagement look like? Certainly not like the formalist models that had straight-jacketed music theory over the twentieth century: the humanist tenor of the Cornell conference had already militated against that. But rather it might offer a taut but flexible dialectical framework that included useful sub-categories ranging from the general to the particular. 'Libretto' would no longer be a matter of words alone, but would rather embrace music, stagecraft and performance. Such a framework, I concluded (admittedly wearing a rather high hat), would both anchor and liberate debate: the medium would stand revealed! Yet things were not that simple; and ever since 'Cornell' I have wrestled with my crisis. This book takes a first step in resolving it.[2]

I begin by defining two kinds of readership for the project: opera lovers who have no specialist knowledge, and connoisseurs who do – those who understand the challenges of the medium from the inside. This is a traditional distinction. At the culmination of Wagner's *Die Meistersinger von Nürnberg* (1868), Walther von Stolzing sings his prize-song before two groups: the ordinary people who are enthralled but cannot quite understand what they hear, and the mastersingers who are equally enthralled but are able to judge the song as 'well-rhymed and singable'. True, Walther has been artfully prepared by Hans Sachs. Yet in the performance he goes his own way: the dynamic interaction with both groups creates a frenzy that grips and transfigures the whole community. So there are really three parties involved: amateurs, specialists and everyone concerned – and that includes singers and players. In the final resort, opera, like theatre, is a kind of group therapy. This book is the first of a pair (the second of which has yet to be assembled). Although it is primarily for the 'opera lovers' (the amateurs) its approach paves the way for the 'connoisseurs' (the professionals), and it ends with a short selection of reviews that should serve the interests of everyone.

My title has a history. Back in the mid-1930s, the Austrian composer
Arnold Schoenberg embarked on a project to map out the topics of musical
composition. These were the general (platonic) 'ideas' that act as vehicles
through which we communicate the particular. Although he left the project
incomplete, his jottings were later assembled as the '*Gedanke* manuscript'
(*Gedanke* meaning 'Thoughts').[3] It was a bold and visionary enterprise. Yet it
was more than a lifetime's work, especially for someone who was primarily
a composer and not a theorist. One of his headings was 'Was ist Steigerung'
(What Intensification Means). Yet below it he left a blank page. So some years
ago I took it upon myself to try to write a fitting entry, and duly published the
outcome in a Dutch journal.[4] Since then I have written on a number of other
'Ideas'. So this volume takes its place in a larger project to build on Schoenberg's
initiative. Its proper title should even be in German, 'Was ist Oper' (What
Opera Means).

The Introduction starts with my own definition of opera and follows it
with a relevant case-study (from Richard Strauss). This sets the pattern for
the book: a category is isolated, and one or more case-studies give varied
instances. There is no attempt to be comprehensive: every opera tells its own
story. There are six main parts, each of which deals with a separate category
(Idea): Sources, Genre, Style, Beginning and End, Invention and Psychology.
After the third part there is an Interlude that deals with Revision – this signals
the importance of knowing that operas can appear in more than one version.
The seventh and last part deals with Performance, and has its own prologue
and epilogue. As has been said, this 'finale' is not an extra but the goal of the
project: the proof of the operatic pudding is in the operatic eating. Opera
is a branch of rhetoric ('applied oratory'), involving authors, performers
and listeners, with all the complexity that that involves. Of course, there
are categories I have not addressed – Versification, Diction, Singing, Form,
Harmony, Line, Instrumentation, Stagecraft and so forth. These belong to the
second book for 'specialists'.[5] Nevertheless I refer to them all throughout the
book. The case-studies deal with operas in repertory, and relate to courses I
gave in the University of London from the mid 1980s on. They were written in
answer to the needs of opera houses and institutions: I avoid referring to works
that audiences have never heard and are unlikely to hear. The concentration
on Wagner, Verdi, Strauss and Britten reflects my own field of specialism
(nineteenth- and twentieth-century music). I regret that I did not have the
opportunity to publish more on opera before Mozart, in which my interest is
less specialized though no less keen. Most of the case-studies have appeared
in print before, though many have been lightly re-edited or amended for the
sake of the overall coherence of this book. Only the prologue to Part Seven
appears for the first time. There are about fifty sub-sections: of these only three

require of the reader some basic knowledge of music. This is in keeping with the 'generalist' tone of this volume.

My critical touchstone is Aristotle's *Poetics*. There are three reasons why. First, many of Aristotle's concepts have stood the test of time: it is hard to deny his six essential components of drama – narrative, character, diction, argument, stagecraft and music.[6] And even when observations have been superseded, they may still embody topics for discussion. For instance, Aristotle argues that, unlike epic, 'tragedy attempts as far as possible to keep within one revolution of the sun or [only] exceed this a little'.[7] Many are the works – operas as well as plays – that have abandoned this 'unity': but 'handling time' is an enduring topic, today more then ever. Second, Aristotle lived in the heyday of Greek drama, from 384-22 BC. He was not shut off from the stage. He wanted to know what did and didn't 'work'. To follow Aristotle's empiricism is to open oneself up to one's own day; it is to follow composers and writers; it is to watch singers, conductors and directors; and it is to be at one with opera audiences. Third, to refer to Aristotle is to re-establish a distance between the past and the present that was already in place at the birth of opera a little over 400 years ago. The earliest creators of opera were mindful of him, and some of their works are still in repertory. Depth of reference is intrinsic to this medium as much as to any other. My enquiry, however, is not circumscribed by Aristotle. In particular I focus on the post-Aristotelian psychological form that has evolved over the last 150 years, and to which opera has made such a striking contribution.

CHRISTOPHER WINTLE
King's College London

Notes

Reading Opera, ed. Arthur Groos and Roger Parker, Princeton: Princeton UP, 1988. The conference was organized by the editors.

1   I was not the only delegate to want to probe the medium further. Carolyn Abbate, with whom I shared the 'Wagner platform', has since published *Unsung Voices* (Princeton: Princeton UP, 1991) and *In Search of Opera* (Princeton: Princeton UP, 2001).

2   The companion volume is *How Opera Works* (forthcoming).

3   Arnold Schoenberg, *The Musical Idea and the Logic, Technique and Art of its Presentation*, trans. and ed. Patricia Carpenter and Severine Neff, New York: Columbia UP, 1995.

4   'Was ist Steigerung' appears in definitive form as 'On Intensification' in: Christopher Wintle, *All the Gods*, ed. Julian Littlewood, London: Plumbago, 2006, pp. 101-10.

5   As an example of my specialist work, see: 'The Dye-line Rehearsal Scores for *Death in Venice*', *Remembering Britten*, ed. Philip Rupprecht, New York: Oxford UP, 2013, pp. 262-83.

6   Aristotle, *Poetics*, trans. and ed. Richard Janko, Indianapolis: Hackett, 1987, p. 8.

7   *Ibid.*, p. 7.

Acknowledgments

Since almost all of the entries have been published before, I owe a debt of gratitude to several commissioning editors and copy-editors: not only did they invite me to write, but they also helped in developing ideas and sharpening expression. The earliest pieces – the reviews in Part Seven – were written in the 1980s and '90s for the *Times Literary Supplement*, where my exhilaratingly exacting editors included Lindsay Duguid, Alan Hollinghurst and Blake Morrison. These are reproduced by kind permission of the *TLS*. When the paper changed direction under a new editor, I wrote mainly for The Royal Opera, with John Snelson as an unusually open-minded editor and Kate Hopkins his assiduous assistant. The Royal Opera pieces are again reproduced by kind permission. But throughout these years and after I also did work for the BBC, for Nicholas John at the English National Opera (his premature death was a great loss), for the Glyndebourne and Longborough Festival Operas, as well as for schools, universities and learned societies. I even acted briefly as a deputy opera critic to Andrew Porter at the *Observer*. All these have brought benefits. As an 'outsider', I am especially pleased to have been able to talk to the British Psychoanalytic Society, and my thanks are due to Michael Parsons and Gerald Wooster for making this possible: Part Six on 'Psychology' shows the fruit of such interest. I know, and have worked with, three of the modern composers I discuss: Alexander Goehr, George Benjamin and Judith Weir. I have had many talks with Harrison Birtwistle, a composer and former colleague at King's College London. And through my academic work in Aldeburgh I have learnt how Benjamin Britten worked: for his sustained support in this I am indebted to the late Donald Mitchell of the Britten Estate.

Finally I thank my editor, Kate Hopkins, who has worked long and hard at the text, the ever-obliging Plumbago type-setter, Julian Littlewood, and the music type-setter, Matthew Rye. The cover image shows Solveig Kringelborn as Countess Madeleine in Richard Strauss's *Capriccio* in a production by Robert Carsen at the Opéra Garnier (Paris). The photograph was taken on 6 September 2007 and appears by agreement with Colette Masson/Roger-Viollet/ArenaPAL. The drawings by Milein Cosman appear by agreement with The Cosman Keller Art and Music Trust.

CW

Editor's Preface

The questions 'what is opera's role in society?', 'who is the natural audience for opera?' and 'why does opera matter?' preoccupy many of today's opera companies, performers and audiences. Behind these stands an even more important question: 'what is the nature of opera?' It is this that Christopher Wintle addresses in his new book, the third in a series of monographs entitled *Defining Opera* launched by Plumbago Books in 2015. Rather than writing yet another history of the art form, Wintle resolves the component parts of opera into distinct categories and supports them with case-studies. These case-studies discuss key operas by Mozart, Verdi, Wagner, Richard Strauss and Britten, along with some lesser-known and contemporary works. They also take care to document each entry: this is a book that uses history rather than rejects it.

Most of the entries have appeared in print before, though in a variety of sources, each with its own house style. So I have attempted to create a consistent style of my own, making minor alterations in addition to the adjustments already made by the author. The headers for each entry give the names of both librettist and composer, as well as an indication of source; I refer to performances at the 'Royal Opera House' or 'Covent Garden' as staged by 'The Royal Opera' (the resident company); wherever possible I give works their original language titles, though occasionally I allow anglicized versions; and I replace 'opera producer' with 'opera director', since the former is now obsolete.

Readers can use the book in a variety of ways. General opera lovers, performers and specialists can dip in as they please and follow their reading with listening before pursuing the relevant topics in works of their own choice. However, the clear demarcation into categories could also make it the basis of weekly seminars in a college programme – indeed, it could usefully complement a conventional course on the history of opera. As Wintle is one of the few writers still to apply psychology to opera, interested readers may be drawn to two entries in Part Six. Both originated in talks: 'Freud on Opera' to the North London Collegiate School for Girls, Edgware and 'Rigoletto's Bottle' to the British Psychoanalytic Society. Performers and directors (established or aspiring) may find the opening entry in Part Seven, 'Alternative Rhetorics', especially thought-provoking: this includes the ironic 'Ten Commandments for the Modern Opera Director'.

KATE HOPKINS
London

Introduction

1 *Defining Opera*

At university we were taught that opera (*'a work'*) *is short for* opera in musica (*'a work rendered in music'*), *and that the term exists in all languages. We also learnt that the earliest operas had various subtitles –* favola in musica (*a story put to music*), dramma per musica (*a drama told through music*) *or whatever.*[1] *Yet the definitions struck me, then as now, as unfit for purpose: the title begins with the work, drama or story which is rendered through music, whereas it is the musical handling to which we attach equal if not more value; and the earliest subtitles conspicuously lack reference to what turned works into 'operas', namely singing. This was, and has remained, essential to the medium. But for all the efforts of generations of scribes, no better term has emerged.*[2] *It seems we are stuck with* opera. *Yet if we are to investigate the medium, as I do here, we need to start with a definition that is fit for purpose – one that should hold good for the future as much as it does for the past (or so we hope).*

My starting point is not to take the harmony of drama and music – words and singing – for granted, as in the popular definition of opera as 'sung drama'. Rather, I see them as rival forces working together for a common good. Again I go back to my university days. The philosopher Isaiah Berlin (whom I met just once) argued that there can be a dialectic field that it is imperative not to resolve, but merely to handle: one party must *not be allowed to win through at the expense of another. Others have written in the same vein. Accordingly I have recast 'opera' as a paradox: music and drama have distinct uses and procedures that often do not mesh, but through a subtle union – a kind of marriage of convenience – can achieve extraordinary effects that would otherwise be unattainable. But the pre-eminence of singing remains. Indeed, when W. H. Auden pondered what need opera serves, he started with the voice. To sing, he argued, is to answer the human need to give universal expression to emotion – and, many would say, to allow art the pleasure of creating that emotion: 'For singing is a form of public outcry: it is on the voluntary level what an ouch of pain or the howl of a hungry baby is on the involuntary.' Opera began when ecclesiastical counterpoint (polyphony) yielded to secular accompanied singing (monody), so its voluntary outcry was both a birth-cry and a cry of liberation.*[3]

Here is my attempt to define what 'opera' means.

Opera is an irreducible field of forces comprising three elements: dramatized music, musicalized drama and the transfiguring power of music and drama working in tandem. All three are governed by song.

1   *Dramatized music* presupposes *fine singing*, whereas relatively untrained singing belongs to popular types such as the musical (or 'musical comedy'). The singing may be for individuals, small ensembles or choruses, and is most dramatic at its most interactive; it requires virtuosity; it may be on-stage or off-stage; and it is normally supported by instruments, which must also be finely played.[4] But sometimes we find instrumental music alone, as in free-standing overtures, interludes and recurrent music; and since music itself has three principal sources – song, dance and mimesis[5] – it may also accompany *ballet* (including less-refined dances) and imitate *Nature* – especially storms and animals – though this often sounds more anthropomorphic than natural.[6] In general, the music may draw on the self-sufficient forms and procedures heard in the concert-hall, in choral and instrumental music as well as in song (which has it own verse-forms); and it also moves at its own speed – normally slower than drama. But once transposed to the theatre, the relatively 'abstract' forms and procedures acquire dramatic purpose, something best achieved through a bespoke libretto.[7]

2   *Musicalized drama*, by contrast, is a staged representation that is wholly or predominantly sung, and can start from a play rather than a bespoke libretto. Mixed representation that alternates between speech and singing has its own classifications – *opéra comique*, ballad opera, operetta, *Singspiel* and so forth – and is differentiated again from a play-with-songs by the scale of the 'numbers' and the character of the singing. Nevertheless, as word turns into music there can be gradations of vocal delivery: from shouting to 'speech-song', from singing to vocalise, with many ranges and voice-types.[8] The purpose of singing rather than speaking is to reveal 'the music behind the words'. Whereas in conventional drama this 'music' is latent, and needs to be conveyed by tone of voice, intensity of feeling and gesture, in opera it is made manifest. Feeling comes to the fore. Music can also expand the range, intensity and character of the normal speaking voice, especially with the help of the accompaniment; it can replicate and amplify theatrical gesture; and it can fill an empty stage with character. In fully through-composed operas, it determines the pacing and emphasis that in normal drama is generated solely by the actors.[9]

3   *The transfiguring power of music and drama working in tandem* is evident in three pre-eminent ways: when it invests gods and heroes with numinosity and authority; when it gives voice to the wonder of the people; and when it supports spectacle. To transfigure is to admit superstition, and superstition

presupposes uncanny force. Such music allows rational man to connect with his primitive roots and all their hopes and fears, and to be ever more aware of his role as an individual in a larger collective. Of course, not all operas include the marvellous, though its presence does not necessarily classify the medium as 'an exotick and irrational entertainment', as Johnson put it. On the contrary, spectacle was one of Aristotle's six conditions of drama,[10] and in opera musicalized spectacle bonds uniquely with dramatized music and musicalized drama. It thus integrates as much as it diverts. Several sub-genres of opera give priority to spectacle, especially when it involves dance – masque, semi-opera, *ballet de cour, divertissement, pastorale, comédie-ballet, opéra-ballet* and so forth. Where there is no *transfiguring power* – in effect magic – an audience will ask why a particular drama or set of musical pieces even needs to be cast as opera.

To say that *all three elements are governed by song* is to acknowledge that the medium is governed by singers. It is they above all who have the ability to enthral and move. Although fashion may give priority to conductors, producers, designers or whoever, it was virtuoso singing that launched opera, and it is live virtuoso singing with all its beauty of tone, skill and dramatic agility that keeps it afloat.[11]

Notes

1   The teacher of opera at Oxford University during the 1960s was Sir Jack Westrup. In his *Encyclopedia* he defines opera as 'A dramatic work in which the whole, or the greater part, of the text is sung with instrumental accompaniment.' ('Dramatic' derives via late Latin from the Greek *dran*, 'to do or act'.) A later Oxford Professor of Music, Reinhard Strohm, writes that the usual generic name for Italian operas from the seventeenth to the early nineteenth centuries was not *opera* but *dramma per musica* (a play through music), *dramma da recitarsi in musica* (a play to be recited in music), *dramma da cantarsi* (a play to be sung) or simply *melodramma*, 'which alluded to the concept of *melos* [music] in Greek antiquity'. However, the philosopher Bernard Williams begins his disquisition on opera with a realistic qualification: 'Opera is by definition staged sung drama, but that leaves many questions unresolved ...' See: J. A. Westrup and F. Ll. Harrison, *Collins Music Encyclopedia*, London: Collins, 1959, pp. 464-9; Reinhard Strohm, *Dramma per Musica. Italian Opera Seria of the Eighteenth Century*, New Haven: Yale UP, 1997, p. 1; Bernard Williams, *On Opera*, New Haven: Yale UP, 2006, p. 1.

2   As an Englishman I turn at once to Samuel Johnson, who writes in his *Dictionary* of 1755: 'An opera is a poetical tale or fiction, represented by vocal and instrumental music, adorned with scenes, machines and dancing.' For a source he cites John Dryden: 'You will hear what plays were acted that week, which is the finest song in the opera.' The citation comes from Dryden's preface to *Albion and Albanius* (1685). Dryden accurately describes this as 'the first all-sung, full-length English opera for which the music [by Louis Grabu] survives'. However, for a more estimable 'first' we might look

to shorter works such as John Blow's *Venus and Adonis* (*c.* 1683) and Henry Purcell's *Dido and Aeneas* (*c.* 1689). We should also acknowledge a handful of semi-operas – plays with at least four episodes or masques – including Purcell's *Dioclesian* (1690), *King Arthur* (1691) and *The Fairy-Queen* (1692). These point to our own operatic pre-history in Elizabethan and Jacobean court entertainments. Johnson's definition has the merit of leaving the topics of opera open: a tale based on either fact or fiction, told in the heightened diction of poetry. In the European tradition this would embrace Ovid's Greco-Roman *Metamorphoses*, Ludovico Ariosto's *Orlando furioso* (1532) and Torquato Tasso's *Gerusalemme liberata* (1581) as well as a line of historical dramas stemming from Monteverdi's *L'incoronazione di Poppea* (1643). But he could – and perhaps should – have extended it to include sacred enactment, *sacra rappresentatione*. This, after all, preceded opera, was 'still around' at opera's official birth in 1597 with Emilio de' Cavalieri's *Rappresentatione di anima e di corpo* of 1600, and has survived ever since in both church and theatre. See: Samuel Johnson, *Dictionary of the English Language*, Librairie du Liban, Vol. 2, 1755.

3   See 'The World of Opera' (1968) in: W. H. Auden, *Secondary Worlds,* London: Faber and Faber, 1968, pp. 76-102. See also: 'Some Reflections on Music and Opera' (1952), *The Complete Works of W. H. Auden, vol. III: Prose 1949-1955*, London: Faber and Faber, 2008, pp. 296-302. Giulio Caccini explains in his *Nuove musiche* of 1602 how the earliest operas set out to promote a new lyric declamation (*recitative*, after 'recitation'). This allows singers clear enunciation of unprecedented flexibility. The semi-improvised accompaniment is raised over a fully-determined 'figured bass'.

4   The late twentieth century saw the emergence of a number of miniature operas for unaccompanied solo voice, including the thirteen-minute *King Harald's Saga* (1979) by Judith Weir. But in general it is hard not to miss instruments in these works.

5   There are also the elemental sources available through electronic music, though in the opera house their effect is usually anthropomorphic – they sound like highly abstracted song, movement or mimesis. Electronics have entered opera in works of Karlheinz Stockhausen, Harrison Birtwistle, Jonathan Harvey and Georg Friedrich Haas, but are problematic in that they necessarily determine the tempo to which the singers and players must respond, and not vice versa.

6   It is possible to construct an operatic bestiary, starting with the cats' duet from Ravel's *L'Enfant et les sortilèges* (1925). However, in a radio interview with Hans Keller, W. H. Auden maintained that 'music cannot imitate nature: a musical storm always sounds like the wrath of Zeus' (1971).

7   Oratorio, which can outwardly share the forms and procedures of opera, differs in that it has no need of costume and make-up. Many operas, of course, can hold their own in concert or semi-staged performance because they are dramatized music as much as, if not more than, musicalized drama.

8   Indeed, Thomas Allen has described singing as 'civilized shouting'.

9   The modern genre of 'music theatre' rebalances the operatic mix in favour of drama. A striking example is *Eight Songs for a Mad King* (1969) to music by Peter Maxwell Davies. Of this, the French composer Olivier Messiaen said it was 'not an opera' and 'unfair to the birds' (personal communication from Peter Maxwell Davies). In some of his generic subtitles Davies alternated 'masque' and 'music theatre'.

10 In the *Poetics* Aristotle asks that drama should have a plot, characters, diction, reasoning, spectacle and music (song). In the introduction to his *Sant'Alessio* (1634), Steffano Landi writes: 'But of the staging, which Aristotle truly allocates to the last [*sic*]

part [of his requirements] but which is nonetheless so important that – as he says – it often takes the prize, what shall I say? The first introduction of new Rome, the flight of the Angel among the clouds, the appearance of Religion in the air, were works of artistry and of machinery vying with nature. The stage [was] most artful; the vistas of heaven and of the inferno wondrous; the changes of the wings and of the backdrop ever more beautiful; but the last one of the [saint's] passing and of the luminous darkness of that portico, with the distant vista of the garden, incomparable.' The costumes were likewise 'sumptuous, opulent, delightful, varied, antique, appropriate and suited to those who wore them' and the dances 'ingenious and lively'. See: Aristotle, *Poetics*, trans. and ed. Richard Janko, Indianapolis: Hackett, 1987, p. 8; and Steffano Landi, 'Il S[ant']Alessio', *Composing Opera. From 'Dafne' to 'Ulisse errante'*, trans. Tim Carter, Kraków: Musica Iagellonica, 1994, pp. 127-35

11 The story of the evolution of the brain reinforces and extends the notion of an irreducible field of forces at the heart of opera. Rupert Sheldrake writes: 'Whereas rhythms are primarily linked to the brain stem and cerebellum, melodies are primarily processed in the right hemisphere of the cerebral cortex, the opposite side of the brain from the primary language-processing areas. And not surprisingly, pleasurable music also activates regions of the brain (in the mesolimbic system) that are involved in arousal and the experience of pleasure.' Rupert Sheldrake, *Science and Spiritual Practices*, London: Coronet, 2017, pp. 148-9.

2 *Opera Defining Opera*

Clemens Krauss and Richard Strauss: *Capriccio*

Consciously or not, every author and composer of a new opera positions their work in the operatic force-field. This is true even if they are merely following the practice of a style, school or sub-genre. Richard Strauss's last work, the one-act Capriccio, *did so more consciously, perhaps, than any other opera. Conceived in the late 1930s, a few years after the death of Hugo von Hofmannsthal in 1929, it was first staged in 1942, during the Second World War. Like his* Ariadne auf Naxos (1912/16), *it dealt with a drama-within-a-drama, though from a new angle: it adapted a tradition of making the art-work self-referential by addressing the nature of the art itself. Not surprisingly, it bears the subtitle, 'A Conversation-piece for Music'. But the initial collaboration between Strauss and his chosen librettist, Stefan Zweig, fell foul of the National Socialists: the project was perforce continued with a new librettist, first Joseph Gregor and then Clemens Krauss (the work's conductor). The searching correspondence between Strauss and Krauss that ensued stands as a counterpart to the dealings of Composer and Poet in the opera. But the project also synthesized past and present by establishing a late eighteenth-century milieu, the era of the operatic-reform-composer Gluck, and then by building forward to the 1940s, absorbing procedures learnt from Mozart, Wagner and others. But in surreptitiously representing the 1940s, Strauss had an agenda of his own: he wanted to face down the frippery of his times. According to our definition of opera, the question whether word or music has priority cannot, and must not, be answered. Yet, guided by a definition of E. T. A. Hoffmann's, Strauss felt that he had come to a resolution of a kind. Even though we might think of it as a third element in a force-field rather than a resolution of the other two elements, his handling of it in* Capriccio *comes close to this book's demand for opera to exercise some kind of transfiguring power.*

1 *From Zweig to Gregor*

To the popular mind, Richard Strauss's *Capriccio* (1942), his 'final' work in one act and thirteen scenes, belongs to that class of opera concerned with the poetics and metapoetics – the making and aesthetics – of opera: Wagner's *Die Meistersinger von Nürnberg* (1868), Pfitzner's *Palestrina* (1917), Schoenberg's *Moses und Aron* (1932/57), Hindemith's *Mathis der Maler* (1938) and Britten's Mann-based *Death in Venice* (1973). It is not a class, of course, that stops with opera – or even theatre (Pirandello) – but one that extends to musicals. In Sondheim's show-biz *Merrily We Roll Along* (1981), the Producer, asked 'which comes first: the words or the music?', replies 'generally, the contract.' In Strauss's opera, the characters ask the same question, only in a Janus-faced context. *Capriccio* builds on its great German predecessors; but by setting itself in '*a chateau near Paris at the time Gluck was reforming opera. Around 1775*', a year after the premiere of *Iphigénie en Aulide*, it also reaches back to a classical, Franco-Italian past close to Strauss's heart. Although it brings together the operatic dialectics of Gluck's day and his own, with copious textual and musical allusions, it outwardly offers no resolution to its central aesthetic and dramatic problems. Yet by the end the work inwardly feels resolved: how can this be?

Completed on 3 August 1941, *Capriccio* (Caprice) was first performed in Munich on 28 October 1942. Yet it is a brainchild of the previous decade. In late 1933, Stefan Zweig, dapper librettist of Strauss's *Die schweigsame Frau* (1935) and *éminence grise* behind several of his post-Hofmannsthal projects, had come across two volumes of libretti by Abbé Giambattista [de] Casti (1724-1803) in the British Museum. These included a short one-act farce, *Prima la musica e poi le parole* (First the Music and then the Words). Originally set to music by Salieri and performed in 1786 at Schönbrunn (near Vienna), it appeared in the same event as *Der Schauspieldirektor* – Mozart's comic, partly spoken occasional piece about an impresario, two squabbling sopranos, a tenor and several actors. Zweig deemed *Prima la musica …* a good starting point for a light comedy (which would eventually include a producer, two squabbling men, a soprano and an actress). Strauss, who had 'read a lot about de Casti in da Ponte's memoirs' and who may or may not have known that Casti's librettist was a parody of da Ponte, leapt at the idea. He also directed Zweig to two essays by E. T. A. Hoffmann, one of which holds the key to the finished work (as we shall see).

However, as a Jew, Zweig was affected by the deteriorating political situation; and in 1935, after the Nazis' interception of an exasperated letter from Strauss ('Do you believe that Mozart composed as an "Aryan"? I know only two types of people: those with and those without talent'), thought it best to join forces with Joseph Gregor.[1] Gregor was a less-than-wholly admired Viennese professor who became librettist for the composer's *Friedenstag* (1938), *Daphne* (1938) and *Die Liebe der Danae* (1940/44). In Strauss's eyes, his crime was to lack 'the ultimate, the decisive'. By the lake of Zurich, and in a frenzy of 'wild dionysiac poetics', Zweig and Gregor produced a draft scenario, inventing La Roche as a 'blunt caricature' of Max Reinhardt, the director and 'revered' dedicatee of the Strauss-Hofmannsthal *Ariadne auf Naxos*. Gregor alone dispatched the draft to Strauss. The composer, who had himself much to say on Goethe, Mozart, Wagner and Verdi, spotted the joint hand. He was disappointed, and despite repeated reworkings, brought the project to a halt. Indeed, in 1939 he tactfully, if guiltily, dropped Gregor (though for a time still thinking of *Capriccio* as a potential curtain-raiser to *Daphne*). Instead, he teamed up with Clemens Krauss, the conductor with whom he had been corresponding on the minutiae of his works from *Die ägyptische Helena* (1928) on. Krauss responded by delivering many volumes of French plays. Strauss was delighted: he was in search of Gallic wit. But he also hankered for the dry logic so appealing to older composers: after all, hadn't Verdi closed *his* final work, *Falstaff*, with a fugue? 'First the form, and then the feeling' would, in effect, be his priority.

2 Strauss and Krauss

For the next decade, Strauss and Krauss sustained a correspondence that ranks among the most fascinating between any composer and librettist.[2] They exchanged scenarios, trawled for sources and refined texts; they discussed line-lengths and musical genres; they honed stagecraft ('good exits are the hardest to write' sighed Krauss, devoting the whole of Scene 10 to the departure of six characters); they pondered lighting (for the Prompter in Scene 12, wrote Strauss, it must get 'spookily' dark); they turned over the 'eccentric' Shavian subtitle ('a conversation piece for music'); and they fine-tuned diction, with Strauss asking for a very free and novel approach to declamation and rhythm, and Krauss for the Director to add 'a bit more pomp' to Clairon's arrival by hailing 'Andromache, Phaedra …' and so forth. Strauss privately thought of himself in the driving seat, though clearly both men held the reins.

The correspondence, moreover, shadowed the Composer-Poet exchanges within the opera, even though Strauss had much to say about the words and Krauss about the music. In Scene 2, for instance, Krauss resisted Strauss's idea that the Count and Countess should together sing 'Brother and sister, united in joy!': 'a little like the *Valkyrie*' he complained. On the other hand, Krauss explained how, in writing Scene 7, he had had in mind Erik's narrative from Wagner's *Der fliegende Holländer*. The composer Flamand, alone with the young widowed Countess, tells how he first watched her, unnoticed, in the library. Whereas Wagner's Erik had asked 'Don't you want to remember that day …?', Flamand declares 'This love, suddenly born that afternoon …'. Krauss originally had Flamand's aria reach its climax with words (by Krauss) from the book she was reading: 'Love has no age, it is always growing.' He later replaced this with a tart epigram from Pascal (c. 1650): 'In love silence is better than speech.' This allowed the Countess's riposte, again from Pascal: 'The joy of love has thorns, but also sweetness.' Flamand withdraws, and the Countess 'remains alone on stage visibly moved'. Here Krauss again steps into the space of the composer by asking for a purely 'orchestral postlude' – a canny request, since the extension of song by wordless music was a speciality of Strauss (witness the closing trio of *Der Rosenkavalier*).

The opera turns on the 'big discussion' of Scene 9, over which the two collaborators worked tirelessly. At its start the Director (La Roche) and others return from rehearsal. On the one hand, Strauss subtly celebrates the very types the 'stage moderns' hope to supersede: three neo-classical pieces for a young dancer (Passepied, Gigue and Gavotte) – pieces that reflected Strauss's work at the time on a Couperin Divertimento (1940-1); a 'Fugue', led by the Poet but continued in the orchestra (there is no vocal polyphony) answering to Strauss's demand for 'a theatre of intellect'; and a duet for two Italian singers on a text by Pietro Metastasio (1698-1782) that asserts the power of *bel canto* that Strauss evidently felt and admired. On the other hand, he has the boastful chattering of the Director and the Actress's dismissal of the Poet push the dances into the background; an orchestral interpolation into the Fugue for the Countess's paean to Gluck finds Strauss doffing his hat to his predecessor by using his own *Krämerspiegel* song – the same that will open the moonlit final scene; and the Countess puts down the rapturous Italian duet for its poor match of words and music. Krauss had been far from sidelined. The dazzling octet that soon follows falls into two parts: the company laughs first at the Director's proposal for an (old-fashioned) allegory on the birth of Pallas Athene from the head of Zeus, and then at his plans for a heroic spectacle on the Fall of Carthage. For his part, Krauss was careful to calibrate the level of humour, setting out the rapid exchanges 'vividly'; whereas Strauss drew on the great ensembles in Mozart's *Figaro* and Wagner's *Meistersinger* to ensure that the hilarity peaked when the Italian singers joined in. Only musicians who knew these works 'as well as the two of us,' wrote Strauss proudly on 7 March 1940, 'could do such things'.

But composer and librettist were divided about the Director's immediate response. Strauss was determined that La Roche's vision for the future of opera should involve, not Greek or Biblical heroes, but rather subjects from the life of the people. These should evince 'indigenous feeling', as did the works of Molière and Goldoni; indeed, by lamenting the general decline of cultural taste, La Roche would act as a mouthpiece for Strauss, whose 'heart' yearned to express the cultural danger emanating 'from films and from Lehár and his gang'. Krauss, though, was alarmed. 'In your draft,' he wrote, '[the Director] is an entirely serious character'; whereas he, Krauss, thought of him as an entirely comic one. After all, La Roche had to take his place in the scheme of things: in 1775, the enlightened Poet and the passionate, high-minded Composer would have been the moderns, whereas La Roche was the traditionalist. Moreover, La Roche's response was fundamentally an act of self-defence, with its comic tone serving to drain the octet's aggression. If the response was long, it was because it had to move from rage to pathos, to seriousness, to solemn request, to vanity and back to parody (for the imaginary inscription on his gravestone): it was thus vital that no-one should interrupt. Strauss duly complied, though only after changes; yet in the music he still preserves something of the seriousness of La Roche's message. Even the Countess, closet arbiter of the 'sharp dispute', applauds.

3 E. T. A. Hoffmann

In a letter of 26 October 1939, Krauss suggested that in the closing scene the Countess should go to the keyboard and sing the music for the sonnet she finds there; later, he had her accompanying herself at the harp. It was a change that completed a large-scale strategy. The sonnet, a love poem by the sixteenth-century writer Pierre de Ronsard, had been chosen by Krauss's friend Hans Swarowsky in the absence of any suitable 'period' alternative: it is addressed to a chaste Florentine lady (Cassandra Salviati) and begins 'No other so burns in my heart, / No, my Beauty, none in this whole wide world.' First declaimed by the Count in a reduced version ('so it doesn't go on too long' warned Strauss), it is then spoken in full by the Poet, with the Composer improvising a setting at the keyboard; a little later, it recurs fully set and performed by the Composer – a subtly phrased piece in a rich key and sensuous waltz-time. Composer, Poet and Countess react in a wondrous trio.

In the closing scene, therefore, the Countess has to extend this rapturous progress from speech to song. This she does at the words 'life or death'. In a different key and metre she now interpolates thoughts of her own, amplifying her remarks in the 'big discussion': 'Words and notes are fused into a single new creation,' she sings, 'the secret of the hour – one art redeemed by another!' She then completes the sonnet. This quasi-Hegelian raising of the words-versus-music antithesis to a higher level chimes in with one of the essays by E. T. A. Hoffmann that Strauss had recommended to Zweig, 'The Poet and the Composer' (1813). To the approval of the Poet, Hoffmann's Composer talks of a paradise where 'poets and musicians are closely kindred members of *one* church' since 'the secret of words and sounds is one and the same, unveiling to both the ultimate sublimity'. True, there remain the Countess's terrestrial problems. She still has to sort out her rival suitors, the poet Olivier and the composer Flamand, and provide them with an end to their 'opera' that her brother, the Count, has proposed: these dialectics are likely to remain unresolved – indeed, the anguish they generate brings her monologue to a head. But *Capriccio's* wry but charming close, a much-postponed perfect cadence, confirms that, although in their letters Strauss and Krauss conversed as two, through their work they became, 'sublimely', one.

Notes

Source: 'Wild Dionysiac Poetics', *Capriccio*, (Richard Strauss), The Royal Opera programme, July 2013, pp. 16-21.

1   For an account of the episode, see 'The History of *Die schweigsame Frau*' (Richard Strauss) in: *A Confidential Matter. The Letters of Richard Strauss and Stefan Zweig, 1931-1935*, trans. Max Knight, Berkeley: California UP, 1977, pp. 107-10.
2   The Strauss-Krauss correspondence has yet to appear in English.

Part One

Sources

1 *Rising to the Occasion*
Antonio Ghislanzoni (after Mariette and Du Locle) and Giuseppe Verdi: *Aida*

Our enquiry begins where opera itself begins – with a work's source or sources. Here already a dialectic field emerges. The librettist will look for a narrative framework, whereas the composer will search out opportunities for music. Both bring experience and knowledge to the task. But even before this, there is the question of cost. Operas are expensive, and grand operas need grand commissions. But at what point do the demands of a public, occasional opera dissolve into the creative – and largely private – expectations of librettists and composers? Unless creators feel that 'there is something in it for them', they may do no more than imitate themselves and pocket the fee.

There are fewer operas more grandly occasional than Aida, and fewer stories more extraordinary than that of the massive turn-round on the part of the composer from lack of interest to intense involvement. Inspiration may come during the creative process: it does not have to initiate it. Still, Verdi recognized that aspects of the project were 'not very new'. So the challenge was all the keener: he would have felt honour-bound to use the source to surpass his own musical achievements. Did he succeed? The great Verdi scholar Julian Budden maintained – plausibly – that, although number-for-number Aida is more achieved than its predecessor Don Carlos, nevertheless Don Carlos (to which we shall return elsewhere) remains more compelling: the Grand March counts for less than the auto-da-fé. Yet Aida may owe its still considerable effect to the very effort it took Verdi to rise to the occasion. In this case-study especially we monitor the pre-natal stages of the medium.

A lavish fee apart, what was in it for Giuseppe Verdi to write *Aida* in 1870 and '71? After all, he had only recently completed *Don Carlos* (1867) for the Paris Opéra and little of interest had come up since. And why try another grand opera? He was now in his late fifties with over 25 years of experience and nothing left to prove: there had been the work of the 'galley years', including *Nabucco* (1842), *Ernani* (1844) and *Macbeth* (1847); a string of pieces that played off public duty against private inclination, ranging from *Luisa Miller* (1849) and *Stiffelio* (1850) to the consummately achieved *Rigoletto* (1851), *Il trovatore* (1853) and *La traviata* (1853); and after that, four challenging masterpieces of distinct character, *Les Vêpres siciliennes* (1855), *Simon Boccanegra* (1857), *Un ballo in maschera* (1859) and *La forza del destino* (1862). True, there would be

an Indian summer ushered in by a new librettist, Arrigo Boito; but this would
be much later, yielding the inspired revision of *Simon Boccanegra* (1881) and
the no less inspired *Otello* (1887) and *Falstaff* (1893). Surely, if ever there was a
time to let go, it was now?

For an answer we must turn to the Middle East. In 1866, Auguste Mariette,
a French writer and archaeologist based in Cairo, had travelled through
Upper Egypt collecting material for a short story, *La Fiancée du Nil*; in 1867, he
took leave in Paris, where he met up with one of the librettists of *Don Carlos*,
Camille du Locle. Du Locle duly paid a visit to Egypt in 1868 and reported back
enthusiastically to Verdi, who at the time was in Genoa. Verdi was unmoved:
'A country which once had a greatness and a civilization I have never been able
to admire,' he wrote laconically. But the Egyptians had Verdi in their sights.
First, the general manager of the new Cairo Opera invited him to compose a
hymn for the opening of the Suez Canal, an invitation Verdi turned down: 'it is
not my custom,' he remarked dryly, 'to compose occasional pieces'. The opera
house and canal were duly inaugurated in November 1869 with a performance
of *Rigoletto*. Then du Locle pestered Verdi for a new work for the Paris Opéra.
Again Verdi resisted: in Paris there were too many cooks trying to spoil the
broth; he wasn't accorded the respect he enjoyed in Italy; he wanted to be the
one and only author; and, in any case, hadn't even the genius of Rossini been
compromised by the 'fatal atmosphere', the whole system of '*la grande boutique*'
(the Opéra)? Finally, late in 1869, du Locle conveyed an invitation to compose
an opera for Cairo from the Viceroy of Egypt himself. The Viceroy envisaged
something sumptuous on an ancient Egyptian theme with sets and costumes
to match. No expense would be spared. Still Verdi showed no interest – and
besides, even though there was a company of Italian singers there, he couldn't
face the sea trip to Cairo. 'Extremely annoyed and chagrined,' the Viceroy
offered to hold the rehearsals 'in Paris or Milan, at the maestro's choice,' using
singers Verdi wanted, on terms of Verdi's choosing. Du Locle pressed Verdi
as never before: 'there might be a nice farm or a nice palace in Genoa out of
this business,' he wrote, 'if you ask for [a pyramid] as a bonus (the biggest, of
course), they may be inclined to give it to you …'

What changed Verdi's mind, though, was the synopsis of the proposed plot.
This had been drawn up by Mariette himself, using an authentic Egyptian name
for the Ethiopian slave girl Aida (softened from Aïta for ease of singing). Verdi
was much impressed. He could see it offered 'a splendid *mise-en-scène*' with
'two or three situations which, if not very new, are certainly very beautiful'. 'But
who did it?' he asked (he knew nothing of Mariette): 'There is a very expert
hand in it, one accustomed to writing … who knows the theatre well.' Out of
this he could indeed see his way to an Italian libretto. He duly set his terms –
he would be paid 150,000 francs and retain 'the rights' outside Egypt – and the
Viceroy accepted, insisting the work be completed for Cairo by January 1871

and allowing Verdi to mount the piece in French whenever the Paris Opéra reopened. It was a tight but manageable deadline.

June 1870 thus saw a flurry of activity. Du Locle travelled to Verdi's Italian home St. Agata to develop the prose scenario; the gifted librettist Antonio Ghislanzoni, who had helped with the first Italian version of *Don Carlos*, agreed to versify the prose. Intense research on Egyptian antiquity, its rites and music, was relayed to the composer, though poetic licence was allowed the upper hand (the Roman god Vulcan co-exists with the Egyptian gods, and priestesses rather than priests celebrate Isis). Mariette went to Paris to oversee sets and costumes, singers and conductors were scrutinized long and hard, and specially extended trumpets were commissioned. Verdi involved himself in the libretto as never before: he demanded of Ghislanzoni, not poetry, but incisive theatrical verses; he established the affective character of 'speeches', specified their syllabification minutely, refined diction, constantly tinkered with the emphases in scenes and acts, argued over when or when not to use conventions (cabalettas), and even added in the famous *romanza* 'Celeste Aida'. His touchstones were his own experience – *La traviata*, *Il trovatore*, *Un ballo*, *La forza*, *Don Carlos* – and tradition: he measured the mezzo range of Amneris against Léonor in Donizetti's *La Favorite* (1840) and took care to suppress any reminiscences of Bellini's priestess-ridden *Norma* (1831). In the meantime the Franco-Prussian War had broken out; and although Verdi had essentially finished the composition by December 1870, Paris was under siege and the sets and costumes were unattainable. So the Cairo premiere had to wait until 24 December 1871. The performance was a triumph, Verdi was invested with the Order of Osman, and a second production soon followed at La Scala.

But Verdi was still right to describe the work as 'not very new'. Love that crossed warring factions had been a commonplace of his early works (in the Peruvian-Spanish *Alzira* (1845), say) as befitted an artist of the *Risorgimento*; nor was there anything so extraordinary in Aida learning that her secret love Radames had to confront her father Amonasro on the battlefield – an Egyptian captain against an Ethiopian king – while she and her mistress, the Egyptian princess Amneris, vied lethally for Radames: power and love have always bred the keenest enmity. Then again, Egyptian settings, like Turkish ones, had been popular for a century or more (through Metastasio's libretto, *Nitteti*) and *Aida*, like Rossini's *Mosè in Egitto* (1818) or Meyerbeer's *Il crociato in Egitto* (1824), was bathed in the local colour that so appealed to Parisians. Mariette's synopsis had already specified harps, trumpets, dancing and chanting, and its three grand scenes allowed Verdi to expand his achievements with, say, the Knights of Death rite from *La battaglia di Legnano* (1849), the 'Miserere' scene from *Il trovatore* and the processional auto-da-fé from *Don Carlos*. And expand them he did. The ritual consecration in Act One involves an uncanny spatial play between invisible priestesses in the distance and visible warriors at the altar; the colossal victory parade and ensemble in Act Two, with its heated debate over the prisoners' fate, incorporates a ballet that allowed Verdi to sustain the French grand opera format without having to interrupt the action; and the hieratic judgment scene in Act Four provides an essay in the macabre far more chilling than the fairground palmistry of *Un ballo*, partly because the offstage trial is experienced through the frantic and impotent reactions of Amneris. The effects are indeed 'splendid'.

Yet it was the intimate side of the opera that contained the 'very beautiful' situations that so thrilled the composer. In Act One, decorum wrestles with suspicion in the first, breathtakingly unsettled trio of Amneris, Radames and Aida; after the King's tub-thumping call to arms (smacking 'a little of the *Marseillaise*', conceded Verdi), Aida, left alone, grapples with her rival affections for Radames and the Egyptians on the one hand, and her father and the Ethiopians on the other: her heart-rending 'Ritorna vincitor' culminates in her rapt 'Numi pietà', a back-to-the-wall prayer for mercy. The first scene of Act Two focuses on the charged colloquy between a febrile Aida and a diabolical Amneris, whose duplicity 'outs' Aida's love: the unsettling play of different speeds and affects, underlined by the sound of victorious soldiers, leads Aida ineluctably back to 'Numi pietà'. After a balmy opening that 'plants' Amneris and the priests on the one hand, and Aida bidding a pre-emptive farewell to her homeland on the other, Act Three turns the screw in a remarkable chain of encounters. Amonasro uses utterly 'savage' emotional blackmail to assure Aida that she can see her homeland once more – she responds with a joyful, passionate prayer to the gods – and then to persuade her to wrest a military secret from Radames: she yields reluctantly in a portentous, gasping conclusion. Radames arrives to assure the shattered and fearful slave-girl of his unblemished, ecstatic love. Now it is Aida's turn to apply the pressure: she invokes an image of paradise back home. Radames is incredulous: how can he be expected to leave Egypt? But he too yields in a fast conclusion (cabaletta) in which their – admittedly stagy – accord is quickly belied by Aida's prising from him the secret her father needs. Amonasro springs out triumphantly: Radames is devastated. But even the ensuing trio is cut short as Amneris bursts in, crying treason: Amonasro threatens to kill her, Radames intervenes and father and daughter flee. In a final, frenetic twist, Radames vows to stay put: the priests take him prisoner.

But if this wasn't enough, the pressure continues into the final act. This begins with a colloquy between Amneris and Radames that Verdi specially prized. Amneris is now as torn as Aida was at the start: her offers to save the proud Radames juxtapose the formal and the frantic, and, when he refuses to yield, do nothing but release her into the violent fury of a woman scorned. What a contrast, though, between this and the closing duet of the incarcerated

Radames and Aida! Verdi had worried that this 'supremely important' final scene might prove

> too abrupt or too monotonous. It must not be abrupt; after such an elaborate setting, it would be a case, were it not well developed, of *parturiens mons* ['the mountains will labour, and a ridiculous mouse is born' (Horace)]. Monotony must be avoided by finding unusual forms.[1]

He therefore renounced the kind of heroics found in the tomb scene from Gounod's *Roméo et Juliette* (1867). He cultivated cavernous silence and transparency as well as sublime awe and cosmic indifference. He divided the set, not just vertically as in the last scene of *Rigoletto*, but rather laterally, with the brilliant Temple of Vulcan above and the gloomy crypt of Osiris below. He then reflected the division in the music: above, the priests and priestesses chant and dance, below, the tender and ethereal Radames and Aida come to terms with burial alive. At the very end, he introduced Amneris to deliver 'a *Requiem*, an Egyptian *De profundis*' from above, ironically recreating the trio with Aida and Radames from Act One. True, his musical design of the scene would have been recognizable in the 1830s, so strict is its control of simple duet form. But what was new was his repetition and attenuation of a single verse of text to sinuous music – as if thought itself has been incarcerated – and the handling of the priests' and priestesses' chant familiar from Act One: its force changes according to the situation of the lovers while appearing to remain immutable. Rarely was Verdi as magical as this – and rarely had he worked at his spells so hard.

Notes

Source: 'A Beguiling Synopsis', *Aida* (Giuseppe Verdi), The Royal Opera programme, May 2010, pp. 13-17, reprinted 2011.

1   *Verdi's* Aida. *The History of an Opera in Letters and Documents*, ed. Hans Busch, Minneapolis: Minnesota UP, 1978, p. 103. This volume offers invaluable insights into Verdi's creative process.

2 A Conundrum and a Problem

Richard Wagner: *Tristan und Isolde*

Emanuel Schikaneder and Wolfgang Amadeus Mozart: *Die Zauberflöte*

Works of art cannot but react to the time, place and circumstance of their birth: hence their unique fascination. However, when their creators face competing pressures, they may embody those conflicts from the outset. The very sources of an opera may be contradictory. The following pair of essays shows how, first in the gestation of Tristan und Isolde, *and second within the story of* Die Zauberflöte *(The Magic Flute), a story astonishing in its array of sources. True, these are extreme cases. But the human mind, as we know from dreams, likes to scavenge and mix opposites: complex artworks reflect that condition. And if, as the Anglo-Austrian music-critic Hans Keller maintained, purity is for the minor master, then complexity, contradictions and all, must be for the major master. Wagner and Mozart were both major masters.*

1 A Conundrum

Wagner posed an unwitting conundrum when, in a famous letter to Franz Liszt of December 1854, he described the inception of his *Tristan und Isolde* – a work, first performed in 1865, for which he would write both libretto and music. In Schopenhauer, he declared, he had found a philosopher whose principal idea, 'the final denial of the will to live, is of terrible seriousness, but … is uniquely redeeming'; at the same time he saw in *Tristan* a distraction from the yet-to-be-completed *Ring* that would stand as a monument to a 'properly sated' love he had never personally experienced – in effect, an act of compensation.[1] But how could this be? Nietzsche, like Auden later, rightly held music to be intrinsically joyous, but never intrinsically tragic: so surely it was perverse to put uniquely life-promoting music at the service of a uniquely life-denying outlook? More still, by August 1856 Wagner had written to August Röckel that he now saw in all his works – including ones he had merely planned – the very same 'high tragedy of renunciation': and it is true, all his heroes retreat (even Sachs), though in the process exuding lofty energy.[2] Of course, the stance reflected something of the Zeitgeist. To his revised *Faust* overture Wagner had appended a motto embodying the death-wish from Goethe (1808): 'This life has taught me, with its weary weight, / To long for death, and the dear light to hate';[3] and this opposition of benign night and tormenting day parallels lines from Novalis (1800): 'Praise to the unending night … / Scorched by the day's anxiety, we bear [its] marks of stress.'[4] Yet, as composition grew, so did Wagner's private ardour for Mathilde Wesendonck, wife of his benefactor Otto: the fraught triangle obviously resonates with that of *Tristan*, though its denouement – separation – was less drastic.

Outwardly, Wagner's operatic triangle is not that special. A young man absconds with the young bride of his old, sexually shy uncle, is caught *in flagrante*, flees and dies abroad of a wound. Since the man (Tristan) is a pre-eminent knight, the uncle (Marke) a King and his wife (Isolde) a key agent for reconciling feuding states (Ireland and England), the political stakes are high – as they always are with Wagner. But the Celtic legend's fascination lies in the quality of the bond between the young. That this is uncanny is already signalled in Wagner's principal source, Gottfried von Strassburg's *Tristan und Isold* (c. 1220).[5] When Gottfried's Tristan is in exile (in Arundel) he invariably inserts into his songs the refrain, 'Isot ma drue, Isot ma mie, / en vus ma mort, en vus ma vie' (Isolde my mistress, Isolde my beloved, in you my death, in you my life). Here, Gottfried both unites and polarizes love and death. That each party feels them equally is clear from an earlier speech of Isolde: 'You and I, Tristan and Isolde, shall for ever remain one and undivided … I am yours … you are mine, steadfast till death …' These oppositions shape the opera, with Wagner making much of the Tristan/Isolde, Isolde/Tristan 'chiasmus'. More still, although his three acts seem to traverse a cycle of 24 hours encompassing evening, night and day, they are in fact significantly separated by several weeks, with voluptuous night in the second act obviously contrasting with scorching day *à la* Novalis in the third. Less obviously, in the first act Isolde tells the couple's fraught back-story and attempts to poison Tristan, whereas in the second act, both lovers ardently revise the same back-story to their advantage (they have drunk the Viagra-like love potion that releases a hitherto suppressed mutual passion). The binary opposites now interweave.

Nietzsche described Wagner as a great miniaturist – and, indeed, fresh study of the opera's details suggests other, quasi-clinical sources. The lovers, for instance, have distinct mental disorders that belie rather than reinforce the conjunction 'and'. Isolde is in the grip of a bipolar disorder. This we learn partly from the manic episode that starts the first act – far beyond a conventional 'rage aria' in its insensitive delusions of grandeur – and partly from a previous depressive episode described by her confidante (and therapist) Brangäne involving inertia, bottling-up and unruly behaviour. Tristan, however, suffers from a persistent depressive disorder. He has had a stressful childhood, losing both parents (as we learn in Act Three), and gaining a surrogate father (Marke) but no stepmother (ironically, a role Isolde could fill). As we see from the outset, he is a loner, his heroism a kind of psychic shield; and his natural habitat being an empty imaginary space (as he explains to his henchman Kurwenal), he progressively sheds his home and his belongings. He also has an eerie 'split-off' persona that throughout monitors his own trajectory. The two disorders, however, overlap: they both indicate a proclivity to suicide. How eagerly Tristan swallows the potion knowing it to be poisoned! And how eagerly Isolde, not to be outdone, joins him! The proclivity, of course, is crucial to dramatizing Schopenhauer's denial of the will to live. But being no absolute nihilist, Wagner further grants his couple the power to effect their own cure. The dying action of Tristan is to re-establish tender eye-contact with Isolde: this was first established before the action began, when she was poised to take revenge for his killing of her betrothed.[6]

It is this tender and redeeming power that allows Isolde to die over Tristan's body in a surge of satiated love. Its music also starts the work's erotically-charged prelude, in particular by looking forward to the lovers' mutual eye-contact late in the first act. At that point, Tristan and Isolde believe they have just drunk the death potion. Yet, as they 'shudder and gaze into one another's eyes with the utmost emotion' to tart and plangent music, their death-absorbed defiance gradually 'assumes the glow of passion'. By drawing on this musical transformation for the opening, Wagner introduces his conundrum; by referring to the same plangent tones at the end as Isolde's soul ascends into the empyrean, he confirms it.

2 A Problem

The elements of *Die Zauberflöte*, 'a large opera in two-acts', suggest that post-modernism was already alive and well in late eighteenth-century Austria: Ancient Egypt, home to the gods Isis and Osiris, merges into a post-Enlightenment Vienna that promoted spiritual wisdom supported by reason and nature; its lofty hero, Tamino, is a Javanese Prince; its comic anti-hero, Papageno, a piping bird-catcher; its villain, Monostatos, a Moor; and its pair of antagonists, Sarastro and the Queen, symbols of light and dark. But the work is also an allegorical celebration of the Austrian Masonic Lodges to which its authors, Emanuel Schikaneder and W. A. Mozart, at different times belonged. It derives its symbolism, trials and ubiquitous 'groups of three' from *Sethos* (1731), a novel by Abbé Therrasson, as well as from an essay on Egyptian mysteries (1784) by Ignaz von Born – though, exceptionally, it allows both hero and heroine (Pamina) to win through in a predominantly-male environment. Starting with fairy-tales drawn from Wieland's *Dschinnistan* (1786-9), including A. J. Liebeskind's 'Lulu *or* The Magic Flute', the authors built on *Der Stein der Weisen oder Die Zauberinsel* (The Philosopher's Stone *or* The Magic Island), another Wieland-derived work on which both had worked. (There were other sources too.) The result was a *Singspiel* – an opera with spoken dialogue in German. For the music, Mozart also drew on a variety of styles, not excluding his own 'Egyptian' *Thamos* (1780). The work was first performed in September 1791 – only weeks before the composer's death – at the Theater auf der Wieden, a populist venue situated in the Viennese suburbs.[1]

Typically, a fairy-tale can reward its conquering hero with the hand of the fair maiden he rescues; it can also confront terror head-on. *The Magic Flute* does both, though it also has to address a problem: if, as it turns out, the young hero moves from darkness in the first act (the Queen of the Night) to light in the second (Sarastro), how can the work develop in intensity (since the devil always has the best tunes)? The answer is threefold, and is central to the work's appeal.

First, the Queen of the Night is initially presented sympathetically, as a mother deranged by the loss of her daughter. Her three attendant ladies are tender and amusing, and Tamino's rescue mission seems eminently worthy; the talismanic flute with which he is equipped, and the Three Boys sent to guide him, are clearly benign. Even his designated helpmate, the delinquent Papageno, is delightful. By contrast, how forbidding is our first encounter with Egypt! We first meet Pamina enslaved by the lascivious Monostatos and calling for her mother; Tamino is repulsed by ominous voices when he approaches the gates of Reason and Nature, and is then held at bay by a mysterious Orator; and Pamina and Papageno try to flee, protected by magic bells. Pamina has then to listen to Sarastro disparage her mother, finding in Tamino's arms only a short-lived refuge. So far, so copy-book.

Second, and to our generic surprise, our sympathies are reversed in Act Two, though the fairy-tale cruelty still intensifies. Sarastro explains why at the outset: he must be cruel to be kind; the trials to which Tamino submits so as to join the priests' order will test the man to the limit. And, indeed, this blend of resolution and tenderness elicits from Mozart the uniquely poignant tone that pervades the various musical 'numbers': the March of the Priests; Sarastro's two dignified arias along with his attempt (in a trio) to calm Pamina; the Two Priests' preemptive warning against women just before the Queen's ladies try to rescue Tamino and Papageno; the Priests' hymn to Isis and Osiris in praise of Tamino; the chorale of the Two Armed Men who prepare Tamino (with Pamina) for his trials by fire and water; the serene flute music that accompanies the trials; and the closing chorus where triumph is initially tempered by prayers to Isis and Osiris. The priests even indulge Papageno for his failures. By contrast, we now see a vengeful Queen urging Pamina to kill Sarastro and recover a shield of the sun once owned by Pamina's father; when foiled, she promises Pamina to Monostatos if he helps her defeat Sarastro. Indeed, so lethal is she that Sarastro confines her peremptorily to oblivion (regardless of any impact on Pamina). More still, we realize in retrospect that when, at the very start, Tamino entered pursued by a serpent, with the Three Ladies appearing fortuitously to save him and then pressing a locket into his hand, the Queen was already manipulating him with her politics of Love and Death.

Third, the constants transcend and unite the feuding parties. This is fundamental: the Three Boys are always benignly interventionist – at their most effective in preventing Pamina's suicide – and the flute and bells always retain their efficacy. More still, the infectiously comic sub-stratum – musically simple, but never simplistic – does not just present Papageno and Papagena as a materialist contrast-pair to the spiritually-minded Tamina and Pamina: rather, it serves to endorse the view that 'Truth, to the initiate, is not for everyone' – a view expressed by a 'highly placed Mason' cited by Stephen Knight in his study of 'the brotherhood'.[2]

After its first performance, *Die Zauberflöte* rapidly acquired the popularity it has never shed. Attracting such artists as Chagall, Sendak and Hockney, it has also prompted creative responses from Goethe, Tippett, Auden and many others. In his cinema version of 1975, *Trollflöjten*, for instance, Ingmar Bergman added to the post-modern carnivalesque by filming the work in Drottningholm, the famous mid-eighteenth-century Swedish theatre, using Brechtian 'epic' techniques. He also alluded to Richard Wagner's hieratic *Parsifal* (1882) and reworked the plot so that Sarastro cedes power to Tamino and Pamina as an act of reparation for his (alleged) failed marriage to the Queen of the Night. That other producers have taken, and continue to take, such liberties, testifies to the enduring stimulus of a 'fantastic' work that may seem a closed period-piece but is in fact open to all times.

Notes

Source: Longborough Festival Opera. 2017 season programme: 'En Vus ma Mort, en Vus ma Vie', pp. 28-9; 'The Pre-post-modernism of *The Magic Flute*', pp. 58-9.

1 A Conundrum

1   Written in Zurich, December 1854, to Liszt in Weimar. *Selected Letters of Richard Wagner*, trans. and ed. Stewart Spencer and Barry Millington, London: Dent, 1987, pp. 323-4.
2   Written in Zurich, August 1856, to Röckel in Waldheim. *Ibid.*, pp. 356-9.
3   Cited in a letter of January 1855 to Liszt in Weimar. *Ibid.*, pp. 324-5.
4   Novalis [Friedrich, Freiherr von Hardenberg], *Hymns to the Night*, trans. Jeremy Reed, London: Enitharmon, 1989, p. 30.
5   Gottfried von Strassburg, *Tristan und Isold*, ed. Friedrich Ranke, Weidmann, 1930/78, p. 243, lines 19409-10. For an English translation see: Gottfried von Strassburg, *Tristan and Isolde*, ed. Francis G. Gentry, New York: Continuum, 2003, p. 253.
6   For a discussion of the relation of the overlapping mental disorders of Isolde and Tristan to musical process, see my study of 'Wagner's Spatial Style' in *The Wagner Journal*, Vol. 9, No. 3, 2015, pp. 4-23.

2 A Problem

1   For details of the opera's progeny, see: W. A. Mozart, *Die Zauberflöte*, ed. Peter Branscombe, Cambridge: Cambridge UP (Cambridge Opera Handbooks), 1991.
2   Stephen Knight, *The Brotherhood. The Secret World of the Freemasons*, London: Granada, 1984.

3   A Perennial Source

Thomas Adès (after Shakespeare): *The Tempest*

There are operatic sources that librettist and composer bring to life; there are those they leave unborn; and there are those they abandon yet can't quite forget. Critics claim that although Claude Debussy never completed his long-pondered opera on Poe's La Chute de la maison Usher *(The Fall of the House of Usher), he still carried its tone into his opera on Maeterlinck's* Pelléas et Mélisande *(1902). Ed Cone's suggestion (cited below) that Giuseppe Verdi composed his Shakespearean* Tempest *even as he wrote his Shakespearean* Falstaff *is by no means an idle one. Indeed, Shakespeare is a special case. For his plays are both a national touchstone for the British and a mysterious site of liberation for post-Enlightenment Europeans, an antidote to Racine. For those who tackle the Bard afresh – and many still do – the attempt inevitably brings to mind those who have assailed his peaks and either succeeded or failed: even to try to 'compose Shakespeare' is to stand in a long shadow. The narrative complexity of the late plays in particular ought to act as a deterrent. But, strangely, it never does. Certain sources will always beguile.*

Ever since its first performance in 1611 Shakespeare's *Tempest* has woven its way through music and the stage like a golden thread: why? Is it because of the wealth of songs, the 'musical' speeches, the vividness of the characters, the mixture of styles and the uncanny sounds of a castaway island? Or is it rather the magical power of Prospero's omnipotence fantasy and Ariel's quest for freedom? As *The Tempest, La tempesta, La Tempête* and *Der Sturm*, as *The Enchanted Island, Die bezauberte Insel, Die Zauberinsel, Die Geisterinsel* and *Prospero's Geisterinsel*, the play has been the source for countless operas, plays-with-music, ballets, intermezzos and cantatas, not to mention free-standing songs and choruses. Their composers have included Robert Johnson (1612), Henry Purcell (1695), Thomas Arne (1746) Johann Rudolf Zumsteeg (1798), Johann Friedrich Reichardt (1798), Jacques Fromental Halévy (1850), Arthur Sullivan (1862), Ernest Chausson (1888), Engelbert Humperdinck (1906), Arthur Honegger (1923), Jean Sibelius (1925) and Frank Martin (1955). More obliquely, the play has also been an inspiration for Michael Tippett's *The Knot Garden* (1970) and Luciano Berio's *Un re in ascolto* (1984). And even when it is not directly invoked, it can assert an undeclared presence, as in the storm that opens Giuseppe Verdi's *Otello* (1887). Indeed, Ed Cone has written: 'There is evidence that Verdi wanted to set *The Tempest*. Perhaps he did – in *Falstaff*.'

Thomas Adès's *The Tempest* (2004) is thus the latest in a long chain. But there is a fascinating missing link. In June 1956 John Gielgud wrote to Benjamin Britten: 'Do you remember once rashly saying you would be interested in doing incidental music for *The Tempest*? … I thought I would write and ask if there is any possibility of interesting you … perhaps in your travels you might look out for a boy Ariel who can both sing and act.' In reply Britten suggested staging it at Covent Garden. Gielgud demurred: 'A small theatre and simple décor is what I am sure is right,' he answered, 'with a bit of a splash only for the masque in the fourth act.' After floating the alternative of Stratford, Ontario, Gielgud wrote that 'what would be wonderful – and has never yet been successfully used – is some sort of wiring which would enable … the music to appear to come from different directions – out of the sky, under the stage and round about.' There would be no 'instruments, stands etc.'.

But Gielgud didn't stop there. What he went on to devise for Britten was in effect a piece of music theatre *avant le jour*: '… a small combination of instruments would be best for Ariel's songs, magic music etc. with a bit more added for storm and masque. The music should permeate the play with beauty, mystery (and terror occasionally) but must not of course dominate the speaking. The occasions for it are implicit in the text, I think, at all times, though the enchanting of Ferdinand in the first act and the final speeches of the play might also be enhanced with strange chords and some kind of simple motifs. There could also be an overture – though the storm scene is really an overture in itself and there music would be an essential and enormous help if it is just right to allow the dialogue to be heard, and one would have some musical links between the scenes.'

Whether or not Britten was happy to play Ariel to Gielgud's Prospero is unknown: the proposal came to nothing. But a decade later, in 1965, the idea turned into a project for a Paramount film involving Gielgud, Richard Atttenborough and Albert Finney (as Caliban), to be shot in Britten's own paradise island of Bali. But the press got wind of the idea. 'I do hope you won't be annoyed at the way it has come out,' wrote Gielgud to Britten after the *Evening Standard* had 'jumped the gun'. Gielgud himself was not too troubled: he had done Prospero for Peter Brook in 1957, would do it again in 1973 for Peter Hall, and film it for Peter Greenaway to music by Michael Nyman in *Prospero's Books* (1991). But Britten was sensitive to advance publicity: and although he went on discussing the project for three or four years it was eventually dropped. *The Tempest* joined *King Lear*, *Anna Karenina* and *The Tale of Mr Tod* in a distinguished cadre of unwritten works.

Is there still a Balinese *Tempest* to be written? What other exotic settings can composers find? The Shakespearean chain, it seems, is far from over.

Notes

Source: '400 Years of Tempests', *The Tempest* (Thomas Adès), The Royal Opera programme, March 2007, pp. 40-1. The Gielgud-Britten letters are kept in the Britten-Pears Library, The Red House, Aldeburgh, but do not appear in *Gielgud's Letters* (ed. Richard Mangan, London: Weidenfeld and Nicolson, 2004) or the six volumes of Britten's selected correspondence (Faber and Faber, Boydell).

4 Play, Intermezzo and Opera

Hugo von Hofmannsthal and Richard Strauss: *Ariadne auf Naxos*

The libretto of an opera, it is said, can best emerge in three stages: the choice of a source reducible to a synopsis (myth, folk-tale, play, novel, sacred story or whatever), the development of a prose scenario with divisions into acts and scenes, and the working-out of a detailed text that balances lyric and dramatic contrast, pitting inner against outer action – all with the requirements of lead and support singers in mind. It may also incorporate the demands of a particular house, not to mention particular soloists. But creation is not always this schematic. And no opera has a more disorderly generative history than Ariadne auf Naxos, *where play, intermezzo and mini-opera, blending ancient and modern figures, coalesced over time into a two-part work that survives in two versions. Fortunately, the disorder is well-documented. The letters of Strauss and Hofmannsthal give invaluable insight into the competing demands of composer and librettist, and thereby help trace the origins of the work's uniquely complex structure and tone.*

To ask a group of opera-lovers, critics and connoisseurs 'Which is the greatest of Richard Strauss's operas?' is to open Pandora's box. There are plenty to choose from – fifteen or so, written between 1894 and 1942. The majority of opera-lovers would hesitate between *Salome* and *Elektra* – the third and fourth – before opting for *Der Rosenkavalier* – the fifth! Whereupon, an old-school critic would cry, 'But don't you see that before *Der Rosenkavalier* – up until 1911 – Strauss was at the cutting edge of uncompromising Modernism, after which he <u>regressed</u> to waltzes, nostalgia and myth?' To this the connoisseurs object. 'Surely Hofmannsthal was right to claim that he and Strauss had really moved on from *Der Rosenkavalier* with *Die Frau ohne Schatten*?' says the first. 'You know, there were already waltzes in *Feuersnot*' – the second opera – 'back in 1901,' adds the second. The third chips in: 'But wasn't Stefan Zweig right to claim that Hofmannsthal became altogether too obscure, notably in *Die ägyptische Helena*?' But the fourth will have none of it: 'Come on! Modernism isn't just about green-eyed monsters. It's also about works of art that reflect upon their own creation – like *Die Meistersinger* or *Palestrina*. *Capriccio*' – the last opera – 'is surely a dazzling addition to that line!' All then ponder the intermittent triumphs of *Guntram, Arabella, Intermezzo* and the lesser-known pleasures of the late 1930s, *Friedenstag, Daphne* and *Die Liebe der Danae*. But no-one can agree. So many of the operas are great! If instead it was asked 'Which of Strauss's operas is at the same time the most entertaining and the most sublime?' then everyone would agree. For nothing beats the sixth opera, *Ariadne auf Naxos*.

The libretto for *Ariadne* is by Hugo von Hofmannsthal. But Hofmannsthal was no ordinary librettist – as he well knew. True, he was Strauss's junior: he lived from 1874 to 1929, whereas Strauss lived from 1864 to 1949. But he had caught the attention of the literary world from the start and never lost it. In his poignant memoir *The World of Yesterday* (1942), Stefan Zweig writes –

> I know of no-one, with the exception of Keats and Rimbaud, who
> so young achieved such a flawless mastery of speech, such elevation
> of ideals, or such saturation in the substance of poetry … as this
> majestic genius, who at the ages of 16 and 17 inscribed himself
> upon the eternal rolls of the German language.[1]

In fact, Hofmannsthal, like Zweig, was a Viennese Europhile. He became a prolific poet, essayist, anthologist, theorist of dance, author of *Jedermann* – cornerstone of the Salzburg Festival – and of many psychologically-probing dramas, some of which were adaptations of earlier plays. Strauss himself collaborated with Hofmannsthal on (principally) six operas, a cantata, a ballet and the *Rosenkavalier* film. Other composers too used his work for operas, ranging from Egon Wellesz to Edgard Varèse. Hofmannsthal's genius was thus a match for Strauss's, and certainly the poet never pulled his punches if the composer disappointed him. *Ariadne* was their third opera and their third project.

Ariadne auf Naxos is brilliant, audacious and subtle, and has an especially complex history. This we may reconstruct from the correspondence between composer and librettist, an exchange that gives us deep insight, not only into their respective personalities, but also into the creative process itself. (But not uniquely: Strauss enjoyed other such exchanges – with Romain Roland, Stefan Zweig, Joseph Gregor and Clemens Krauss.) In fact, *Ariadne* appeared in two versions, the first in 1912, and the second in 1916. It is the second we usually hear. The 1912 version was a one-act opera appended to Molière's *Le Bourgeois Gentilhomme* (The Bourgeois as a Would-be Gentleman). Molière's play dated from 1670 and originally included dances and songs; it also closed with a 'Ballet of Nations' to music by Lully, a ballet unrelated to the main action. In the 1916 version, Molière's play was replaced by a long Prologue. But only when both versions are taken together can we grasp the *Ariadne* project as a whole.

In fact, the idea for an opera preceded any thoughts about the play. In March 1911 Hofmannsthal told Strauss that he wanted to follow up *Der Rosenkavalier* with a fairy-tale opera. This eventually became *Die Frau ohne Schatten*. But he needed time for gestation. So in the interim he proposed an opera of just thirty minutes, *Ariadne auf Naxos*. This he described as

> a combination of heroic mythological figures in eighteenth-century
> costume with hooped skirts and ostrich feathers, and, interwoven

in it, characters from the *commedia dell'arte*: harlequins and scaramouches representing the *buffo* element [the comic] which is throughout interwoven with the heroic.[2]

Such a work would represent

a new genre which to all appearance reaches back to a much earlier one, just as all development goes in cycles.[3]

It was indeed new to do this in opera in such a way. And it would certainly have been anathema to Wagner, who complained of the mixture of tragic and comic in Shakespeare. *Commedia dell'arte* means 'professional' theatre rather than a theatre of aristocratic amateurs; it flourished in the sixteenth and seventeenth centuries; it involved small troupes of stock figures who sang and danced; and its theme was love, whether serious or playful. But a *commedia dell'arte* scene could also serve as an intermezzo – an insertion between scenes or acts of serious plays; and, as everyone knows, in the late sixteenth century the Florentine intermezzo was an important precursor of opera. So, by dropping into a drama an intermezzo with five characters who merely sing, dance and engage in flirtatious banter, Hofmannsthal was indeed 'reaching back'.

It was only two months later, in May 1911, when he was in Paris, that Hofmannsthal had the idea of inserting this little opera into *Le Bourgeois Gentilhomme*: it could replace Lully's ballet as a closing divertissement played before Monsieur Jourdain. Jourdain is Molière's bourgeois tradesman 'crazily' determined to acquire the refinements of a gentleman: he hires music teachers, dancing masters, tailors, lackeys and so forth. Needless to say, this creates consternation in his family, especially as there are serious matters of the heart at stake. The action culminates in a dinner at which his daughter's lover, dressed as the son of the Grand Turk, tricks Jourdain into surrendering him his daughter's hand. But the idea didn't stop there. Hofmannsthal would eventually reduce the play to two acts, to each of which Strauss would append an overture, bits of entrance music and extensive background music for the dinner. He would also set three songs and include several dances over which the actors spoke. The style would be loosely neo-classical, the whole play to last seventy-five minutes. Finally, to connect play and opera, Hofmannsthal would preface the opera part with a spoken 'transition', or a getting-ready scene, and give Jourdain some words to close the entire work; whereas Strauss would give the play's main songs to Ariadne's three attendants, Naiad, Dryad and Echo, and at the end of its first act have offstage instrumentalists rehearse the last nine bars of the overture to the opera part.

But back to 1911 … Hofmannsthal urged Strauss to get the 1751 translation of Molière's play. Strauss did. But after reading it he was only cautiously enthusiastic and pointed to alleged weaknesses: indeed, it would be several months before Hofmannsthal had him fully on board. Nevertheless, Strauss did at once produce an outline of numbers, vocal casting and instrumentation that already bears the stamp of the final work. The star role would be for one of the *commedia dell'arte* figures, Zerbinetta: her coloratura soprano would stand in the line of Bellini's *La sonnambula*, Donizetti's *Lucia di Lammermoor*, Verdi's *Rigoletto* (Gilda), Hérold's *Le Pré aux Clercs* (Isabelle) and certain Mozart rondos. Her central *pièce de resistance* would comprise a recitative and aria, a dazzling rondo, a cadenza and, to crown it all, a duet with her enamoured Harlequin. Strauss imagined the death-devoted, lamenting Ariadne as a contralto, though this he later changed to a soprano – obviously more suitable for the radiant finale. He proposed giving the 'light baritone' Harlequin his own song and the comic men a trio and a quartet (they also have a quintet with Zerbinetta); and he wanted the long, unbroken finale to be introduced by the Naiad and continue in earnest with Bacchus's entry. His idea of the orchestra already included harp, harmonium, celeste, trumpet and percussion (but not yet piano).[4]

Hofmannsthal acceded, but insisted that the work should be staged by Max Reinhardt rather than by members of the stuffy court opera. Reinhardt, in fact, would be its first producer. Yet Hofmannsthal was startled about Strauss's star choice of Zerbinetta, and over several long, pained letters explained why. For him, Ariadne was central to the opera part of the work. Ariadne it was who had brought back Theseus to live with her in Naxos, after helping him destroy the bloodthirsty Minotaur in Crete. After Theseus had slipped away perfidiously in the night, she had been devastated and sang a passionate lament. But when Bacchus, the god of revelry arrives, she is redeemed. Of supreme importance, therefore, would be the exchange between Bacchus and Ariadne. As he pleaded with Strauss:

> [The] essence of the relationship … stands before my mind's eye so finely graded, so delicately animated, so psychologically convincing and at the same time so lyrical, that my execution would have to be wretched indeed if at the end it failed to arouse your interest as much as the lyrics of your songs, or the scenes [in *Der Rosenkavalier*] between the Marschallin and Octavian.[5]

Bacchus would have to be a rather 'boyish' lyric tenor, since 'he is but lately fledged [and] has had his one involvement with Circe and is shy'. Despite escaping her clutches, Bacchus is 'wounded', something evident from his entrance aria in which he repeatedly calls for Circe. More still,

> The strange aura of the fabulous East … surrounds Bacchus, the vibrating sense of the realm of death and shadow, that delicate, lyrical, unearthly atmosphere to which Ariadne clings – and all this

in most distinct contrast to the melodically pellucid world in which Zerbinetta and Harlequin have their being.[6]

This unbridgeable contrast, this mutual incomprehension between Ariadne and Zerbinetta – so redolent of the contrast in an earlier work of theirs between the obsessive Elektra and her bland sister Chrysothemis – was indeed of the essence. As the poet put it,

> the group of heroes, demi-gods, gods – Ariadne, Bacchus, Theseus – [face] … the merely human [group] consisting of the frivolous Zerbinetta and her companions, all of them base figures in life's masquerade.[7]

Ariadne herself

> could be the wife or mistress of *one* man only, just as she can be only *one* man's widow, can be forsaken by only *one* man [Theseus]. One thing, however, is still left even for her: the miracle, the God. To him [Bacchus] she gives herself, for she believes him to be Death: he is both Death and Life at once; he it is who reveals to her the immeasurable depths in her own nature … who conjures up for her in this world another world beyond, who preserves her for us and at the same time transforms her.[8]

This is the work's central statement. Ariadne first mistakes Bacchus for the returning Theseus, and then re-casts him as Hermes, the messenger of Death. She never asks him who he actually is, nor does Bacchus think to enlighten her. When at the close he gathers her up into the canopy of night, taking her to his ship, the action symbolizes just the *living* death the poet describes. And as for Bacchus – well, he too is enriched and transfigured by this encounter.

Though impressed by Hofmannsthal's explanation, Strauss found it a bit obscure. Certainly, for the conclusion he wanted a 'bigger crescendo'.[9] With the long Bacchus-Ariadne exchange he may have had in mind the model of Wagner's great duologues: at the end of *Siegfried*, for instance, Siegfried wakens Brünnhilde and gradually turns the tables between his inexperience and her experience so that at the close the two are level, joining in a laughing, death-defying duet. So for the end of *Ariadne*, Strauss created just such a process. The music leads to a duet and a blazing climax suitable for Hofmannsthal's transformation of Death into Life-embracing Death – a climax in no way diminished by the use of a chamber ensemble of just thirty-six players, a stark reduction from the huge forces Strauss had used for their *Elektra* and *Rosenkavalier*.

The first performance of this first version took place on 25 October 1912. Generally the work had a mixed reception, partly because German actors had

had little experience of Molière. So in due course Hofmannsthal and Strauss went back to the drawing board. But the reception was not the main catalyst. For, already in July 1911, Hofmannsthal had thought of replacing the play-part with an act-length prologue more closely linked to the opera-part. This, he explained to Strauss, could

> offer the opportunity of stating quite plainly, under cover of a joke, the symbolic meaning of the antithesis between the two women [Ariadne and Zerbinetta].[10]

'Brilliant', replied Strauss –

> provided that you develop the two parts of the Composer and the Dancing Master in such a way that everything is said that can be said today about the relationship of public, critics and artist. It could become a companion piece to *Meistersinger*: fifty years on.[11]

He also proposed a liaison between Zerbinetta and the Composer 'so long as he is not too close a portrait of me.' The Prologue could thus become a trenchant critique of modern art and Strauss's position within it – as indeed it did.

But Strauss needed more convincing: in 1913, he was still thinking of the first version 'as the only valid and definitive' one. However, in April 1916, after concentrated work on *Die Frau ohne Schatten*, he turned his attention to the revision, asking, among other things, that the Composer should be a female trouser role. 'Operetta,' cried Hofmannsthal, 'odious!'[12] But Strauss dug in, and a trouser role it was – an inspired piece of casting, one that emphasizes how the Composer is but a pupil of the Music Master, endearingly intense and a touch comic. 'Appalling' too was how Hofmannsthal described Strauss's ideas for a new end to replace that of 1912 (where Zerbinetta, her troupe and Jourdain had returned after the end of the *Ariadne* opera). Here Strauss buckled: 'Do whatever you like.'[13] So Hofmannsthal closed the new version with the exit of Ariadne and Bacchus, though not before Zerbinetta has observed tartly 'when a new god steps forward, we stand back in silence'. He explained to Strauss that

> such spicing of the sentimental with its opposite is quite in your spirit … [as] at the end of *Rosenkavalier*.[14]

They now worked up the Prologue. This emerged as a huge expansion of the 'getting-ready' scene that had prefaced the 1912 opera part. For Hofmannsthal, it had advantages. It retained some of Molière's characters and even a speaking role, the Haushofmeister; it explained the Ariadne back-story and the symbolic significance of her liaison with Bacchus; it created the required dalliance between Zerbinetta and the Composer by having Zerbinetta insist she is not the coquette she has to act; it conducted the socio-artistic critique with an on-stage disparagement of the 'boring' *Ariadne* opera; and, through Jourdain, now the wealthiest man in Vienna, it epitomized a public more interested in fireworks than in high art. More still, it showed the origin of the mixed genre: it showed how Jourdain overturned his initial idea for the *commedia dell'arte* frippery to follow the serious *Ariadne* opera with a later command for the two to be played concurrently. For Strauss, too, there was the advantage that the music of the Prologue could now comprehensively foreshadow that of the *Ariadne* opera. After further changes, including the deft scaling back of Zerbinetta's coloratura aria, this new *Ariadne auf Naxos* was mounted in Vienna on 4 October 1916. Its music now lasted two hours.

And what of the music that had been lost by dropping the 1912 play part? Hofmannsthal promised to use it in a new 'half-fantastic, half-realistic *Singspiel*'. This duly became the three-act *Der Bürger als Edelmann* of 1918, from which Strauss devised the famous orchestral suite.[15] And where, aesthetically, did the composition of *Ariadne* leave Strauss? 'I [now] hope,' he wrote,

> to move forward wholly into the realm of un-Wagnerian emotional and human comic opera.[16]

Whether or not he did quite that is another story.

Notes

Source: 'Play, Intermezzo and Opera', *Ariadne auf Naxos* (Richard Strauss), talk to the Friends of The Royal Opera, 12 June 2014.

1   Adapted from: Stefan Zweig, *The World of Yesterday* (1942), trans. Anthea Bell, London: Pushkin, 2009.
2   *The Correspondence between Richard Strauss and Hugo von Hofmannsthal* (1952), trans. Hanns Hammelmann and Ewald Osers, London: Collins, 1961, p. 76.
3   *Idem.*
4   *Ibid.*, pp. 81-3.
5   *Ibid.*, p. 86.
6   *Ibid.*, p. 90.
7   *Ibid.*, p. 94.
8   *Idem.*
9   *Ibid.*, p. 95.
10 *Ibid.*, p. 99.
11 *Ibid.*, p. 100.
12 *Ibid.*, p. 242. A curious reaction, since Hofmannsthal had derived part of the scenario for *Der Rosenkavalier* from private reports he received of a French operetta, *L'Ingénu libertin*. See: Michael Reynolds, *Creating 'Der Rosenkavalier'. From Chevalier to Cavalier*, Woodbridge: The Boydell Press, 2016.
13 *Ibid.*, p. 243.
14 *Ibid.*, p. 247.
15 *Ibid.*, p. 256.
16 *Ibid.*, p. 262.

Mariano Stabile as Falstaff
(Milein Cosman, 1948)

Part Two

Genre

1   *Tragedy of Affliction or Bourgeois Drama?*

Francesco Maria Piave and Giuseppe Verdi: *La traviata*

In handling a source, creators must always ask, what is to be its genre? But how are they to think of genre? Let us go back to Aristotle and his discussion of tragedy. In the Poetics, *he advances four types: of 'complexity' (involving reversal and recognition); of 'suffering' (specifying individuals); of 'character' (including groups); and of 'spectacle' (as when, for example, the work is set 'in Hades'). Nowhere does he suggest that tragedy should involve death (a common misunderstanding).* Rather, he asks for 'terrifying and pitiable events', 'complication and resolution', 'moral satisfaction', 'catharsis' of terror and pity, and so forth. Now it is true that Aristotle was addressing ancient Greek drama whereas we are dealing with modern opera. But the distance of time, place and circumstance is no argument against the kind of inquiry in which Aristotle was engaged. Genre – in his case, tragedy, comedy and epic – and its impact on an audience will always matter: indeed, it is one of art's most liberating restrictions. Of course, it is bad practice for creators or critics to take a generic type 'off the shelf' and apply it like a mould or yardstick: any work worth its salt 'starts over' with its premises, which must bow to the demands of the moment: modern times in particular prefer mixed genres. The issue is especially pertinent to* La traviata, *an opera that has always enjoyed great popularity. Aristotle might have complained that its characters are of dubious moral worth and that Violetta's suffering is as much a 'given' of the drama as an element arising from it, but today we ask, is it not this very generic complexity that is so appealing?*

'A perfect expression of an imperfect society' was how tuberculosis was known until the advent of streptomycin, PAS *et al* in the late 1940s: after that, other fatal illnesses seized the public imagination. But at the time of (Alphonsine) Marie Duplessis (d. 1847), of Dumas *fils*'s Marguerite Gautier (novel and play, 1848 and 1852) and of Francesco Maria Piave and Giuseppe Verdi's Violetta Valéry (1853), the 'white death' – to borrow the title of Thomas Dormandy's history of TB – held pride of place.[1] As stunned Parisians discovered, never was tuberculosis more terrifying than when it carried off a young hostess whose commanding looks and vivacity seemed blessed by the gods.[2] But what of TB in the theatre? We are bound to recognize, of course, that though a serious affliction may be a feature of a drama, a 'given', it cannot play a role in it. That is to say, *La traviata* is a tragedy of affliction, biological destiny has supplanted Fate, and Violetta's tuberculosis is irreversible (as in the case of Duplessis). Nevertheless, the drama plays with the illusion that, on the contrary, consumption can be delayed or reversed, if not downright denied: for the bourgeois mind – and bourgeois drama – cannot rid itself of the superstition that the illness is well-earned, a just reward for a courtesan. Only cure Violetta's circumstances, thinks her lover Alfredo, and the colour will come back to her cheeks. How mistaken he is!

Everything in the music of *La traviata* grows out of this dichotomy. Back in 250 AD, Aretaeus the Cappadocian had noticed in advanced tuberculosis the co-existence of lassitude and hoarseness with bursts of excitement and 'foolish gaiety'. Not surprisingly, after the prelude (a tender memorial postlude to the heroine) the first scene in Violetta's house begins with dance music of such manic energy that even her seasoned friends are disconcerted: *allegro brillantissimo e molto vivace* is a step on from the festive *allegro con brio* that opens *Rigoletto*. Then, reluctantly, Alfredo steps forward. His carefully shaded drinking song, a *brindisi*, is graceful and alluring, just as Violetta's response is graceful and defensive. Already the two have set themselves apart. A waltz strikes up from within: it is the most erotic of dances, the epitome of licentiousness, yet it halts Violetta, who lets the others disappear. Pallid and faltering, she lingers with Alfredo, the frivolity of the off-stage band throwing into ironic relief the seriousness of her condition. In the duet that follows, Alfredo transmutes the waltz into a slower expression of devotion, 'Un dì felice' (One day, happy and ethereal, you appeared before me), only to be resisted by Violetta who bids him return the next day. The vivacious choral close of the introduction also rounds off the duet. The guests and Alfredo depart. Both the affliction and the drama have been well established.

Violetta reflects ambivalently on the action in her famous double aria: it is the first of many passages in the opera that seeks a return to a pre-consumptive state of unblemished health and happiness. Her shyly tender (minor-mode) 'Ah fors'è lui' (Ah, perhaps it is he who has sown confusion in my heart) already bears the imprint of Alfredo's earlier music; its continuation yields to an open reiteration of his (major-mode) 'Di quell'amor' ([waking me] to that love which is the pulse of the universe): in her future lover she recognizes the hero of her girlish dreams.[3] However, she quickly counters this by recalling and defending the frivolities of the *demi-monde*. Her closing music (the cabaletta) is a vocal *pièce de resistance* doubling as a Freudian piece of resistance: part enhanced waltz and part a deployment of the full range of *bel canto* scales, trills and roulades, it is again carried off with a consumptive's energy. Yet it is compromised by the return of Alfredo's music. This we in the audience hear as a *Trovatore*-like serenade rising from outside but Violetta hears as a repetition of Alfredo's earlier 'words' rising from within herself (he sings in her key). We thus witness love's putative medicine seeping into her soul, almost despite herself.

In Abbé Prevost's *Manon Lescaut* (1731),[4] a touchstone for Dumas, the central couple elope. Likewise by the start of Verdi's Act Two, Violetta and Alfredo have eloped. We meet them in the rural retreat they have inhabited for three months. Alfredo is happy and expansive: she has done as much for him as he for her. Yet his aria shows that he is every bit as volatile as Violetta. On the one hand, his 'De' miei bollenti spiriti' (The youthful ardour of my ebullient spirits she tempered with her calm smile of love) is forceful yet tender; on the other hand, his reaction to the news that Violetta has been in Paris selling up her possessions to pay for their 'pastoral and ethereal' fantasy (the words of Dumas) is brash and impulsive: 'O mio rimorso!' he sings (Oh my remorse! Oh my disgrace!). He rushes out, determined to buy back her things.

The ensuing meeting between Violetta and Germont, Alfredo's ponderous but not unfeeling father, is the turning point in the drama, a peripeteia from which she never recovers, socially or physically. It is, in fact, a traditional double duet (which Violetta leads in both the andante and the cabaletta) though the long opening section comprises a chain of verse-and-responses that allows, for Verdi, an unparalleled ebb and flow of emotions. (Verdi had already explored such chains to good effect in *Macbeth*, *I due Foscari* and *Stiffelio*.) Here we listen to bourgeois rectitude fully arrayed against the *demi-monde*. Germont does not want Violetta as a daughter-in-law; Violetta is emphatic that she is not after Alfredo's fortune; in Germont's God-given view, her past is ineradicable and compromises the marital prospects of Alfredo's sister, a girl 'pure as an angel'; in Violetta's view, her blessed life with Alfredo has wiped out that past; he insists she must renounce Alfredo; she argues frenetically that he doesn't know how much she lives for him, she who has neither family nor dependents. When Violetta asks if he knows of her horrible affliction, Germont remains unmoved. She is compelled to recognize that for the fallen woman, the *traviata*, there is no reprieve. It is she, then, who must make the sacrifice.

Here, the slow part of the duet proper begins, with a purified (6/8) version of the pervasive waltz music (originally Verdi had written this E♭ major passage in the more 'vulnerable' E major):[5] Violetta now reveals a wholly uncontaminated moral dignity, something Franz Liszt also observed in Duplessis. Friedrich Schiller once argued that we grasp dramatic characters more by their restraint of emotion than by their release: yet with Violetta we are privy to both restraint and release, feelings that are dispersed across two consecutive 'numbers'. On the one hand, her poignant instruction to Germont, 'Dite alla giovine' testifies to the force of her dignity: 'Tell the young girl, so beautiful and pure, there is a victim of misfortune who has a single ray of happiness … which she sacrifices to her and who will die.' On the other hand, once Germont has departed and Alfredo has interrupted her letter-writing, her ardent outburst, introduced by a Rossini-like crescendo of unparalleled pathos, is a valediction to both Alfredo and the love she believes might have cured her. 'Amami, Alfredo,' she sings – 'Love me, Alfredo, love me as I love you … farewell'.

The scene ends with a new confrontation, between Germont and Alfredo. Eloquent and authoritative though Germont's aria may be, it cannot control Alfredo who, at its end, races off to Paris: he thereby denies his father the gratification of 'closure'. Out of this flight grows Alfredo's no less impetuous behaviour in the second scene of Act Two, the magnificent, though essentially traditional, central act finale involving the whole company. We are back in the *demi-monde*, artistically reliving the diversionary aspects of Parisian opera, with playful choral dances that share in the Andalusian world of *Il trovatore*. Violetta arrives with the Baron to whom she has now returned: in Dumas's play, they have been to Donizetti's *La Favorite*, another opera about a young woman torn between an older and a younger lover who dies of a fatal illness. Tension mounts during the 'card episode', a magnificent demonstration of how a single 'shuffling' figure in the orchestra can act openly as a diversion (directing everyone's attention to gaming) but subcutaneously as an expression of the community's agitation as Alfredo and the Baron square up (the music is in the portentous key of F minor). After Alfredo has released his pent-up fury by hurling his winnings at Violetta – his money, his love, and his cure all in one – the company appear to sing as one, though each of its members has his or her own viewpoint: Alfredo is consumed by remorse, Germont by guilt, the Baron by vengeance and Violetta's friends by sympathy. But the main part of the ensemble is led by Violetta in a slow song that appropriately blends debility (a sad reminiscence of a waltz) and passionate remonstration: the soft-loud, private-public music infects all.

Soft-loud too is the prelude to the last act. This depicts on the one hand the hushed sickroom, its faltering patient and the benign absolution of the priest, and on the other the force of Violetta's hope, passion and terror. What follows charts her decline by way of conflicting emotions – memories of Alfredo as (quite literally) she reads his father's letter of reconciliation, and expressions of renunciation, lament and prayer in her plangent 'Addio, del passato' (Farewell, lovely, happy dreams of the past), a gaspingly dysfunctional waltz. Then follows the extravagant excitement of her reunion with Alfredo, his tender, healthily waltzing promise to re-enact their flight from Paris – as he quickly discovers, his reparation is too little, too late – and her loud-soft acknowledgment of impending death. After the arrival of the guilt-ridden Germont, she passes her portrait to Alfredo as a keepsake for the pure virgin he will one day surely marry: it is an act of metempsychosis, as if Violetta is passing on her own soul, now purified. Throughout this, Death stalks the orchestra with a muffled, inexorable tread.

In the last moments of the opera, Violetta suddenly revives and in a state of extreme frenzy (*agitatissimo*) cries 'gioia' ('joy') and, horrifically, collapses lifeless. Her final word is not merely the affirmation of the courtesan's 'pure' devotion to Alfredo in face of the brittle Parisian revelry that has impinged briefly from outside with such heart-rending irony; nor is it just the defining moment of *spes phthisica*, that astonishing terminal illusion of the tubercular that quite suddenly they are cured; rather it is the point when the inexorable tragedy of affliction, sensed throughout the act, steps out from behind the bourgeois drama to claim its victim. Even Aristotle, who considered recognition at its finest when combined with reversal, would have gasped at this generic 'switch'.[6] The remorse of the bystanders is proportionate to the shock it induces.

Notes

Source: 'Tragedy of Affliction or Bourgeois Drama?', *La traviata* (Giuseppe Verdi), The Royal Opera programme, January 2008, pp. 32-6, and subsequently revised during several re-printings. It has again been reworked for this book.

* The important preface by a Venetian academician to the lost opera *Le nozze d'Enea con Lavinia* (1641) by Monteverdi, though acknowledging the authority of Aristotle, prefers a tragedy with a happy end (*lieto fine*) to one with a sad end. It contains the following remark: '[On account of Aristotle's preference for a sad end] ... this word tragedy – which signifies the action of an illustrious person – ... has commonly been taken as something mournful and grievous, contrary to its proper meaning.' Anon. 'Argument and Scenario: *Le nozze d'Enea in Lavinia* [sic], Tragedy with a Happy Ending', in: *Composing Music*, (Practica Musica 2), trans. and ed. Tim Carter, Krakow: Musica Iegellonica, 1994, pp. 151-3.

1 *The White Death. A History of Tuberculosis*, Thomas Dormandy, London: The Hambledon Press, 1999. PAS also came too late to save the tubercular Mimì: Puccini's *La bohème* (1896) is set in the Paris of c. 1830.

2 For a recent biography see: René Weis, *The Real Traviata. The Song of Marie Duplessis*, Oxford: Oxford UP, 2015.

3 Julian Budden draws an important parallel here with Isabelle's music from Meyerbeer's *Robert le diable* (1831). See: Julian Budden, *The Operas of Verdi* (3 vols.) vol. 2, London: Cassell, 1978, '*La traviata*' pp. 113-66, especially p. 134.

4 Abbé Prévost, *Manon Lescaut* (1731), trans. Leonard Tancock, London: Penguin, 1949/91. The full title is *L'Histoire du chévalier des Grieux et de Manon Lescaut*.

5 See Julian Budden: 'The Two *Traviatas*', *Proceedings of the Royal Musical Association*, No. 99, 1972-3), pp. 43-66. This is discussed later in 'From 1853 to 1854'.

6 Aristotle, *Poetics*, trans. and ed. Richard Janko, Indianapolis: Hackett, 1987, section 3.4.2, p. 14: 'A recognition is finest when it happens at the same time as a reversal, as does the one in *Oedipus*.'

2   A Comedy of Psychopathologies

Eric Crozier and Benjamin Britten: *Albert Herring*

For 'comedy' Aristotle suggests a deeper origin than mere 'revelling': comedians were those who 'wandered round the villages ejected from the town in disgrace' causing affront. However, there developed a hierarchy of types: comedy became 'greater and more honourable' than 'lampoon', just as tragedy became more honourable than epic. Homer was the first such comedian, the earliest connoisseur of the merely laughable, 'a sort of error and ugliness that is not painful and destructive'. In early times, Aristotle claimed, grander people celebrated the actions of fine people, ordinary people composed invectives, and the forms and language reacted accordingly. And although, we might add, later writers have moved between tragedy and comedy, comedy has continued to probe the interplay of the social strata, often (but not always) watching from below. Nor do we forget Aristotle's maxim that tragedy presents people as better than they are, comedy as worse, though even in the bad there must always be something good for us to hold on to. Comedy versus lampoon, the co-existence of comedy and tragedy, the corresponding variety of musical forms and language: these are our co-ordinates as we approach one of the most accomplished operatic handlings of genre in recent times.

'A Comic Opera in Three Acts' is how Benjamin Britten described his chamber opera *Albert Herring*. We therefore think we know what to expect: witty situations, sharply-drawn types, varied diction, wacky stagecraft, topical musical reference and light but confident handling. Yet the comic must be played for serious. The singer Janet Baker recalls how Britten 'once gave the cast of *Albert Herring* a piece of advice':

> in playing comedy one must not think the situation amusing oneself … the characters were not in the least amusing or eccentric *to* themselves, which is precisely why an audience thinks them to be so.[1]

However, comedy can have many strains. *Herring* has a period setting – spring, 1900 – that is sufficiently distanced, even by Britten's 1947, to allow audiences to smile benignly over a vanished world even as they compare it meaningfully to their own. It includes picture-post-card innuendo, as with the refrain 'have a nice peach?', and an orgiastic kiss for Sid and Nancy; and it indulges in outright lampoon with its allusions to Wagner's *Tristan und Isolde*, the magic love-potion now trivialized into the lemonade laced with rum that makes Albert hiccup.

The title page of the score describes *Albert Herring* as being 'freely' adapted by Eric Crozier from a short story by Guy de Maupassant, 'Madame Husson's May King'.[2] The story was written in 1887. It is told in flashback, Maupassant's 'May King' ending up as an old soak who dies of 'the DTs'. By contrast, Crozier's libretto unfolds directly, with his youthful May King, Albert, triumphantly facing down the ossified ethical code of the community in the market-town of Loxford. The moral focus of both story and opera is twofold. First, there is the formidable busybody Madame Husson, the opera's Lady Billows. Maupassant writes: 'She was very virtuous herself and was keen on the cause of virtue in others.' Indeed, in the opera Lady Billows and her housekeeper note down every sexual transgression in town. By contrast, Maupassant's chaste Isidore, the opera's Albert, has 'an unhealthy fear of woman': he is 'modesty's litmus paper' and the butt of every licentious joke. Albert's casting as a May *King* thus brings together two psycho-pathologies: in the story, Madame Husson and Isidore – in the opera, Lady Billows and Albert.

In fact, *Herring* is Britten's only comic opera, and in both its jocular and serious aspects proceeds by hyperbole – exaggeration. This is clearly the case in Act One. The first scene, a kind of muster, introduces the local dignitaries, each of whom has distinct music – the frantic, servile housekeeper Florence, the fussy, unctuous vicar, the ponderous superintendent, and so forth. As a group they sing sycophantically in unified harmony or buoyant fugue, and propose various May Queens to an ingratiating waltz. At their centre stands the domineering and effusive Lady Billows, whose emphatic voice swoops, slides, leaps and is given to self-righteous bravura. Her rage aria is in the classical tragic key of D minor: 'Is this all you can bring?' she cries, '… are Loxford girls all whores?' Florence officiously echoes her final phrases, to our amusement, though not, of course, to hers. By contrast, the second scene, which is set in a grocery, defines Albert negatively: he has never sung ball-games in the street like Cis and Emmie, or stolen apples like Harry, or courted a girl as the cocky butcher's boy Sid does right under his nose with the tender Nancy. None of their music is his; thanks to his mother, another Lady Billows, he is an arch goody-goody. And when the Loxford dignitaries arrive to invite him to be their May King, it is his mother who does the negotiating, and when they have left it is she who bludgeons him into accepting. No wonder Albert reflects that it's time to get away: the social strata and their suffocating constraints are there for all to see.

The second act develops the first with a witty range of musical reference. We are now in a marquee in the Vicarage garden, laid out with food and drink. In the horn, the May King motif tells us the great day has come – but it has acquired an extra, cautionary note: we wonder why. In a passage reminiscent of Wagner's *Die Meistersinger*, the schoolteacher assiduously rehearses her children in a greeting song, which is also oddly reminiscent of 'Hark, the herald angels sing'; the guests respond to this and other presentations in a controlled hubbub – a witty foretaste of the 'aleatoric music' of the 1960s. In her address, Lady Billows duly billows, closing with echoes of 'Rule Britannia', and soon after Albert is presented with *Foxe's Book of Martyrs*. Now Albert rises. As the angst-ridden string music tells us, he is tongue-tied and confused. His eventual speech, '… 'er … thank you very much', reduces the company to laughter. After drinking the lemonade Sid has laced, his hiccups again make him ridiculous. But he is not left humiliated. For by consuming alcohol at the very moment he celebrates abstention, he is finally liberated: 'I feel brisk like a rocket', he sings in the final hubbub, and the orchestra follows suit with a riotous interlude.

The second scene takes us back to the shop. It is late in the evening. A slow, beguiling duet for alto flute and bass clarinet frames the action and comes as a welcome contrast to the preceding fast music. We now follow Albert into a dark night, in every sense. There is still humour, of course – Albert fumbles with the gas lamp and tosses a coin before setting off on the razzle. But there is also self-recrimination – so fierce, indeed, that we wonder if, after all, we really are set for a dire outcome. His music is structured like an intense double aria in Verdi. First, he arrives and reflects on the day's events – the *scena*; thinking of Nancy, he launches into a slow aria comparing his shyness with Sid's whistling bravado – the *cavatina*; Sid and Nancy appear outside, singing a duet on which Albert eavesdrops – the middle section, or *tempo di mezzo*; and now, thoroughly goaded, Albert rapidly takes stock, and whistling like Sid races off into the night – the *cabaletta*. In a slow, poignant close, Albert's mother returns, unaware that she has been comprehensively abandoned.

The third act now gathers all parties into a single scene – all, that is, except Albert, who is missing, presumed dead. The people of Loxford, bar the children, break into the work's famous threnody. This is both tragic and comic. On the one hand it has the high pathos appropriate to the commemoration of an illustrious figure; it gathers force as it grows from four to nine real parts; over a relentless choral chant – 'In the midst of life is Death, Death awaits us one and all' – each of the nine singers superimposes a poignant, characteristic solo; and after another hub-hub, the group bursts out, ironically in full voice, with the impressive 'Grief is silent, Pity dumb'. The key, moreover, is the conventionally morbid B♭ minor. On the other hand, the music exultantly mocks its own high solemnity: for at its end, Albert returns. His appearance – 'back from the dead' – riotously punctures the gloom, and most of the 'mourners' react with vicious prurience. Loxford grief is exposed for what it is: wounded pride.

The close of the opera points to the importance in comedy of tone-of-voice. Albert tells us of his drunkenness and debauchery – decorously sparing us the details – and then upbraids his mother: '[You] did up my instinct with safety pins, kept me wrapped in cotton wool,' he cries. Then we hear an amiable, cool cantilena in the strings. It is a sign that Albert has found his independence. Above it, he soaks up the rage of Lady Billows and his mother, and asks the crowd to leave. He has now faced down the matriarchal society: one day, we imagine, he will surely be Grocer, Father and Mayor. Nancy gives him a kiss, and the children turn their mocking chorus into an approving one. Reversing the authority of the generations, principally from the vantage point of the young or disadvantaged, is a challenge we find in most Britten operas. But never is it accomplished with such aplomb as it is in *Herring*. At its end Sid and Nancy murmur 'Good old Albert!', and, indeed, the community will now have to move on. We in the audience also nod approvingly, knowing that it is the spirit of comedy that has triumphed, even though it has had to borrow a few clothes from tragedy.

Notes

Source: 'The Comic in Opera', talk commissioned by BBC Radio 3 and recorded on 23 November 2013. By prior agreement, only extracts were used for a 'sound-bite' documentary.

1   Janet Baker, in: *Britten's Century*, ed. Mark Bostridge, London: Bloomsbury, 2013, p. 43.
2   'Madame Husson's May King' in: Guy de Maupassant, *Madamoiselle Fifi and Other Stories*, trans. and ed. David Coward, Oxford: Oxford UP, 1993, pp. 167-84.

3 A Generic Puzzle

Richard Wagner: *Die Meistersinger von Nürnberg*

In Ancient Greece, a short and amusing satyr-play could follow a set of three serious tragedies; and, as we have said, Aristotle located the pre-history of comedy in just such revelling. A much-cited example is Cyclops *by Euripides: here, the bibulous Silenus heads a chorus of satyrs imprisoned by the man-eating Cyclops (Polyphemus), and the wily Odysseus, finding himself during his voyage back from Troy on 'danger's very altar-base', has to plot an effective escape. The semi-human satyrs may be wise and knock-about, and their eventual master the god Dionysus, but the terror they face is genuine. Not for nothing did Wagner think of his* Meistersinger *as a quasi-Greek pendant to* Tannhäuser *(itself a tragic action with a happy end): disorder erupts in Nuremberg in Act Two and the orderly revels unfold by the banks of the Pegnitz in Act Three. But comedy hardly suited his essentially serious nature, and the scale of the pendant he planned was even larger than what it followed: so in wrestling with the competing demands of tragedy, comedy and satire he was perforce returning to the very origins of drama.*

Audiences are entitled to ask, just what *kind* of piece is *Die Meistersinger von Nürnberg*? It is a question Wagner asked himself, and answered differently at different times. In July 1845 he first sketched a 'Comic Opera in 3 Acts'; in a letter of 1861 he referred to a 'popular' comic opera; and in 1861-2 he turned his sketch into a libretto for a 'Grand Comic Opera'. However, the bill for the first performance in Munich on 21 June 1868 merely announced an 'Opera'; and the published score (in the Peters Edition) makes no mention of genre whatever. *The New Grove Dictionary of Opera* (1992) follows suit, listing *Die Meistersinger* as the only generically unclassified work in the Wagner canon.[1]

Inevitably, scholars have had their say. Carl Dahlhaus claimed that despite the operatic 'monologues, songs, ensembles, choruses and dances' with a 'massed finale' at the end of each act, Wagner's treatment was a 'total musico-dramatic conception' in line with the music dramas he was, or had been composing at the time (the *Ring* and *Tristan*).[2] The musical materials indeed spin an intricate web of cross-reference over the work so that, say, we hear elements of the closing Prize Song even as the young lovers meet in church during the opening scene. Likewise, Theodor Adorno argued that, despite appearances, *Meistersinger* depends on magic: how could a woman from Nuremberg be dispatched to meet John the Baptist on the banks of the

Jordan (as Sachs's apprentice David relates in his Act Three song)? 'Beneath [Wagner's] gaze,' he remarked, 'everything becomes mythological.'[3] Certainly, the famous Act Three quintet celebrates Walther von Stolzing's Prize Song not as artifice, but as the interpretation of a sacred (morning) dream. Art comes from the unconscious. Yet *Meistersinger* is not just a 'Festival Stage Piece' (*Bühnenfestspiel*) or an 'Action' (*Handlung*), later categories that roll back Wagner's earlier operatic genres up to *Lohengrin* (1850): Grand Romantic Opera, Grand Comic Opera, Grand Tragic Opera and so on. Its roots are demonstrably less in myth, the context of music drama, than in history, the context of opera: the work is specific to Nuremberg in 1560 or '61. And as such its basic plot had been around for twenty years: Adalbert Gyrowetz's 'Romantic, Comic *Singspiel* in 2 Acts', *Hans Sachs im vorgerückten Alter* (Hans Sachs in Later Life), appeared in 1834; and Albert Lortzing's three-act 'Comic Opera', *Hans Sachs* (1840), a work derived from a dramatic poem by J. L. D. von Deinhardstein (which Wagner knew), was revised and restaged in May 1845. (In Gyrowetz, Sachs helps a young nobleman and prospective Mastersinger to win his lady whereas in Lortzing he is himself the lover.)

Wagner himself revealed the source of the confusion in a key passage from his 'Communication to My Friends' of 1851. For him, Hans Sachs, leader of the Mastersingers, was 'the last manifestation of the people's creativity (*Volksgeist*)'; he stood

> in contrast to the pettifogging bombast of the other Meistersingers, whose absurd pedantry, in tabulator and prosody, I embodied in 'The Marker', an examiner appointed to mark each breach of the rules in singing. It is also 'The Marker' who courts the young lady offered by her father, a senior Mastersinger, as prize in 'a forthcoming singing contest'. [4]

The Marker, though, has a rival in a young nobleman who has come to Nuremberg from 'the ruined castle of his ancestors' to learn the art of the Mastersingers. His aim is to sing 'enthusiastically' in praise of Woman; and this he does with conspicuous success. Eros drives Art. 'Just as, in Athens, a jolly satyr-play could follow a tragedy,' wrote Wagner, so too could his 'comic' *Meistersinger von Nürnberg* act as a 'pendant' to his *Sängerkrieg auf Wartburg* ('The Wartburg Singing Contest' is part of *Tannhäuser's* title). The song contest thus became the fulcrum of a shift from potential catastrophe to triumph, from 'tragedy' to 'comedy' (in the modern sense of both terms). However, Wagner declined to name *Meistersinger* after Hans Sachs or the Marker's young rival, Walther: rather he focussed pre-eminently on the community and its rebirth through song.

Yet there was a fly in the ointment. Wagner explained how, after mapping out *Meistersinger*, 'peace forsook me until I had sketched out the more detailed plan of *Lohengrin*'; he had had to recover 'the earnest, yearning mood' wherein lay 'the core of Art rooted in Life itself', whereas the satirical spirit in which he had conceived *Meistersinger* was voguish, superficial and un-natural. But yearning (as he had previously shown) leads to revolt, and revolt to the tragic (which for him entailed self-sacrifice and death, albeit death endowed with vital significance); and since the earnest and the satirical were incompatible, he abandoned the latter. The implication was that if he was to rescue *Meistersinger*, he would have to subsume elements of the tragic into the comic.

This, in fact, was what Wagner did, consciously or not, between 1851 and 1868. He integrated aspects of the *Tannhäuser* 'tragedy' with the elaborate details of the Nuremberg 'comedy'. He moved the singing competition from inside the Wartburg castle, where it was introduced by stiff pageantry, to the open meadow beside the river Pegnitz, where it is preceded by popular festivities, jubilant trumpet calls and a procession of three guilds, each with a male-voice chorus; he substituted the frenzied bacchanal of the Venusberg with the playful dancing of young men and women (though keeping it sufficiently licentious to disturb Sachs's apprentice); and in place of the Thuringian Court saluting their political leader with 'Landgraf Hermann, Heil!', he has the Nurembergers greet their cultural leader with 'Heil Nürnberg's theurem Sachs!' They even sing back to 'the dear Sachs' his *Wittenberg Nightingale* poem as a radiant chorale. Where *Tannhäuser* pitted sacred Catholicism against profanity – the Pope and the Virgin Mary against Venus –, *Meistersinger* sustains an unchallenged panegyric to Luther and Lutheran music; and just as in *Tannhäuser* the Landgrave pronounced music as essential to the health of the body politic and offered his niece as a competition prize, so too in Act One of *Meistersinger* does the goldsmith (Pogner) follow suit with his daughter. But the *Meistersinger* competition doesn't collapse in turmoil, as it did in *Tannhäuser*, but rather is marked, even before the end of the Prize Song, by general rejoicing (the uproar is reserved for the collective reaction to the young man's Trial Song at the end of Act One). It is as if the characters from *Tannhäuser* have come back to make reparation in *Die Meistersinger*.

But they have also come back changed. Ritchie Robertson writes that '*Humor* (humour) in German denotes neither comedy nor wit, but a resigned acceptance of life's imperfections.'[5] The much-vaunted 'humour' Sachs acquired during the years from 1851 to 1868 pays testament to just this: it is as if Wagner had moulded a national character out of a whole tradition of German history and letters. From Goethe's poetic interpretation of a fictitious old woodcut, *Hans Sachsens poetische Sendung* (1776), he took the 'skilful … full and loving' cobbler, a favourite of the Muses steeped in learning and wise to the follies of the world; he followed J. G. Herder in directing Sachs's attention to German art and 'natural' popular culture (*Von deutscher Art und Kunst* (1772) and *Stimmen der Völker in Liedern* (1778-79)); and from Schopenhauer's perception of the illusory nature of the world and art ('*Wahn*') he not only enriched Sachs's musings on poetry (planned in 1845) but also anticipated Nietzsche's ideas of sublimation (of aggression into creativity). By referring in Act Three to the real Hans Sachs's play on *Tristan und Isolde*, he drew some sly but significant parallels: his own Sachs relinquishes his pursuit of the younger woman as a correction of King Marke's failure to give up Isolde, just as he, Wagner, the supreme Mastersinger of *his* day, had relinquished the young Mathilde Wesendonck. More still, he indicated how the nub of the aesthetic confrontation in *Meistersinger* lies between the fervent Tristanesque eroticism of the young knight ('the Wagner style') and the stiff formality of French court music, including the Marker's song, a rickety Franco-Italian serenade. *Meistersinger* is as much a pendant to *Tristan* as it is to *Tannhäuser*.

Yet Wagner never jettisoned his original satire. In the completed work, the creator still avenges his critic, Sachs marks the Marker's song with jocular sadism and the Marker walks straight into Sachs's humiliation trap in the prize contest. Not for nothing did W. H. Auden point to the severity of the treatment of Beckmesser as Wagner's 'one artistic mistake'.[6] Indeed, when the Marker's repetitive caterwauling is taken up in the orchestra for the Nuremberg riot, we understand his 'wrong' music as a disease in the body politic. Wagner certainly lined up his *dramatis personae* on a combative basis. He turned the Marker briefly into Veit Hanslich (lampooning Eduard Hanslick, the formalist Viennese music critic) before settling for Sixtus Beckmesser ('Beck the Knife'), a name derived from J. C. Wagenseil's book on the Mastersingers of 1697; on the other hand he endowed Beckmesser's young rival, Walther von Stolzing, with pride (*Stolz*), nobility ('a Franconian knight') and resonance (Walther von der Vogelweide, a minstrel from *Tannhäuser* whose very name signalled affinity with Nature and the birds). By calling Pogner's 'prize' daughter Eva, he turned her union with Walther into a pre-lapsarian fantasy of Adam and Eve in Paradise; and by signalling how Sachs shares his name day with John the Baptist, he makes us ask if Walther is a new Messiah, no less.

Jungians will quickly point to Beckmesser as Sachs's 'shadow', 'the 'negative side' of his personality, 'the sum of all those unpleasant qualities we like to hide'. Latent in Sachs is indeed an officious pedant, an inappropriate suitor and even (as we learn from the ardour of his – possibly inaccurate – transcription of Walther's prize song) a pilferer. Freudians, on the other hand, will share Hans Keller's view that Sachs 'is a projection of Wagner's own mind ... Walther is [his] ego, Sachs his enlightened super-ego':[7] certainly, Walther is still an impulsive Tannhäuser, and though he has Sachs to rein him in, goes his own way when it comes to performing the prize song in public (necessarily, for performance is nothing if it doesn't mould itself to an occasion); and though Sachs shows mature restraint in resisting Eva, he copes with the ensuing bitter disappointment through bursts of self-contempt. Walther and Sachs will always have a troubled relationship. Others, like Juliet Mitchell, will locate the comedy in David's narcissistic delight in listing all the Mastersingers' rules and types; and Kleinians will point to the moment when Sachs, hailed in Act Three by the Nurembergers, instantly relates the group joy to the group madness of the previous night, revealing through the music a realistic ('depressive') understanding of ubiquitous illusion (*Wahn*). It is the complexity of the psychological traits that distinguishes the finished work.

Nowhere, though, is it more essential to retain a dual perspective (of the 'depressive' and the 'illusory') than at *Meistersinger's* much-sensationalized close. Hans Sachs's startling address derives from a 'humorous' couplet Wagner appended to his 1845 sketch sometime before 1851:

> The pride of the Holy Roman Empire may depart,
> But we'll still hold on high our holy German Art.[8]

The harnessing of song to the defence of the realm had been a topic of the Landgrave's address in Act Two of *Tannhäuser*: Sachs's couplet merely recast it in prescient form (Charlemagne's Holy Roman Empire would survive only up to Napoleon). By 1868, however, things had changed. France was threatening Bavaria, and political tensions were soon to erupt in the Franco-Prussian War of 1870-1. No wonder Wagner felt the need for a specifically German Art (the focus of his writings in the 1860s)! No wonder, too, that Sachs's less-than-humorous warning of 1868 – '*Habt acht!*' (Beware!) – served to rally the '*deutsches Volk und Reich*', the community of German-speaking people west of the Rhine (Wagner's definition from his essay '*Was ist deutsch*' of 1865)! Sachs's couplet of the late 1840s had thus been adapted to the political realities of the late 1860s. As with the work of J. G. Herder (1744-1803), what had started as an outward-looking treatment of the people had over time become inward-looking.

So, what kind of piece is *Die Meistersinger von Nürnberg*? Perhaps the best we can say is, *Grosse romantische Komödie im vorgerückten Alter* – a Grand Romantic Comedy Grown Old. But we still need the rider that advancing age can bring the wisdom to deconstruct that Romanticism unflinchingly, even when celebrating it most forcefully.

Notes

Source: 'Wagner's Satyr Play', *Die Meistersinger von Nürnberg* (Richard Wagner), The Royal Opera programme, December 2011, pp. 28-33.

1   I am indebted to the excellent contributions of John Warrack and Lucy Beckett to: *Richard Wagner: Die Meistersinger von Nürnberg*, ed. John Warrack, Cambridge: Cambridge UP, Cambridge Opera Handbooks, 1994. I am also indebted to the essays in *The Mastersingers of Nuremberg*, ed. Nicholas John, London: ENO/ROH Opera

Guide, John Calder, 1983. As noted, I have referred to the multi-authored entries on 'Wagner, Richard', and '*Die Meistersinger von Nürnberg*' in *The New Grove Dictionary of Opera*, 4 vols., London: Macmillan, 1992.

2 Carl Dahlhaus, '*Die Meistersinger von Nürnberg*', *Richard Wagner's Music Dramas* (1971), trans. Mary Whittall, Cambridge: Cambridge UP, 1979, pp. 65-79, especially p. 75.

3 Theodor Adorno, *In Search of Wagner* (1952), trans. Rodney Livingstone, (n.p./UK): New Left Books, 1981, p. 120.

4 Richard Wagner, 'A Communication to my Friends' (1851), *The Artwork of the Future and Other Works*, trans. William Ashton Ellis (1895), Lincoln: Nebraska UP, 1993, pp. 328-33.

5 Ritchie Robertson, *Kafka. A Very Short Introduction*, Oxford: Oxford UP, 2004, p. 44.

6 W. H. Auden in a transcribed but unpublished radio interview with Hans Keller, 1971.

7 Hans Keller, review of Egon Wellesz's handbook on *The Mastersingers* (London: Boosey and Hawkes, 1948), *Music Review*, October 1949, pp. 146-7.

8 Richard Wagner, 1851, p. 331.

4 Boccaccian Comedy

Arrigo Boito (after Shakespeare) and Giuseppe Verdi: *Falstaff*

We have already noted that Aristotle introduces social status into his discussion of genre: the comedians were those who had been 'ejected from the town in disgrace'. As it evolved, opera first became increasingly alive to national differences, notably with regard to singing; then, in the late nineteenth and early twentieth centuries following the political turmoil in Europe, it took on a further distinction: comic opera was perceived as the province of the French and Italians, and tragic opera, with its weighty emphasis on myth, the specialism of the Germans. Of course, there are plenty of exceptions to prove, if not invalidate, the rule, and there is no pretending that comedy doesn't depend upon a dark underside (as we have seen with Britten's Albert Herring *(1947)). Yet it took a Puccini to set the witty* Gianni Schicchi *(1918) and a Ravel to compose both the wry* L'Heure espagnole *(1911) and the poised* L'Enfant et les sortilèges *(1925) – all three, significantly, short works in one act. There are also delightful miniatures by Poulenc and Martinů. Verdi's last opera, still concise but on a larger scale, was deemed to play its part in such generic politics. Without immediate context, comedy is nothing.*

Those who attended the first performance of *Falstaff* at La Scala in February 1893 were overwhelmed by the opera's novelty and zest. Verdi's wife Giuseppina hailed it as 'a whole new art of music and poetry', and the librettist Boito saw in it 'a real outburst of grace, power and gaiety': indeed, 'by the miracle of sounds, Shakespeare's sparkling farce is returned to its clear Tuscan source of "Ser Giovanni Fiorentino"' (*Il Pecorone* – the Outsize Sheep-man – of 1558).[1] It was a work, Boito further claimed, to purge Milan of 'ultramontane fog' (Wagner's *Der fliegende Holländer* was in repertory at La Scala) and 'mediterraneanize' the human spirit (echoing Nietzsche's promotion of Bizet's *Carmen* over Wagner's *Ring*); and it would throw down a gauntlet to the French who habitually bowdlerized the Bard in the theatre and would surely tone him down in the 'deeply academic' Opéra. The French critic Camille Bellaigue likewise set the lightness of *Falstaff* against the 'heavily Germanic joy of [Wagner's] *Die Meistersinger*'; and from the first Verdi himself aimed at a new kind of intimacy by wanting to stage Boito's 'incomparable' lyric comedy in his own home (St. Agata): 'I am afraid the ambience of La Scala may be too vast for a comedy in which the rapid flow of the dialogue and the play of facial expressions are the principal features.' A 'last opera' though it may have been, *Falstaff* nevertheless set Italy a fresh agenda.

Almost a century later, that agenda was refined by Italo Calvino.[2] In a posthumous essay of 1985 he upheld 'the values of lightness'. Lightness removes 'weight' from stories; it transforms language; it manifests itself in thoughtfulness as much as in frivolity; it is a 'vector of information'; it 'goes with precision and determination'; it reveals itself in motion, leaping and hovering uncannily; in a nutshell, it is Boccaccian. Above all, it is a reaction to the unbearable weight of being (to adapt a term of Milan Kundera's) – so much so that lightness and weight have constantly to be understood in opposition. Indeed, this fundamental insight holds the key to Boito and Verdi's achievement at the most literal level. The opera falls into three acts, each of two scenes. The first scene in each act focuses on the manifestly weighty Falstaff and his circle (the cupidinous, compromised men), the second on the nimble Alice Ford and hers (the streetwise but morally punctilious 'merry wives'); the finale of Act Three resolves the conflict not just by spooking Falstaff with the (supposed) supernatural, but also by uniting the company in a choral celebration of the lightness of being ('All the world's a farce'). The first scenes address suffering in private, the second gaiety in the community; and because the opera belongs to the Shakespearean 'theatre of masks', Falstaff and Ford on occasion speak the language of light even when their motives are cloaked in dark. *Falstaff* owes its lightness to the deft handling of weight.

In fact, Boito and Verdi began work in 1889 with a debate on genre. In comedy, Boito noted, our interest wanes as the end approaches (the audience says 'it is finished' before the plot is done), whereas in tragedy it grows ('because the end is terrible'). They should therefore make their own 'last scene' brisker and less fragmented than in their source, just as they should invest it with warmth and a new 'light' tone for the fantastic elements. Verdi also acknowledged the problem: 'even Shakespeare could not escape this law.' Within weeks he was writing a comic fugue, and in due course added a choral fugue to the close to make a rumbustious climactic 'curtain', uniting a typically fast conclusion (*stretta*), an epigrammatic statement directed at both cast and audience (*parabasis)* and a modern libation to the contrapuntal spirit of Palestrina.

But the musical challenges went deeper. While admitting that the orchestra now had greater importance – an importance he certainly exploited – Verdi still gave pride of place to the voice. In 1892 he wrote: 'The music is not difficult but will have to be sung differently from other modern operas and from the old [comic] *buffo* operas … [not] like [Bizet's] *Carmen*, and not even like [Donizetti's] *Don Pasquale* … there is need for study, and that will take time. Our singers, in general, can only sing with big voices; they have neither flexibility nor clear and easy diction, and they lack phrasing and breath.' When it came to rehearsal, he devoted hours to encouraging precise enunciation and bodily expression without compromising the tempo. Yet, although he developed a conversational style (*parlante*) in the music, he still retained vestiges of *bel canto*: Alice's role was to be 'very agile', Ford's highly dramatic, Fenton's lyrical, Nannetta's 'delicate', especially in her fairy song. He used rhythm to 'code' these types: for the most part Alice and the women sing in teasing Beethovenian scherzo metres (6/8, 9/8, 12/8), Falstaff and the men in combative duple metres (2/4, 4/4) and Fenton and Nannetta in a sensual triple metre (3/4); he made the vocal casting more or less traditional (though, significantly, Falstaff and Ford – the two deceived men – are both baritones); and, very roughly, he centred the keys on a rotund C major for Falstaff, going sharp-side for the women and flat-side for the lovers. The opera revels in its demarcations.

Clearly, the principal action of *Falstaff* involves a double plot: Falstaff's attempt to seduce Alice Ford ('Potbelly' needs money to fund his gluttony) and Ford's attempt to marry his obstinate daughter Nannetta to Dr. Caius. Both ventures are foiled by the 'wives'. But weaving through this is the burgeoning romance of Nannetta and Fenton, which, by guile, leads to their marriage in Windsor Park at Herne's Oak. Boito was clear how we wanted to handle this: their love should serve 'to refresh and solidify the entire comedy'; it should appear in each ensemble scene; and it should be 'as sugar is sprinkled on a cake' without gathering at any point into a 'real duet'. Verdi took him at his word. Love moves furtively in the margins of the action, and – apart from a tiny formal duet embodied in the second act finale – the lovers share a single line rather than sing in tandem. Yet, paradoxically, the romance provides the work's most stable music, deploying fixed forms that nevertheless respect the unstable action. In the second scene of Act One, Nannetta and Fenton share a two-verse aria: towards the end of the first verse they are interrupted by the arrival of women, whereupon they complete their verse with Fenton in hiding; after a short scene for the women, they sing the second verse (expanded as the flirtation mounts): only now it is Nannetta who moves away to complete the verse off-stage – whereupon four men arrive. Similarly, at the start of the second scene of Act Three: when Fenton sings his famous solo 'sonnet' (a piece Verdi originally thought expendable), Nannetta comes out of the forest to join him. Although together they complete the fourteen lines of text, Alice arrives to interrupt them at the apex of their melodic line (the concert version shows the music still had two bars to go). Even when, later in the scene, Nannetta does sing her melting two-verse aria without interruption, it is as the Queen of Fairies putting on a performance with her nymphs. Here stable form is placed in inverted commas.

But there was a further complication. Boito was not only a fervent Italian and Shakespearean but also a Germanist and a composer-librettist. So it is hard not to make ultramontane comparisons in the musical schemes he devised for the ensembles. As a type the *concertato* ranks among the glories of Italian opera, and its elements are still present in *Falstaff*; yet, as in *Die Meistersinger*, the three act-finales are as brilliant as they are varied. In the third scene of his own *Mefistofele* (1868/75) Boito had combined two amorous couples – on one hand the light Faust and Margherita, and on the other the dark Mefistofele and Marta. In the second scene of *Falstaff*, he likewise combines contrasting factions after presenting them independently: four vengeful women pitted against four circumspect men (each faction retaining its distinctive metre), with Fenton floating a serene melody over the hubbub (since each of nine strands has its own text, there can only be Babel). At the end of the second act of *Die Meistersinger*, Wagner had supported the riot in Nuremberg with constantly-moving music (*moto perpetuo*) derived from Beckmesser's song. Verdi likewise gathers his second act to a tumultuous head with constantly-moving music in the orchestra. But in his case he changes the quality of the movement with each character: after the arrival of Meg come Mistress Quickly, Ford and then, following a snatched aria from the two lovers, Ford again as he returns in a jealous rage. For the scourging of Falstaff at the climax of Act Three Boito reduces the text to vicious little taunts, allowing Verdi to recapture something of the wild energy of the 'Walpurgisnacht' in *Mefistofele*. Verdi's intention throughout was to keep the ensembles flowing – and indeed, he revised part of the Act Two finale with just that in mind.

True comedy, though, stands or falls by its handling of linguistic small-change. For Shakespeare that meant word-play, punning, double entendre and delight in the quirks of speech. Little of this, though, can survive into opera. So Boito's task was threefold. First, to invent memorable phrases that could dissolve into witty musical motifs, as with Mistress Quickly's mock-obsequious greeting, 'Reverenza', her conspiratorial 'dalle due alle tre' (from two to three) and her 'povera donna' (poor woman) that lures Falstaff to the forest. Alice's 'Se ne ritornerà', which looks forward to the general return, transforms into the airy dance-like figure that closes Act Three. Second, to generate situations that would repeatedly exaggerate Falstaff's size and self-esteem (*hyperbole*) only to debase him with laughter (*tapinosis*) – and what a weight to tip into the Thames! This is also true of how the characters behave in Falstaff's presence (witness the comedy of manners as Ford comes and goes in Act Two) or discuss him in his absence: the wives' letter-reading unfolds his aria-like *billet-doux* with melting affect before gleefully deriding it. Third, to create for Falstaff a double-sided diction that constantly juxtaposes extremes, pitting the suavely debonair against the coarsely priapic, the mutter against the roar. His 'Va, vecchio John' (On your way, old John) may issue his body a stately call to new erotic ventures, but the music that flanks it is grossly triumphalist. Nevertheless, the irony has its delights: Falstaff's reminiscence of his slim self, the dainty 'Quand'ero paggio del Duca di Norfolk' (When I was page to the Duke of Norfolk), was the most encored 'number' in the work's early history.

For his part, Verdi also pushed in three different directions. First, he delights in allusion: Bardolph and Pistol's bogus ecclesiastical 'Amen' has the technical function of closing the instrumental (sonata) form underpinning Dr. Caius's confrontation with Falstaff and his crew; Falstaff's pseudo-madrigal with Ford in Act Two, 'L'amor, L'amor', seems to parody Carmen's 'L'amour, l'amour'; Alice's 'Elizabethan' guitar-playing launches Falstaff into a snip of serenade; and Dr. Caius 'marries' Bardolph to the sounds of a decorous 'air'. Second, he deploys an abundance of small 'classical' instrumental forms, sometimes presented simply, but sometimes subverted according to context: the women's quartet in Act One owes its wit to the crystalline structure. And third, he ventures into the dark with genuinely weightier music. In describing 'the Black Hunter', Alice so spooks her friends that she has at once to un-spook them with a blithe mazurka; the company's torment of Falstaff ('Capron! Scroccron! Spaccon!') borders on the downright vicious; and the three great dramatic monologues – a type Verdi had all but perfected by the time of *Rigoletto* (1851) – show Falstaff and Ford attaining a near-tragic stature. The genres manifestly switch when Ford discovers that Falstaff has already made an assignment with his wife: for a telling instant his abrupt shriek of 'Chi?' (Whom?) lets the comic mask slip. His jealousy is now for real.

Some months after the first performance, Boito tried to turn Verdi's thoughts to a *King Lear*. Verdi resisted, pleading (to Mascagni) age and terror at 'the scene when Lear is alone on the heath'. Composing such tragedy would overwhelm him. Yet back in 1850 Verdi had thought of *Lear* as the ideal subject to release him into 'a completely new manner', a fluid dramatic style. In declining Boito, did he also sense that with the comic *Falstaff* he had finally achieved that manner?

Notes

Source: 'Verdi's Boccaccian Comedy', *Falstaff* (Giuseppe Verdi), The Royal Opera programme, 2012, pp. 31-6; reprinted 2015, pp. 31-7.

1 Quotations from Boito and Verdi are drawn from: *Verdi's 'Falstaff' in Letters and Contemporary Reviews*, trans. and ed. Hans Busch, Indiana: Indiana UP, 1997.
2 Italo Calvino's undelivered Charles Eliot Norton lecture on 'Lightness' appears in: *Six Memos for the Next Millennium* (1988), trans. Patrick Creagh, London: Penguin Classics, 2009, pp. 3-29.

5 Epic Opera

Bertolt Brecht and Kurt Weill: *Aufstieg und Fall der Stadt Mahagonny*

Among theatrical innovators of the twentieth century, pride of place must go to Bertolt Brecht. Along with others, he developed an 'epic' style of drama in Munich and Berlin during the years that followed World War One, motivated in part by stodgy performances of Wagner in Munich in the early 1900s. However, it would be as wrong to equate Aristotle's 'epic' with Brecht's 'epic theatre' as it is to ignore their areas of overlap. Aristotle compares the varied episodes of Homer's large epics – the Iliad, *say – with the tightly focused progression of scenes in the relatively short tragedies of Sophocles (and for Aristotle, tragedy here subsumes comedy): 'what is more concentrated is more pleasurable than what is diluted with a lot of time.' While Brecht could assemble varied short scenes, as in his* Fear and Misery of the Third Reich *(1935-8), he could also write historical plays that were conspicuously long, notably* Mother Courage *(1941) and* The Life of Galileo *(1943). 'Epic theatre' set out to create a pervasive sense of detachment (or 'alienation') by presenting each scene as a moral picture for the audience to reflect upon; and it preceded each picture with a title. Yet the scenes could also be intensely moving, just as they contributed to a political (anti-fascist, communistic) agenda. However, Brecht's methods were not wholly new: Cammarano and Verdi added titles to each of the three acts of their Schiller-derived* Luisa Miller *(1849); Leoncavallo appended a distancing prologue to his verismo opera* Pagliacci *(1892); and Prokofiev gave his* War and Peace *(1944/59) the generic subtitle 'opera in 13 lyrico-dramatic scenes'. Likewise, Stravinsky, working with Cocteau, prefaced each of the six episodes of his wilfully cool opera-oratorio* Oedipus rex *(1928) with a spoken introduction. In this he may not have owed directly to Brecht, but his intention was similarly motivated by a determination to resist Wagner.*

Aufstieg und Fall der Stadt Mahagonny, an 'opera in 3 acts' about a beguiling 'City of Nets', received its eagerly awaited first performance on 9 March 1930 at the Neues Theater in Leipzig; indeed, so eager was the anticipation that the performance yielded the greatest operatic scandal of its century. Ronald Sanders reports how Nazi Brown-shirts were demonstrating 'in front of the opera house' early in the day; Alfred Polgar recalls 'war cries' and whistles echoing through the house; and H. H. Stuckenschmidt describes how the tumult in the third act was such that the conductor could barely end the work – indeed, the uproar lasted fifteen minutes and spread to the stage. Kurt Weill, the work's composer, was there; Bertolt Brecht, its playwright-cum-librettist, stayed away. If that was unprecedented, so was the staging in Frankfurt that October when storm troopers burst in and hurled stink-bombs. Worse still, during rehearsals for the first (modified) Berlin performance in December 1931, the already shaky relation of librettist and composer fell apart, with Brecht denouncing Weill as a 'phoney Richard Strauss' and quitting the show. (They were back together, however, for *The Seven Deadly Sins* of 1933.) Tensions, that is to say, were forever at breaking point – but why?

From the first, the *Mahagonny* project had been conceived as politically and aesthetically iconoclastic. It followed Brecht and Weill's short but sharp *Mahagonny-Songspiel* of 1927, an 'American' songs-only music-theatre piece they cannibalized lavishly for the opera, and their marginally less strident *Dreigroschenoper* (Threepenny Opera) of 1928, a German version of John Gay's populist *Beggar's Opera* of 1728. Yet though the Communistic, no-holds-barred side of Brecht took America and its *laissez-faire* capitalism for his target, the witty, poetical side succumbed to the culture's narcotic appeal: his German text is pervaded by catchy Americanisms. No sooner have Jenny and the girls arrived in Mahagonny than they sing (in English) the Alabama Song – 'Oh, show us the way to the next whisky-bar, Oh, don't ask why!'; much later, finding 'There is no money in this land', they cry (again in English) 'Let's go to Benares'; and at the end, as Begbick, Fatty and Moses reprise 'Aber dieses ganze Mahagonny war nur, weil alles so schlecht ist' (But this entire Mahagonny existed only because everything is so lousy), Jenny and the girls respond 'Oh moon of Alabama. We now must say goodbye'. The macaronic chaos epitomizes Brecht's ambivalence: he may have hated dollars, poker and telephones but he just loved the sounds of those words.

This double standard pervades the project. Commentators have always insisted that Weill, who was only just 30, was less strident than Brecht. Certainly, he asked that the published score would offer German alternatives to the English names – 'Johann' for 'Jimmy', say – with an instruction, contra Brecht, that 'the typical American milieu' should be avoided. He believed that by returning the action from Florida to Leipzig (or wherever) he would universalize 'greed'. (Whereas Aristotle argues that *any* particular story should mask a universal one.) But Weill also caught the Brechtian mood. On 31 January 1930, weeks before the first night, he wrote to Lotte Lenya, his '*Rehbeinchen*' (little doe): 'we'll play the entire piece in masks, completely rigid ones ... they will really hamstring those over-emoting singers ... at the end, the "Gott in Mahagonny" must tear the masks off the men's faces. After that, the revolution starts'. The masks never materialized, though later the charismatic but vocally limited Lenya would herself play Jenny. Soon after, Weill wrote an article describing the opera as a series of twenty-one 'moral pictures of our time', presented in the purest form of 'epic theatre' with each 'picture' introduced by a title card (the 'pictures' were later introduced by a speaker). The music, too, would unfold situation rather than probe character – and this despite the fact that it still relied on familiar operatic types (recitative, melodrama (speech over music), aria, ensemble). In all this Weill manifestly succeeded: the work's transparent textures and clearly-etched repetitive rhythms exude 'new objectivity' from start to finish. The score's energy is nothing if not infectious.

In his 'Notes' on the work, Brecht took the challenge still further: 'The opera *Mahagonny* pays tribute to the senselessness of the operatic form.' If in a (socially probing, realistic) libretto 'rational elements are employed' then 'it is all washed away by the music.' Indeed, a conventional audience's hedonistic pleasure grows with the ensuing 'unreality'. The new task for music, therefore, was to act *against* its traditional self by exposing just that unreality. It had to make the strange *seem* strange. If the music still remained enjoyable, then, as the Marxist theorist Theodor Adorno put it so approvingly, the pleasure served to introduce 'the terrors of a perceived demonology into the human consciousness'. Certainly, in *Mahagonny* Brecht's most ruthless couplet is sung to Weill's most enticing melody. This comes towards the end of both the first and second acts: 'and if someone kicks, then that's me, and if someone gets kicked, then that's you'; and when the men of Mahagonny listen languidly to Weill's kitschy piano version of the popular Polish song 'The Maiden's Prayer', Brecht has one of them remark 'This is eternal art'. The ironies serve to unsettle (*épater*) the audience with exquisite effect. It was a stance, indeed, that Brecht pursued in the cinema a year later with Hanns Eisler in their *Kuhle Wampe, or Who Owns the World?*, Eisler proving a more compatible partner for Brecht than Weill.

Yet if Brecht reviled Weill for musical excess, it was one he himself had encouraged: for the work is designed on two planes throughout. Act Two, for example, presents a set of tableaux of life in a city spared from destruction. At first, the tone is gleefully callow. Under the banner 'anything goes', and to a racy refrain that drives us from horror to horror, the scenes seem to act out four of the seven deadly sins – *Gluttony* (fearless eating to fatal excess), *Lust* (paid sex), *Anger* (a lethal boxing match) and *Greed* (Jim will die because he can't pay for three bottles of whisky). For these, Weill uses tart on-stage music and popular genres. Yet as in other operas that revel in licence – Tannhäuser in the Venusberg or Tom Rakewell in Mother Goose's brothel – a steely reaction also gathers head. Jimmy falls in love with Jenny; he shares memories of foresting in Alaska with Joe and ruinously stakes his wealth upon him in the bout with Trinity Moses; and when he finds he cannot pay the bar bill, he imagines escaping to Alaska with Jenny and Bill by ship – only to find that their turbulent journey leads straight back to Mahagonny. Jimmy's Alaska is not just a psychic retreat – a rural heaven to counter an urban hell – but also a testament to the residual Romantic in Brecht. No other German poet can ever have fêted this far-flung state so flatteringly. The lyric aspect comes to a head after the tableaux. Jimmy is alone in chains (a wilful parallel to Beethoven's incarcerated Florestan): although the music retains its 'alienating' anapaest rhythms, Jimmy's vocal line appeals to night in the face of encroaching day with all the passion of a Tristan.

In Act Three, by contrast, the moral reaction assumes a perversely divine authority. In this it follows on from the close of Act One, where, as the hurricane bears down on Mahagonny and Jimmy asks, what can a typhoon bring compared to the horrors of man?, the distant men sing, in a numinous chorale, 'fear not'. In the surreal show-trial of Act Three, Trinity Moses, who killed Joe in the bout, acts – of all people – as judge, first accusing Jimmy of Joe's death and then condemning him, through Begbick, to the electric chair. More still, Moses then plays God in the story of how, 'one grey morning, in the midst of whisky, God came to Mahagonny' to order its inhabitants to put away their cigars ('Virginias') only to be told that they were in hell anyway. This story, recounted to music of mounting ferocity, is the opera's goal: after this, Mahagonny burns and its now-confused inhabitants parade with competing placards to a relentless death-march. It is a secular hell-fire sermon to match any from the pulpit. (Directors, of course, adjust the placards to their times. At Leipzig in 1930 one banner declared 'For the Just Distribution of Worldly Goods', another 'For the Unjust Distribution of Worldly Goods'; whereas at Sadler's Wells in 1963 one proclaimed 'Better Dead than Red', another 'Better Red than Dead'.)

Constant Lambert saw Alban Berg and Kurt Weill as the two counter-poles of pre-war 'highbrow' opera. Yet to the extent that Wozzeck and Jimmy lay bare the plight of the 'arme Leut' – the poor people – they are two peas in a pod. These protagonists both go under, tragic victims of circumstance. Wozzeck murders the woman who betrays him with a Drum Major and drowns. Jimmy has earned the cash to quit his manual labour in Alaska, comes to Mahagonny in a gold-rush, but when he realizes that its laws won't save him from the typhoon, urges the people to throw inhibition to the wind, and when they do just that loses money, friends, the love of Jenny and his life. There is no way back for either. In our own post-war, recessionary times, when the gap between rich and poor shows no sign of closing, *Mahagonny*, a *sui generis* epic that gathers all other genres into its fold even as it disdains them, has lost none of its sting.

Notes

Source: Programme essay for a King's Opera (student) production of *Aufstieg und Fall der Stadt Mahagonny* in the Desmond Tutu Bar of King's College London, March 2013; subsequently reprinted in reduced form for The Royal Opera *Mahagonny* digital app in 2015.

The information owes to the following sources: (a) 'Kurt Weill' and '*Aufstieg und Fall der Stadt Mahagonny*' from (respectively) *The New Grove Dictionary of Music*, ed. Stanley Sadie (London: Macmillan, 1980) and *The New Grove Dictionary of Opera*, ed. Stanley Sadie (London: Macmillan, 1992); (b) Joy H. Calico, *Brecht at the Opera*, Berkeley: California UP, 2008, pp. 34-9; (c) David Drew, *Kurt Weill: A Handbook*, London: Faber and Faber, 1987, pp. 171-87; (d) *Speak Low (When You Speak Love). The Letters of Kurt Weill and Lotte Lenya*, trans. and ed. Lys Symonette and Kim. H. Kowalke, London: Hamish Hamilton, 1996, pp. 62-5; (e) Ronald Sanders, *The Days Grow Short. The Life and Music of Kurt Weill*, London: Weidenfeld and Nicolson, 1980, pp. 145-58; and (f) Ronald Taylor, *Kurt Weill. Composer in a Divided World*, London: Simon & Schuster, 1991, pp. 149-66.

Part Three

Style

1 The Style of the House
Eugène Scribe and Giuseppe Verdi: *Les Vêpres siciliennes*

The time, place and circumstance of an opera's intended first performance can be, and often is, central to the way the opera is conceived, to its style. It is a bold creative team that writes an opera of any scale 'on spec'. It is partly a matter of material resources – the stage facilities, the number and calibre of singers and musicians the management can afford, and so forth – and partly of tradition: each house has its heroes, each its history of works that demand somehow to be 'answered'. Only a master as established as Wagner can design a Bayreuth from scratch. Verdi's work became intimately bound up with not only the Paris Opéra, to which, in fact, he held ambivalent feelings, but also its towering masters: the librettist Scribe and the composer Meyerbeer. As noted elsewhere, his involvement with the house culminated in the premiere of Don Carlos *in 1867 and continued to a staging of* Aida *in 1880 that broke all box-office records. Here we meet Verdi with his first commission for the house, the style of which became integral to his own mature style.*

'It is to be hoped that no one will try to learn history from the libretto that Scribe wrote for Verdi.' Thus Sir Steven Runciman in the preface to his monumental *The Sicilian Vespers* of 1958.[1] For not only did the 'unfortunate' opera of 1855 offend Italians with its (inauthentic) portrait of a 'sly' Giovanni di/da Procida and his 'cruel and cowardly' Sicilians, but it also showed Parisians a deserved massacre of the occupying French, and by inference their 1855 counterparts, the Austrians. Far better to understand the Easter Monday massacre in Palermo of 30-31 March 1282 – which, as Runciman goes on to show, was but the start of an uprising that swept Sicily for weeks – as 'one of those events in history which altered the fate of nations and of world-wide institutions'; indeed, although the massacre may integrate the story of a brilliant but arrogant prince, the pluck of the Sicilians and the massive conspiracy plotted in Barcelona and Byzantium, it marks above all 'the gradual suicide of the grandest conception of the Middle Ages, the universal papal monarchy'. Its effects are still with us.

Obviously, no opera can or should be a history seminar: events in life are complex, chaotic and often fraught, whereas art is relatively direct, ordered and intrinsically pleasurable.[2] And however much we may now want to rein in Runciman's flamboyant judgements, the 'truth' of Verdi's opera is something different. The key lies in the work's origin. In 1852-3, Verdi, turning forty, had the opportunity to collaborate with Eugène Scribe (1791-1861) on his first bespoke work for the Paris Opéra, an opera he conceived in five acts with the traditional ballet. Indeed, he welcomed it with all the enthusiasm of a young man absconding with his father's mistress. For it was Scribe who had written libretti for the towering father-figure Meyerbeer, notably the three 'grand operas' in five acts – *Robert le diable* (1831), *Les Huguenots* (1836) and *Le Prophète* (1849); and it was Meyerbeer whom Verdi, like Wagner, had a lifelong ambition to emulate if not surpass. It was Scribe, too, who had written the bulk of his works for Halévy in five acts, just as he had cast his *Dom Sébastien, roi de Portugal* (1843) for Donizetti in five; and it was to Halévy in 1838 and Donizetti soon after that Scribe had originally offered the source of Verdi's opera, *Le Duc d'Albe*. By accident or design, and to his liking or not (Verdi was initially uncomfortable with a Donizetti 'cast-off'), the collaboration gave Verdi poll position within one of the greatest traditions opera has known. What he wanted from the 'intoxicating' (but weary) Scribe was 'the grandiose, impassioned and original', the 'imposing and overwhelming'. That it would prove 'work enough to kill a bull' was no inhibition; that he revised extensively comes as no surprise.

So what did he do? First, for the public, political aspects of the piece Verdi exploited to the full the Opéra's choral and instrumental forces – notably its agile wind and brass. He composed an elaborate formal overture that treated contrasting themes from the opera symphonically, something he had recently avoided. For the obligatory ballet (nowadays often omitted), he wrote thirty minutes of music: introduced by the God Janus, each of the 'The Four Seasons' included several classically-cut dances, the whole offering an astonishing lexicon of dance types available in the 1850s. The scale was nothing if not ambitious: his charming 'harem' ballet for *Jérusalem* had lasted ten minutes, and even Donizetti's witty, colourfully orchestrated dances for *Dom Sébastien* had taken only twenty. In *Jérusalem*, moreover, the ballet of Act Three, scene 1 had led in scene 2 to a trial (of a kind) before an executioner with lugubrious monks chanting in Latin. In *Les Vêpres*, the comparable episode occupies two acts: in Act Three, scene 2 the ballet is followed by a masked ball that culminates in a huge chorus after the foiled assassination attempt (the obligatory *concertato*); whereas in Act Four, the prison appearance of the French, the executioner and the intoning monks leads to a big chorus that seemingly unites the rival factions after an eleventh-hour reprieve.

For the choruses generally, Verdi followed Gluck's recommendation of 1770 that rival forces should have distinctive music.[3] This he exploited to the utmost. At the start of Act One, for example, the drinking song of the full-throated French is answered by and combined with the seditious murmurings of the Sicilians; this is reinforced after the agile-voiced Hélène has arrived, though a massacre is forestalled by the entrance of the terrifying French governor, Montfort: a numbed, unaccompanied quartet greets his arrival. At the end of Act Two, the Sicilians dance a tarantella, during which the French soldiers abscond with the Sicilian women (they are mindful of the Rape of the Sabines – the opera's key image). Not only does Verdi float distinct music for the rival forces over the whirling dance, but he also draws it to a spectacular climax: after a stunned silence, the Sicilians give voice to their shame in the anapaest (rat-a-tat) rhythms that conventionally signify mortal threat but in *Les Vêpres* also stand for profound shock. After another climax, a delicate barcarolle is heard from across the waters: the French are ferrying Sicilian women to Montfort's ball. As this song unfolds, the Sicilians resume their menacing rhythms, ready, like Etna, to erupt. Whereas in Act Three of *Les Huguenots* Meyerbeer had likewise combined the music of celebration and dissidence, Verdi is more effective in isolating and sustaining the sounds of rival factions. The strategy comes to a head in Act Five. With castanets clicking, the chorus opens with decorative but charged nuptial music, first for the men, then for the women and finally for both together. The bride, Hélène, enhances this with a catchy bolero (Verdi had already used Iberian colour in *La traviata* and *Il trovatore* and would do so again in *Don Carlos*). At the act's end, however, after the bell has struck, the Sicilians launch their massacre to a chorus of astonishing energy. Verdi had taken pains to plot the act's trajectory from one extreme to another.

Of course, the opera's building-blocks are not choruses, but structural units. These Verdi described – disparagingly – as the typical progression of aria, duet and finale so evident in Acts Two, Three and Four, and still latent in Acts One and Five. Certainly, they include familiar things: the triumphalist drinking song (as in *La traviata*); the dramatically pertinent stage song (for Hélène – as in the first-act ballad of *Robert le diable*); the controlling presence of the dead – Hélène's brother and Henri's mother (as in *Stiffelio*, *Rigoletto* and later *Simon Boccanegra*); and the violent disruption of ceremony and festivity (as in the last two acts of *Le Prophète*). Yet, although they are not our concern here, the arias, duets and small ensembles contain the work's best music, with, for Verdi, newly flexible and focussed lines, French aria-types (mixed-mode 'couplets'), and a readiness to push back rapid Italianate exit music (*cabaletta*) with scenes that close with dramatic recitative (*scena*).[4]

But what of the grand ensembles that befit grand opera? Only twice do the protagonists join forces. In Act Four, Procida launches a lament for his unliberated Sicily after Montfort has openly revealed that Henri is his child; Montfort joins in, relishing his lethal power; the newly defiant Henri lines up with Procida; and Hélène bids farewell to Sicily in an ethereal melody. It is an intimate quartet that replicates the conflicts polarized in the big choruses; it also a worthy match for the sublime final-act quartet from *Rigoletto*. In Act Five, circumstances have changed. Procida begs Hélène to join him in striking the French at the wedding now that they have lowered their guard. She finds herself in an impossible position: if she cancels the wedding, she loses Henri and betrays Procida; if she goes ahead with it, she betrays the political truce and unleashes cruelty against her new family. She appeals to her dead brother; Procida urges her to think of her brother's commitment to Sicily; and Henri is bewildered by her unforeseen hesitation. This superb trio builds to an appropriately forthright climax, and reflects Verdi's determination to make the plight of individuals the focus of his final acts – as he had done in, say, *Ernani* (1844).

However, the wedding proceeds, the bell tolls and the consequent massacre ensues. The carnage lasts barely twenty-five seconds. Originally there was a final twist: as the slaughter raged, Procida, seeing Hélène protecting Henri and Montfort, ordered the Sicilians to 'Strike the lot down. Who cares – French or Sicilian? Let God choose.' Verdi, however, was patriotically committed to the Sicilians, and, evidently deeming Procida's ruthless brutality excessive, cut it out.

In any case, the events were factually wrong. What had triggered the 1282 uprising was neither a plot nor a ceremony, but the seizure of a married Sicilian woman by a French sergeant whom her husband then stabbed to death. Whereupon, as Runciman writes,

> the Frenchmen rushed up to avenge their comrade and suddenly found themselves surrounded by a host of furious Sicilians, all armed with daggers and swords. Not one of the Frenchmen survived. At that moment the bell[s] of the city began to ring for Vespers.[5]

Yet the historical facts hardly collapse the opera's fiction. For *Les Vêpres* remains loyal to the root cause of the massacre: it isolates the sexual contempt of an occupying force for an occupied people and tenaciously unpacks its lethal effects. Indeed, what Scribe and Verdi produced so magnificently for the Paris Opéra was not so much 'unfortunate' truth as 'fortunate untruth'.

Notes

Source: 'Fortunate Untruth', *Les Vêpres siciliennes* (Verdi), The Royal Opera programme, October 2013, pp. 36-41, reprinted 2017.

1   Sir Steven Runciman, *The Sicilian Vespers*, Cambridge: Cambridge UP, 1958. pp. ix-x.
2   On this issue, even Aristotle (384-22 BC) admitted flexibility: 'The poet cannot undo traditional stories ... but he should invent for himself, i.e. use the inherited stories well.' *Poetics*, trans. and ed. Richard Janko, Indianapolis: Hackett, 1987, p. 18.
3   In the preface to his opera *Paride ed Elena* (1770) Gluck writes: 'I was obliged to exert myself to find some variety of colour, seeking it in the different characters of the two

nations, Phrygia and Sparta, by contrasting the rude and savage nature of one with all that is delicate and soft in the other.' Reproduced in: '*Paride ed Elena*', *The New Grove Dictionary of Opera* (4 vols.), ed. Stanley Sadie, London: Macmillan, 1992, vol. 3, p. 853. Gluck set a bench-mark. Fromental Halévy, for instance, has attracted criticism for not using sufficiently distinctive music for both camps in *La Juive* (1835), in particular for passing up the opportunity for exploring Jewish musical sources.

4   At this point, two paragraphs have been dropped from the original. These dealt, respectively, with the work's arias and duets.

5   Runciman (1958), p. 215.

2   A Melodrama of Two Styles

Francesco Maria Piave and Giuseppe Verdi: *Rigoletto*

When any art is sufficiently developed to call on different styles, past or present, national or international, it will ineluctably mix them. In opera the mixture can have explosive musico-dramatic effect. In Rigoletto, *Verdi's 'ottocento' style has an admixture of Viennese classical style, not just to differentiate character, but also to signal that this work is positively not Mozart's* Don Giovanni: *the Duke of Mantua is not dragged off to hell by his accuser but escapes the curse imposed upon him. By being enhanced, the moral outrage also shifts the question of responsibility from victor to victim (Rigoletto himself). There is a further internal change going on in both* Rigoletto *and the contemporaneous* La traviata: *Verdi was trying to forge a new style for himself that would relax the formal musical conventions of Italian opera in favour of a less formal, dramatically-orientated approach. In his middle years, we find him achieving this most effectively in the last act of* Rigoletto *and the central act of* La traviata. *With the arias of Gilda and Violetta, indeed, we hear the heyday of bel canto drawing to a close. Verdi's style was in a state of constant becoming.*

Back in 1969, Pierluigi Petrobelli drew a parallel between the finale to the first act of Mozart's *Don Giovanni* (1787) and the opening scene of Verdi's *Rigoletto* (1851).[1] In the Mozart ballroom scene, three stage orchestras play three dances concurrently – a minuet, a *contredanse* and a *teitsch* (or allemande). In the Verdi scene, which is set in the sumptuous Ducal palace, the stage orchestras are reduced to two. An out-of-sight *banda* sets the tone with festive dances and a brash refrain for the entire company (a sort of vertiginous gavotte that creates a paradigm for later choruses). By contrast, a stage orchestra plays two archaic dances. The first appropriates the four-square minuet from *Don Giovanni* and turns it into a serenade for the Duke, replete with an infectious lilt and a heart-wrenching sob. As it unfolds, the Countess Ceprano, to whom it is addressed, first resists and then responds to the Duke's adulterous advances under the very nose of her husband. It is an informal duet overlaying the minuet, partly 'spoken', partly 'sung'. Of course, the allusion to *Don Giovanni* is one that only we in the audience can pick up: the sixteenth-century Mantuans knew nothing of Mozart. But its message is clear to all: temptation is never harder to counter than when it comes from a figure of absolute power and Orphic eloquence. Similarly, when the stage orchestra accompanies the following *perigordino*, we relish the antique charm of the dance: it is less Mantuan *tinta* (local colour) than Mozartian pastoral. Tchaikovsky would likewise plunder *Don Giovanni* for the pastoral divertissement in *The Queen of Spades* (1890).

Nor does Verdi's awareness of Mozart stop here. When Monterone bursts into the jollifications in the middle of the scene, he curses both the Duke and his jester Rigoletto (a kind of hunchback Leporello), one for philandering, the other for encouraging it. Although Monterone conveys his holy wrath in the lethal repeated monotones and charged rising chromatic lines familiar from Italian opera in general, his presence and music can only recall the return of the Commendatore at the close of *Don Giovanni*. Unlike his Mozartian counterpart, though, Verdi's Duke holds out. He is untouchable. He is the dissolute who cannot be punished. There will be no fiery death to match the horrors of his life. Monterone is summarily clapped into prison: later he will rue the futility of his curse. Only Rigoletto, who has goaded Monterone beyond endurance, feels the force of the malediction, and will continue to re-enact it to the end. But then, Rigoletto is merely compelled to acknowledge what he already knows: Fate has deprived him of a wife just as Mother Nature has cursed him with a hump on his back (in Freud's terms, his is the rage of a congenital 'exception', the disappointment of one who continually tries but fails to become 'normal').[2] On the other hand, the Duke is blessed with egregious good looks and success with women, and seems protected by Apollo himself. Throughout the opera this polarity never changes. There is no resolution as in Mozart.

But the classical reference goes further still. Another, darker set of allusions surround Rigoletto and his entourage, whose *fons et origo* is Beethoven. (The earliest listeners, in fact, were alive to his presence.) Although these allusions are more oblique, they act as a foil to the Mozart ones. The first instance comes in the second scene. Rigoletto is alone in the deserted street outside his walled house and in a state of shock. He has been cursed. An assassin appears, almost out of the air; he is Sparafucile, whom later Rigoletto describes as his alter ego, 'Pari siamo!' (we are equals). Sparafucile offers to rid Rigoletto of a dangerous rival, a potential predator on the woman Rigoletto keeps locked in his house (in fact, his daughter Gilda). Rigoletto stores up the information.

Now, much has been written about this 'spoken' duet – a kind of duologue sung so quietly as to be almost imagined (*ppp*) and floated over the background of a muted melody for solo cello and double bass. The late Julian Budden, for instance, found a stylistic precedent in 'Qui che fai?' from Donizetti's *Lucrezia Borgia* (1833/40). But the early Verdi scholar Abramo Basevi put his finger on the matter when in 1859 he stopped over the form. What, he asked (in effect), is an Austro-German classical ternary form (A-B-A1-Coda) doing in an Italian opera? The answer is simple: Rigoletto and Sparafucile's classical code is a riposte to the similar classical code the Duke used to seduce the Countess Ceprano. It takes a decorous assassin to avenge a decorous philanderer. This

F major 'duet' can find a small-scale parallel in, say, the F major ternary-form that opens the slow movement of Beethoven's Piano Sonata op. 2, no. 1 (1795).

The next allusion is surely direct. Rigoletto enters his house in a state of turmoil to be greeted by Gilda. They launch into one of Verdi's greatest duets. Rigoletto is so pathologically protective of his daughter that he has never told her his name. For her part, Gilda has just come back home from her convent education and now longs to see the world: her mother is dead, and her most urgent task is to get away from her father. Necessity, though, has already turned her into a sharp psychologist: 'If you won't talk about yourself,' she says, 'tell me about my mother.' The question is well directed. As she puts it there is a hush in the orchestra. We hear a sad falling figure for a pair of lonely horns. It is stated twice, the second time in the key of E♭. The figure is traditional enough but here divulges a secret meaning: for the same figure appears at the opening of Beethoven's Piano Sonata in E♭ major, op. 81a ('*Les Adieux …*') (1810): this is specifically marked 'Lebewohl' (farewell). Gilda recognizes the loss her father has never worked through and his need to 'talk' for both their sakes. The outpouring of grief she unleashes takes even her by surprise.

A third allusion is more iconic. At the height of the final act, Gilda sacrifices herself on behalf of the Duke whose mistress she has become: Sparafucile's dagger at last strikes home. But this is not the elegant assassination Rigoletto had planned for his master. Rather it is a murder of utmost brutality coinciding with the peak of a storm, one already foreseen by the chorus at the opening. The operatic storm, of course, finds a locus classicus in Rossini's *Guillaume Tell* (1829), just as the theatrical one does in *King Lear*, a dramatic paradigm for Verdi in the early 1850s: however indirectly, *Rigoletto* owes to both. But we also sense the storm music from Beethoven's 'Pastoral' Symphony (1808), not just through shared storm-figures (which are commonplace) but because the tempest has a cosmic fury previously known only in Beethoven. Verdi's storm, indeed goes further: it is the 'objectification' of an impotence – Rigoletto's – that cannot discharge itself outwardly but is compelled to turn itself inwardly, thus destroying its bearer's most cherished object. The classical diction of Rigoletto's first-act meeting with Sparafucile finds its tumultuous counterpole in Sparafucile's Act Three meeting with Gilda. The extremes find a precedent in Beethoven, in whose creative personality they co-exist.

These allusions to 'Mozart' and (more symbolically) 'Beethoven' are, of course, local. But they mark out the opera's two stylistic poles. On the one hand, the Duke's seductive diction ('Mozart') finds a counterpart in the archaic dotted rhythms associated throughout with the courtiers' levity. They are heard when Gilda recalls the handsome man at the church, when the courtiers arrive to abduct her, when they recount the abduction to the Duke, and, ironically, when Rigoletto affects their manner, first as he mocks Monterone, and later as he searches for the abducted Gilda ('La ra, la ra'). On the other hand, the trajectory of poise and tenderness leading to storm ('Beethoven') creates a template for all of Rigoletto's music: it is heard in his labile *scena* before Gilda first greets him, 'Pari siamo', and in their following duet; in the anguished outburst when he finds himself duped over her abduction; in his challenge to the courtiers as he searches for her, with agitation, 'Cortigiani' (Courtiers!), leading to confrontation, 'quella porta assassini, m'aprite!' (open this door for me, assassins!), and eventually to imprecation, 'Signori, perdon!' (My lords, forgive me!); and in the self-pity, tenderness and rage of his reaction to Gilda's plangent account of her abduction. It reaches its apex in his pitiful discovery of Gilda's mutilated body, when, indeed, his Promethean anguish exceeds even Monterone's.

These poles also stand behind the stark juxtaposition at the start of the opera, where the pathos of the orchestral prelude cedes at once to the frivolity of the music for the off-stage band. Even more importantly, they invade the background of formal conventions that operate here as they do through most of early nineteenth-century Italian opera. Gilda's simple bel canto aria, 'Caro nome' (Dear name), is elongated as she dotes on the Duke whom she supposes to be a 'poor student', watched by an abduction party of courtiers; like Don Giovanni, the Duke sings in an extravagant variety of forms and tones-of-voice according to whichever woman he has in mind or is trying to seduce – the little minuet for Countess Ceprano, a full duet with Gilda, a full aria when he imagines he has lost her, a two-verse solo *ballata* to boast of his contempt for women, 'La donna è mobile' (Women are fickle), and a heart-melting Orphic song in the great last-act quartet as he tries to lure the assassin's street-wise sister, Maddalena. Rigoletto, by contrast, positively has none of this, but reveals himself reactively, mainly in duets and extended recitatives. Although the chorus has a strong presence in the first act (as in the preceding *Stiffelio* (1850)), there is no formal gathering of forces into one large, central ensemble as would happen again in *La traviata* (1853); and although Verdi had already developed chains of loosely-linked pieces, nothing before or after compared with the loose form of the final act of *Rigoletto*, a looseness that allow the poles to be pushed to extremes as Rigoletto tries but fails to vanquish the Duke.

Rigoletto has been variously described as a political allegory, the fruit of a long stay in Paris in the late 1840s, and the work in which Verdi worked through his earlier loss of wife and daughter. But it is also a triumph of the mix of styles he had started to develop in *Macbeth* (1847) and would continue to refine over the next decade. Ralph Vaughan Williams considered *Rigoletto* Verdi's greatest achievement: from this point of view he may well have been right.

Notes

Source: 'Rigoletto: A Melodrama of Two Styles', *Rigoletto* (Giuseppe Verdi), The Royal Opera programme, February 2009, pp. 28-35; subsequently reprinted on four occasions, with minor changes. It is itself a revision of '*Rigoletto*: A Melodrama in Three Styles', *Rigoletto* (Giuseppe Verdi), The Royal Opera, July 2007, pp. 29-35.

1   Pierluigi Petrobelli, 'Verdi and *Don Giovanni*: on the Opening Scene of *Rigoletto*' (1969), *Music in the Theater. Essays on Verdi and Other Composers*, trans. Roger Parker, Princeton: Princeton UP, 1994, pp. 34-47.

2   The issue is addressed in *Part Six: Psychology*, under 'Encapsulated Repression'.

3 New-old Style

William Plomer and Benjamin Britten: *Gloriana*

Costume drama, with its historical figures and settings, invites meticulous research for both libretto and staging. That it does not always achieve this is down to the need for effective staging and the scale of resource: excessive outer attention to 'period' can inhibit the flow of the inner drama. In opera of the twentieth century, the reclamation of historical style can be more thorough-going than mere allusion or local colour: in The Rake's Progress, *the librettist W. H. Auden deploys Augustan diction and the composer Stravinsky adopts the manner of Mozart to promote a stagecraft rooted in the tableaux of William Hogarth: however, the creative situation is more complex, the allusions wider, and the musical thought at heart more Russian than Viennese. There is no question of 'pastiche'. The carefully researched* Gloriana *was devised to celebrate the coronation of the new queen, Elizabeth II. It was first performed at the Royal Opera House, Covent Garden, on 8 June 1953. Here we find an abundance of period songs and dances redolent of the age of Elizabeth I: but these integrate with Britten's post-Verdian, vocally-led style, itself rich in allusion to other contemporaneous music. The attempt to create a new-Elizabethan national style, in contrast to the folkloristic style epitomized in the music of Ralph Vaughan Williams, was subtly internationalist.*

Gloriana's extraordinary new-old music owes its character to five extraordinary factors, all of them extra-musical. First, the 'opera in three acts' fêtes a new monarch – Elizabeth II – by celebrating her older namesake: in Rossini and Donizetti she was Elisabetta, here she is Gloriana. Based on Lytton Strachey's colourful *Elizabeth and Essex* (1928) and J. E. Neale's more scholarly *Queen Elizabeth I* (1933),[1] it is Britten's only overtly historical opera, and necessarily focuses on a woman more than the man she loves – Donizetti called his version of the story *Roberto Devereux* (1837) (Devereux was the Earl of Essex). Second, it exaggerates the composer's habitual blend of middle and late Verdi techniques by marking separate numbers in the score and treating them with a considerable measure of self-sufficiency without sacrificing dramatic flow. This allows Britten to assimilate his recreation of 'period' (sixteenth-century) songs and dances into the action – and 'period' numbers he knew well from his version (1949) of John Gay's *The Beggar's Opera* (1728). Third, it includes something of French Grand Opera's diversionary singing and dancing, while offering itself as England's answer to Italy's *Aida*, Czechoslovakia's *The*

Bartered Bride and Russia's *Boris Godunov*. It is nothing if not public, national and monumental. Fourth, it extends the composer's distinctive canon: like *Peter Grimes*, *The Rape of Lucretia*, *Albert Herring* and *Billy Budd*, it explores the conflicting emotions of an essentially modern individual, though here it is not a crushed victim but a fraught ruler – like Captain Vere in *Budd*, who also makes a political sacrifice against private instincts. Fifth and finally, it adapts Stravinsky's multi-levelled harmony for dramatic purpose, and follows modernist predecessors in rebalancing the orchestra in favour of forceful wind, brass and percussion, without compomising the clear and essentially vocally-led style. For listeners, it is well-nigh impossible to isolate these strands: the 'givens' of the commission and the pursuit of the dynamics of modern drama pull in tandem with impressive assurance.

1 Act One: Public versus Private

As a projection of the conflict within Elizabeth, the scenes alternate between the public and the private throughout, though – inevitably – the two interact. This was also a technique of Verdi. Act One begins publicly in a tilting ground, with the unseen jousting and triumph of Mountjoy before the Queen. The excitement is conveyed by the music and off-stage chorus, and reported on-stage to the jealous Essex by Cuffe. The jousting ends as the chorus turn to Elizabeth and sing what will be the work's protean, charismatically gawky refrain: 'Green leaves are we, red rose our golden Queen.' The librettist, William Plomer, derived the words from an Elizabethan boy's school-book: 'The rose is red, the leaves are green, long live Elizabeth, our noble Queen.' After Mountjoy has entered and been challenged by Essex, the Queen arrives in a blaze of pomp, hears a report from Raleigh and reins in the hotheads. The assembly then sings a staunch hymn of praise to their protectress. It is the work's largest ensemble. In Italian opera at least one such *concertato* would have been obligatory, and its function here is to assert the work's constant: that Gloriana's authority is unassailable.

The end of the next scene offers us a stark contrast. Now in 'a private apartment in Nonesuch', we find Elizabeth with two men who represent the twin poles of her sympathy. First, the canny Cecil instructs her in *Realpolitik*; and then the younger Essex reveals himself, as Strachey puts it, as both a scholarly melancholic and a restless, full-blooded Romantic. The real Queen had loved music, played the lute and, according to Neale, was still dancing the *coranto* up to her death (Strachey notes 'she danced, after the Florentine style, with a high magnificence'). So it is no surprise that Gloriana tells Essex, 'There lies my lute; take it and play'. At the close of their elaborate, part-erotic, part-courtly Italianate full duet (of which more later), she is left alone. After reflecting on the conflict of Duty and Inclination – one of opera's oldest topics –

she prays for divine help. It is Elizabeth's 'Numi pietà' (*Aida*) – and no matter that, according to Strachey, this outward Protestant was at heart 'profoundly secular'.

2 Act Two: Masque in the Modern Age

If Act One is exposition, then Act Two is development. Taken together its three scenes watch the growing interaction of public and the private: public in the Guildhall at Norwich (scene 1) as well as inside a great room at Whitehall (scene 3), and private in Essex's garden off the Strand (scene 2). Indeed, the three scenes unfold as if in a single sweep. The first presents a masque before the Queen, with mutterings 'aside' from Cecil, Essex, Mountjoy and Raleigh: Essex is impatient to lead troops against Tyrone in Ireland. In the second, Essex's impatience turns into outright sedition as he plots with his sister, Lady Rich, and her illicit lover, Mountjoy, to 'seize the reins of state': only his young wife, Lady Essex, urges caution. The third forms the goal of the act, as the challenge erupts during a set of courtly dances: Essex has forced his hapless wife to dress up to rival the Queen, the Queen wins the showdown, but with diplomatic acumen grants Essex the Irish commission: peace is restored. The disruption of ceremony, of course, is an operatic cliché, never handled better than by Verdi in *Don Carlos*. Yet the historically well-grounded showdown in *Gloriana* is unique in that it is between two women: by donning Lady Essex's dress, not only does Elizabeth expose the plotters, but she also throws her old age and misshapen carcass back in their faces. Hers is a sado-masochistic triumph, as biting now as it was then.

The musical diversions are in effect spread across the act. Masque, which flourished in late Elizabethan and Jacobean times, was normally built round a theme with five dances (or 'entries') involving the courtiers. In *Gloriana* the Spirit of the Masque announces the theme in scene 1: Time. A mixed semi-chorus sings five choral dances (the choral dance itself being a period genre, as well as a feature of very early opera): Time, Concord, Time and Concord, Country Girls (women only) and Rustics and Fishermen (men only); a finale unites the Spirit and full chorus. Flanking the scene are stylized cheers for the chorus (in which one early critic heard the bells of *Boris Godunov*) and the 'Green leaves' refrain. The whole recalls the historical Elizabeth's rapturous coronation procession on 15 January 1559. The City had prepared a number of pageants along the route, the first on 'Unity and Concord', the fourth on 'Time': '"Time!" exclaimed Elizabeth' (according to Neale) '"and Time hath brought me hither!"'. Britten's numbers also allow him to permute possibilities in terms of speed, tempo and variety of ensemble. However, dances involving the courtiers come only in scene 3: *pavane, galliard, lavolta*, morris dance (a solo) and *coranto*, with an added march. All are written as stage-music in a persuasive new-old style. For his sources, Britten depended upon direct instruction from Imogen Holst, who had researched the matter in Oxford, and Thoinot Arbeau's dance manual of 1588, the *Orchésographie*.

This meticulous approach to musical colour – Verdi's *tinta* – was nothing exceptional: Britten had used sea shanties in *Billy Budd*, and would use schoolroom rhymes in *The Turn of the Screw* and Venetian types in *Death in Venice*. But the 'Tudor music' also acted as backdrop to more modern inventions, some startling. Scene 2 opens with the waiting Mountjoy: like Fenton's sonnet in Verdi's *Falstaff*, his song is interrupted at its climax when Lady Rich arrives. Although their subsequent love-duet offers a stable counterpole to the mercurial duets of Elizabeth and Essex, a subversive accompaniment (an ostinato tritone) reminds them and us that the 'angel' Rich is fleeing from a 'brute' of a husband; and in the quartet that follows once Essex and his Lady have joined them, Lady Rich's subtly ornamented vocal line becomes Amazonian as she urges revolt, a line that contrasts vividly with Lady Essex's muttered qualms. In scene 3, when Elizabeth returns wearing Lady Essex's dress, clumsy tubas and leering trombones play a savage burlesque of the *lavolta* à la Mahler or Bartók; and at its end, as the courtiers dance the *coranto*, the orchestra plays a minor mode version of their preceding ensemble 'Victor of Cadiz', in a different key à la Stravinsky: Essex's commission may not, after all, be quite what it seems. In each case, new musical practice dramatically challenges or qualifies the Elizabethan types.

3 Act Three: a Sane Mad-scene

By contrast, Act Three presents two interior, private scenes flanking an exterior, public one. The exterior scene is set in a street in the City and charts the people's response to Essex's fatal uprising. As at the work's opening, the events are told at a remove. Plomer was himself a ballad-writer and provided a five-verse ballad interspersed with comments and action; whereas it was Britten who asked for the singer to be blind (like Tiresias). Ballads were integral to Tudor politics, and the off-stage cries of 'Saw! Saw! Tray! Tray!' came from Sir Christopher Blount. If this inner scene chronicles a key process, then the two outer scenes pivot round single events: in scene 1, Essex's impetuous arrival and discovery of the bald Queen, and in scene 3, the Queen's signing of Essex's death warrant. Both scenes prepare for and react to these events meticulously. In scene 1 the musical excitement and confusion of the opening 'chatter' for the Maids of Honour in attendance will carry through the scene, and a tender chorus for the ladies-in-waiting literally and metaphorically puts a good face on their humiliated monarch (as in *Lucretia*: after the rape, flower music). In scene 3, the portentous opening male chorus 'Essex is guilty and condemned to die' forms the backdrop to the political confusion: Cecil in particular urges the Queen not to defer the signing (in Strachey's words, she had an 'innate predisposition to hedge'). Yet left alone, the Queen sings an essentially traditional antithetical aria ('I grieve, yet dare not show my discontent'); and then, faced with pleas for clemency, she shows a feminine side to Lady Essex and her children, and a masculine side to Lady Rich, whose pompous music proves aggressively, and fatally, more regal than her sovereign's. Elizabeth is piqued to the quick by the superciliousness of the Essexes, and there is no hint that she has 'condemned her lover to her mother [Anne Boleyn]'s death', as Strachey suggests. (Strachey's brother James was a Freudian.)

But it is the close of scene 3 that plays the opera's trump card: it brings back Essex's Second Lute Song. This had initially appeared in the Earl's first duet with Elizabeth in Act One, scene 2, using a text penned by the original Robert Devereux on his return from Cadiz. It begins 'Happy were he' – an echo of Horace and Virgil (*Felix qui …*) – and includes a reference to himself as 'harmless Robin'. The music in turn borrows an opening contour from 'Happy, O happy he' from John Wilbye's *Second Set of Madrigals* (1609). The Dowlandesque languor of the music is significant, for it was Elizabeth herself who had set the mood. Having rejected the First Lute Song, 'Quick music is best when the heart is oppressed', as too bright (a sustained, dissonant bass note shows her keeping her distance), she had demanded something 'to spirit us both away'. What Essex provided may have been a callow paean to death (in a skilful new-old style), but what her political side understood was a potential blueprint for action. It is no surprise that she demanded the song to the most lethal harmony of all (an F minor triad).

In fact, in Act Three this music returns twice. In scene 1, it forms a slow, surprise ending to Essex and Elizabeth's second – and again Italianate – duet, replacing a traditionally fast close (*cabaletta*): sensing he is losing out to the wigless Gloriana, Essex introduces his signature phrase 'Queen of my life' and gradually wins her round: when he remembers 'Happy were we', Elizabeth joins in (in musical canon). Momentarily she succumbs. But later in the scene, after Cecil has arrived and delivered his report in a tiny aria, she orders the 'rebel' Essex to be placed under house arrest. According to protocol, her wish is Cecil's command and he offers no response. But she still gives vent to her distress at having to destroy what she loves.

So when, in scene 3, the Lute Song makes its final appearance, now as an expanded, saturnine orchestral song, the irony is awesome: Essex will perforce act out his own fantasy. As the music unfolds, Britten asks for the stage to darken and 'time and place' to become 'less and less important to her'. The Queen, he wrote, should stand 'like some majestic fowl' as a few spoken, historically authentic interpolations compress the subsequent events as they relate to herself, Essex, Cecil, and Parliament (using a fragment of the 'Golden Speech'). The technique suggests both cinematic montage and a mad scene from Italian opera: yet – remarkably – she is wholly sane. In this lies the work's novel, unsparing, tragic-triumphant critique of the demands of power. Yet the song in the orchestra is also Elizabeth's threnody for the hubristic Essex. This we learn from the only two phrases she sings with the orchestra: 'In some unhaunted desert … There might he sleep secure.' (A third phrase, 'mortua, sed not sepulta' (dead but not buried), refers to herself, and is separate.) As the darkness gathers, we further recognize the final re-working of the off-stage chorus's 'Green leaves are we' as a threnody for the dying Queen herself. As in Verdi's *Otello*, it is left for a refrain to bring an extraordinary work to a fitting end.

Notes

Source: 'Happy Were He?', *Gloriana* (Benjamin Britten), The Royal Opera programme, June 2013, pp. 32-8.

1   Lytton Strachey, *Elizabeth and Essex. A Tragic History* (1928), London: Harvest (Harcourt), 1969; J. E. Neale, *Queen Elizabeth I* (1933), Chicago: Academy Chicago Publishers, 1952/2001. See also: *Britten's Gloriana. Essays and Sources*, ed. Paul Banks, Woodbridge: The Boydell Press, 1993.

4 Old-new Style
Ottavio Rinuccini and Alexander Goehr (after Monteverdi): *Arianna*

Each art not only enjoys seeking out its origins but evidently feels an imperative to do so: new work has a need to set itself against old work. The first opera was La Dafne *(1598), with an Ovidian libretto by Ottavio Rinuccini set to music by Jacopo Peri and Jacopo Corsi. It told of the metamorphosis of Dafne into a laurel tree as she sought to ward off the amorous ardour of Apollo. Little of its music survives. But some ten years after its first performance, one of Peri's associates, Marco da Gagliano, re-used the libretto, now revised by Rinuccini himself, to produce a new score. This had a prologue and six scenes and formed part of the celebrations for the wedding of the Infanta of Savoy. The score includes various types of 'number': solo recitative, aria duologue, short duos and trios, madrigal-like chorus and ritornello; and it used lavish vocal embellishments where appropriate (for Venus and Apollo). Now, there is nothing to prevent a modern composer from returning to an early libretto and following the example of da Gagliano; and this is what the contemporary composer Alexander Goehr has done. But since the libretto – again by Rinuccini – came from the dawn of opera, and the composer wanted to incorporate the only surviving part of Monteverdi's original score – the lament – into his own, there were striking contrasts of style to negotiate. Unlike Britten who built back from the present to the late sixteenth century with his* Gloriana, *Goehr built forward from the early seventeenth century to the present with his* Arianna. *The ensuing 'old-new' style is thus of a different order to Britten's 'new-old' style.*

We are all fascinated by torsos, fragments, ruins, lost works – anything, in fact, that demands restitution or recovery. So the description inside the score of *Arianna* (1995), 'Lost opera by Claudio Monteverdi composed again by Alexander Goehr (1994-5) [to a] libretto by Ottavio Rinuccini (1608)' at once grips us. There are two reasons why. First, 'composed again' suggests that the work that brought fame to its composer in 1608 on account of its affecting lament has against all odds been restored; and second, it reminds us that the restorer is not so much a scholar as a composer. As is well known, Goehr (b. 1932) has a long and rich experience of writing music for the stage. Though he has described *Arianna* as a special undertaking, the matter was by no means simple. So what exactly was involved in the restitution? Why did this composer want to undertake it at this time? And how should we receive the result?

In fact, the three questions belong together. Although in recent years others have produced versions of extant Monteverdi works – Dallapiccola, Maderna, Berio and Henze among them – Goehr's 'composing again' has a motivation of its own. In two early pieces for the Music Theatre Ensemble, *Naboth's Vineyard* (1968) and *Shadowplay* (1970) he drew on Monteverdi's introduction to the *Combattimento di Tancredi e Clorinda* (1624): the two contestants, says Monteverdi, 'should make their steps and gestures in accordance with the text, not more not less, whereby they must observe the tempos, the beats and the steps carefully'. Monteverdi's stagecraft forms part of this new *Arianna* too: at certain points mime is crucial, musical gesture introduces each singer and the actors are all present throughout. (In Monteverdi's Mantua staging there was also 'one unchanging scene': all 'mountains, rocks and sand' with waves in the distance 'constantly in motion' creating a 'charming effect'.)

In the *Combattimento*, furthermore, the narrator (Testo) merely describes the principal actions – which, classically, take place off-stage – but allows the indirect speech of the principal characters to be taken directly. The same is true of Goehr's handling of Rinuccini's messengers: Arianna breaks into the report of her attempted suicide with complaints and screams, as do both Arianna and Bacco into the closing account of their meeting. As in Monteverdi, choral parts are taken by soloists, who may number from one to five; and the (presumably) relatively small ensemble of instruments and 'continuo' used in 1608 is matched here by the same kind of modern Monteverdian ensemble Goehr had devised for his cantata *The Death of Moses* (1992). There are two flutes doubling sopranino recorders, a bass clarinet doubling contrabass clarinet, one bassoon doubling contrabassoon, two trombones, two percussion players and three upper strings; continuo functions are shared among harp, amplified guitar and sampler (which creates a range of imaginary instruments such as metal organ, *organo di legno*, electric piano, celesta and glockenspiel).

Goehr's restored work also follows principles described in Monteverdi's Eighth Book of Madrigals (1638): contrasts in vocal tessitura between high, middle and low are used expressively, and the tone of utterance includes the agitated as well as the soft and moderate (*concitato*, *molle* and *temperato*) – perhaps necessarily so in a drama that, although about a 'betrayed woman', also involves 'warriors and kings', gods, goddesses, messengers and choruses. Goehr also sought guidance from scholars: Eric Chafe, in his *Monteverdi's Tonal Language* (1992), demonstrates the expressive use of mode ('sharp side' versus 'flat side'); his father, Walter Goehr, who edited Monteverdi's *L'incoronazione di Poppea* (1643), makes the upper lines of the accompaniments independent of the vocal ones; and in his edition of Monteverdi (1926-42), G. F. Malipiero creates a style of realization that offers a starting-point for *Arianna's* restitution as a whole. Both Walter Goehr and Malipiero were themselves composers.

So how exactly did Goehr set *Arianna* anew? First, he pruned the eight scenes of Rinuccini's libretto – the new version lasts about two hours against the two-and-a-half of the lost original. He then set the remaining text as an imaginary Monteverdi opera in a Malipiero-type realization. In so doing he incorporated in the sixth scene the lament Monteverdi wrote for Arianna (as has been said, the only extant part of the original score): this occupies the same pivotal function as did the hero's entreaties in Monteverdi's *L'Orfeo* (1607); in the vocal lines he preserved the scrupulous sensitivity to prosody and feeling (*parlar cantando* – 'sung speech') which for Monteverdi defined the crucial difference between opera and theatre music; he indulged madrigalian word-painting throughout to match Rinuccini's inspired rhetoric; he introduced vocal ornamentation where appropriate; and he used short dance-like instrumental pieces (*sinfonie*) to introduce the scenes and bind them together through repetition (*ritornello*).

All of this, then, marks roughly the boundary of what might have been achieved by scholarship alone. But the instinct to compose a new work as well as to recreate an old one presented other challenges. These Goehr conceived in terms of a paradox: as a young composer, in order to refer to Monteverdi's style in *Shadowplay*, he had worked backwards from modernist 'serial' procedures; whereas to create a modern idiom for *Arianna* he had to work forwards from Monteverdi/Malipiero. Instead of moving from the new to the old, he now worked from the old to the new.

Underlying the difference between the two are social and cultural contrasts. The Monteverdi-Rinuccini *tragedia* was written as a court piece to celebrate the marriage of Margherita, daughter of the Duke of Savoy, to Francesco Gonzaga, elder son of the Duke of Mantua. Its first performance took place on 28 May 1608. It was introduced by Apollo, a figure possibly familiar from *L'Orfeo*, 'king of the sweet choir [of Muses]' and symbol of the highest civilization, who invited the audience of (allegedly) thousands to admire the restitution of the 'ancient glory of the Grecian stage'. The tragedy typically showed noble but faltering humanity in thrall to merciful gods; as the drama unfolded between Teseo, Arianna, Bacco, confidantes, messengers and groups of soldiers, the choruses – mainly of fishermen – reacted to the changing events (the fishermen being there to form a pastoral contrast); and the resolution of the human drama was crowned with a wondrous display of numinosity: Venere rose from the sea with attendant nymphs and goddesses, Amore descended from the clouds, and, 'heaven having opened', Giove himself predicted happiness for his children. According to a contemporary account, one part of the soldiers sang while the other part 'performed a very delightful dance, weaving in and out a thousand ways'. The work ended happily (in a *lieto fine*) with a celebration of Arianna's rejection of mortal beauty for the love of a god.

The new work, by contrast, was a public opera commissioned by the BBC to celebrate the heritage of British music. Since it reclaims Mantua in much the same way that Apollo reclaimed ancient Greece, Goehr's first idea was to replace the 1608 Prologue for Apollo with one featuring an encounter between himself and Monteverdi. The idea was soon abandoned. But given that Rinuccini's text could not be changed, he necessarily had to convey any new interpretation through music and additional stagecraft. His reading of the libretto was influenced by the work of Bertolt Brecht and the Berliner Ensemble (his first opera, *Arden Must Die* (1967) had already shown such an influence): he specially admired Brecht's ability to analyse characters who belong to an alien culture (*The Good Person of Szechwan*) and invest them with feelings that we ourselves might recognize. On the other hand, he was less concerned with 'alienation' techniques.

Fundamental, then, to the newness is the rebalancing of the relationship of gods to humans. In the opening scene, Venere (Venus) is now an aged goddess, and her son Amore (Cupid) still carries 'the tattered remains of his bow and arrow', though his wings 'no longer function'. For the most part, indeed, they have lost their efficacy. On the other hand, Arianna, who appears in the second scene with Teseo (Theseus), turns out to be much more a woman of our time: she is in command of her destiny, and like Debussy's Mélisande (whose sighs Goehr will quote) speaks with a low, dignified restraint. Vocally she is as much a mezzo as a soprano. The effect of the rebalancing emerges most strikingly in the final tableau with the arrival of the gods. In *Ariadne auf Naxos* (1912/16), Hofmannsthal and Strauss had interpreted Bacco (Bacchus) as a figure of death as much as of love; earlier dramatists still might have presented him as the compensatory hallucination of a deranged, suicidal heroine. Goehr, however, views him as an androgynous figure, a corrupter of the order of things, like Dionysus in *The Bacchae* of Euripides: accordingly, he casts him as a male alto, and his soldiers as a chorus of children. As Bacco arrives to stake his claim and Amore proclaims 'proud glories', Arianna, for all that she is verbally acquiescent, 'emblematically rejects her good fortune'. She has been deceived once before and will not be deceived again. Goehr's stage direction shows that in her own understated way she is as morally courageous as Kattrin who, at the end of Brecht's *Mother Courage* (1941), fatally defies the soldiers (and all they stand for) with her wild drumming.[1] In the music, beneath the celebrations we hear dark inflections in the harmony.

For his part, Teseo is tortured by the awareness that his debt to and love for Arianna – who saved him from the Minotaur in Crete – must take second place to the political need to abandon her. He emerges as a figure even more fraught than he would have done in 1608. The second scene offers a paradox: he addresses his soldiers 'wearily but in a kind manner'; whereas he deals in private with Arianna imperiously, so that 'the notes belie the words', he is carried away by his own rhetoric', and when he takes his leave 'he embraces her, perhaps too vehemently'. And in the third scene, when his counsellor 'emerges from the shadow' as a timeless personification of Realpolitik, he accedes to the view that he should not 'make himself a vile slave to his own pleasure' while uttering his words 'feebly and banally'.

Other figures, including messengers and chorus, are also scrupulously differentiated in style – necessarily, perhaps, given the many doublings in the vocal casting: each has their own tempo, instrumentation and set of musical figures, and deploys modern, and therefore complex, tones of voice.

The overall design, with its strong progression to Arianna's lament, also recalls other modern operas cast as a single act with a clear climax (Strauss's Sophocles-derived *Elektra* (1909), for instance, pivots on Elektra's poignant greeting to Orest on his long-awaited return). The progression is achieved in part by the handling of the choruses, which in themselves have a madrigalian richness beyond what is found in Monteverdi's few extant operas. Partly because Rinuccini follows classical precedent by ending all scenes but the first with a chorus, these are fully integrated into the score – more so, indeed, than their statuesque counterparts in Goehr's previous opera *Behold the Sun* (1985). In fact, there are two kinds of chorus: one that participates in the action (Teseo's and Bacco's soldiers) and the one that both participates and stands apart (the fishermen in scenes 3 to 6 and the chorus that cross-questions the messenger over Arianna's attempted suicide in scene 5). Sometimes choric comment is consigned to one singer; elsewhere it gathers other voices, a gathering that creates forward momentum. For example, scene 3 culminates in the four-part aubade 'Stampa il ciel', scene 4 in the five-part madrigal 'Avventurosa genti' embodying the pastoral message 'Love guides and governs us', and scenes 5 and 6 most powerfully in another five-part madrigal, 'Su l'orride paludi', which proclaims, centrally, that 'a woman's virtue has won such clear renown' – renown that transcends even that of Orfeo.

The greatest novelty, however – and in Goehr's view the one by which the work stands or falls – is the reworking of Monteverdi's music for the great lament. A clue to the new conception lies in what will not be heard in the opera house, the 'concert ending'. This is included in the score: for the operatic lament is now a modern set-piece aria in five sections, interspersed with newly-composed choruses for the fishermen, and concluding with a short coda. Goehr worked this in three stages: the first is Monteverdi/Malipiero as before; the second an enrichment of the harmony and alteration of the lines in the later, less well-knows passages, partly to match the enriched harmony and partly to create a more forceful climax; and the third a still further elaboration of the harmony, rhythm and instrumentation – the original lament appears to have been supported by strings alone.

That the new lament marks the extremity of *Arianna*'s modern style creates an entirely new situation: whereas all earlier serious opera, including Monteverdi's, distinguishes social status and significance by differences of idiom and complexity within a given style, Goehr's does so by invoking different degrees of elaboration between old and new styles. That is to say, certain passages – some of the *sinfonie*, or the children's chorus (for Bacco's soldiers) – remain remarkably close to 'Monteverdi' (there was no direct modelling), and others – the music for Arianna's confidante, Dorilla, for instance – are of intermediate complexity. The more intricate writing, though, shows some stylistic eclecticism – Wagner (in the harmony), Stravinsky (in the opening scene), Fauré (in the little nocturne for Arianna at the end of scene 2), and so forth – yet the effect is quite other: the writing testifies to the remarkable development of the art of accompaniment since Monteverdi. Rhythmically, instrumentally and expressively, this is music of quite new sensibility. At an extreme from Monteverdi, indeed, Goehr allows himself a single, startling moment of modernist dislocation to signal the beginning of Arianna's lament.

So how, finally, do we react to Goehr's composing again of Monteverdi's lost opera? Comparisons will inevitably be drawn with prominent 'new-old works', among them Pfitzner's *Palestrina* (1917), Stravinsky's *The Rake's Progress* (1951), Britten's *Gloriana* (1953) and Maxwell Davies's *Taverner* (1972). Yet *Arianna* stands apart: it is, not 'new-old', but 'old-new'. Scholarship favours period stagings, reduced ensembles and historical sensitivity to vocal and instrumental style; opera houses like to invigorate old works with new styles of production. Goehr has reacted to both tendencies; his opera is firmly rooted in our time. The acid test, though, lies in performance. Here, the benchmark was set in 1608. Federico Fellino reported that 'no-one hearing [Arianna] was left unmoved, there was not one lady who did not shed a little tear at her beautiful plaint'. We too are allowed to shed a tear at the poignant events before us.

Notes

Source: 'Towards a New Prologue (1995)', *Arianna* (Alexander Goehr), The Royal Opera programme, September 1995, pp. 29-33. The essay introduced the opera for the first time, and was printed alongside Ottavio Rinuccini's verse prologue of 1608 in a translation by Patrick Boyde. It has been slightly adapted here.

1   In a letter to this author written after a performance in Konstanz, Goehr explained his intentions with regard to the end, where the music darkens and appears to go in an opposite direction to the text:

'Why is Arianna's D major coloured by flat notes belonging to F major/minor, and why does she sing in the lower part of her register in her last appearance? When the opera of *Arianna* is over, the wedding duly celebrated, Arianna will be deserted again. Ovid writes (*Fasti* III, 459 *segue*): 'Already had she exchanged a perjured spouse for Bacchus, she who gave to a thankless man a clue to gather up. "Why like a rustic maiden did I weep?" quoth she: "His faithlessness [*perfidus*] has been my gain." But already there's a girl who "pleased Bacchus all too well". Arianna sings a second lament: "Lo yet again, ye sands, receive my tear." I used to say, I remember, "Forsworn and faithless Theseus! He deserted me: now Bacchus does me the same wrong." ' Frank Kermode in *The Sense of an Ending* tells us about the fiction of time and end. My (as opposed to Rinuccini's) Arianna wants to stray out of the opera (not *back* to Theseus, but *forward* with me). She can quite reasonably love a new lover, but she cannot accept reintegration into the order of things. She has to say 'Rejoice at my great fortune', otherwise the particular opera couldn't end. She understands that, as did I, with a heavy heart. But don't ask us to be happy about it: we say the words because we have to, but don't expect our hearts to be in it. The resulting tension is the fingerprint of a lost opera composed again in 1994.'

This text appears in a letter of mine to *The Musical Times*, printed in the December 1996 issue (p. 2) in response to my essay in the November issue, 'A Fine and Private Place' (this had dealt with operas by Harrison Birtwistle and Alexander Goehr). It has been corrected here in one or two particulars.

5   *Constant Flux*

Martin Crimp (after de Cabestanh) and George Benjamin: *Written on Skin*

The three temporal styles of opera reflect its three irreducible conditions: the real-time dramatic comes from theatre, the suspended-time lyric comes from music (song), and the out-of-time epic from (authorial) commentary. They normally infiltrate the three basic domains of opera: word, music and stagecraft. Traditionally, we are used to recognizing the styles interweaving, now one assuming ascendancy, now another. But in Written on Skin, *a striking early twenty-first-century opera, the styles are radically mixed and proceed concurrently. The thirteenth-century past and our present constantly interpenetrate in a mixed handling of time, place and circumstance; the intensely involving dramatic action is saturated in distancing epic speech; the mortals double as Angels, and even return from the dead as Angels; the orchestral forces, themselves large in number but chamber in their use, blend sounds ancient and modern – and so forth. This premise, of constant flux has roots in contemporary music. But it also mirrors what contemporary producers try to achieve as they invest old works with new images to create a novel stylistic fluency.* Written on Skin *is nothing if not of our time.*

A friend of George Benjamin's, the late French composer Gérard Grisey, said of his own music that he wanted everything to be in 'constant flux'. His material would have minimum character to be maximally malleable; his wave-forms would encompass large acoustic spaces; and his writing for instruments would not just deploy 'pretty colours' (the French stereotype), but rather probe sonority itself. His music was almost entirely instrumental, and as for opera, 'it would take me 10 years to write one' – as long as it took Debussy to write *Pelléas et Mélisande*. Like Grisey, Benjamin is a pupil of the French composer Olivier Messiaen, resists over-defined musical ideas, projects across large spaces and has an exceptional, Ravel-like affinity for instrumental sounds. But there the parallel stops. For Benjamin also conducts modern concerts and operas (like Pierre Boulez or Oliver Knussen) and writes for different voice-types: *A Mind of Winter* (1981) for soprano (on Wallace Stevens), *Upon Silence* (1990) for mezzo-soprano (on W. B. Yeats) and *Sometime Voices* (1996) for baritone (on Shakespeare's *Tempest*). His music, though modernist, and sometimes challengingly so, can still refer to elements of older music, especially in its clear diction, euphonious triads and key centres. And his dramatic instinct, already in evidence in his *Three Inventions* for chamber orchestra (1995), has led to two operas in less than ten years: *Into the Little Hill* (2006) and the more elaborate *Written on Skin* (2012) – both to words by the contemporary British playwright Martin Crimp. Just as Goethe claimed that Meyerbeer blended an equable German temperament with an Italian affinity for voice, so could it be claimed that Benjamin blends a dramatic English temperament with a French affinity for timbre. But even so his sympathies extend more widely.

For the operatic Benjamin, 'constant flux' begins with the drama. Crimp describes his *Written on Skin*, not as a libretto, but as a 'text'. Avoiding the conventions of opera, he gathers the basic kinds of theatrical time into a constantly shifting unity – the dramatic (for action), the lyric (for reflection) and the epic (for explicit free-standing commentary). It is a blend that goes even further than Brecht's – in, say, his *Rise and Fall of the City of Mahagonny* (1930) – by *continually* distancing the audience in order to engage it more intensely. At the core he places a triangle of husband, wife and lover – the Protector, Agnès and the Boy – each of whom refers to him- or herself in *both* the first and third persons. In the second of the fifteen scenes, for instance, we meet the Protector (a baritone). He sings a conversational arioso, equating his property with the paradise he wants the Boy to paint: 'And day by day – says the Protector – fruit-trees … turn towards the sun.' The Boy answers 'A book costs money, says the Boy. A book needs long days of light.' In both cases, 'says the Protector' and 'says the Boy' are set as musical asides, staccato. Similarly when the Protector's wife Agnès (a soprano) reacts: 'No! says the woman. Nobody here starves.' The effect is of a Brechtian rehearsal where singers constantly remind listeners of the characters they represent. Only here, the mechanism of rehearsal becomes the manner of performance.

In Scene 4, however, Agnès makes her first lone visit to the Boy: she is predatory but circumspect, while he becomes aware of a 'situation'. Both start to absorb asides into the main text: the Boy utters 'You're in my light says the Boy' as a single melodic arch that shores up his identity. At first Agnès still refers to 'the woman' to promote a link between herself and the figure in the Boy's picture: 'She doesn't look real, laughs the woman, that's not how a woman looks.' But in Scene 6 – the finale of the first act – she again visits the Boy, now by night. She finds the Boy has redrawn the picture in her favour. 'I've painted the woman's heart,' he sings; she replies, 'No! not "the woman" – I am Agnès. My name's Agnès'. She and the music begin to throb. Significant naming, of course, is Wagnerian. Yet because the text has started from further out, this individuation of 'Agnès', if anything, comes closer in. Similarly in the penultimate scene, the Protector insists on calling his wife 'the woman' until he reveals she is eating the Boy's heart, whereupon he calls her, with sadistic intimacy, 'Agnès'.

This novel approach to identity works in with the fluid handling of time, place and circumstance. This is crucial. The Boy is cast as a counter-tenor – a modern operatic voice well known from, among others, Britten (*A Midsummer Night's Dream*), Ligeti (*Le Grand Macabre*) and Birtwistle (*Gawain*): he is close to Agnès in age, hence the simulation of an unbroken voice – and the pictures he paints 'on skin' will capture the thirteenth-century action for posterity. But he also doubles as one of three Angels. These are the deathless Fates. They deliver the vehement time-travelling prologue, they are choric chroniclers of human horror and serve as unsparing catalysts of an appalling tragedy (there is no chorus *per se*). They also act as actual or imagined *dramatis personae*. The second and third Angels, for instance, double as Agnès's sister Marie and her husband John (mezzo-soprano and tenor), uncannily warning the Protector both in person and in dreams of Agnès's infidelity. They act out the Boy's mendacious account of a dysfunctional marital relationship (ruthlessly holding up a mirror to the Protector's) and of Marie's (alias Agnès's) desire to play Venus, a decadent artist's model ('feed me pomegranates and soft-cooked eggs') and the devil's whore ('shut me in eternal darkness with the devil'). And finally, though not without internal dispute, they whip up the Protector's lethal vengeance against the Boy. Whereas in the first two acts the Boy describes his pictures in a musical 'miniature', at the end of the third act he does so posthumously, as an Angel. This enables him to complete the narrative and return it to the present: he shows 'the woman' leaping to her death to escape the Protector's knife, falling not just to the ground but rather to a modern car-park.

Bohuslav Martinů once described the deep processes of opera as constituting its 'psychological form'. Certainly, audiences will experience *Written on Skin* in part as a case-study in polarized personality: the narcissistic 'Protector' expresses his 'purity' in unchallengeable control of others and his 'violence', once roused, in pathological destruction of those whom he most protects. The source of his disorder – if not its effect – is sexual terror. Agnès, the once child bride whom he insists on keeping as a child (and virgin?), looks elsewhere for her gratification: she seduces the Boy, taunts the Protector with her newly acquired sexuality and, revealing a startling pathology of her own, demands that her young lover uses his pictorial skills to 'push our love into that man's eye like a hot needle … make him cry blood'. Indeed, she has a 'mad scene' of a kind. The Protector slaughters the boy and bakes his heart in a pie that, with sadistic relish, he has Agnès eat. Agnès in turn commits pre-emptive suicide as the angels look on with 'cold fascination'.

These stark extremes define the musical boundaries – purity, violence, sexuality, wrapt indifference – and explain why the vestigial duets and trios are so minimally interactive (and there is no full ensemble). They also build on the historical achievements of music drama: the Protector's cross-examination of the Boy recalls Golaud's pressure on Yniold in Debussy's *Pelléas et Mélisande*, and the lover's congress at the Act One curtain recalls the impetuous first-act curtain to Wagner's *Die Walküre* as brother and sister start to make love (and conceive Siegfried).

On the other hand, the time-travelling of both drama and music enrich this process by way of the contemporary context it drives through a story that is itself rooted in an anonymous thirteenth-century *razo* (Guillem de Cabestanh – *Le Coeur mangé*). Ancient and modern constantly interpenetrate. The result is a highly compressed musical language of extraordinary contrasts and energy that would have made even Mascagni or Puccini gasp. Indeed, the score unfolds in a suspended time held together by threads of slow sustained notes, whether high, middle or low, through which different kinds of music, slow or fast, pass fleetingly. For the second and third of the Angel/Boy's miniatures, for instance, Benjamin draws on the uncanny glass harmonica and the archaizing antique viol (viols also provide the accompaniment to his *Upon Silence*). By contrast, he has the Angels sing right from the start with a wholly contemporary 'strident' force (*fff*) – sounds of a dysfunctional mechanism redolent of Birtwistle or Stravinsky. But these modern sounds return at the end of Scenes 5 and 13 to enrich the violence of the thirteenth-century Protector, albeit a violence the Angels have themselves whipped up. Indeed, the crazed Scene 13 music is positioned pivotally like the D minor interlude in Act Three of Berg's *Wozzeck* (a work close to Benjamin's heart). And at the very end, after the Boy-Angel has brought the fallen woman to rest in the 'Saturday car-park' – his lethal repeated monotone a stock-in-trade of Italian opera – the 'choric' music exudes an even greater force: as it splinters into peremptory jabs (*fff*) over a throbbing bass, with its note D exerting its traditional high pathos, the ferocity now speaks for *all* times.

But Benjamin also finds ferocity in extreme restraint. The music for *Written on Skin* charts the movement of passion through silence and the barely audible with a relentlessly bated breath. In Scenes 4 and 6, Agnès's seduction of the Boy is slyly under-spoken. In Scene 12, the cuckolded Protector reads to his illiterate wife what the Boy has 'written on skin' with a 'barely repressed rage': his final 'this is what the woman, what Agnès, what your wife, your property – writes the Boy – asks me to say to you' touches the work's quietest moment (*pppp*). It is only when he charges into the wood at the end of the next scene to make 'one long clean incision' into the Boy's bone that the sound and fury break loose. Yet even this hubbub is thrown into relief by the 'tense' stillness of the start of the next scene (14): the Protector shows Agnès the 'silver dish' containing the Boy's cooked heart to music marked *keck* (feeling as if about to vomit), with the sporadic clashing of two pebbles breaking the silence like the proverbial drop of two pins. It is a far cry from Shakespeare's 'cook' Titus Andronicus who watches Tamora eat her sons amidst murder and mayhem.

Pebbles, though, are the smallest part of an orchestra whose sheer size belies any definition of *Written on Skin* as a chamber opera. Benjamin seeks out the right sound – *le son juste* – just as Crimp hunts down the right word – *le mot juste*. He even invents new 'instruments': when the Boy describes the two Angels in the 'shopping mall', it is 'fast random typing from a computer keyboard' that links past and present. We also hear sleigh-bells, bowed cow-bells and cymbals, a huge percussion section and a lexicon of modern instrumental devices. Furthermore, multiple divisions within each orchestral family serve a word-painting as assiduous as anything in Richard Strauss. When, in Scene 4, Agnès's heart 'shook at the sight of a boy, the way light in a bowl splits and shakes on a garden wall', Benjamin gives overlapping patterns to six divided violins (muted and pizzicato) supported by three solo second violins (*tremolando sul ponticelli*), flecked by flute, harp and contrabass clarinet. There are many inventions of this kind, made possible by the flexibility of the lyric recitative they support. They also build on tradition: Benjamin once expressed admiration for the four divided double basses in the first act of Pfitzner's *Palestrina* (1917). On the other hand, the orchestra helps articulate the overall design. Act One ends with an eroticized silence into which Agnès drops her lowest note ('Love is an act'); Act Two ends with an overwhelming force through which Agnès releases her highest note ('Make him cry blood'); and Act Three ends by alternating a barely containable force with a barely audible high violin supported by maracas. If the history of opera can be measured by the development of 'the accompaniment', then Benjamin's score certainly extends that line.

In times dominated by standard repertory, opera directors have struggled to apply post-modern fluidity to pre-modern stability. But Crimp and Benjamin's new work throws down the gauntlet: *Written on Skin* positively demands contemporary staging. Indeed, its stylish demonstration of constant flux may well set a benchmark for the future.[1]

Notes

Source: 'Opera in Flux', *Written on Skin* (George Benjamin), The Royal Opera programme, March 2013, pp. 25-31, reprinted 2017. Katie Mitchell was the producer. The essay also appeared as a liner note in the subsequent Opus Arte DVD of the same production (2013).

1 At the time of writing, Crimp and Benjamin are at work for The Royal Opera (with six other houses involved) on a third opera, *Lessons in Love and Violence*. Their subject is Edward II and his entourage.

Tony Sympson as Bardolfo
(Milein Cosman, 1948)

Interlude

Revision

Introduction

Meet a composer entering an opera house with a freshly-composed score under his arm. He has a spring in his step. Meet him again once the work has been given, and he will be staggering home, fazed, with a patchwork of cuts, paste-ins, re-orderings, re-orchestrations and even transpositions under his arm. He has discovered that 'the work' is no longer his (or the librettist's) but also the management's, the director's, the designer's, the conductor's and the property of every singer and player. Nor is that the end of the matter. If the work is staged elsewhere, the process can easily start again. An opera is an open-ended project: a composer's work is never done. An egregious case is that of Musorgsky. He wrote his Pushkin-derived Boris Godunov *in 1869. In 1871 he had it turned down for performance on the grounds that there was no female lead. So in 1872 he not only obliged by inserting a brand-new act (Act Three) but also comprehensively rethought and revised the whole thing. This second version was accepted and staged in 1874, and generally well received. Even so, after the composer's death in 1881, his devoted friend Rimsky-Korsakov made two further versions, staged in 1898 and 1908 respectively. (Rimsky had also completed and orchestrated Musorgsky's* Khovanshchina *(1886) and put on the road his earlier Gogol-derived* Marriage *(1868/1908).) If a composer won't bring his work to a satisfactory state, then others will.*

Throughout this book there is constant reference to different states of an opera. So before exploring any work, we must make ourselves alive to the potential instability of its text. This part offers three token entries on revision, dealing with three 'problematic' scores in the modern repertory – La traviata, Tannhäuser *and* Don Carlos. *The entries don't just chronicle two or more versions, but also discuss what differences the changes make to our dramatic and musical understanding. Only one of these, on* La traviata, *requires any technical knowledge of music. In this case the differences between the two versions may be small, but their significance is great.*

1   From 1853 to 1854 (on Keys)

Francesco Maria Piave and Giuseppe Verdi: *La traviata*

It may seem odd to suggest that one way of getting to the heart of *La traviata* is to think about those parts the modern audience doesn't usually hear. These are not only the arias, or sections of arias, that tend to be cut (sometimes to help singers), but also certain passages from the original version of the opera of 1853 that Verdi replaced in 1854. It is the 1854 version that forms the basis of modern published editions. Yet one of the achievements of modern musical scholarship is to have unsettled the notion that a masterpiece has by definition an immutable text. As long as the reasons for a composer's alterations are understood, there should be nothing to prevent a performer or director from consulting an earlier version, using it, or even making a new one, if he or she considers it to be in the best interests of staging the work.

Such thoughts are prompted by an important article that appeared in the *Journal of the Royal Musical Association* in 1973 by the distinguished Verdi scholar, Julian Budden.[1] Entitled 'The Two *Traviatas*', it compares the two versions from 1853 and 1854 principally in terms of alterations to the vocal lines. In the 1854 version, these serve to highlight climaxes, ease tessituras and undeniably improve characterization. Verdi also helped his singers by transposing certain arias down a semitone. To many opera-goers, these transpositions will seem insignificant. Budden, indeed, suggests that in choosing a key a singer's convenience was Verdi's main concern: 'To Wagner, a difference of key in relation to the surrounding material means a difference of emotion. Verdi and the Italians were so used to adapting their music for different performers that they did not allow their ideas of music drama to evolve on these lines.' But how true is this? Was Verdi really so cavalier in choosing his keys, and relating them one to another? Or should we not relax traditional national distinctions and look for a sharper understanding of *La traviata*, its characterization and balance, by asking whether Verdi wasn't, in fact, using key association in a more considered way?

The issue of balance inevitably raises questions of proportion and pacing. The familiar cuts to the opera for the most part reflect the taste of later generations for a less stylized, more 'realistically' paced opera. From this point of view some of the *traviata* cabalettas – the rousing closes to large arias or ensembles of the *scena-andante-tempo di mezzo-cabaletta* kind – can still seem misplaced. But a cut may also impair understanding as much as does a transposition, and we need to take the two issues together.

Budden's claim referred specifically to Violetta's 'Dite alla giovine', the Act Two cavatina that typifies the poignant vocal restraint of the work as a whole. By agreeing to forego her claims on Alfredo at the insistence of his father, Giorgio Germont, Violetta senses that she is relinquishing not only her love, but also her life: rightly or wrongly she believes that Alfredo alone could have sustained her through her consumptive illness. In 1853, Verdi set this cavatina in E major. The 1854 transposition to E♭ major was intended, it seems, to make Germont's subsequent reply, a continuation of the aria, that much easier to sing. Why, though, did Verdi originally choose E major? One of its traditional associations is with the poise and tenderness that can arise in the face of adversity. This is the case with the stand Fiordiligi takes against Ferrando in *Così*, with Leonore's invocation of hope in *Fidelio*, and Sarastro's defence of his sacred halls in *Die Zauberflöte*. The same association holds good for *La traviata*, with one difference: whereas Violetta's poise and tenderness are conveyed by the blend of vocal line, tessitura and key, the tragic consequences of her sacrifice are not left implicit but are articulated forcefully by Germont, whose reply 'Piange, piange' responds directly to the tone of her cavatina.

It is important to see that there are two other, comparable treatments of this key in the work. First, the orchestral prelude assembles a portrait of Violetta by taking her impassioned but desperate expression of love for Alfredo from Act Two and transposing it from the infectiously bright F major with which he is associated into the (sharp-side) intimacy of 'her' E major. It then amplifies this music in two ways: by adding to this theme of love a violin countersubject suggestive of her role as hostess to the Paris *demi-monde* – indeed, Act One will reveal how she uses this role to mask her deeper fears and aspirations; and then by prefacing it with the etiolated strains of the sick-room music, taken from the last act, where it appears in the more portentous (flat-side) C minor.[2] In this prelude, therefore, death, love, tenderness and gaiety are united within the same key (E major). Second, in the last act, the dying Violetta's selflessness emerges in the poignant restraint of her 'Se una pudica vergine ...' (If, some day, a modest virgin ...): she encourages Alfredo to take a young bride if the opportunity arises. Once again, the latent anxiety behind the poise of her E major music finds manifest expression. The discreet, muffled funereal rhythms in the wind testify to the anguish underpinning her generosity.

The original choice of E major then, for the Act Two 'Dite alla giovine' epitomized Verdi's entire characterization of Violetta: he invokes an extraordinary range of subtle but intense feelings to portray a love blossoming under the shadow of death. The contrast between her, Alfredo and Germont is thrown into relief by the original key-relations and proportions. For example, the fluid emotions of the later part of the labile Act Two interview between Violetta and Germont were represented in 1853 by a series of regular modulations through the unstable 'diminished seventh', from C♯ to E to G to B♭, mixing major and minor in each case. The substitution of Violetta's E by E♭ obviously obscures this scheme. More still, it dissolves the significance of the 'diabolical' tritone relation between her E and Germont's concluding B♭. The British theorist Donald Francis Tovey would have seen this as the most alienated opposition of two keys. Verdi had intended that the next scene, in which Germont attempts unsuccessfully to draw Alfredo back into the bosom of the family, should also end with an aria in B♭ ('No, non andrai rimproveri'). This is often cut, and the force of the parallel between the endings of the two interviews is again obscured. Germont is trying to square things with both Violetta and Alfredo, and in both cases he betrays their most vital interests.

The ramifications of these points are considerable. Key association of all kinds permeate the work. For example, the other traditional association of E major is with bright, rapid movement: this occurs here in the gypsies' interlude in the second scene in Act Two. The two associations, however, are brought together in the passionate, doomed E major reunion of Alfredo and Violetta in the last act. Whereas F major is consistently irradiated with Alfredo's love, the traditionally portentous F minor is used no less motivically. It links Violetta's hesitations about Alfredo in Act One ('Ah, forse lui'), Germont's attempt to subvert her position early in Act Two ('Bella voi siete') and the card scene that causes Violetta such distress later in the same act. C major and minor ('dominants' to F) are also used by Alfredo and Violetta to express various shades of consternation. D♭ major, on the other hand, along with its dominant A♭, consistently promotes the allure of bourgeois harmony. It is entirely logical, therefore, that the work should end in the minor of D♭, when this harmonious image has proved so unattainable. This D♭ minor, moreover, is first heard in the first scene of Act Two at just the point where Violetta perceives the hopelessness of her situation with regard to Alfredo ('Così all misera'). Even the extraordinary passage in which the dying woman imagines herself strangely cured (the tubercular's *spes phthisica*) elaborates the same harmony used by Alfredo when, in Act One, he first sings of the mysterious power of love.

Does all of this imply that we should return to the original version in its entirety? Hardly. As Budden points out, there are also many gains in the revisions and cuts. It does suggest, however, that we should think twice before assuming that the need for change in 1854 necessarily pointed to looseness of thought in 1853. It could also mean the opposite, that there was a tension between what Verdi wanted ideally and what the singers could manage practically. Yet even this argument should not be pressed too far: the pattern of key associations outlined here is actually strengthened by one later transposition. Violetta's 'Ah! Gran Dio! Morir si giovine' (Ah! Good God! To die so young) is made to fall from the 'bourgeois' D♭ to the more directly turbulent C. Yet the basic point stands: the definitive *La traviata* lies somewhere between what we are and are not likely to hear in the opera house. Its passions need to be understood as well as experienced.

Notes

Source: 'Which *Traviata*?' *La traviata* (Giuseppe Verdi), English National Opera programme, 1988, n. p. Appended to the essay was a further note by the ENO conductor, Mark Elder: 'In the final moments of the opera, when Violetta imagines that she is recovering, Verdi originally scored the string passage an octave higher than we are accustomed to hearing from the 1854 full score. We have opted to retain his 1853 intentions, which are, indeed, still what are written in modern vocal scores.'

1   There was some tension between members of staff in the music department of King's College London and the late Julian Budden, who was their frequent and welcome visitor, over the importance of large-scale 'tonal architecture' in Verdi's oeuvre generally. In fact, it is a paradox of both Wagner and Verdi that, however much they may have planned large-scale key-relations, they were both amenable to transposition if a singer needed it: the show was always the thing. Budden responded to the present essay with a slightly tetchy letter to *The Times*.

2   In other words, the C minor chord that opens Act Three is transposed down a semi-tone to form the B minor chord that opens the work's Prelude. B minor, of course, is the dominant minor of E major.

2   *From Dresden to Paris*

Richard Wagner: *Tannhäuser und der Sängerkrieg auf Wartburg*

Few operas can boast a stable text, least of all Richard Wagner's *Tannhäuser und der Sängerkrieg auf Wartburg*. Originally conceived as *Der Venusberg* (The Mount of Venus), a title that excited ribaldry among medics, the work underwent many changes over 30 years. It was first given on Sunday 19 October 1845 at the Königlich Sächsisches Hoftheater in Dresden as a *Grosse romantische Oper* in three acts and immediately revised for subsequent performances. Further alterations followed between 1847 and 1852, notably to the beginning and end of Act Three. All these were incorporated in the published score of 1860, now known as the 'Dresden version'. Almost immediately, the work was translated for the Paris Opéra by Charles Nuitter and four others and significantly reworked. This was partly to meet the director's demand for a ballet, which Wagner added in (unusually) to the start of Act One – too early, alas, for influential diners who liked to arrive late. In Act One the reworkings embraced the bacchanalian ballet planned to follow straight on from a truncated overture (a plan that didn't materialize), the whole of the second scene between Venus and Tannhäuser (which Wagner had thought too 'sketchy' anyway), the start of the third scene on the approaches to the Wartburg (the music for the Shepherd Boy gave him surprising trouble) and a later adjustment as Tannhäuser agrees to be led to Elisabeth in the fourth scene. Much of this was expansion and enrichment of existing material. In Act Two, Walther von der Vogelweide's contribution to the singing contest was cut for reasons of vocal casting (it is now often restored) and the end of the act reworked. There were no further changes to Act Three, the orchestration of the end apart (Wagner added four harps).

Thanks to the noisy attentions of the Jockey Club, the Paris production, which opened on 13 March 1861, survived for just three nights. This version was then given in Munich on 1 August 1867 in a German translation by Wagner himself; and at a subsequent Vienna performance on 22 November 1875, where the overture was at last elided with the start of the opera, Felix Mottl took down a number of instructions from the composer and included them in the republished score. This Vienna score is now known as the 'Paris Version'. Not surprisingly, the accumulated discrepancies of style left Wagner dissatisfied and he had thoughts of returning to the score. But he never did. Would a 'final version', though, really have solved the problem? And what changes would he have made?[1]

Notes

Source: 'Note on the Edition', *Tannhäuser* (Richard Wagner), The Royal Opera programme, December 2010, p. 51, reprinted 2016. This was written after consultation with David Syrus (Head of Music for The Royal Opera) and Reinhard Strohm (Professor of Music at the University of Oxford). The final sentences have been adapted.

1   For instance, undoubtedly conventional though the Act Two Tannhäuser-Elisabeth love duet now appears, its very formality can be made to signal the emotional precariousness of the situation. This was how it was produced by Tim Albery in 2010. At the revival in 2016, however, the duet was compressed. Both versions were effective. There is no record that Wagner proposed to revisit this 'number'.

3 *From Paris to Modena … and Back*

Joseph Méry and Camille du Locle (after Schiller) and Giuseppe Verdi: *Don Carlo(s)*

Most audiences know something of the complex history of Verdi's *Don Carlos*. First performed in Paris on 11 March 1867, the year of the *Exposition Universelle*, its libretto by Joseph Méry and Camille du Locle took as its starting point Schiller's play of the same name (1787). Indeed, it was the intimate aspect of the play – the King's separate meetings with the lethal Grand Inquisitor and the revolutionary Marquis of Posa – that had fired the composer in the first place. Yet the five-act work Verdi delivered to the Opéra in 1866 was still on the grandest scale – Giacomo Meyerbeer, who had died in 1864, still cast a long shadow. After a bleak first-act preface in the forest at Fontainebleau, a succession of sumptuous tableaux paid tribute to a mid-sixteenth-century Spain, where, typically, religion and love shared the same 'natural ferocity' (as Baudelaire put it). There was a cloister around the tomb of Charles V, a shady place by the monastery for the women to sing in, and a square in Valladolid, the centre of government, where a grand procession outside the church heralded an auto-da-fé – an 'act of faith', often involving the burning of heretics. More still, the Queen's gardens included a fairy grotto of mother-of-pearl that would be home to *La Peregrina*, a ballet that flattered the King of Spain as lavishly as any Florentine intermezzo. Mediating between religion and love, and conducted with no less ferocity, were the politics of church and state. These were thrashed out in the most forbidding of places: the gloomy study of the ageing King and the dark dungeon where Don Carlos is incarcerated. Musically too, Verdi had met all the challenges of grand opera while boldly reinventing some of them for his own ends.

Yet it was all too long, and during the 270 rehearsals substantial cuts were made: the opening of the first act was dropped as were some of the duets in part or whole (there were cuts after the premiere too). When the opera was duly translated into Italian as *Don Carlo*, principally for performances in Naples (1872), Milan (1884) and Modena (1886), further authorized changes followed (unauthorized changes had been made elsewhere). For Naples Verdi altered a pair of numbers, including the charged final duet of Act Two, which in fact he had rewritten at every stage. For Milan he was more radical. He mainly reworked three duets, turned the five acts into four by jettisoning the whole of Act One with the exception of Carlos's aria, which he skilfully adapted and relocated in Act Two; and he abandoned two scenes from the start of Act Three as well as a chorus from Act Five. This time the new material was provided by the surviving French librettist, du Locle, and the original

Italian translation was revised. Verdi had found preparing all this a 'rather tedious and lengthy job'; yet in 1886, even this version was altered, though less drastically: the shortened Act One given in Paris in 1867 was restored and the original start of Act Two reinstated. It is this five-act 'Modena' version, Verdi's last thoughts, that modern productions often follow.

But the story doesn't end there. For, over the last forty years scholars have been busy unearthing the material jettisoned on the way to 'Modena', most notably the music cut from the first production. This was retrieved in 1970 by Andrew Porter and David Rosen; a reconstruction of the Paris 'original' was broadcast by the BBC in 1973 and staged without the ballet in Paris and London; and after Ursula Günther and Luciano Petazzoni had edited the work for Ricordi in 1980, conductors felt free to pick-and-mix from any of the sources – as they still do: there are now four printed versions. Yet audiences are less concerned with edition than effect, and their question will always be, what is gained and lost by any one version? The more complex question as to why no version seems definitive takes us back to Schiller's play; but even this needs interpretation, as Schiller himself found when critics impelled him to write a series of explanatory *Letters on Don Carlos* in 1788, a document remarkable for its acuity.[1] So the way back has increasingly been the way forward.

Let us look at some of the main changes. It is usually argued that the first act, even in its reduced form, is necessary to establish the love at first sight of Carlos and Elisabeth before the intervention of the 'cruel destiny' that re-attributes her hand in marriage from Carlos to his ageing and despotic father, Philip II: and it is true, the trauma of this reversal pervades the opera. But to leave it at that obscures the underlying situation. For the original 'Paris' version begins with the French woodcutters ravaged by the war with Spain and then shows Elisabeth's bond with a 'good mother' who has lost her sons in battle: peace is their demand, something that only she, Elisabeth, can secure through political marriage – a pressure to which she yields. The people's progress from despair to hope, moreover, is beautifully crafted in the music. However, the reduced Paris version, like the 'Modena' one, begins with the next event, the arrival of Carlos himself. This narrows the focus. But how do we see him? Lost in a wood, risking the wrath of his father by having slipped off to seek out the fiancée with whom he has long been obsessed, and, according to the 'Paris' staging instructions, 'drawn this way and that by mixed emotions, trusting only in Rodrigo [the Marquis of Posa]'. The librettists clearly knew of the historical Carlos's instability; but why Rodrigo? How could any audience grasp this subtlety when Rodrigo is never so much as mentioned in Act One? Yet, oddly, this is the crux of the matter. For in Schiller's eyes 'Posa' (Rodrigo) was the stronger and more significant figure, a worldly republican who has inflamed the impressionable Carlos with his plans for redeeming the oppressed people of Flanders.

In fact, Rodrigo's domination of Carlos comes to the fore in the first scene of Act Two (where significantly the Milan version opens). At first, we find the traumatized Carlos at the tomb of his grandfather Charles V, whose voice he thinks he hears emanating from a monk. Yet the monk's advice, that the only peace of mind is in heaven, is an oblique encouragement to Carlos to renounce the world altogether, a prod in the direction of death that will finally prove self-fulfilling. Then Rodrigo arrives. Not surprisingly, he is aghast to find his royal friend infatuated with Elisabeth to the exclusion of all else: after all, she is now Carlos's stepmother. How could they ever achieve their political ends in such a dangerous situation? So he urges Carlos to abandon private cares for public ones – in other words, to adopt his own agenda. Carlos now finds himself pulled in two ways: 'Charles V's' and Rodrigo's; yet between them, nothing is left for himself. In both the 'Milan' and 'Modena' revisions, Verdi took pains to heighten the urgency of this meeting and thereby throw the extremes into relief. No wonder in the next scene Carlos will even simulate death to regain Elisabeth's love, a love that alone gives him identity!

The scene ends with a duet embodying Verdi's famous recurrent theme of the mutual loyalty of Rodrigo and Carlos. We should pause over this. For despite all its genuine (if laddish) camaraderie, the theme distils a field of fiercely conflicting forces. For Schiller argues that the bond that will finally impel 'Posa' (Rodrigo) to sacrifice himself on behalf of Carlos in Act Four is not just evidence of fanaticism, or of someone imbued with the image of Plutarch's heroes, but also a deeper sign of obligation. He writes:

> from the very day when Carlos [as a boy] offered himself voluntarily to receive a painful punishment on his [Posa's] behalf, the desire to reimburse him for this magnanimous deed troubled [Posa's] soul, tormented him like an unpaid debt, and thus must reinforce no less the importance of the preceding reasons [for the sacrifice] at this moment.[2]

And why did Carlos offer himself? Because, as he says in the play, he recognized in Posa the stronger spirit: '[I] resolved to love you without measure, because I lacked the strength to be like you.' This never gets into the opera, of course. Yet it remains crucial for our understanding of the whole project.

The most substantial cut for Milan and Modena was that of the first two scenes of Act Three. These could easily be passed over as 'dull' Parisian divertissement (the term is Stendhal's). The first contains a choric paean to the balmy summer evening, the Queen's Gardens being perfect for Iberian *fêtes galantes*, and the pivotal moment where the weary Elisabeth retires for the night and passes her veil to the Princess Eboli. Eboli then declares her intention of 'inebriating' Carlos, whom she mistakenly believes to be in love with her (there is also an open reference to her veil song from Act Two). The second comprises the ballet *La Peregrina*, which ends by glorifying the King and Queen, the latter, of course, now played by Eboli, who thereby hopes to inflame Carlos all the more. It is after these two scenes that Eboli writes the *billet doux* to Carlos which he opens at the start of the next scene, the beginning of the 'Modena' Act Three. The two abandoned scenes, though, are delightful and all of a piece: the ballet music in particular is beautifully formed and gathers in complexity to its closing grand hymn; and long though they may be, they provide an excellent demonstration of the reverse side of Verdi's aesthetic: for although he was as keen as Wagner to drive on the drama, he still wanted to succeed when there was 'no action', as he wrote in 1870. Just to keep the first scene with Elisabeth and Eboli and drop the ballet, as is sometimes done, may seem sensible, but in practice leaves the audience feeling short-changed.

In Act Four, we pass over the first scene with its effectively rewritten encounter between the King and Elisabeth, its quartet, and the Queen's dismissal of Eboli (which in 1866 had been a full duet), and go to the more challenging second scene. Here there are two stark choices in what to do after the death of Rodrigo. The original Paris version of 1866, cut in 1867, marks this most definitive event – the obliteration of the republican spirit – with a fierce exchange between an implacable Carlos and a remorseful King. This leads to a duet supported by a chorus of courtiers: both men stand united in grief before a man who has inspired them in opposite ways. The final versions for Milan and Modena, however, first compress the reactions of Carlos and Philip II (the King) into a short, sharp exchange; then, after Philip has delivered a searing, mournful phrase that sounds as if it is about to launch a duet, they interrupt the flow with the insurrection of the people. There is no longer time for grief. The interruption, in fact, is less peremptory than it sounds. For Rodrigo's preceding full aria is itself very long: he is shot and fatally wounded just at the point we expect the second verse of the closing fast music, and thereafter sings an extra two-verse andante, complete with re-workings of the bonding theme, as he dies. After this, we feel that all the necessary mourning has been done. Both choices, however, remain open.

What, though, of the 'problematic' ending? After Elisabeth's 'Tu che le vanità' sung at the tomb of Charles V, we hear the duet between her and Carlos. This itself was revised many times. As Carlos is now determined to make the mission to Flanders his own, the two bid each other a lingering farewell. But the King now bursts in with the Inquisitor. In the play he utters the lethal closing words:

> KING *(coldly and quietly to the Grand Inquisitor)*: So, Cardinal.
> Now I have done my part. See you do yours! *(He exits. Curtain.)*

The opera, however, extends the moment. In the Paris version, the King and the Inquisitor accuse Carlos three times; then, in a shock reversal, the Charles V monk appears (is he actually from beyond the grave?) and gathers up Carlos to the quiet intonations of the fraternal order. (The moment has uncanny origins: the real Charles V had rehearsed his own funeral, first lying in a coffin beside his own tomb and then rising out of it.) This 'salvation' is a trump card prepared in the first cloister scene as well as at the end of the *auto-da-fé* when a consoling angel sings; it is to *Don Carlos* what Fate and Malediction are to Verdi's earlier works: the assertion of an ultimate, transcendent will. In the later versions, including 'Modena', the accusations are dropped with the now more rapid appearance of 'Charles V' unleashing turmoil (the music for the praying monks is reassigned to the brass): the effect is utterly vertiginous. In his Tenth Letter Schiller argued that 'if fraternal orders have a moral purpose ... then it must be at least very closely related to the one Marquis Posa proposed.'[3] Yet is an assertion of a higher moral order what the Modena ending intends? And when the monk sings so lugubriously that earthly sorrow follows us into the cloister and will abate only in heaven, is such a promise really salvation, or is it just the final coup de grâce?

Notes

Source: 'From *Don Carlos* to *Don Carlo* ... and Back', *Don Carlo* (Giuseppe Verdi), The Royal Opera programme, June 2009, pp. 15-20; reprinted September 2009 and April 2013; revised May 2017, pp. 15-19. The revision is followed here, with slight amendments.

1   'Letters on *Don Carlos*', trans. Jeanne R. Willson, in: Friedrich Schiller, *Plays. Intrigue and Love* and *Don Carlos*, ed. Walter Hinderer, New York: Continuum, 1994, pp. 305-46.
2   *Idem*, p. 345.
3   *Idem*, p. 337.

Richard Strauss conducting
(Milein Cosman, 1948)

Part Four

Beginning and End

1 *The Title*

Hugo von Hofmannsthal and Richard Strauss: *Der Rosenkavalier*

An opera's title is the first thing to catch our attention. Yet it is not necessarily where the librettist or composer begins. Nor even is it what an opera house's management – or sponsors – might accept. It can be a last thing, and even so, not always the right thing. It can always be changed, and sometimes is. Obviously, a title may refer to time, place or circumstance (especially an event); to one or more named characters; to character-types; to attributes; to stagecraft; to music or musical instruments; and so forth. Some words and topics will have a greater 'pull' than others. Alternatively, or additionally, the title may be philosophical, referring to an internal argument or an authorial point of view. An interesting case of an unsettled title is that of the first grand opera, given in Paris in 1828. The librettist was Germain Delavigne and the composer Daniel Auber. Originally called Masaniello ou la Muette de Portici, *it indicated not one but two points of focus: a named revolutionary leader (the fisherman Masaniello), and an unnamed type (the mute girl from Portici, in fact Masaniello's sister Fenella). When Eugène Scribe joined the project, the censors asked for the work's revolutionary aspect to be toned down. 'Masaniello' was thus dropped, leaving 'La Muette de Portici'. However, by indicating that the lead role couldn't sing, the title became even more arresting – in fact, the mute is taken by a dancer who communicates through pantomime. The 'matter' of the opera had thus perforce given way to the 'manner' of its presentation. Ironically, through one of its duets the suppressed revolutionary aspect would still fire the founding of Belgium in the 1830s.*

By contrast, the double titles of Da Ponte's libretti for Mozart celebrate events: Le nozze di Figaro *(The Marriage of Figaro) (1786) was a contraction of the double title of Beaumarchais' source play* La Folle journée, ou Le Marriage de Figaro *(The Crazy Day, or The Marriage of Figaro) integrating time, event and a lead role (the subject had revolutionary overtones, so it too required special pleading before the Emperor, Joseph II);* Il dissoluto punito ossia Il Don Giovanni *(The Rake's Punishment or Don Giovanni) (1787) retains the sense of the double title of Tirso de Molina's source play* El burlador de Sevilla y el convidado de piedra *(The Trickster of Seville or The Stone Guest) (c. 1625), which indicated that the fiendish trickster (not yet a named 'dissolute') can be overcome only by a supernatural figure; and* Così fan tutte *ossia* La scuola degli amanti *(Thus do All Women or The School for Lovers) (1790) embodies the old philosopher Don Alfonso's laconic perception of women, while also hinting at the ensuing action, the schooling of young lovers through a wager (the title is provocative and has often been replaced).*

Most common is for an opera to have a generic subtitle. This may indicate a category within theatre (dramma per musica)*, a sub-category of the same (*tragédie lyrique *or* comédie mise en musique*, opera seria or* opera buffa)*, or simply a hybrid (*opéra-ballet, radio opera, opera for television *and so forth). Cavalli's* La Calisto *(1651) is an example of the first, Grétry's* Andromaque *(1780) and* Richard Coeur-de-lion *(1784) are examples of the second, and Rameau's* Les Indes galantes *(1735-61), Thea Musgrave's* An Occurrence at Owl Creek Bridge *(1981) and Britten's* Owen Wingrave *(1971) examples of the third. There are countless other instances and variants extending back to the dawn of opera, just as there are a number of bespoke alternatives: Gustave Charpentier called his* Louise *(1900) a* roman musical *(a musical novel), Ravel his* L'Enfant et les sortilèges *(1925) a* fantaisie lyrique *(a sung fantasy), and Henze his* We Come to the River *(1976) actions for music.*

But there is also a reverse angle. Titles and subtitles may set the character of the action, but music will set its tone. And if the music is complex – generically, stylistically or both – audiences will expect the complexity to be reflected in the work's description. But titles do not always meet expectations. For example, audiences might well ask, aren't Wagner's 'Romantic Operas' really about Senta and the Flying Dutchman, Elisabeth and Tannhäuser *and* Elsa and Lohengrin *– and does the music-drama duo* Tristan and Isolde *deserve to be so privileged? And why is Harrison Birtwistle and David Harsent's* The Minotaur *(2008) not called by its mythologically accurate title* Ariadne and Theseus in Crete*, a latter-day prequel to Strauss's* Ariadne auf Naxos *(Harsent's Minotaur being of no especial interest)?*

The most striking dilemma over title-and-subtitle, however, arises when both creators and audiences find themselves on shifting ground. This is not necessarily a fault, but rather an indication of complexity. There are few cases as challenging as that of Der Rosenkavalier *(1911). The following study looks at the work's title and genre, first from the point of the poet Hugo von Hofmannsthal and then from that of the composer Richard Strauss, assessing how the competing internal forces are balanced in each act. What emerges is a map of the work's contrasts. It is these that best form the basis for debate over its title and genre. For many theorists, indeed, the first way to touch base with any opera is to stake out its field of contrasts.*

In opera, titles can set the tone of the music. They often appear in duplicate – a topic and a genre – and can change before the premiere (and sometimes even after). *Der Rosenkavalier* received its first performance early in 1911, and bore the generic subtitle 'comedy for music in 3 acts'. The subtitle, preferred to 'burlesque opera in 3 acts', already reflects Hugo von Hofmannsthal's priority: a play to which Richard Strauss would add music – which he did, after having Hofmannsthal turn parts of it into an operatic libretto with duologues that glide seamlessly into 'numbers'. But the topic was originally *Ochs von Lerchenau*, a vehicle for an incorrigible, well-connected, up-from-the country lothario in the line of Molière's Monsieur de Pourceaugnac and Verdi's Falstaff, who has his own dialect, features centrally in each act and is shamed in a final masquerade. True to type, Baron Ochs is entertaining but sinister – all the more so for being carefully removed to the Vienna of the 1740s (in the 'early years of the reign of Maria Theresia'), even though his music celebrates the Viennese waltz as received a century later. However, the change to *Der Rosenkavalier* (The Cavalier of the Rose) answered a growing sense in both authors that Ochs was not their main focus. It signalled a shift from history to fairy-tale, from a named protagonist to a symbol. It did not call itself *Octavian*, after Ochs's young and 'noble' cousin who is the only other 'lead' to appear in each act, but underscored Octavian's role as cavalier in a fictitious ceremony. By bearing a rose to Ochs's intended bride, he enters a triangle involving an older woman, a younger woman and himself as the 'man' who has to choose between them (his being a trouser-role that further asks him to appear disguised as a maid). This entangled trio had its roots in a risqué French operetta of 1907 by Louis Artus and Claude Terrasse known to Hofmannsthal through his friend and invisible collaborator Count Kessler, and the title of which also focussed on an Octavian figure, *L'Ingénu libertin* (The Ingenuous Libertine).[1]

Just as the dramatic sources for *Der Rosenkavalier* reach back over three centuries, so do the musical sources. This depth of reference is crucial to defining the multifarious character of the project. The comedy begins with an orchestral 'introduction'. This uninhibited representation of the sexual act involves distinct musical figures for each lover complemented by a joint 'lovebird' figure (eighteenth-century 'parallel thirds'); it is marked, not just 'stormy … agitated and highly exuberant', but also, as it gathers to a joyously whooping climax, 'parodistic'. Here is a priapic teenager – Octavian – in the first flush of manhood, answered, during the following amorous repose, by a married woman in her thirties – the (Feld)Marschallin. The situation may derive from the start of the third act of *L'Ingénu libertin*, yet the shape of the music brings to mind the orchestral introduction from *Tristan und Isolde*. This likewise depicts the act of love. Strauss's pair emerge as a witty riposte to Wagner's personality-disordered couple, with Octavian asking 'Was heisst das "Du", was "Du und ich"? … Ich will nicht den Tag!' (What means that 'thou', what 'thou and I'? … I don't want the day!) and the Marschallin responding gently though not in kind. Fittingly, Strauss writes the music in E major, a key with traditional connotations of energy and vulnerable tenderness. The shadow of *Tristan* falls over other parts of *Der Rosenkavalier* too, especially those generating erotic intensity. The fervent duet of Octavian and Sophie, for instance, is interrupted by Sophie's intended husband, Baron Ochs: they have been betrayed by the two *commedia dell'arte* figures, Valzacchi and Annina. Ochs's response is to turn more than a blind eye: 'Ich muss ihm gratulieren!' (I must congratulate [him]!) he sings admiringly of his bewildered cousin. This *interruptus* parodies the moment in Act Two of *Tristan*, when the lovers' impassioned duet is halted by the sudden appearance of Isolde's new husband King Marke, guided by Tristan's jealous 'friend' Melot: Marke's response is far from admiring, and, indeed, his shaming of Tristan proves lethal.

The first act of *Rosenkavalier* is bounded, not by Ochs, but by the Marschallin and Octavian. At its opening, their privacy is interrupted three times by people who bring with them three kinds of music. First, the blackamoor servant with a delicate scherzo. Second, Baron Ochs with a pompous entrance figure that gives way to a double duet – one with the Marschallin, the other aside with 'Mariandel' (Octavian) – followed by a provocative dramatic monologue that parades the scale of his philandering (invariably sung with a cut). And third, the throng of visitors to the Marschallin's levee who interleave a trio for three orphans, a minuet for a hairdresser, a *bel canto* arietta for an Italian tenor and so forth, the levee being derived from William Hogarth's *Marriage à la mode* (No. 4). This heady mixture throws into relief the following long monologue. Prompted by the morning's events, the Marschallin reflects poignantly on mortality. Her mood continues into an intense duologue with the returning Octavian – she will have to renounce him – and touches bottom as she reveals her piety and sense of social duty (here the music regains E major). The style crosses that of Verdi's Shakespearean monologues from *Falstaff* with Strauss's version of Wagnerian speech-song nimbly supported in the orchestra by recurrent motifs.

The second act is Wagnerian by moving from one extreme to another – though it pulls back at the end – and Italianate by including a large ensemble, a central-act *concertato* of a kind. To our surprise, it does not include the Marschallin. The presentation of the rose, the most fêted enactment of adolescent love at first sight in the repertory, is an oasis of calm in the midst of turmoil. Preceded by preparatory bustle artfully interwoven with the devotions of Sophie, it is followed by an exposé of Vienna as gossipy, snobbish and mercenary, centred on Ochs and his proposed father-in-law, the newly ennobled and obsequious Faninal. The presentation is not a duologue but a duet, as formal as it is liberating, as archaic as it is enchanting. It casts its spell in three ways: it overlays an eighteenth-century dance type, a dignified *siciliano*, with surging but restrained waves of Tristanesque feeling; it depicts the silver rose, a catalyst in the developing drama between Octavian and the two women, with a touchingly sentimental tinsel of harps, celesta, flutes and solo violins; and it unites Octavian's mezzo-soprano, not just with a soprano (the Marschallin's vocal type), but with a high soprano: for the first time, Sophie's vocal lines soar into the empyrean, reminding us that opera is never more itself than when its music touches the sublime. We in the audience soar with her.

Baron Ochs arrives to claim Sophie. By contrast, his bass reveals itself best when set against his fêted waltz tune 'Mit mir' (With me). This emerges in the middle of the Act Two in riposte to Sophie's demand 'Was ist denn er zu mir?' (So what is he to me?) and takes its place in a network of waltzes spanning the opera. Strauss uses the dance to epitomize the Viennese conversational mode – in Act One as the Marschallin and Octavian bask in a post-coital glow, in Act Two as Sophie and Octavian shyly get to know each other, and parodistically in Act Three as Ochs dines with 'Mariandel', their waltz gliding out of the banal waltzes played by a Mozartian off-stage band. But Ochs's waltz significantly breaks the mould. At first marked 'rocking and sentimental', it becomes harmonically unstable and indulges briefly in 'impudent and coarse' rhythms for 'mit mir keine Nacht dir zu lang' (With me no night will seem too long): all this depicts Ochs's radical disregard of 'the other' (he will be Sophie's 'all'). Indeed, the coarseness is enhanced when, soon after, his followers rampage in pursuit of the servant girls to music of near-expressionist violence. These features are accentuated in the quiet ending to the act, after Ochs has been wounded by Octavian. This embodies another Falstaffian monologue, again with interjections from onlookers. Shockingly, his 'Mit mir' refers no longer to Sophie but to 'Mariandel', with the waltz tune marked 'very sickly'. Strauss's musical portrait of Ochs confirms what Carl Jung would observe in 1932, that 'sentimentality is the superstructure erected upon brutality'.

The tone of this second act has shifted startlingly from that of the first. So it is fitting that the third act seeks a denouement on two overlapping fronts, both with distinct music. First, the dazzlingly intricate orchestral introduction, along with the subsequent 'pantomime', depicts the busy preparations for the Windsor Forest-style trick to be played on Ochs. To be performed 'as fast as possible', it dresses up Octavian's priapic opening theme from Act One as a popular folk-song to characterize the rough-spoken 'Mariandel'. Once the attempted seduction gets underway (now to a string of waltzes), the theme returns partly 'undressed' as Ochs comes close to rumpling Mariandel's disguise. Second, the Marschallin sweeps in to an expansive version of her own music, the sustained poise of which transfigures the circumstance just as does the emergence of the Countess at the end of Mozart's *Figaro*. Other issues have now to be resolved. Sophie arrives to give Ochs a voluble come-uppance, the Marschallin takes stock of her '*charmant*' rival, and 'Mariandel' reveals 'herself' as Octavian (whose theme is now fully restored). But the most poignant passage is musically the sparsest. Ochs realizes that the disconcerted Marschallin is herself compromised with Octavian: both negotiate to each other's advantage, with the Marschallin insisting that Ochs renounce Sophie (to Sophie's bewilderment). Theirs is a morality 'beyond good and evil': in this Vienna, there is no stone guest to drag Don Juan into punitive hellfire. Instead, the real people burst in to have their say, tearing off masks, demanding payment, and using Ochs's signature waltz to mock the 'Luck of the Lerchenau'. There is a hard edge to this chaotic ensemble, yet the comedy never oversteps its limits.

After the throng leaves, the two fronts converge. Octavian, Sophie and the Marschallin now find themselves alone. Separately and together, to themselves and to each other, they unite in their confusion. Privately steeling herself for the blow to come, the Marschallin sings in duple-time against the triple-time of the waltz. This splitting of tempi marks the preparation for the great formal trio that follows, and will return at its climax. When the trio starts, the Marschallin and Sophie sing holy thoughts 'to themselves' – as befits two ex-convent girls – while Octavian expresses his amazement 'with great feeling': all this is in slow triple-time. The tempo then quickens into a transfigured waltz as the music intensifies and Octavian and Sophie now address each other. But at the trio's climax, the duple time returns. It marks the moment the Marschallin steps out of the love triangle: to a sweeping statement of her theme, she gives the young couple her blessing 'in the name of God'. In Kleinian terms, she has embraced the 'depressive' position with a dignity that restores the social equilibrium.

But this is not quite the end. The Marschallin leaves Octavian and Sophie alone. For their closing duet Strauss wrote out rhythms for Hofmannsthal to complete with words. There are three verses. In the first and third, both rhythm and tune recall the passage from Mozart's *Die Zauberflöte* where Pamina and Papageno trust in the sound of enchanted bells to banish their fears ('Könnte jeder brave Mann …'); but in their transfigured simplicity they are also redolent of the lost-in-the-woods duet from Humperdinck's 'fairy-tale' *Hänsel und Gretel* (of which the admiring Strauss conducted the first performance in 1893). More still, the duet 'dreamily' recalls the sound world of the presentation of the rose. The central verse, by contrast, anchors the music in the present: Octavian lays bare his worries, Sophie reveals her vulnerability and even the Marschallin and Faninal put in a final appearance, not unlike depth-psychology parent-figures there to endorse the match. The young lovers have created an enchanted psychic retreat that will do at least for now – though we wonder whether, given time, Octavian too might not travel down the same path as Ochs.

So what title would best suit the opera? *The Luck of the Lerchenau*, an ironic insight grounded in Ochs's invincible waltz? *Octavian and Sophie*, celebrating two named adolescents caught up in (and protected by) a fairy-tale ritual? *Marie Theres'*, charting how an intimately-described Austrian princess comes to recognize that her waltzing years are over? Or, after all, *Der Rosenkavalier*, an unnamed figure who embodies a Viennese type? And what generic subtitle should go with it – comedy, operetta, music drama …? If these establish an irreducible force-field, then that in part pays homage to the power of Strauss's complex and enthralling music.

Notes

Source: 'The Tone in the Title', *Der Rosenkavalier* (Richard Strauss), The Royal Opera programme, December 2016, pp. 30-4.

1   For this I am indebted to a recent study by Michael Reynolds: *Creating 'Der Rosenkavalier'. From Chevalier to Cavalier*, Woodbridge: The Boydell Press, 2016.

2 A Name

Francesco Maria Piave (after Gutiérrez) and Giuseppe Verdi: *Simon Boccanegra*

*One way of getting into an opera is to see how its names are handled –
what role they play in the drama and how they are set to music.
Throughout his later works, Wagner consistently invested naming with
the highest significance, never more so than with Kundry's expansively
seductive call of 'Par – si – fal'; Britten used the repeated 'Grimes' as the
hunting cry of an incensed Borough, one that Peter Grimes eventually
turns against himself; and in* Der Rosenkavalier *Hofmannsthal and
Strauss have Sophie litanize all Octavian's names – not just 'Octavian,
Maria Ehrenreich, Bonaventura, Fernand, Hyazinth', but also 'Quinquin',
the term of endearment we have already heard from the lips of the
Marschallin (whom Octavian calls 'Bichette'). Yet for a composer there
are many aspects to a name: vowels, consonants, accents, tempo, rhythm,
intensity and tone-of-utterance. All require careful handling, though all
can bend to circumstance. For instance, there is no more affecting or
dramatically progressive isolation of a name than in the outer acts of
Gluck's* Orfeo ed Euridice *(1762). Act One begins in medias res. Euridice
has already been fatally stung and borne off to the underworld. We
meet a chorus of mourners. Chief among them is Orfeo, who is set apart.
Whereas the chorus sing decorously of 'Euridice, ombra bella', Orfeo
can only utter the name 'Euridice' – which he does three times. The
chorus have two accents for 'Euridice', Orfeo has one, the more pitiful
'Euridice'. His naming becomes even more pitiful in Act Three when he
loses her for the second time. At the centre of his famous lament, 'Che
farò senza Euridice', he cries out to her twice, achieving high pathos as
the continuity is broken and the overall tempo stalls. Does he believe she
is still there, we wonder? Yet there is no answer to his call. Irrevocable
loss suddenly strikes home. It is one of the great 'moments that matter' in
opera, psychologically and musico-dramatically.*[1]

*The following note takes things further by showing how, for dramatic
reasons, Verdi played with two versions of his lead character's name.*

The title of the Spanish play on which Verdi based his opera for Venice in
1857 was *Simón Bocanegra*, its author Antonio García Gutiérrez. Gutiérrez
had also written the not dissimilar *El trovador*, the source for Verdi's *Il
trovatore* (1853), which was also heard in 1857 (in Paris) as *Le Trouvère*. Either
Verdi, his librettists Piave and Montanelli or his lifelong-partner Giuseppina

Strepponi translated *Simón* to *Simon* and *Bocanegra* to *Boccanegra* (literally, black-mouth), though, as Eduard Hanslick noted in the early 1880s, 'Italian historians [of the fourteenth century] sometimes spell the name "Boccanigra", and at other times "Boccanera"'.[2] The historical Simon had also been known as Simonino, on account of his tiny stature. However, since Simon and Simone were (and still are) available Italian names, and because it had been the historical name for Boccanegra, Verdi used both – rather as a modern opera composer might use Joe or Joseph for 'Stalin'. At the end of the Prologue, for instance, the people of Genoa hail their newly elected Doge to the cry of 'Viva Simon!' (Long live Simon!), where the masculine (*tronco*) ending Simòn clinches his newly-bestowed authority. On the other hand, when earlier in the Prologue the manipulative Paolo steps out of the shadows to divulge his choice of leader to the people, the chorus of men cry in astonishment and wonder 'Simone! Il corsaro!' (Simone! The corsair!). Here the two feminine (*piano*) endings establish a parallel rhythm – Simòne / Corsàro – that deftly positions Boccanegra as a pirate or outsider – a parallel Verdi exploits keenly in the music. (Simone-the-heroic-corsair is Byronic poetic licence, not historical fact.) The publisher Ricordi followed suit: in the vocal score, the list of characters refers to Simon, whereas the stage directions refer to Simone.

Not surprisingly, the name has come in for some banter. When the opera, in Boito's inspired revision, was in rehearsal at La Scala, the conductor Franco Faccio wrote to Verdi on 16 February 1881: 'Early next week I'll devote myself body and soul to the *Bocca* (so-called) *Negra*, which will be rosy instead, fresh and full of promises like the mouth of a young bride.' Another title, then – *Simone Boccarosa*?

Notes

Source: *Simon Boccanegra* (Giuseppe Verdi), The Royal Opera programme, June 2010, p. 45.

1   I have amplified the concept of 'moments that matter' in a separate essay: ' "Suddenly finding it really matters": Psychology, Verdi and Aristotelian Form', *Open Spaces*, issue 7, Fall 2005, pp. 225-40'. *Open Spaces* is supported by the Department of Music, Princeton University (NJ, USA). 'Che farò ...' sometimes attracts criticism for being initially too perky, overly major-mode. Yet the major-mode poise of the outer sections throws into relief the minor-mode suffering of the inner section that comes with Orfeo's calls for Euridice. A century later, a composer would have been unlikely to accept the return to the major mode for the reprise of the opening but rather might have progressed to a new position. That is to say, Gluck's ternary scheme A-B-A is essentially *dramatized music*, whereas our later composer's putative dramatic monologue A-B-C would have been essentially *musicalized drama*. Ironically, Gluck himself was alive to just such an anomaly when he wrote in the preface to his later

Alceste (1769) 'I did not think it my duty to pass quickly over the second section of an aria of which the words are perhaps the most impassioned and important, in order to repeat regularly four times over those of the first ...' (*Source Readings in Music History. From Classical Antiquity through the Romantic Era*, ed. Oliver Strunk, New York: Norton, 1950, p. 674.)

2 Hans Busch, *Verdi's* Otello *and* Simon Boccanegra *(revised version) in Letters and Documents*, trans. and ed. Hans Busch, Oxford: Clarendon Press, 1988, p. 673.

3   The Prelude

Antonio Somma (after Scribe) and Giuseppe Verdi: *Un ballo in maschera*

It was in 1769 that Christoph Willibald Gluck threw down a gauntlet, not just for himself, but for all later generations: 'I have felt,' he wrote in the reforming preface to his Alceste, *'that the [opera] overture ought to apprise the spectators of the nature of the action that is to be represented and to form, so to speak, its argument.'[1] In other words, the overture should no longer be a distinct, all-purpose* sinfonia *(or* introduzione*), with slow-fast music (as in the French style), fast-slow-fast music (as in the Italian style) or other arrangements of tempo; it should establish the character (genre and style) and focus (topic) of the work in hand; and it should take the place of a dramatic prologue. It was indeed a watershed moment. Historians can reasonably speak of an overture as being pre-Gluck or post-Gluck, or even in the case of the neo-classicists, pre/post-Gluck – Stravinsky's* The Rake's Progress *(1951) opens with a playful fanfare redolent of the toccata that introduces the prologue to Monteverdi's* L'Orfeo *(1607).*

Now, 'post-Gluck' much has happened to the overture: it is more likely to have a single tempo (Bellini's Norma *(1831)) or several tempi (Rossini's* Guillaume Tell *(1829)); it may preview the music to come (Weber's* Der Freischütz *(1821) or the medleys of operettas and musicals); it may lead straight in to the first act, with or without a change of tempo (Donizetti's* Lucia di Lammermoor *(1835) follows a 'maestoso' with an 'allegro'); it may seem free-standing at first but then turn out to be a feature of the drama (Flamand's 'prologue-sextet' in Strauss's* Capriccio *(1942)); it may be delayed (in Britten's* Death in Venice *(1973) the overture follows scene two and acts as a lead-in to scene three); it may be pithy (the three 'Scarpia' chords of Puccini's* Tosca *(1900)); it may be dropped altogether (Schoenberg's* Moses und Aron *(1932/57)); or it may be replaced by the introductory character of an opening scene (Strauss's* Elektra *(1909), significantly prefaced by the pithy but dominating 'Agamemnon' motif). In terms of character and topic, there are many ways of tailoring a bespoke overture, if indeed such a thing is still needed.*

However, Gluck also demanded that the overture should represent the opera's 'argument'. This was a daunting demand. Instrumental music may be 'argumentative' in character, but it cannot 'argue' as can spoken language. It cannot tell a back-story, or describe a social circumstance, or advance a moral or aesthetic outlook. The most it can hope to do is to indicate an argument by arranging musical ideas or motives associated with forthcoming characters or situations in a suggestive manner. Even so, such an argument becomes clear only when the work has progressed or finished: it is strictly incomprehensible at the start. It is no match for a theatrical argument. The overture thus acts as a prologue (in musical terms a 'prelude') and the prelude becomes a prefatory postlude. This is the issue with which Verdi grappled in the 1850s.

Most opera-goers know that the orchestral prelude was usually the last part of an opera that Verdi wrote. They also know that Verdi composed various kinds of prelude, and even dispensed with preludes altogether (as in *Il trovatore*, *Don Carlos*, *Otello* and *Falstaff*). But how many know just how the type he developed in the 1850s actually worked? In fact, it had four main tasks: to focus on the central character, to look deep into the future of the action, to map out musical extremes, and to make a whole that was greater than its parts. The prelude to *La traviata*, for example, anticipates the etiolated sick-room music of the final act and then allows 'sick' harmonies to subvert the playful society music that follows: these two types of music, the sick and the gay, define the two aspects of the heroine, the loving, tubercular courtesan, Violetta. Similarly, the portentous opening of *Rigoletto* leads to a tormented outburst of a kind we associate with the death of the hunchback's daughter at the close, even though this music never actually appears in the opera; its pathos is then thrown into relief by the 'trivial' party music that opens the first act. That is to say, Rigoletto's paranoia and suffering are played out against a background of frivolity.

But what of the prelude to *Un ballo in maschera* (1859)?[2] This is far from the decorous blend of festivity and tenderness that characterizes Auber's prelude to *Gustave III* (1833), an earlier work on Scribe's *Ballo* libretto. On the contrary, it lays out the work's extremes. Of its four sections, the first three anticipate the opening scene. There is a delicate lullaby that will be associated with the courtiers: 'Posa in pace a'bei sogni ristoro, O Riccardo, il tuo nobil cor' (May your noble heart rest in peace, O Riccardo), they sing to their Governor. Then there is furtive music to be associated with the conspirators who are pursuing a vendetta against Riccardo for his political murders: this comprises five overlapping entries. Third, there is the typically effusive music associated with Riccardo's illicit love for Amelia, his loyal henchman's wife: this falls into a unit of its own, as self-contained as it is self-absorbed. But what of the final section? Here the conspirators' music returns, now worked up into a forthright climax. We hear two violent, stabbing chords followed by a stunned silence; then the kind of tender music we associated with the court and its love-struck Governor returns, as if nothing had happened. The prelude closes more or less as it began.

Violent, stabbing chords? This, of course, has nothing to do with the first scene. Stabbing, rather, takes place in the final scene, when once again the court is assembled and Riccardo rashly seeks out Amelia. But *violent* stabbing? Hardly. As the final scene is a masked ball, the conspirators, now led by Amelia's enraged husband Renato, act surreptitiously. There is no musical representation of the knifing. The tone simply switches from festivity to horror. The horror, indeed, takes time to sink in and is compounded when the courtiers discover the assassin's identity. And now we see Verdi's strategy with regard to the musical design of the whole: the violence that will be masked in the opera's finale stands revealed in the stabbing chords of its prelude.

However, we should pause over the fact that at the end of the prelude, after the stabbing chords, the tender music returns. Now, in terms of the prelude's wholeness this is unremarkable: closed forms like to end as they begin. But in terms of the opera's drama, nothing could be more astonishing. In the finale, once the assassin has been unmasked, the dying Riccardo urges clemency. In an arioso of utmost desolation he asserts Amelia's unblemished honour and reveals that he has arranged for her and Renato to be sent abroad: out of sight, out of mind. The court is astonished. From behind a mask of playboy irresponsibility Riccardo emerges as a paradigm of the Enlightened Ruler: the sane part of his personality has won through. Everyone joins in a prayer of utmost intensity, but to no avail: Riccardo's words collapse into a shout as Death itself unmasks his singing voice. And only now do we understand the true import of the end of the work's prelude, which celebrates the placing of duty before love and self-interest.

But if the sane part of Riccardo wins through, what of the insane part? Again, the prelude gives the clue: Riccardo's ring-fenced love music for Amelia stands in a reciprocal relation to the conspirators' music that surrounds it. That is to say, whenever in the opera Riccardo declares his passion for Amelia and vows to protect her, he is in effect asserting self-love and self-defence. For Amelia is his secret talisman against catastrophe: even the courtiers mistake his love for her as love for them. For her part, Amelia reluctantly responds to Riccardo's ardour; but she is frantically aware of the dangers their situation poses, and risks anything to dissolve it honourably. After all, in choosing her as his love-object, Riccardo is taking up the wife of the very man, Renato, on whom his survival depends. Yet Riccardo wilfully ignores every warning that comes his way. In Act One, he eavesdrops on Amelia's fretful meeting with the witch Ulrica. In Act Two, he intrusively joins her by the gallows at midnight as she looks for the herb that will save her; and in Act Three, despite her pleas, he approaches her at the masked ball. When finally he bids her farewell, he implicitly bids himself farewell: and it is at just this point that Renato, now head of the conspirators, stabs him. In the words of the psychoanalyst Gerald Wooster, it is as if Riccardo has unconsciously willed his own destruction.[3]

Not surprisingly, the relation between Riccardo and Amelia yields extraordinary music: rarely have two operatic lovers been so uncomfortable together. At the start of Act Two, Amelia sings an aria of abject terror, 'Ma dall' arido stelo divulsa' (But when, plucked from the withered stem) that ponders the meaning of life after love; Riccardo bursts in impetuously, and although their formal duet ends, not in rejection, but in celebration of love, he sings with joy and she with shame. When at the masked ball, the lovers bid each other farewell against the 'banal' background of a ballroom minuet, he exudes ardour, she desperation. Only in his dying moments does Riccardo sing as if she is a meaningful 'other'.

Before this, Riccardo's frivolity and self-absorption is thrown into relief by two other characters whose love turns lethal. Renato may be humourless, more loyal than a dog and more vengeful than any woman scorned, but his case is real enough. In the first scene of Act Three, his confrontation with Amelia yields not only her most tortuous aria, 'Morrò, ma prima in grazia' (I will die, but first in mercy) but also his anguished soliloquy, 'Eri tu' (It is you). In terms of suffering, this cedes nothing to the parallel soliloquy in the next scene when Riccardo articulates his foreboding, 'Ma se m'è forza perderti' (But if you are lost to me forever). Similarly the brilliant, Gallic singing of the page Oscar (a light trouser-role who plays fool to his master's Lear) matches Riccardo's levity, notably when Riccardo shows the fortune-telling Ulrica his hand. Yet by fatally revealing Riccardo's identity at the ball, Oscar conspicuously acts as his master's Own Worst Enemy.

Out of such extremes, indeed, Verdi moulds the play of light and shade (*chiaroscuro*) for which the work is famous. The lightness emerges especially in the work's dazzling choral ensembles, notably those that end the first two scenes, through which, nevertheless, there run sinister undercurrents. Luigi Dallapiccola once noted that Verdi's assassins, rather than exuding cloak-and-dagger villainy, cultivate an air of macabre jocularity (as in *Nabucco*, *Macbeth* and *Rigoletto*): in the opening scene of Act One of *Un ballo*, the conspirators may provide a discreetly subversive counterpoint to the lullaby of the courtiers, but at the end of Act Two they burst out into a laughing chorus, one almost unique in opera.[4] Whereas in *Rigoletto* Verdi devised a broad Shakespearean tragi-comic mix to replace the 'single-string' diction of *I due Foscari*, here in the first scene of Act Three we can watch him working up the mix by stages: the vengeance of Renato and the conspirators in a trio is enhanced by the suffering of Amelia in a quartet, and then brilliantly offset by the joy of Oscar in a quintet. And whereas in the ball scene of his *Gustave III*, Auber had already pitted tragedy in the orchestra against banality in the stage band, in the comparable final scene of *Un ballo* Verdi achieves one of his greatest triumphs when he allows the musically portentous to infiltrate the band music without compromising its ballroom function.

But it is the sorceress Ulrica who casts the darkest shadow of all. The scholar John Rosselli wrote that what had attracted Verdi to the subject of *Un ballo* was 'the contrast between a brilliant civilized society on the one hand and the possibility of superstition on the other'. Acquiescence in superstition, representative of the unyielding, primitive Freudian super-ego, has many outcomes in Verdi's operas: fatalism, vendetta, ostracism, and an irrational propensity of the guilty to accept their malediction. But nothing is more compelling than Ulrica's entranced invocation of the powers of night in the aria that opens the second scene of Act One, 'Re dell'abisso affrettati' (Lord of the abyss, reveal thyself). Her three acts of clairvoyance climb through the social ranks: the sailor Silvano is of the people, the terrified Amelia is of the court, and Riccardo is the ruler of them all. But her acts also conform to the Freudian 'rule of three' by which the third in a series may stand for Death. Ulrica predicts Riccardo's end: he may greet her prediction with mockery, yet there is no escaping it – die he will.

Although it may be an exaggeration to say that in the mixed-style prelude to *Un ballo*, we recognize, not just the play of the hunter and the hunted, but also the will of the Prince of Darkness himself, nevertheless this is how things eventually turn out. A Comedy of Love is unmasked as a Tragedy of Fate.[5]

Notes

Source: 'The Enlightened Sounds of Fate: the Prelude to *Un ballo in maschera*', *Un ballo in maschera* (Giuseppe Verdi), The Royal Opera programme, December 2014, p. 41-5 (revision of the original 2005 version).

1   In: *Source Readings in Music History. From Classical Antiquity through the Romantic Era*, ed. Oliver Strunk, New York: Norton, 1950, pp. 673-5.
2   There are different versions of this text, involving settings in Stockholm or Boston, with the central figure either the King of Sweden (Gustav III) or Riccardo, the Count of Warwick and Governor of Boston. The move from Sweden to the United States was a response to the objection of the censors at staging a regicide. The first performance was at the Teatro Apollo in Rome. Previously, when Verdi was expecting the first performance to be given in Naples, the authorities had suggested the title *Adelia degli Adimari*. This essay follows the American setting.
3   Private communication.
4   There is also a laughing chorus in scene 10 of Britten's *Death in Venice* (1973), though there the laughter turns into 'wild' mockery, and the chorus laughs with Adèle in Act Two of Johann Strauss's *Die Fledermaus* (1874).
5   In the music of the prelude, the B major of the tender first and fourth sections is unmasked as B minor in the violent third section. This B minor in turn has unmasked the amorous D major of the second section.

4   Multiple Beginnings

Richard Wagner: *Das Rheingold*

Like an overture, a theatrical prologue can act as a call to attention; it can flatter the audience while asserting the modesty of the performers; it can set the scene and provide back-story; and it can indicate the work's genre. In the prologue to Shakespeare's Henry V *(1599), we all sense some inverted pride as the 'Chorus' transports the audience from the poverty of the theatre to the richness of the imagination: '... pardon, gentles all, / The flat unraisèd spirits that hath dared / On this unworthy scaffold to bring forth / So great an object. Can this cock-pit hold / The vasty fields of France? Or may we cram / Within this wooden O the very casques / that did affright the air at Agincourt?' Now, such prologues may also appear in operas, from the earliest to the most recent, sung by a figure who may or may not go on to join the action. In Monteverdi's* L'Orfeo *(1607) La Musica decorously asks the illustrious audience to listen in silence; in Leoncavallo's* Pagliacci *(1892) an 'actor' expounds the new aesthetic of realism (verismo); and in Britten's* The Burning Fiery Furnace *(1966) 'The Abbot' tells his (stage) monks of the condition already imposed upon the three Babylonians Ananias, Misael and Azarias: 'Their fathers blest them, Only made one rule Binding upon them all: They never must in any way Betray their faith. How could they know What testing lay ahead?' All then dress up to set off the action.*

Wagner had no such prologues. Rather, he was obliged to subsume their scene-setting function into the work itself. In the first act of Parsifal *(1882), he has Gurnemanz relate the back-story of Klingsor, Titurel and Amfortas to the Four Squires. It is egregiously long. However, the question of prologue in* Der Ring des Nibelungen *(The Ring of the Nibelungs) is more complex. In 1848, he compiled a libretto for* Siegfrieds Tod *(Siegfried's Death). In 1851-2, to articulate the back-story thoroughly, he added three works,* Der junge Siegfried, Die Walküre *and* Das Rheingold. Der junge Siegfried *(The Young Siegfried) and* Siegfried's Tod *then became* Siegfried *and* Götterdämmerung *(Twilight of the Gods), preceded by* Das Rheingold *(The Rhinegold) leading to* Die Walküre *(The Valkyrie Woman). Of these* Das Rheingold *was presented as a* Vorabend, *a prelude to the three remaining evenings. More still, he gave* Götterdämmerung *an act-length prologue in two parts. In the first part the Three Norns (or Fates) stand outside the action to assume the function of a Chorus, whereas in the second part Siegfried and Brünnhilde continue their story from the previous evening, breaking off as Siegfried sets off on his Rhine Journey.*

The journey itself is an orchestral passage that will abandon Siegfried and leap ahead in time and place to act as an overture leading straight into Act One. But this is not the end of the matter. For, before we hear the first notes of Das Rheingold, *things have already happened: a narrative start is never the beginning of a story.*

Much has been made of Richard Wagner's comment to Franz Liszt in 1853 that *Der Ring des Nibelungen* 'contains the world's beginning and its end'.[1] And when we hear the first low E♭ of *Das Rheingold*, so powerful is our sense of setting forth that it is easy to overlook three qualifying factors: first, that the drama meaningfully begins at several points; second, that it celebrates an integration, or love, that has neither beginning nor end but stands outside time; and third, that it signals the beginning of a new aesthetic venture. All three, it should be said, can find endorsement in Wagner's writings.

In the first draft of *Rheingold*, the *Gesamtentwurf* of 1853, Wagner appears to have thought of the opening music as no more than an introduction to the first scene (in fact, he claimed to have dreamt it at La Spezia). Over a softly undulating background, rippling strings outline a long, unbroken E♭ major chord that prepares for the arrival of the Rhine-daughters: at this stage the music is featureless and does not even (yet) sound like the opening of Felix Mendelssohn's *Das Märchen von der schönen Melusine* (The Tale of the Fair Melusine) of 1833, an alleged 'source'. However, when he revised the work in 1854, Wagner remodelled the ascending contour in view of the later music of Erda, whose surprise appearance in *Rheingold*'s fourth and final scene is the work's supreme *coup de theâtre*. Erda prophesies the end of the all-too-human gods, and accordingly her contour ascends and descends. The revised start of the first scene thus absorbs her ascent, and thereby adumbrates the topic that preoccupies the *Ring* as a whole: the coming to terms with the end, with death. It also establishes the impassive authority of those who, like Erda and the Rhine-daughters, speak for timeless 'Nature'. With the subtly overlapping entries of the eight horns, it now lasts longer and is vastly more intricate than before – Wagner complained to Liszt that he could find no 'other way of writing out the prelude' than in full score. Indeed, the revised prelude, which gathers movement as the texture rises, prepares us for the following scene: we are in the depths of the Rhine, which is 'darker below' and 'lighter above' (where the waters billow): the music guides the eye from bottom to top. The curtains should open shortly before the singers enter.[2]

Now, a new set of aesthetic beginnings is signalled by Woglinde's opening words, 'Weia! Waga! Woge, du Welle, walle zur Wiege! Wagala weia! Wallala weiala weia!'. For they introduce Wagner's archaic, alliterative head-rhyme (*Stabreim*) together with his novel principles of accentuation; they establish the genre of a cosmic lullaby (Welter, you wave, swirl round the cradle!);

and at the same time they blend an ancient type of watering song with the *eia popeia* (hushabye) of a children's nursery rhyme. Even more, they enact the birth of language from vocalization, itself a vehicle of pre-verbal affect. Yet Woglinde is just the first of three Rhine-daughters; and as we eavesdrop on their conversation, we realize much has already happened. 'You guard the sleeping gold badly', chides Flosshilde, reminding her carefree companions that their Rhine-father has bound them to guard the 'bright hoard' so that 'no false thief should filch it from the flood'. Fear and suspicion, that is to say, are already well rooted.

In itself Flosshilde's warning is significant. For she is the third of the Rhine-daughters, and according to Sigmund Freud in the 'The Theme of the Three Caskets' (*c.* 1913), the third in a chain of three can portend a fatal reversal.[3] Unlike the light-headed sopranos Woglinde and Wellgunde, Flosshilde is a darker dramatic mezzo. And in *Das Rheingold* she is the first in a chain of three mezzos that includes Fricka (Wotan's chiding wife) and the sybilline Erda. (Correspondingly, our third light-headed soprano will be Freia, the fairy-tale princess taken hostage by the giants.)

But why should the Rhine-father be so concerned? Is it just because he knows of Alberich, the squat, amphibious dwarf who, goaded beyond endurance by the Rhine-daughters, is shortly to commit the highest sacrilege by stealing the gold, an action that threatens the gods? Wagner has various answers. The first comes in a seminal letter to August Röckel of January 1854. 'It is not the fact', he writes, 'that Alberich was repulsed by the Rhine-daughters that is the definitive source of evil – for it was natural for them to repulse him; no, Alberich . . . could not have harmed the gods unless the latter had already been susceptible to evil.'[4] And why were the gods susceptible to evil? Here Wagner directs us to scene 2 of *Das Rheingold*. Wotan, the head of the gods, and Fricka are locked in 'the mutual torment' of a loveless marriage; they are unable to yield to the necessity of 'change, variety, multiplicity and the eternal newness of reality and life'; they too have sacrificed love, only this time for contracts. In the celebrated musical interlude between the first and second scenes, Wagner clinches the parallel between dwarf and gods by transforming Alberich's music into Wotan's.

Two other symbols in *Rheingold* take us closer towards an understanding of the 'source of evil'. The first is the ring the dwarf has fashioned from the stolen gold. As we learn from scene 3, this gives Alberich the power to terrorize his fellow dwarves who no longer pass their days as 'carefree smiths' fashioning 'trinkets' for women. Indeed, Wagner sees in the ring all 'the pernicious power that poisons love': its descending and ascending musical contour is a mirror image of the contour through which Erda proclaims 'the end'. The second symbol is the spear that denotes Wotan's position as lawgiver and head of the gods. It is a position the gods and giants gradually discover to be deeply compromised. But what is the origin of the spear? For an answer to this, we have to wait until scene 1 of the last part of the cycle, *Götterdämmerung*. There, the first of three ancient Norns will describe how Wotan had long ago desecrated Paradise by tearing a branch from the 'World Ash-Tree': from this he had made his spear. As a result, tree and garden had withered. Strikingly, the Norn's music draws on material from *both* the first and second scenes of *Rheingold* – dissolving the Rhine-daughters' fluid music (Nature) into the rocky-steady music of Valhalla, Wotan's newly-built 'fortress against fear' – the rhythm (a stately sarabande) tells us of the god's self-regard, the key (D♭ major) being the 'relative' of the bleakly portentous B♭ minor.

The conclusion is obvious: the drama of the *Ring* is launched by two parallel acts of vandalism, Alberich's and Wotan's. And it is no surprise that throughout the cycle we follow the stories of Wotan and Alberich and their respective progeny. But this bi-focal context is also central to our view of the *Ring* as a new aesthetic venture, the outcome of years of reflection. However, the character of this venture can easily be misrepresented. True, Wagner moved back from the Romantic medievalism of *Tannhäuser* (1845) and *Lohengrin* (1850) to myth. Yet in *Rheingold* we still meet the magical figures beloved by the early Romantics (even Schubert wrote music for a dwarf).[5] True, Wagner developed a pliable, expressive vocal line that mediated between declamation and song (*Sprechgesang*) to create 'drama transfigured by music' (as Cosima Wagner put it). Yet this line had sources in accompanied recitative and in the adding of vocal counterpoint to instrumental melody. These point to the continuing mix in *Rheingold* of loose sections (matching the to-and-fro of dialogue and action) and stable ones (songs, instrumental pieces, and tonally closed units). True too, Wagner focussed the time-honoured principle of recurrent material into *Leitmotiven* – memorable and affecting thematic fragments associated with people, things, or ideas that could be juxtaposed, combined and transformed to create the illusion of a 'symphonic web'. Yet again, most of these fragments are potential building blocks of larger, stable pieces, some of which are elaborated – as with the 'Golden Apples' folksong from scene 2 – and some not – as with the clumping music for the giants.

The aesthetic departure, rather, lies in the relation of all this to the strongly directional shaping of scenes, acts and works, the overall handling of keys, and the deep interconnection of thematic and harmonic materials – all serving a bi-focal drama that constantly probes psychological cause-and-effect. In scene 1, for example, the Rhine-daughters' opening 6/8 lullaby (in E♭ major) leads on to a second song in 9/8 celebrating the shining gold (in a brighter C major). As he steals this (C major) gold, Alberich renounces love in the very key (C minor) that he has learnt from the Rhine-daughters' threats. When in the final scene he is forced by the gods to yield the gold, he sings another stable unit, an outburst of rage in the bleak, flatter key that traditionally spells doom (B♭

minor). On the one hand this outburst extends the 'ring' music from scene 3; but its newly brazen climax sounds for just what it is, a hideous and loveless distortion of the Rhine-daughters' (C major) music reflecting the perversion of their gold into his ring. The outburst is chillingly accompanied by the anvil motif, which is associated with the enthralled dwarves who now pile up the gold. There are countless relations of this kind.

To ask, 'How will the drama end?' is eventually to take us back to the beginning. 'The source of all lovelessness,' wrote Wagner in 1854, is 'fear of the end', and we fear the end 'only when love itself is already beginning to wane'.[6] This, then, was Wotan's original undoing: the fading of his capacity to love. The only way to counter the fear is for Wotan to 'will' his own destruction and yield to a new, 'totally unconscious', *fearless* human being', a child of Nature 'who never ceases to *love*'. This child would be '*Siegfried*'. Siegfried, though, cannot embody such love alone, but needs the support of 'a suffering, self-immolating woman'. Such a woman is Brünnhilde, '"the eternal feminine" itself'. In the final scene of *Rheingold*, Wotan grasps this 'grandiose' insight to the sound of a motif that will come to be associated with Siegfried's sword; and the next three parts of the cycle put his insight into practice as they trace the conception, growth and maturity of Siegfried, along with the development of Brünnhilde and the decline and end of Wotan. However, even Siegfried cannot survive in a world that includes Alberich and his son Hagen. After Hagen has slaughtered Siegfried, Brünnhilde recovers the ring (with the help of some post-mortem magic from Siegfried via Wotan) and returns it to the Rhine-daughters. It is the only possible thing to do. This 'redeeming' action thus confirms the efficacy of the pure love depicted at the start of *Rheingold*: the long E♭ chord, we remember, pulses but never changes, the gold gleams but may not be sullied. By returning to the beginning, the end promotes an image that by definition has neither beginning nor end.

For Wagner, art was both a re-enactment of life's sufferings and an escape from them. Composing in penury, he too had 'learned what distress is caused by gold', had yearned for 'annihilation' (he was reading Schopenhauer) and had hoped, like Wotan, to 'perish in the flames of Valhalla'. His *artistic* solution – regression – was, of course, fantasy: even in the Book of Genesis an angel with a flaming sword blocks the return to Eden. But the impulse behind it wasn't. In 1853 he also wrote to Liszt: 'Though [a hereafter] lies beyond *my life*, it does not lie beyond the limits of all that I can feel, think, grasp, and comprehend, for I believe in *humanity* – and have need of naught else!'[7] It is above all this supra-mortal humanity that the opening of *Das Rheingold* celebrates.

Notes

Source: 'The Beginnings of *Das Rheingold*', *Das Rheingold* (Richard Wagner), The Royal Opera programme, 2004, pp. 32-5. Translations of Wagner's libretto are taken from: *Wagner's 'Ring of the Nibelung': The Full German Text with a New Translation and Commentaries*, ed. Stewart Spencer and Barry Millington, London: Thames and Hudson, 1993.

1   Letter to Franz Liszt, 11 February 1853, *Selected Letters of Richard Wagner*, trans. and ed. Stewart Spencer and Barry Millington, London: Dent, 1987, p. 281.
2   I have described the physical use of the stage and the imaginative spaces it can suggest – outer and inner spaces – in: 'Wagner's Spatial Style', *The Wagner Journal*, Vol. 9, No. 3, 2015, pp. 4-23.
3   Sigmund Freud, 'The Theme of the Three Caskets' (*c.* 1913), trans. C. J. M. Hubback, *Standard Edition* 12, London: Hogarth, 1958, pp. 289-310 (reprinted in: Pelican Freud Library, London: Penguin, 1985, Vol. 14 (*Art and Literature*), 1985, pp. 233-47). The topic is discussed more fully in the next part, under 'Freud and Opera'.
4   Letter to August Röckel, 25/26 January 1854, *Selected Letters of Richard Wagner*, 1987, p. 300-13, especially p. 307.
5   Franz Schubert's Lied 'Der Zwerg' is to a text by Matthäus von Collin.
6   *Selected Letters of Richard Wagner*, 1987, pp. 306-7.
7   Letter to Franz Liszt, 13 April 1853, *Selected Letters of Richard Wagner*, 1987, pp. 284-5.

5 *The Denouement*

Arrigo Boito (after Shakespeare) and Giuseppe Verdi: *Otello*

Narrative theory draws a distinction between close and closure.[1] A close may be a conventional ending in which all conflicts are resolved: in Milton's Aristotelian words, the audience is left 'calm of mind all passion spent'.[2] In opera such a close may be sealed with a chorus, as with the moralizing ensemble in each of Mozart's Da Ponte operas or the universalizing chorus at the end of Beethoven's Fidelio *(1814); it may be affirmed by an individual, as with Hans Sachs's paean to 'sacred German art' before the community in Wagner's* Die Meistersinger *(1868); and it can be preceded by a vertiginous series of twists and turns, as with the slaughter of the protagonists in the closing seconds of Meyerbeer's* Les Huguenots *(1836) or the mass decapitation of nuns in Poulenc's* Dialogues des Carmélites *(1957). On the other hand it may be happily sealed with one or more dances, as in Gluck's* Orphée et Eurydice *(the 1774 Paris version of his* Orfeo ed Eurydice*). But 'closure' – in the modern sense of intellectual and affective satisfaction – is not always achieved: the action may not be quite over, serious issues have still to be addressed, and an audience may be left in meaningful confusion. However, this is more characteristic of modern than of ancient practice. In the final scene of Berg's* Wozzeck *(1925), for instance, the children tell Wozzeck's boy that his mother Marie is dead. As they all go to find her, the curtain falls. In the strings quiet but stable ('tonic') chords signal the work's end, but in the winds unstable figures contradict their authority. A close may be achieved, but closure isn't.*

In their endings, Verdi's operas form a site of extraordinary innovation. And with Otello *(1887) Boito and Verdi lavished the closest possible attention on its final minutes.*

1 *Verdi's Endings in General*

Stravinsky said: endings matter. Schoenberg said: great composers compose great endings. And Verdi demonstrated that, however shackled he could feel by operatic convention, once it came to the final act he was out there on his own, free to forge the ending that belonged exclusively to the work in hand. Some of the dramatic situations, of course, were unique: Violetta's momentary *spes phthisica* (the false hope of the dying tubercular) in *La traviata*, the *deus ex machina* rescue of Don Carlos by Charles V, or the interment of Aida and Radames below the feet of Amneris, a startling resolution of a 'core triangle'. Other endings, though, owed their effect to music: the heart-rending repetitions of Stiffelio's cry of 'Perdonata!' (Forgiven!), the radiant chorus that greets the dying King's (or Governor's) clemency in *Un ballo in maschera*, the witty fugal conclusion to *Falstaff*, 'Tutto nel mondo è burla' (all the world's a jest), not to mention the ferocious energy of the last-minute revelation of Azucena, the 'witch' from *Il trovatore* whose tragedy was to burn the wrong baby. After Verdi, any ending was possible.

Yet the last acts of *Rigoletto*, *Simon Boccanegra* and *Otello* form a special group. In the case of *Rigoletto* (1851), the librettist was the accomplished Francesco Maria Piave; for *Simon* it was again (mainly) Piave, though his libretto of 1857 was revised in 1881 by the no-less accomplished Arrigo Boito; and for *Otello* it was just Boito, a composer-librettist willing to spend several years from 1879 to 1887 coaxing the score out of a stubborn Verdi. Each work examines the vicissitudes of power in a historical context (from the fourteenth to the sixteenth centuries); each explores the tragic situation of an outsider – a hunchback, a corsair (or sea-pirate) and a blackamoor; and each holds the outsider responsible for the death of a young woman – a daughter, another man's daughter, a wife. And although in the first two works the title role is a baritone (neither Rigoletto nor Simon is a romantic lead) and in the third a tenor (Otello is a lover-husband), Verdi invariably demands a forceful but sensitive upper range (from middle C to top G for the baritone, up to top B for the tenor). Only a versatile singer can navigate these challenges – but then, it was always the dramatically-gifted singer whose interests Verdi had at heart. For lavish documentation of what Verdi wanted from a performer, we must turn to the fourth and final act of *Otello*.

2 Otello

In England, critics love to ponder how faithfully Boito condensed Shakespeare's five-act tragedy into a four-act libretto (which begins with the play's tempest from Act Two); on the continent, they rejoice in the homecoming of a story that originated in Italy, Cinzio Giraldi's 'The Moor of Venice' (1565) set around 1520; they also salute Boito for making good the 'fiasco' of Francesco Berio di Salsa's three-act libretto for Rossini's *Otello* (1816), only the last act of which they are prepared to recognize (and rightly so). Musicians, on the other hand, admire Boito for shaping Verdi's suave late style without wholly sacrificing earlier conventions and for meeting the composer's demand for clear, taut diction. And singers note how exactly Verdi wanted them to sing.[3] For instance, at the opera's close, after killing Desdemona, Otello must be 'breathless':

> he is weary, physically and morally exhausted; he cannot and must not sing any more, except with a *half-muffled, veiled voice* ... [albeit] a reliable one.

As he dies, and the music of the three kisses returns,

> between the second kiss and the third, there are four bars for the orchestra alone, which must be filled with delicate, moving gestures that I imagined as I was writing the notes.

And his very last syllable, 'bac<u>io</u>' (kiss), was to be no more than a sigh.

In fact, Boito lived dangerously in compressing the last scenes of the play's fourth and fifth acts into the single action of *Otello*'s finale. Gone is the banter between Desdemona and Emilia; gone is the murder of Roderigo and the wounding of Cassio (which are now known by report); gone is the murder of Emilia by Iago (a parallel to that of Desdemona by Otello); heavily reduced are the revelations that gather up loose ends (some, like Iago's recapture, stay loose); and gone is the final exchange between Cassio and Lodovico that sets wrongs to rights. Instead, Boito begins the act midway into a conversation between Desdemona and her maid Emilia, and thereafter dwells at length on Desdemona's dignified but frantic preparation for Otello's arrival. He amplifies her Willow Song, a re-enactment of the *canzona* sung by her mother's morbid maid (a distanced narrative can bring pathos closer home), and after the departure of Emilia inserts her prayer (only alluded to in the play), interpolating into a dramatically recast version of the ecclesiastical *Ave Maria* her hopes for herself and her husband. Indeed, song and prayer together form her psychic defence against what is to follow: one recalls her mother, the other the Virgin Mary – both 'absent' figures. For the exchange following the arrival of Otello and the vertiginous business following Desdemona's murder, Boito provides even tauter dialogue than did Shakespeare; and although he still allows Otello to speak out at the end, he admits no choric response to his suicide (at La Scala in 1887 Otello's corpse simply 'rolled down the steps'). He jettisons convention. Indeed, Boito's charged selectivity laid the ground for what Milan Kundera would later describe as modernity's *ethics of the essential*.

Verdi, by contrast, located his drama in the play of voices. Desdemona was 'a type … the type of goodness, of resignation, of sacrifice! Such beings are born for others, unconscious of their *own self*: therefore she had to sing with a 'calm, aristocratic passion', adopting one manner for the sad Willow Song, another for the urgent talk with Emilia or Otello, and a third for the prayer, the *Ave Maria*. 'The perfect Desdemona will always be the one who sings best,' he wrote. The more primitive Otello, on the other hand, 'loves, [grows jealous], kills and kills himself' and is 'now the warrior, now the passionate lover, now crushed to the point of baseness, now ferocious like a savage': so 'he must sing and shout'. Indeed, Verdi's idea of handling words went beyond Shakespeare's or Boito's: the changing repetition of 'Salce' (willow) 'does not, and must not, make any sense; it's a vague voice, one that is neither Desdemona's or Barbara's'; it is a 'fading away [*smorzato*]' best done 'as much as possible with the head voice'. When, towards the close of his 'towering melody', Otello sings 'Desdemona! Desdemona! Ah! morta! morta! morta!' (dead! dead! dead!) he must emit unaccompanied sounds 'that have almost no tonality … there must be neither a poetic nor a musical phrase'. Verdi also built on the orchestral experience he gained in revising *Simon Boccanegra*. For Otello's entrance into Desdemona's chamber, he writes a long double-bass solo, a kind of thematic 'mime', in which he specifies exactly how Otello should move. He then extracts from it a 'sabre figure' to drive the action to its lethal climax. Both for the dialogue between Otello and Desdemona and the subsequent 'business', the verses are entirely 'blank [*sciolti*] and broken [*spezzati*]'; yet Verdi showed that 'set to music' a text can be 'shorter and quicker than if it were spoken'. More still, he used the orchestral music to throw a penumbra across the entire act: during the prelude, before Desdemona's pitiful farewell to Emilia and at the start of Otello's peroration, there are stark repeated chords that sound like the heavy tread of a cortège, or, as Boito said, like shovels of earth on a coffin.

With *Otello* (1887) Verdi extended the bounds of musical tragedy by gathering into it portentous monotones, orchestral shrieks and dazed silences. Yet the key to this ending (as to the endings of *Rigoletto* and *Boccanegra*) lies in a work Verdi often pondered but never composed: Shakespeare's *King Lear*. 'Moving scene between Lear and Cordelia,' he wrote in 1850 of his proposed denouement, an ensemble that Lear was to lead:

> Cordelia begins to feel the effects of her poison … [others rush in]
> … Lear, unaware of their arrival takes Cordelia's corpse in his arms,
> and cries 'She's dead as earth. Howl! Howl!'

Verdi openly compared Desdemona with Cordelia; and we wonder whether, at the very end, his distraught Lear, like Otello, would have gasped the name of the woman he most cherished? Whatever the answer, it was through Shakespeare that Verdi learned to heighten pathos even as he closed the action.

Notes

Source: 'Verdi's Endings', *Plácido Domingo Gala Performance*, The Royal Opera programme, 29 October 2011, pp. 27-33. This is a shortened and slightly modified version of the original essay, which also dealt with the endings of *Rigoletto* and *Simon Boccanegra* (works discussed elsewhere in this book).

1   'Closure', *Routledge Encyclopedia of Narrative Theory*, Abingdon: Routledge, 2005/8, pp. 64-5.

2   Itself the closing line of Milton's *Samson Agonistes* (c. 1671).

3   Citations are taken from: *Verdi's Otello and Simon Boccanegra (revised version) in Letters and Documents*, 2 vols., trans. and ed. Hans Busch, Oxford: Oxford UP, 1988, vol. 1, pp. 301, 306, 310-11, 330; vol. 2 (*Otello* Production Book: Act IV) pp. 597-628.

6   Peroration (Cadence)

Richard Wagner: *Götterdämmerung*

The introduction to 'Multiple Beginnings' (section 4) charted the growth of the Ring *from one to four evenings. But this growth itself raised a new issue. The central figure of the back-story of the first two evenings, Wotan, emerged as more complex and fascinating than that of the third and fourth evenings, Siegfried, whose death, indeed, had been the* raison d'être *of the cycle. Unsurprisingly, there has been much debate as to whether the* Ring *is 'about' Wotan or Siegfried, or both.[1] Yet there is another way of grasping the work. On the one hand, Wotan is the human god who has to face up to his end (and, indeed, to the end of all the old gods); on the other hand, his fantasy creation Siegfried is the godly human whose notional invulnerability will defend him against such an end. The real and the fantastic, the outer and the inner, merge into a single action. In the* Ring, *psychological form, modernity's greatest achievement, finds an early locus classicus.*

How, though, could Wagner bring such a double-headed action to a close? And did he achieve 'closure'? For our answers we must look to the musical score and the handling of cadence and key. (It is this entry that asks of its reader a little knowledge of the workings of harmony.) Wagnerians will notice that the argument is built around a sub-thematic motif – a conventional cadence figure treated as a motif. This incorporates recurrent thematic motifs of reminiscence (leitmotifs), but is of a different order to them. To chart such a play of thematicism and sub-thematicism is the critical agenda of our time.

1   The Two Cadences

The musical correlative of a dramatic ending is a perfect cadence. Yet, when we listen for a definitive cadence in the 'home key' of D♭ major at the end of *Der Ring des Nibelungen*, we face a paradox: there are two such cadences. Both occur during the course of Brünnhilde's concluding monologue, and together they celebrate the conclusion of the two interlocked narratives that make up the cycle: the 'tragedy' of Wotan and the 'fairy-tale' of Siegfried (as Carl Dahlhaus puts it).

The first cadence is grave and tenebral (Example 1): the motion draws towards, and eventually achieves, the repose that Brünnhilde invokes for the head of the gods. Its last two bars are marked 'sehr langsam' (very slow), and

Example 1: Götterdämmerung, *Act Three, scene 3.*
The first cadence: Brünnhilde's farewell to Wotan.

Translation: 'Rest now, rest now, thou god!'

the utterance is characterized by a *pp* restraint appropriate not only to a child's final benediction of its parent, but also to our foreknowledge of the combustion that awaits Valhalla (it will blaze to the Neapolitan harmony marked ∗ – in effect, to D major). Moreover, the funereal brass instrumentation is epitomized by the wan sonority of the bass trumpet, which plays the cadence figure (x) from the Valhalla 'theme' first heard in the second scene of *Das Rheingold*: Wotan is laid to rest to his own music.

On the other hand, the second cadence is jubilant and impetuous (Example 2): the motion intensifies, the string lines soar, the dynamics swell to *ff* (and immediately after will burst into a series of *sforzandi*), while Brünnhilde's words are snatched, syncopated and set in the radiant upper register of her voice. As the examples show, both cadences trace an upper line that descends

Example 2: Götterdämmerung, *Act Three, scene 3.*
The second cadence: Brünnhilde's greeting to Siegfried.

Translation: 'Siegfried! Siegfried! See! Blissful[ly] greets thee thy wife!'

from A♭ to D♭ (a journey through a fifth), and both are followed by actions: the first by the preparation of Siegfried's funeral pyre, and the second by Brünnhilde's leap into the flames on the back of her steed Grane. But beyond this, the contrasts are so great as to seem reciprocal; and if we think of the second cadence as a *transformation* of the first, we may begin to understand the peroration to the *Ring*.

Let us look more closely at Example 1.

There is an irony to this passage that emerges only when its musical and dramatic functions are taken together. Formally, the music recapitulates a passage from Act One of *Götterdämmerung* where Waltraute begs Brünnhilde to return the ring to its owners. Waltraute relays Wotan's words from Valhalla, whispered 'as if in a dream': 'If she [Brünnhilde] returned the ring to the daughters of the deep Rhine, god and the world would be redeemed from the burden of [Alberich's] curse' (Example 3).

Example 3: Götterdämmerung, *Act Three, scene 3. The distinctive cadence figure of Wotan's Valhalla Theme is left significantly unresolved.*

Translation: 'Redeemed were god and world!'

At that point, of course, nothing is further from Brünnhilde's mind: to restore the ring would be to cede her most cherished token of Siegfried's love. So the music significantly fails to proceed to a close (as it did in Example 1): Waltraute's request is left unanswered, the rocking motif (y) freezes into a *ppp* chord, and the subsequent comforting cadence figure (x) is disconcertingly absent. In any case, Brünnhilde has already acquired too much wisdom not to recognize Valhalla for what it is: an emblem of Wotan's worldly authority to be sure, but also the kitsch, chauvinist paradise that had already been rejected by the discerning but doomed Siegmund, and from which, indeed, she herself had been harshly expelled.

However, there is more to all this than mere pomp. The Valhalla theme itself shows why. We first meet it in scene 2 of *Das Rheingold* (Example 4). At its conclusion, the rocking motif (y) and the subsequent cadential figure together depict its regressive nature: the gods are cradled 'safe from fear and dread', and their portals are closed (cadentially) against the threatening outer world of 'dark elves'. Indeed, Wotan himself had willed and dreamt its design. So in Act One of *Götterdämmerung* it is this false domestic and psychological security that Waltraute seeks – and fails – to shore up.

Eventually, in her concluding monologue in Act Three, Brünnhilde complies with Waltraute's entreaty. She will bequeath the ring to the Rhine-daughters. Yet her outlook has changed utterly. 'All is now clear' to her, the falseness of Valhalla is irredeemable. Her words purge the world of the illusions harboured by the gods. As we see from Example 1, the rocking motif (y) now lulls Wotan to the eternal rest he once dreaded, a rest Brünnhilde seals with the cadence figure (x).

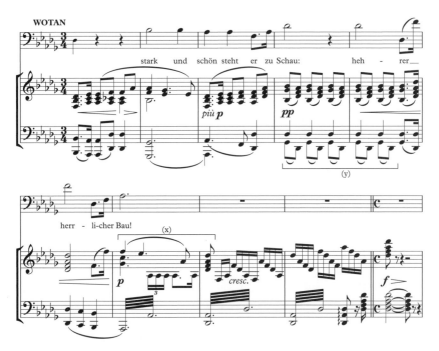

Example 4: Das Rheingold, *Scene 2.*
Close of Wotan's Valhalla theme with its distinctive cadence figure.

Translation: 'Fit and fair for all to see: mighty and marvellous pile!'

2 Laughter

In fact, this cadence figure has had an illuminating history during the course
of the cycle. But before tracing it any further, we must look again at Example 2.
Here the cadence shows Brünnhilde's concluding actions recalling her former
self: the anticipated D♭ major harmony beneath the final word *Weib* (wife)
is replaced by the augmented harmony C♯/F/A, a harmony associated with
Wotan's band of immortal Valkyries back in *Die Walküre*. A little earlier in
her *Götterdämmerung* monologue, Brünnhilde had turned to her steed: 'Are
you enticed,' she asks confidentially, 'by the laughing flame?' The question
drew a caustic comment from Theodor Adorno: 'in the teeth of the cult of
the prevention of cruelty to animals,' he declared, 'she even insists that her
horse should neigh for joy as it leaps into the flames'.[2] The jibe, however,
should not deflect our attention from the importance of the keyword *laughing*.
Brünnhilde's joy is far from that of a willing accomplice to an ostentatious
act of Indian self-sacrifice (suttee), as Adorno claimed. In fact, it marks the

culmination of another process that extends over the *Ring*. Laughter abounds in the cycle, and is of essentially three kinds. The first is both literal and brutal, and reveals all that is craven, malevolent and avaricious in the male psyche. It includes Mime's pathetic tittering as he unwittingly informs Siegfried of his treacherous designs on his life ('kichernd'); Alberich's jeering at Mime's death ('hohnlachend'); and the strident Schadenfreude of Hagen as he hears of Mime's death from the lips of the fated Siegfried ('grell lachend'). Fricka, too, complains to Wotan that it is his 'laughing lightness' that has brought the gods into disrepute. By contrast, the second kind of laughter is metaphorical, and is born of the eternally-feminine nature of Brünnhilde, which in turn represents Wotan's 'laughing joy'. This finds its fullest expression in the concluding love duet of *Siegfried*: 'Laughing must I love you,' sings Brünnhilde, 'laughing will I lose my sight, laughing shall I go into the ground.' Back in *Die Walküre*, moreover, Wotan had even asked Fricka to rejoice laughingly in the pure, incestuous love of Siegmund for Sieglinde ('lachend der Liebe'). There can be no more tangible affirmation of her death-defying love, therefore, than Brünnhilde's laughing leap into the flames.

The third, and most interesting, kind of laughter, is the callow mirth of Siegfried. This knows no restraint. It functions in the narrative as an agent of truth and, in one central instance, mediates between the concerns of the two cadences. We encounter it at the young hero's first appearance in Act One of *Siegfried*, where his rollicking guffaws mock his guardian Mime – the bear he has brought in from the forest is pursuing Mime round their cave. Later in this act, Siegfried's description of his re-forged sword's participation in the laughter posits an image of radiant rebirth ('nun lacht ihm sein heller Schein'). In Act Two, his first contemptuous response to Fafner indicates the length to which the giant has been driven in his determination to guard the gold (he has become a dragon). But, most strikingly, in Act Three, the confrontation between Wotan and Siegfried provokes laughter on both sides that is mutually incomprehensible. At first, Wotan, cannily disguised as 'the Wanderer', takes pleasure in his surrogate son (in fact, his grandson). He breaks into a contented laugh. The wholly naïve Siegfried takes offence. Why should he be mocked by such an old man?, he asks. Wotan advises him to hold his tongue, and hints at their blood-relationship: one of Siegfried's eyes, he remarks, compensates for his own missing eye. The music reinforces Wotan's warning by deploying the power of the Valhalla theme, which proceeds to its affirmative cadential figure (x) (Example 5). But all this is too much for Siegfried, who refuses to allow the cadence to complete its course and disrupts its flow with a guffaw (the bass remains on the dominant before moving to the subversive tritone F♯). Siegfried has grasped intuitively the illusory nature of Wotan's power, which he shortly confirms by breaking the god's spear with his sword (ironically, a gift to

Example 5: Siegfried, *Act Three, scene 2. Siegfried's mockery of Wotan.*

Translation: '[The one eye] that for me to see with remains.'

his father from Wotan). Later, of course, the rawness of his humour will be tamed by the love of Brünnhilde.

We may usefully compare this moment with another at the end of *Das Rheingold* (Example 6). This enshrines an irony that will become evident only in time. For, as they prepare to cross the rainbow bridge into Valhalla, the assembled gods mock the Rhine-daughters for the loss of their gold. Theirs is the most brazen laughter in the cycle, combining the protectively affirmative cadential figure of the Valhalla music (x) with the laughing figuration of the fire-god Loge – the same who at the end of the cycle will consume the lot of them.

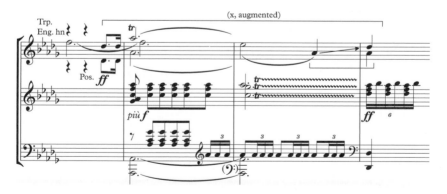

Example 6: Das Rheingold, *Scene 4. The contemptuous laughter of the gods.*

3   A Further Perspective

So let us think again of our two related cadences in Brünnhilde's closing monologue to *Götterdämmerung* (Examples 1 and 2). As we have said, both mark the end of the era of Valhalla and both look forward to a new world of love purified by laughter that has itself been purified. However, there are other, less obvious links that put them into a still further perspective. In the second cadence (Example 2), Brünnhilde's greeting to Siegfried, her dead husband, is accompanied by two motifs. These first appeared in Act Three of *Die Walküre*. The first comes near the start of the act (Example 7a). It shows a leitmotif that will be associated with Siegfried himself, made explicit as Brünnhilde reveals to Sieglinde that she carries in her womb 'the world's greatest hero'; this is set in C minor and opens out into E♭ major where it closes. The second is the leitmotif of 'sublime wonder', heard as Sieglinde reacts to the news (Example 7b). She thanks the 'glorious maid' Brünnhilde for the comfort she brings: 'May the recompense of my thanks laugh for you some day.' The music is now in a higher, more charged G major. In Brünnhilde's monologue towards the

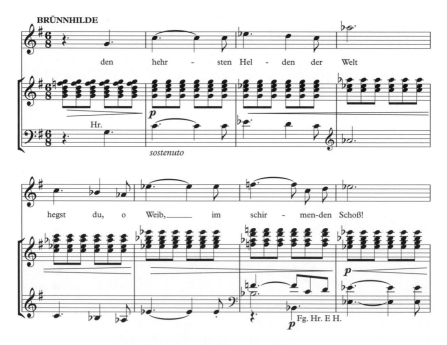

Example 7a: Die Walküre, *Act Three, scene 1.*
Siegfried's motif as Brünnhilde reveals the hero Sieglinde carries in her womb.

Translation: 'The proudest hero the world knows, O wife, you guard in your womb.'

end of *Götterdämmerung*, both motifs are combined: Siegfried's motif is in the trumpets, Sieglinde's in the strings (as we see in Example 2). The fluid harmony, though, moves towards the D♭ major in which the *Ring* will end.

Example 7b: Die Walküre, *Act Three, scene 1.*
The motif of 'sublime wonder' as Sieglinde reacts to Brünnhilde's news.

Translation: 'O highest wonder! Proudest maid!'

However, in Example 7(a) it is important to pause over the fact that Brünnhilde's revelation gravitated towards E♭. Of course, this note and its tonality recall the unbroken integration of the opening of *Das Rheingold*, as well as the supremely integrated love-duet between Brünnhilde and Siegfried from the Prologue of *Götterdämmerung*. It also embraces the E♭ major in which the First Norn describes the woodland paradise where the World Ash-Tree once flourished, the terrestrial equivalent to the original state of Nature.

Example 8: The Prologue to Götterdämmerung *(first part). The First Norn describes the pre-lapsarian woodland paradise.*

Translation: 'At the World-Ash-Tree once I wove (…wood).'

Example 8 shows the beginning and end of the first part of her music, in which she describes this paradise as irretrievably lost. This broadly traces a modulation from E♭ major to its dominant. Bar 1 establishes the connection with the Rhine music from the opening of the cycle: Norns and Rhine-daughters evidently share the same pre-lapsarian state. Bar 3, on the other hand, establishes the narrative position of the Norn. Her vocal line adopts the falling-and-rising 'circular' contour of the 'ring' motif, and the chords in the orchestra are cast in the portentous key of E♭ minor – sounding the same stark harmony to which Hagen will justify the slaughter of Siegfried as the 'holiest right of the hunter'. Especially revealing is the closing music at bars 8 and 9. Back in the major, this follows on from the description of the woodland as it once was: astonishingly, however, the closing formula is that of the Valhalla music, figure (x). This is not fortuitous. Six bars later, this formula will be repeated, to be followed at once by the description of Wotan's appearance in the wood: he has sacrificed an eye in exchange for wisdom and fatally broken a branch from the World Ash-Tree to form his spear. The implication is clear: Valhalla, which Wotan conceives the moment he drinks from wisdom's well, attempts to recreate the security of this woodland paradise by harnessing its (cadential) symbol of stability. Wotan is in the grip of a regression.

When at the end of *Götterdämmerung* Brünnhilde closes the Valhalla music (as we see in Example 1), she does not merely purge figure (x) of its false security, but thus restores it to its natural state – the very state for which Wotan himself yearned.

4 Two Interpretations

How, then, do these detailed observations illumine our understanding of the *Ring* as a whole? In fact, two interpretations emerge.

The first asks us to accept the simple transformation before our eyes. This is not only epitomized by the move from the solemn cadence of Example 1 to the exuberant one of Example 2, but is also summed up in the last minute or so of *Götterdämmerung*. Valhalla has fallen before the new order ushered in by Siegfried, the gods burn in the heavens, and we are left to contemplate Brünnhilde's uplifting self-sacrifice. Significantly, the key of D♭ major in which we end was once associated with the corporeal Valhalla in *Das Rheingold* and is now re-assigned to the theme of the incorporeal 'sublime wonder' celebrated by Brünnhilde. It is hard not to see a Biblical model behind this, with Wotan's Old Testament 'letter of the law' ceding to Brünnhilde's New Testament 'spirit of love'. Yet it is the Old Testament parallel that is the more striking: most of the protagonists (above all, Wotan) are guiltily preoccupied with the need to regain their lost Eden; the burdens incurred by this loss are passed through the generations and are epitomized by the loss of the gold from the Rhine; and most live under the shadow of a determinism as inexorable as it is apocalyptic. One may compare Erda's 'all of the past I know: all thing that are, all things that shall be – all I know… all things that are, perish', with Isaiah 37: 'have you not heard that I determined it long ago, I planned from days of old what I now bring to pass, that you should make fortified cities crash into heaps of ruins, while their inhabitants, shorn of strength, are dismayed and confounded?' However, from a New Testament point of view it is harder to think of Siegfried as the Redeemer of Man: not only is his love consummately sexual, but unlike Brünnhilde, he is not prey to the full gamut of human sufferings and temptations (erotic fear notwithstanding). Moreover, Brünnhilde's 'redeeming' acts of restoration and self-sacrifice, though promoting the harmony of man-and-woman, in Wagner's cosmology are essentially feminine.

The second interpretation arises out of the ramifications of the two cadences shown in Examples 1 and 2, and appears to contradict the first. The history of figure (x) has taught us that Valhalla represents, in part, an attempt to retrieve a lost paradise. This effort at reparation on Wotan's part, however, has been laughingly brushed aside by Siegfried, who later achieves reparation for himself by celebrating his consummate love for Brünnhilde back in the paradise key of E♭ major. Yet, despite the efforts of the narrative to persuade us otherwise, we can understand neither Siegfried (Wotan's blood-relation) nor Brünnhilde (his 'eternal side') as entirely free agents: they are as much an extension of Wotan's all-too-human eugenic fantasy as they are of his loins. (Through magic Wotan constantly interferes in their story – in Hunding's hut, in the forest with the Woodbird, with the ravens in the denouement.) So it comes as no surprise that their love turns out to be as doomed as the Ash-Tree itself. In this world, it appears impossible to sustain E♭ major for very long – and, significantly, Wagner deliberately chose not to end the cycle in this key. As audience, therefore, it seems the best we can do is to purge ourselves of the worldly illusions attendant upon our own D♭ major existence, just as Brünnhilde purged Wotan (in the first of our cadences). Our *idea* of paradise, as Brünnhilde demonstrates, can at best only lead to a 'laughing death' and a denial of ordinary human life. From this point of view, the deaths of Siegfried, Brünnhilde and Wotan in the last act of *Götterdämmerung* serve only to confirm the pessimism and renunciation that Wotan increasingly embraces over the whole *Ring* cycle.

Neither interpretation, of course, stands happily on its own. In the *Essence of Christianity*, which (according to Ernest Newman) Wagner read around 1850, Ludwig Feuerbach maintained that 'every advance in religion is a deeper self-knowledge', and that religion itself is no more than 'the dream of the human mind'. From this standpoint, the profundity of Wagner's humane, atheistic portrayal of the pagan god Wotan must place the *Ring* among the most important contributions to the anthropology that Feuerbach insisted that theology must become. Hence, the second interpretation must hold good. But Wagner's mythic dreams may still testify to the irrepressible, quasi-religious, redemptive aspirations of a suffering humanity; and it is these love-imbued hopes that are enshrined in the story of Siegfried and Brünnhilde. The first interpretation, therefore, must also hold good. But for the audience, the psychological dependence all this suggests of the lovers' aspirations upon the nihilism of Wotan is not that clear-cut. We empathize equally with Wotan and Brünnhilde. Thus, by asking us to respond to the tragedy of Wotan and the fantasy of Siegfried equivalently, Wagner creates in the *Ring* a work of extraordinary ambiguity. And this, perhaps, is what our two cadences eventually signify.

Notes

Source: 'The Questionable Lightness of Being: Brünnhilde's Peroration to *The Ring*', *Twilight of the Gods/Götterdämmerung*, English National Opera/Royal Opera Guide 31, ed. Nicholas John, London: John Calder, 1985, pp. 39-48.

1   For an overview of the reception of Wagner's works, see: Arnold Whittall, *The Wagner Style*, ed. Christopher Wintle, London: Plumbago, 2015.
2   Theodor Adorno, *In Search of Wagner* (1952/74), ed. Rodney Livingstone, n.p.: New Left Books, 1981, p. 146.

Peter Pears as Peter Grimes
(Milein Cosman, 1947)

Part Five

Invention

1 *Topic and Time*

Ronald Duncan (after Obey) and Benjamin Britten: *The Rape of Lucretia*

The Rape of Lucretia (1946) is an extraordinary masterpiece that has never had its full due. The 'problem' lies with the Male and Female Chorus, two solo singers with key roles: by appearing to take sacred advantage of a secular tragedy, they can all too easily sound sanctimonious. (A production at Glyndebourne in 2013 tried to overcome this – with some success – by casting the Chorus as a pair of quaint characters <u>within</u> the action, rather than outside it.) Yet it is the handling of different time scales along with dramatic topics that make this chamber opera so arresting: there is conventional lyric and dramatic time, 'epic' observation of the drama, and a transfiguring 'supra-historical' epic reaction to it all. It is the supra-historical that gathers the audience into a wider collective action – a kind of therapy we meet again in Britten's openly sacred Noye's Fludde *(1958). With his own version of 'epic' drama, Britten may owe to Brecht, but his sacred aims were quite other – Brecht was an arch-secularist. In* The Rape, *the dramatic topics address both a charged outer world of politics and an expanded inner world of suffering – Lucretia's and the Chorus's. As elsewhere in Britten, the framing device serves to enrich an inclusive 'innerness' rather than (as in Brecht) to distance it for whatever purpose.*

Benjamin Britten's *The Rape of Lucretia* opens up three dramatic topics: crime, politics and self-punishment. Around 510 BC, Prince Tarquinius, the impulsive son of an Etruscan tyrant, criminally rapes Lucretia, the pure wife of Collatinus, a Roman General: Tarquinius appears to assert the absolute sexual rights of an occupying force – the Etruscans – over an occupied people – the Romans. However, it was another Roman general, Junius, who had sensed a political advantage. He has subtly encouraged Tarquinius to visit Lucretia in the absence of Collatinus; he wilfully fails to warn Collatinus until it is 'too late'; and when Lucretia is dead, he races to the window and cries, 'Romans arise! … Their throne will fall. I will rule!' Junius senses correctly. Livy records that the rape did indeed trigger the ejection of the Etruscans. For her part, Lucretia feels that Tarquinius has irreparably destroyed her loyalty to the tender Collatinus; and partly because she cannot turn her aggression outwards against the Etruscans, she turns it inwards against herself, with fatal consequence. As the arts have shown, the rape – the crime and the self-punishment – has left a scar ever since: where does this desecration of decency leave our civilization? What ethical system can handle it? In the opera these questions are turned over to a chorus. As in the source play by André Obey, *Le Viol de Lucrèce* (1931), this comprises just two figures, a male and a female. Psychologically, they are time-travelling 'good parent' figures, who will interpret the action within a Christian framework. Their words bring a measure of catharsis to an immeasurable tragedy.

As we expect, the three topics interweave, though they do so on three temporal plains. There is the *dramatic present* for the Roman and Etruscan characters, incorporating dramatic and lyric music in the normal way. There is the *historic present* for the Male and Female Chorus: they describe or report the actions of the characters, occasionally sing their lines and even try to advise them – to no avail, of course, since only we can see and hear them. And there is also the *supra-historical present*: the Chorus moves between 500 BC, the time of Christ and the present – specifically 1946, though by extension 'today'. For Britten, this threefold time-frame was new. It was also unique – though he did go on to use simpler time-frames in *Billy Budd*, *The Turn of the Screw* and the three Church Parables. The Chorus introduces both acts and adds an epilogue (in Brechtian terms, their function is 'epic'); and each act comprises two scenes divided by an interlude. Let us take each topic in turn.

About Tarquinius, the perpetrator of the *crime*, we learn two things. On the one hand, he is utterly impetuous. In the first-act interlude, the Male Chorus describes Tarquinius's ride into Rome to ravish Lucretia. It is a thrilling passage that invests the horse with a rampant eroticism unprecedented in music: when Tarquinius succeeds in crossing the Tiber, we know he will succeed in overcoming Lucretia. On the other hand, he can show princely restraint. This matches the Female Chorus's diagnosis of the Etruscan character as blending the primitive and the refined. At the end of Act One, he and the women utter the words 'good night' with exaggerated decorum: it is only in the orchestra that we hear the predatory tread of his motif, part of a falling scale. When, later, Tarquinius approaches Lucretia's bed, he sings a small aria whose tenderness extends the beautiful lullaby of the Female Chorus, 'She sleeps as a rose upon the night'. As a result, his subsequent assault on Lucretia is all the more shocking.

As often in life and art, *politics* wears two faces. The *collective* face of Roman fury emerges at the start of Act Two, where the Chorus's back-story includes off-stage cries of 'Down with the Etruscans' and 'Rome's for the Romans!' But the *private* agenda has been revealed at the start of Act One. Junius is piqued that Collatinus alone has not been cuckolded by his wife: Lucretia's virtue, he sings in a short rage-aria, 'is the measure of my shame'. Tarquinius's rape of Lucretia will thus alleviate that shame. In fact, her very name maddens both Junius and Tarquinius, and the 'Lucretia motif' pervades the score.

Lucretia's self-punishment shows her polarized between the extremes of hate and love. After she has told Collatinus of the rape, he responds with mature advice: if she hasn't yielded to Tarquinius in spirit, 'there is no need of shame'. But she is unmoved: there is nothing conciliatory in her nature. Indeed, she and Collatinus have already admitted, 'To love as we loved / was to live on the edge of tragedy'. However, polarized extremes make for strong musical contrast. In the second scene of Act Two, the morning after the rape, Lucretia enters and sings from the bottom of her voice. Her *self-lacerating* aria inverts her attendants' paean to the sun: psychoanalytically, she is no longer a madonna but a whore. How much, critics have asked, was she unconsciously attracted to Tarquinius? By contrast, when offered a vase for her flowers, she sings a *tender* aria. Making 'a wreath with the orchids', she notes that 'flowers alone are chaste'. Lucretia withdraws and Junius and Collatinus arrive. But when she returns, she is dressed in 'purple mourning' and moves to music redolent of a Bach Passion: a plangent cor anglais supported by a bass with a heavy tread accompanies her aria. Indeed, Britten draws heavily on traditional types for what follows: Lucretia's Italianate monotones portend death, and a little aria introduces her taut account of the rape. After Collatinus's tender response, she stabs herself fatally, gasping like any doomed opera heroine as her line plunges from high to low. There follows a funeral march, whose lugubrious rat-a-tat figure is now focussed into the singers' bewildered, 'it is done', 'it is all'.

Lucretia is a contralto, and her dark hues contrast with the bright, expansive music for her maid Lucia, a light soprano, and her nurse Bianca, who is a mezzo. This contrast reflects the large-scale handling of voices: Junius and Tarquinius are baritones, Collatinus is a bass, whereas the Male and Female Chorus are a tenor and a soprano. The first scene of Act One uses three male voices, and the second three female voices. Act Two, however, pits Lucretia against Tarquinius in the first scene, and balances Lucia and Bianca with Junius and Collatinus in the later part of the second. The work's finale duly unites men and women in a powerful sextet. We also see the same fastidious planning in Britten's handling of the instruments of his orchestra, which is small.

However, Britten and his librettist, Ronald Duncan, show their greatest skill in their decorous handling of the rape itself – a novel challenge in opera. They create a broad action which they divide in three. First, as 'Tarquinius pulls the coverlet from the bed and threatens [Lucretia] with his sword', we hear the thrusting of priapic horns; second, after an awe-struck silence, Tarquinius, Lucretia and the Male and Female Chorus describe, prospectively, how 'the great river underneath the ground flows through Lucretia'. At this juncture, their slow, unaccompanied ensemble is a master-stroke. And third, as Tarquinius extinguishes the candle and the curtain falls quickly, we are left to imagine the assault from the violent music in the orchestra: as the energy gradually subsides, the Male and Female Chorus sing a hymn invoking Christ and Mary. The singing embodies a universal truth that, *in extremis*, witnesses of horror will turn for support to religion of any kind.

The handling of this central episode has its cake and eats it: it represents rape in the music graphically, but suspends time in the drama reflectively. The theorist Theodor Adorno complained how Britten loved to play the trump card. We can only be thankful that he did so, and did so this well.

Source: 'Topic, Time and Decorum', Britten-Centenary talk for BBC Radio 3, 28 December 2013. Collatinus is pronounced 'Collàtinus'.

2 Sources of Musical Invention

Myfanwy Piper (after Mann) and Benjamin Britten: *Death in Venice*

The quality and character of invention stands at the heart of every operatic score. But invention itself has three constituencies: the different kinds of music suggested by the drama; the different kinds of forms and processes peculiar to music, including recurrent and 'epic' factors; and the sense of the rhetorical effect achieved only when music and drama work together. This entry on Death in Venice *(1973) focuses mainly on the first constituency, but touches on the third, where the tone of the purely instrumental peroration – elegiac but not sentimental, dignified but quietly celebratory – takes us to the heart of the work at the very point Britten closes it.*[1]

Any opera composer will scour his or her subject for sources of musical invention. These may respond to genre – tragedy, comedy, epic or whatever; they may relate to the time, place and circumstance of the action; they may grow out of individual or group psychology; they may explore the abilities of singers and the requisite dramatic diction; they may draw on instrumental colour; they may adapt musical forms and processes; they may introduce stage music; they may react to the resources of 'the house'; and they may build on 'other music'. The title of Thomas Mann's novella of 1912, *Death in Venice*, is already rich in potential: on the one hand there is Venice, or *La serenissima* as the young call her; and on the other the process of an articulate author dying in a city where the pervasive water already implies death and renewal.

Benjamin Britten's opera of 1973 responds to all this. At its simplest, it listens to Venice in high season: gondolier cries, barcarolle rhythms, the beach-calls of the old to the young, a melodious strawberry-seller, strolling players, popular songs in dialect, a comic porter and hotel guests who converse in many languages at once. It evokes wind and sea, and, through a soaring theme, helps us marvel at the view of the beach. And it brings all this to a head in a diversionary set of five choral dances representing a beach contest for the young (the choral dance being a type already known from early opera). Of course, Britten would have learnt Venetian colour from other composers too – from Chopin and Mendelssohn, or Verdi and Offenbach. But he also knew Venice first hand: it was where he first performed his chamber opera *The Turn of the Screw* in 1954. He recreates the café music in the Piazza; he invokes the bells and 'Gabrieli' brass music of St Mark's, working heterophony into the sacred singing – distortions that suggest the building's resonance; and in the languid, irregular metres of the ubiquitous gondola music, he lets us imagine, on each last beat, a gondolier pulling up his pole.

But the situation in the Venice Mann envisaged is less simple. For, increasingly, it is a city in the grip of a plague; and, as in the Thebes of Sophocles's *Oedipus Rex*, the outer plague is a projection of the inner sickness of the central character. Mann's hero, of course, is not a king, but the author Gustav von Aschenbach. He is thus especially sensitive to changing circumstance, which, of course, he sees only from the outside. At the start, he journeys south from Munich and complains of the low-lying cloud: 'Where is the welcome that my Venice always gave me?', he sings pitifully to murky lines in the music. Off to the Lido, he reflects on 'ambiguous Venice'; on his arrival, he sings 'How black a gondola is … coffin black'. The air strikes him as 'heavy' with 'a hint of sirocco'; and he notes 'a stagnant smell from the lagoon'. Importuned by vendors and beggars, he cries 'O *Serenissima*, I fear you in this mood', and when the sun does appear, he complains of the heat. Later, he hears the citizens intoning public warnings from the Venetian authorities, and soon discovers there is an epidemic of Asiatic cholera. Not surprisingly, the hotel guests quit; and after Aschenbach has, in effect, sung his own threnody, the orchestra bursts out with a twisted, violent handling of the 'marvellous view' theme in the brass. This Venice is anything but serene.

Now, in general, drama comprises a range of characters. There are those that develop with the action, and those that don't (some may appear just once); those that belong to everyday life, and those to history, myth or imagination; and those that merely interpret the action, such as Prologues, Choruses or allegorical figures. In his novella, Thomas Mann invents these kinds afresh; and, through his music, Britten brings them to operatic life.

In fact, the turbulent protagonist Aschenbach integrates three of these kinds. First, he is a lonely German widower who travels south to Venice, becomes erotically obsessed with a beautiful male adolescent, fails to leave the infected city when he can, and dies there. From this viewpoint, his character develops through events that, for opera, are novel and audacious. Typically for a lover, Aschenbach is a tenor. The work's seventeen scenes show him constantly on the move, latterly in pursuit of his quarry. Aschenbach sees in the adolescent, the Polish Tadzio (or sometimes 'Tadziù'), the incarnation of the beauty of ancient Greece. Britten, though, cocoons him in exotic sounds – Venice, after all, is where East meets West – and, in a master-stroke, casts him as a dancer who never speaks (similarly with his entourage). Communication between the older man and his junior is thus by furtive look and gesture. Not surprisingly, Aschenbach's greatest expression of love is wordless: at the start of Act Two, the orchestra alone enlarges on his words 'I love you'; this music returns when Aschenbach watches the boy disappear into a hotel bedroom.

Second, Aschenbach is a man driven by ineluctable Destiny to die in a remote place. From this viewpoint, his character never develops. Such Destiny is often projected into the mythic figure of Hermes, a 'psychopomp' recognizable by a wide-brimmed hat, winged shoes and staff. Remarkably in *Death in Venice*, this figure is split into six characters, all taken by one singer, a bass-baritone. Each of them subcutaneously attacks Aschenbach's pride. The first, the Traveller, significantly appears in a Munich cemetery: his aria entices Aschenbach with images of an East that turns out to carry a mortal plague. On the steamer, the Elderly Fop taunts Aschenbach in a rapid, squeaky diction, and offers himself as a role model that Aschenbach will later adopt. The Old Gondolier proves gruff and autocratic, the Hotel Manager stolid but formidable, and the Hotel Barber, with his busy musicalized scissors, jocular and macabre. Worst is the satiric Leader of the Strolling Players. In an 'infantile' singing voice, he strikes up a laughing chorus, whose refrain, 'how ridiculous you are', pointedly isolates Aschenbach and Tadzio. These six roles share musical material and demonstrate Britten's superb art of dramatic variation.

Third, Aschenbach writes up his experiences in a notebook, in effect observing himself like a chorus – the function of his diary is 'epic'. The self-reflective, 'split-off' music is set as a rhythmically-free recitative accompanied by the piano, whose matter-of-fact sound instantly shifts the expressive register from action to interpretation. There are several such recitatives in the opera. Their musings on the challenge to the artist of physical beauty stand at the heart of the work's aesthetic enquiry – one that positions *Death in Venice* alongside Wagner's *Die Meistersinger* and Richard Strauss's *Capriccio*.

Psychologically, Aschenbach's task is to negotiate the rival pulls of Apollo and Dionysus, the gods of reason and sensuality. This marks the boundaries of the work's energy, a key source of invention, albeit a relatively abstract one. At the start, Aschenbach sings how his 'mind beats on' to nagging repeated notes and crazed swooping figures in harp and, later, strings: a self-disciplined, Apollonian master-writer he may be, but emotionally he is withered. However, lurking in the orchestra is the yearning, Dionysiac harmony borrowed from Wagner's *Tristan und Isolde*. This intimates love and death. On the Lido, we now hear the voice of Apollo, an ethereal counter-tenor who sings an old Delphic hymn. Tadzio wins at Apollo's games, and the thrilled Aschenbach is rejuvenated: 'Eros is in the word,' he proclaims in the key central aria. But this Nietzschean epiphany is short-lived. It is now that Aschenbach oversteps the mark, confessing breathlessly of Tadzio, 'I ... love you'. Thereafter the senses take over. In a nightmare, Dionysus gets the upper hand, Apollo departs for good, and wild revels painfully pervert the sounds of 'Tadziu's' name – 'aa – oo'. (Britten habitually explores the musical potential of names.) Aschenbach wakes, a broken man. In a final, deeply affecting aria, he engages in an imaginary Platonic dialogue that plays off the rival pulls: 'Does beauty lead to wisdom, Phaedrus?' 'Yes, but through the senses.' Aschenbach, though, has learnt that the senses lead to passion, to knowledge, forgiveness and compassion with the abyss ... he is utterly bewildered.

Soon after, Aschenbach expires on the beach, his spirit led out to sea by the now-Hermes-like Tadzio. Yet the opera does not end as a private tragedy or a tragedy of circumstance. Rather, it offers a quiet epilogue in the orchestra celebrating Aschenbach's key aria 'Eros is in the word', a paean to the sublimation of libidinal instinct that for the audience offers moral guidance. Aesthetically, his death in Venice has bequeathed an insight by which we may all live.

Notes

Source: 'Sources of Musical Invention', Britten-Centenary talk for BBC Radio 3, 9 October 2013.

1   I have written a detailed study of the work's musical poetics in: 'The Dye-line Rehearsal Scores for *Death in Venice*', *Rethinking Britten*, ed. Philip Rupprecht, New York: Oxford UP, 2013, pp. 262-83. By showing how a lead singer (Peter Pears) helped shape his role, these scores appear to be unique in the history of opera.

3 *Colloquy*
Richard Wagner: *Parsifal*

During the opera conference at Cornell I mentioned in my preface, I heard it suggested that the defining element of an opera was not the aria but the duet. Whereas the aria, like the chorus, the dance and different kinds of processional music, can always be played at a concert, and often is, the interactive duet tests the crucial dimension of drama and positively demands a stage (as do other interactive ensembles). I have since travelled with this thought. From about the middle of the nineteenth century, the duet with all its types of sympathy and opposition, has tended to give way to, or been supplemented by, the duologue. Whereas the duet is on the side of dramatized music (the two singers usually sing consecutively and then concurrently), the duologue is on the side of musicalized drama (the two singers only sing consecutively): music has retrenched before drama, closed form has given way to open process (though there are plenty of exceptions to prove the rule). Following the lead of Henrik Ibsen and Tennessee Williams, the long, searching duologue has also become staple fare in the theatre – even in the cinema, which resists 'talking heads', we find it in full flower in the later work of Ingmar Bergman (in, say, Scenes from a Marriage (1973)). However, opera of the last thirty years or so has tended to eschew the interactive in favour of independent, non-communicative assertion on the part of two or more characters. Whether this signals a negative virtue – a stylistic stance promoting peremptory statements – or a serious limitation of language and technique depends upon the composer and work in hand. This entry charts the evolution of Wagner's handling of colloquy from Tannhäuser *to* Parsifal: *it could have been extended to include the extraordinary colloquies found in Hofmannsthal and Strauss's* Elektra *(1909).*

1 *Tannhäuser to Parsifal*

On Friday 15 March 1878, Cosima Wagner recorded in her diary that

> [Richard] says he is nervous about the great scene [in Act Two] between Kundry and Parsifal; he has already done several things in this style, among others the Venus scene [from Act One of *Tannhäuser*]. Mozart only once did a scene such as the appearance of the Commendatore [in *Don Giovanni*], and it is impossible to imagine that he would have done something similar a second time.[1]

What was good for Mozart should also be good for Wagner: lightning must not strike twice in the same place. 'Several things in this style', of course, refers to Wagner's long dramatic duologues, or colloquies. With the exception of the exchanges in *Die Meistersinger* (a generic anomaly), these are conducted between couples at least one of whom has magic gifts – not surprisingly, since the context of Wagnerian myth is the uncanny. This is true, say, of all Wotan's colloquies in *Der Ring des Nibelungen*, even of the urgings of the love-forsaking Alberich to the half-sleeping Hagen in *Götterdämmerung*, and of the nuptial exchange between the hero and his uncannily-attuned Elsa in *Lohengrin*. Magic may still enmesh two characters even when neither is magical – as when Wotan stage-manages the first encounter of Siegmund and Sieglinde or the love-potion releases the mutual passion of Tristan and Isolde. Moreover, many of the colloquies move from one extreme to another and can have lethal consequences: by upending Wotan in their only encounter, Siegfried expedites the fall of the gods.

The parallel scenes, however, between Kundry and Parsifal in Act Two of *Parsifal* (1882) and Venus and Tannhäuser in Act One of *Tannhäuser* (1845) are not just 'great' in extent and stature but also unique. Both involve an enchanted seductress and a knight; both counter extreme erotic enticement with extreme restraint; and both epitomize a broader social-cum-political conflict between the pagan, or infidel, and the Christian. They also have a life-and-death consequence: at their respective ends, Venus will vanish and Tannhäuser die, his soul saved by the heavenly intercession of the departed Elisabeth; and Parsifal will wander but return to Monsalvat, redeeming Kundry before she too dies (blessedly released from relentless re-incarnation, not unlike Wagner's Dutchman). Both Venus and Kundry curse their respective knights when they fail to yield, and the arduous working-through of the curse is central to the psychological drama in each case. The Venus colloquy comes embryonically in Wagner's source *Das Lied von dem Danheüser* (1515); yet the Kundry colloquy is Wagner's alone, for all that the 'harsh-featured' sorceress 'Cundry' features in his main source, Wolfram von Eschenbach's *Parzival* (c. 1205), and his Kundry also absorbs Wolfram's much-courted 'Orgeluse'.

From another, lesser perspective, the scenario is older than opera itself, as several scholars have noted. Wagner had conducted Gluck's spectacular 'heroic drama' *Armide* in Dresden in March 1843 – doing it better, according to his autobiography, than Meyerbeer had done in Berlin. Like *Parisfal*, *Armide* was about a sorceress and seductress riven by love and hate who attempts to ensnare a Christian knight, Renaud, in a beautiful oasis. Set at the time of the First Crusade, its origins lie in Torquato Tasso's *Gerusalemme liberata* (Jerusalem Liberated, 1581). Tasso's epic had in fact prompted a host of operas, the episode with Armida and Rinaldo appealing to Lully (1686), Handel (1711), Haydn (1784) and Dvořák (1904) among others. Sometimes the Christians are supported by a magician (Handel), and Armida by Hatred and her demons (Lully and Gluck). When magic fails, the enchanted place can turn instantly into open countryside (Handel) or collapse into ruins (Gluck). Wagner too draws on these conventions: the first half of Act One of *Tannhäuser* ends with Venus vanishing and Tannhäuser finding himself suddenly in a beautiful valley; and Act Two of *Parsifal* closes with the collapse of the sorcerer's castle and the withering of the magic garden into a desert. This collapse also parallels that in Gozzi's *La donna serpente*, the play from the 1760s on which Wagner drew for his first opera, *Die Feen* (1834).[2]

However, Wagner succeeded in making the *Parsifal* colloquy significantly more complex than the *Tannhäuser* one (even in its enriched Paris version of 1861). *Tannhäuser* opens in a magic grotto with the goddess Venus revealing her domain to her mortal lover. Naiads, Sirens, Nymphs, Satyrs, Fauns, Cupids, the wild Bacchantes and the three restraining Graces lead on to a 'vision' of the Rape of Europa. Act Two of *Parsifal* likewise opens in a magic domain, though here the atmosphere is deeply fractious: Klingsor exudes universal contempt, arousing from sleep the death-demanding seductress Kundry, who gaspingly rends the air with shrieks enhanced by wild, mocking cascades in the orchestra; his Flower Maidens not only try to seduce Parsifal to a waltz 'in the American style' (Wagner's term), but also squabble among themselves and abuse him petulantly when they fail. Wagner ascribes Klingsor's hatred to sexual self-mutilation driven by envy of the (relatively) chaste knights of the Grail. (Wolfram von Eschenbach, on the other hand, had told a richer story: 'Clinschor' has had his manhood 'justly' incapacitated after a King has caught him in bed with his Queen; so he travels to 'Persida' (Persia), the *fons et origo* of magic, to acquire formidable powers with which to avenge himself on all other lovers; he then receives from the fearful King Irot an impregnable mountain on which to build a castle. Only the Godhead can vanquish him.)[3]

2 *Tannhäuser*

At the opening of the *Tannhäuser* colloquy, Tannhäuser awakens: he has been dreaming of long-lost sacred bells and the outside world. At Venus's command, he sings a song. It falls into three verses, all roughly parallel, in each of which a paean to love precedes a plea for release. After the first verse, Venus asks tenderly, what has she done wrong? After the second, she angrily accuses Tannhäuser of having grown bored with her and then woos him with a new erotic vision, more kisses and the promise of physical union. Tannhäuser springs away and launches into the third verse. Hearing that he still rejects her, Venus launches into a contemptuously dismissive 'rage aria' that includes an imagined enactment of Tannhäuser's futile return to her, followed by a piteous appeal laced with dire threats. After a final tussle, Tannhäuser appeals to 'Maria' (the Virgin), and Venus, recognizing *force majeure*, vanishes.[4]

3 *Parsifal*

In essence, this three-verse scheme forms a template for Kundry's seduction of Parsifal, even though it is now the woman (Kundry) who takes the lead, and there is no longer a formal strophic song to act as backbone. The first part opens with Kundry calling Parsifal by name (in Wagner, to name is always to appropriate). She then induces and exploits Parsifal's guilt at having youthfully abandoned his mother Herzeleide, fatally breaking her heart. In seductive triple time, Kundry sings five rhyming stanzas of different length, so fluidly composed as to prevent any audience from spotting the formality. Parsifal is duly mortified. (In fact, the problem is social as well as personal: in *Parzifal*, Eschenbach explains how 'Herzeloyde' is the sister of 'Anfortas', giving 'Parzival' a dynastic claim to power.)

In the second part, Kundry presses her advantage, again in triple time and rhyming stanzas, albeit with a new scheme. She will console him with love; she will let him experience vicariously the passion of his (dead) father for his mother; and she will offer him, as his mother's final greeting, a kiss. As the orchestra plays the yearning harmony from *Tristan und Isolde*, she 'presses her lips to his mouth'. In 1878 Wagner described this slow, Oedipal kiss as demonic, poisonous and 'serpentine'. This is certainly how Parsifal receives it. Recognizing only a re-enactment of Kundry's damaging and wounding seduction of Amfortas, he blazes with compassionate fury. The force of his reaction recalls what in 1859 Wagner had said of Amfortas – like 'my third-act Tristan with incomparable intensification'. Parsifal even imagines himself in conversation with the Grail.

Parsifal again resists, so Kundry moves to her third wave of seduction, with a Venus-like appeal to pity. Although her words still rhyme, she no longer sings in triple time, but in Parsifal's common time (four-in-the-bar), even taking for herself the sacred Dresden Amen and Grail motifs. In fact, her delirium is in part genuine: she has been condemned down the ages for mocking Christ on the cross, and, despite her subservience to Klingsor, yearns for Parsifal to redeem her by granting her death. The situation is thus far more complex than in *Tannhäuser*. Now comes the final tussle. Kundry rages; Parsifal insists he will redeem her his way and not hers; and she again tries to embrace him. Finally, she summons Klingsor to endorse her curse on Parsifal's wanderings. He appears. 'Halt there!' he cries, revealing himself as the power behind Kundry. (The moment is not unlike the close of Act Two of *Die Walküre*, when Wotan emerges to countermand Brünnhilde's submission to Siegmund after their great colloquy on the field of battle.) Klingsor hurls his spear – the same that wounded Amfortas. But Parsifal does not die: the spear merely hangs in the air. Parsifal seizes it, and, with the sign of the cross, condemns Klingsor and his environs to 'misery and ruin'. The Grail has intervened, revealing itself as the power behind Parsifal. But what is it, and what is its music?

4 The Grail

Legend has it that the Grail is the cup used at the Last Supper in which Joseph of Arimathea is said to have caught Christ's blood from the Cross. But in Eschenbach's *Parzifal*, it is a stone, *lapsit exillis*, that extends lives, answers prayers and issues decrees (including the dispatch of the swan-knight 'Loherangrin' to Brabant). It is visible only to those whose loyalty has been secured through baptism – hence the intense rites that open Wagner's Act Three, rites that, to radiant music, help restore the 'waste land' into which Monsalvat has fallen under Amfortas. In Eschenbach's closing ceremony, it is carried by the sister of 'Anfortas', Repanse de Schoye, 'a maiden most rare' who appears alongside other maidens; and it provides choice sustenance for the inhabitants of 'Munsalvaesche': 'meats both wild and tame … mulberry wine, tinctured, clary'.

Musically, Wagner represents the Grail by distributing its voice across three levels of the dome that covers the Knights' dining hall, the setting we first meet at the end of Act One. The boys and youths 'in the middle height' remind their stricken leader Amfortas of what, according to the all-wise Gurnemanz, the Grail has ordered: he must wait to be redeemed by the pure fool 'whom I have chosen'. The Knights on the ground demand the Grail be revealed. Now voices from 'on high' sing the communion injunction 'Now take my body, now take my blood, as token of our love' (we in the audience have already heard its floating, questing music in the work's Prelude). A light shines down on the cup. After the Knights have eaten and left to the sound of bells, and Gurnemanz has dismissed the foolish Parsifal for not asking what he has seen, a solo female voice from the very top of the dome repeats the Grail's prediction. This essentially three-tiered arrangement returns at the end of Act Three, now preceded by two litanizing choirs of Knights angry at the death of Titurel. (Wagner has Titurel as Amfortas's father, whereas Eschenbach had him as his grandfather who lives on.) Instead of a female voice, an intensely illuminated white dove appears from on high as Parsifal reveals the Grail: it 'redeems the redeemer', releasing Kundry from life in the process, and is supported in the orchestra by the no-longer questing Grail music. The dove is an emissary of the Grail's supreme authority, the Holy Ghost, and bears the (mass) wafer that is to be the mysterious source of sustenance for Monsalvat: it descends only on Good Friday. Its appearance is Wagner's final *coup de théâtre*, one that, for Jungians, signifies deep integration. Yet this too builds on his experience with *Tannhäuser*, at the end of which we also hear sacred, redemptive voices.

The Act Two colloquy between Kundry and Parsifal, like that between Venus and Tannhäuser, thus masks and integrates a colloquy between the pagan and the Christian, the profane and the sacred, Klingsor and the Grail.[5] Conceived in 1857, when the composer was in his early forties, it stands as one of the greatest achievements in dramatic art.

Notes

Source: 'Voicing Parsifal', *Parsifal* (Richard Wagner) The Royal Opera programme, November 2013, pp. 47-50.

1 *Cosima Wagner's Diaries, vol. 2, 1878-1883*, London: Collins, 1980, trans. Geoffrey Skelton, pp. 40-1.

2 Some of my information comes from the valuable discussion of sources in: William Kinderman, *Wagner's Parsifal*, New York: Oxford UP, 2013.

3 We may draw a further parallel between Klingsor at the start of Act Two of *Parsifal* and the sorceress Ortrud at the start of Act Two of *Lohengrin* (1850).

4 There is an argument, much treasured by musicologists, that Tannhäuser's song to Venus is in fact in four strophes, since Tannhäuser returns to the music of his song for a fourth time in Act Two during the singing contest in the Wartburg. See: Werner Breig, 'The Musical Works' in: *Wagner Handbook*, ed. Ulrich Müller and Peter Wapnewski, Cambridge Mass.: Harvard UP, 1992, p. 424. The argument rests on what appears to be an unbroken ascent of keys: in Act One, as Tannhäuser sings to Venus, the three strophes rise from D♭ to D to E♭, all in major; in Act Two, a further 'strophe' appears in E major. But there are three arguments against this notion of a four-strophe song: (1) In Act Two, scandalously, Tannhäuser only sings the first half of the strophe, that which praises Venus; he misses out the second half, which informs her that he must abandon her (2) this is because a dramatic event, a *peripeteia*, has intervened between the two acts, namely the curse that Venus has put on the world (including Tannhäuser) – a curse that Elisabeth understands and sacrifices her life to combat: the situation in Act Two is quite other than that in Act One (3) The status of E♭ and E is deeper than that of mere progression: they are the two dialectically engaged keys of the entire work: E♭ major is sacred, and E major profane, the first is Elisabeth's key, the second Venus's. The tendency of the work is to raise the two keys to a higher synthesis, to advance an image of the sacred transfigured by the profane, though the tonal system can only suggest this but not achieve it. When, therefore, in Act Two, under Venus's spell Tannhäuser sings the first part of his song in E, it is as much as a *substitution* for the E♭ in which he ended the third strophe in Act One as a logical *continuation*. The key conflict comes to a head at the end of the third and final act: Venus reappears in E, but she is overcome by the community which sings with full force in E♭. From this point of view the E major in which Tannhäuser sings the first half of a strophe in Act Two is an anomaly, a fly in the social ointment that it takes the rest of the work to

correct (technically an F$\flat$ neighbour-note!); yet it does set him apart, and it is to this apartness that Elisabeth responds. There is a study to be written on Wagner's pervasive use of the rules and rites of three (as described in Part Six under 'Freud and Opera').

5   The Christian voices also have a background in Buddhism, as Wagner himself indicated. I have amplified this in: 'Kundry's Baptism, Kundry's Death', *The Wagner Journal*, Vol. 8, No. 3, 2014, pp. 4-18. To enrich the field of allusion further, we may remember Wagner's observation on 14 September, 1882, that '... Kundry already experienced Isolde's *Liebestod* a hundred times in her various incarnations'. *Cosima Wagner Diaries Vol.* 2, p. 910.

4 Sacred and Secular

Francesco Maria Piave (after Souvestre and Bourgeois) and Giuseppe Verdi: *Stiffelio*

Music touches the dynamic essence of our being. This essence, of course, is neither sacred nor secular, but still finds its purest embodiment in prayer and solemn ceremony, which both stand at a remove from everyday life. Not only is sacred representation a precursor of opera, but its rituals and music are frequently harnessed by this overtly secular medium. Indeed, the different kinds of sacred music, from different religions and denominations, are a rich source of invention for a composer. Opera abounds in religious figures, among them a vestal virgin (Spontini's La Vestale (1807)), a Druidess (Bellini's Norma (1831)) and a nun (Puccini's Suor Angelica (1918)); there are operas about composers of sacred music, including Pfitzner's Palestrina (1917) and Peter Maxwell Davies's Taverner (1972); and Arnold Schoenberg gives voice to God himself in two concurrent six-part choruses, one sung, the other spoken, at the start of Moses und Aron (1932/57). The conflict of the sacred and the profane has also been a vital source for composers, especially when one openly erupts into the other. This was a commonplace in grand opera. For instance, in the sumptuous scene in Münster Cathedral from Act Four of Le Prophète (1849), Meyerbeer has John of Leyden, with ecclesiastical choruses ringing in his ears, compel his forthright mother to disavow him after she has stepped forward with a challenge. The action of Verdi's inventive but little-known Stiffelio (1850) likewise comes to a head inside a church, when the zealous pastor is compelled to accommodate the private and the public, the secular and the sacred, in a poignant act of forgiveness.

Verdi's *Stiffelio* (1850) may have been 'rediscovered' back in 1968, yet audiences have still to get its measure. True, the work is overshadowed by the force of *Rigoletto* (1851) and the poignancy of *La traviata* (1853): the need for a Protestant minister to exercise in private the compassion he preaches in public engages a rite that leaves little room for sentiment even if it offers a fascinating portrait of a contrite 'woman taken in adultery'. Yet *Stiffelio* is far from being a curiosity, or just the missing link between *Luisa Miller* (1849) and the famous trinity of *Rigoletto*, *Trovatore* and *Traviata*, not to mention other works of the 1850s – Lina's prayer at the tomb of her mother paves the way for both the dying Gilda in *Rigoletto* and the terrified Amelia in *Un ballo in maschera* (1859). On the contrary, *Stiffelio* deserves recognition in its own right. But why?

To begin at the beginning. In general Verdi likes to get to the core of his dramas as quickly as possible: yet nowhere does he move as fast as in *Stiffelio*. After the sinfonia, which in part prepares for the bright choruses of the first act, we meet the solitary figure of Jorg. He is the daunting 'wise old man' who decrees with the voice of God that society should live by 'the holy book': more still, it is for the zealot Stiffelio to enforce his will. In fact Jorg's first three words, 'O santo libro!', embody the task of the drama: to uncover the spirit of the Bible rather than to hide behind its letter. As Stiffelio and his wife approach, we hear the buoyant music of the household: everyone rejoices at the homecoming of the 'mighty orator' Stiffelio. Only Jorg hopes that love will not dampen the minister's zeal. The music seems trite – but is deliberately so: it speaks naïvely for the people. Indeed the contrast between Holy Wrath, 'banal' festivity, and what will follow – a fraught amorous intrigue – establishes three strands that develop across the act in a rich counterpoint. It is often claimed that Verdi used this Shakespearean mix for the first time in *Rigoletto* (albeit foreshadowed in *Macbeth* (1847)): yet here he already handles it with astonishing skill. If anything, it is *Stiffelio* that blazes the trail.

Now, it is well known that in the early 1850s Verdi wanted to set Shakespeare's *King Lear* in such a way that abandoned the conventions of Italian opera for a more direct musical drama. The project came to nothing, but for the rest of his life Verdi continued to struggle with his heritage, only rarely 'succeeding' (as in the first act of *Falstaff* (1893)). Yet it was the struggle that produced the best results, and the opening act of *Stiffelio* shows why. At first the 'banal' happiness of the community engulfs Stiffelio to the extent that he tears up unread the adulterer's notes that have come his way. The action releases the work's first *concertato*. By convention this is an extended slow passage in which a company reflects upon a situation and what it means to each of its members. Here, Stiffelio's wife Lina renounces sin, whereas Lina's father, Stankar, voices his suspicions: yet only the seducer Raffaelle remains untouched by the situation. He merely continues the unwanted intrigue with a promise of another *billet doux*. This capacity of a villain to sustain dramatic action through a conventionally lyric moment finds its locus classicus in the third act of Verdi's *Otello* (1887) where Iago cruelly schemes right through the huge *concertato* that follows Desdemona's humiliation: *Otello's* precedent lies in *Stiffelio*.

A greater test for Verdi in the 1850s came as he tried to turn operatic duet into musico-dramatic duologue – a return, in fact, to the ideal of early opera. At the centre of the first act we find Stiffelio alone with Lina. Stiffelio pretends not to make the very accusations he furtively advances; he bestows such nobility on Lina that her speech becomes every bit as confused as, secretly, he expects. The exchange culminates in a broken arch of melody as Stiffelio notices that Lina's ring is missing: tenderness becomes confrontation, the two wrestle over melodic shapes, and *affettuoso* becomes *cupo con ire* (dark with rage). After this, Stiffelio can no longer wear the mask of goodness. What we hear throughout is a chain of textures and tempi that create a 'loose form' (or large *scena*). Yet all this is still embedded in a 'strict form', a conventional aria with slow and fast sections. The technique, to be used so effectively in the second act of *La traviata* for the meeting of Violetta and Germont *père*, is already deployed here for the same reason: to chart a slow process of accumulation.

It is often claimed that Verdi had ushered in a new kind of intimacy in *Luisa Miller*. However, he also found new ways of uniting the public and the private in *Stiffelio*. At the height of the first act finale, Stiffelio declares that his sermon will be on Judas's betrayal of Christ: with barely concealed animation he sings of the horrors of Raffaelle. He finds a book of his locked. Lina has the key: he demands she open it. Inside, as we all know, is a *billet doux*: Stiffelio predicts the uncovering of the betrayer (Raffaelle alias Judas). Here the act's second great *concertato* begins, a *sotto voce* adagio in which the entire company holds its breath. Stiffelio, Raffaelle and Lina each take the minor melody in turn: theirs is a trio within the ensemble. As the music turns to the major, there is a build-up to the key phrase, 'fatal mistèro'. Stiffelio bursts open the book, and the note falls out. But, in a *coup de théâtre*, Stankar, Lina's father, tears it up (repeating Stiffelio's action at the outset). This releases Stiffelio's pent-up anger and launches the frenzied *stretta*, the conventional fast ending to a finale. Yet inside the following turmoil, the arguments continue: Lina begs Stiffelio to turn his rage on her and Stankar arranges a duel with Raffaelle. Once again private action invades public reaction.

And what of the second act? In Italian opera we are familiar with situations where the protagonists' sufferings at the front of the stage are thrown into relief by the benign sounds of a distant choir. At the end of Donizetti's *La Favorite* (1840), for instance, we see the distressed Léonor arrive at the Monastery of St James to hear the monks and her vengeful lover pray for the soul of the dead Queen. In the *Miserere* scene from *Il trovatore* (1853) another Leonora suffers as she hears a distant male chorus praying for the soul of her lover Manrico. Manrico, in fact, is heard resigning himself to death inside a tower. The two unwittingly sing a duet. And at the close of the first act of Puccini's *Tosca* (1900) Scarpia reveals his evil machinations to the sound of bells, cannons and a full chorus intoning 'Te Deum laudamus'.

Yet the situation in *Stiffelio* is more complex. We find ourselves in a moonlit graveyard: there is a cross in the middle and a church to the side. The church is lit up. Lina prays at the tomb of her mother and is then joined by the persistent Raffaelle. The two argue. The commotion draws Stiffelio from the church, and his suspicions of Lina's adultery are confirmed: he seizes a sword to fight a duel. But suddenly the mixed voices of the congregation are heard from inside the church, the distance adding intimacy to their gentle plea for forgiveness. Stiffelio is beside himself with fury and curses Lina. But now the sturdy Jorg comes from the church and reminds Stiffelio of divine mercy. In effect he creates an altar round the cross while the unseen choir continues to sing. Stiffelio collapses and the others take pity. Over the course of the scene the service has migrated from church to graveyard. The prayers are offered where they really matter.

More important still, this makeshift ceremony prepares the way for the second scene of the third act. We are now inside the church, a gothic edifice with 'huge arcades'. What is striking here is Verdi's handling of diction (tone of voice). This leaves convention far behind to concentrate on the fine workings of an exceptional denouement. At the start the muted company offers up the last and most focused of the work's many prayers: 'Non punirmi, Signor, nel tuo furore' (Spare me, O Lord, in thy wrath). Here the music again seems artlessly simple: yet it is most effective in supporting Lina's delicate appeals for mercy on the one hand and Stankar's expansive contrition on the other – after all, he has just killed Raffaelle. When Stiffelio crosses the church to ascend the pulpit, everyone holds their breath: he alone has shown no change of heart. Even the music walks on eggshells: chorus and soloists sing breathlessly, and the orchestra restricts itself to repeated patterns, a device of Rossini's put to new use. Then, to a barely audible halo of winds and the sparsest of bass accompaniments, Stiffelio reads the Biblical story of the woman taken in adultery. There is general astonishment. Finally he puts his hand on the book and declares 'with full force': 'Perdonata. Iddio lo pronunzio.' (Forgiven. Thus I decree). He has made Christ's forgiveness his own. Everyone brazenly repeats the absolution, none more so than Lina: 'Gran Dio!' she shrieks, hitting her highest note, C. Turbulence, group pressure and a death have done their work: the private and public Stiffelio, the secular and the sacred, are finally at one.[1]

Notes

Source: 'Why Stiffelio Matters', Stiffelio (Giuseppe Verdi), The Royal Opera programme, April 2007, pp. 17-20.

1 In fact, throughout Stiffelio Verdi pursues extremes of expression. Although he is usually fastidious in marking his vocal lines, he is never more so than at the start of the third act. Here Stankar is alone. Such is the impact of his daughter's adultery that he considers suicide: 'Disonorato io son!' (I have been dishonoured) he cries 'with desperation'. In the elaborate scena that precedes his andante he reaches for his pistol: 'Oh quanto sei tu grande, o dolor!' ('Oh how great you are, my grief!') he exclaims 'with great force'. When he hears of the approach of the doomed Raffaelle, his voice becomes 'suffocated', 'convulsed', 'abandoned' and 'panting'; and he concludes his solo with 'full force'. Stankar's suffering marks the high point of Verdi's daring in Stiffelio. In the next scene, when at last Stiffelio and Lina are alone together, it legitimates Stankar's horrific

murder of Raffaelle, an off-stage act that saves the face of his family just as Lina's no less horrific signing of divorce papers saves her face before Stiffelio. The work's 'happy end' is all the more affecting for it.

Afterword: In May 2007 I attended a group discussion in South London between psychoanalysts and therapists. They had all been to see *Stiffelio*. Their over-arching question testified to a vital aspect of any operatic or dramatic experience: how does the work leave the audience once it has ended? They asked: 'Where is the ring – lost with Raffaelle's death?'; 'If Lina has been forgiven, where does it leave Stiffelio, and everyone else, with regard to the murder of Raffaelle?'; 'Are Stiffelio's cries of "Perdonata" more of a statement of intent than a sea change?'; 'In the final scene, isn't the father imago split four ways – Jorg, Stankar, Stiffelio and the hand of God?'; and 'Since the work includes a death, isn't it at best a tragi-comedy?' There was also reference to Mary-Jane Phillips's programme essay on the tricky context of forgiveness in the Catholic community of the time, with special reference to Verdi and Giuseppina Strepponi's difficult return to Busseto.

5 The Force of the Outsider

Salvadore Cammarano (after Gutiérrez) and Giuseppe Verdi: *Il trovatore*

*Opera, like drama, habitually deals with the outsider, and behind the outsider can stand an uncanny power. As we have seen, this is especially true of Wagnerian music drama, where myth goes hand in hand with the supernatural (*The Flying Dutchman, Lohengrin, Parsifal*). Many of Verdi's greatest operas also deal in rank outsiders. Yet because they are social or political outcasts, they are perceived as differently uncanny, as emanating their own kind of power. Indeed, they can become the source of superstition. Reciprocally, the sense of being set apart also heightens their own feelings, just as it attracts sympathy from each member of the audience who feels that he or she is somehow an outcast. The following entry focuses on a so-perceived 'witch' in Verdi's* Il trovatore *and charts the musical effect of her isolation. On the one hand, Verdi follows nineteenth-century Italian conventions to the letter, and on the other he subverts them to accommodate her music. This is driven by a double passion inspired by a dead mother and a dead son – forces from beyond the grave. Such insider-outsider tension has been a key source of invention for opera composers of all periods.*

In his 'History of Modern Pagan Witchcraft', *The Triumph of the Moon*,[1] Ronald Hutton suggests that the 'classic' description of magic for modern scholars is James Frazer's. Frazer held that magic involves practices designed to bring the supernatural 'under the control of human agents'; and since the agents were 'witches', the control was deemed to be potentially if not actually malign. The witch was thus the focus and source of a society's irrational fears. Only name the witch and destroy her, so the thought went, and the black magic would disappear.

Such superstition, and everything that flows from it, stands at the core of *Il trovatore* (1853). It is the first of Verdi's operas without a full orchestral introduction; yet the opening scene substitutes for it, acting as a 'topical' prelude of the kind Verdi had just used in *Rigoletto* (1851) and would use again in *La traviata* (1853). The setting is suitably remote: the time is the fifteenth century, the place the Aliaferia palace in Aragon, and the situation a group of guards listening to an old captain. Ferrando is explaining what happened twenty years before when a witch came to the palace to tell the fortune of the old Count's youngest son. The scene is an exercise in group hysteria, whipped up by soldiers (of all people), and fuelled by Ferrando's account of how the woman was immolated for allegedly casting a spell on the child. He also describes how her avenging daughter (Azucena) subsequently stole the child and (apparently) tossed it into the same fire. The scene culminates in blood-curdling cries as the guards hear unexpected bells. In all this, the music moves between extremes: a rousing martial call with uncanny echoes is followed by the urbanely-told story of the old Count and his two sons. Dropped into this is a precisely tailored two-verse song about the horrifying 'witches' themselves. The song, 'Abbietta zingara' (There stood a gypsy woman), carefully prepares for the later triple-time gypsy music without stealing its thunder. Incensed, the guards demand that the witch's daughter should burn too: after all, she is known to turn into an owl, a black cat and a vampire. No wonder they end up shrieking – and no wonder, when they catch her in Act Three, they are so eager to commit her to the flames!

It is important to see how the opera unpacks the polarities of this 'prelude': for there has never been a consensus on just how this marvellously crafted work is actually balanced. Verdi himself thought outwards from Azucena, a complex, stigmatized figure hounded by society – like Rigoletto or Violetta, in fact. Inevitably, a woman who has failed to avenge her mother by inadvertently immolating her own baby (and not someone else's) has a dual burden of guilt. In Azucena's case it expresses itself as exaggerated love: for the old Count's son, Manrico, whom perforce she has raised as her own (*amor filiale*), and for her immolated mother (*amor materno*). Indeed, in a letter to the librettist Salvadore Cammarano (1851), Verdi spoke of 'this woman's two big passions: her love for [Manrico] and her wild desire to avenge her mother'.[2] Of these, the deepest passion is for her mother, expressed in music that simply won't go away. In Act Two Azucena twice re-enacts her mother's death at the stake: first as she 'performs' the lugubrious canzone 'Stride la vampa' to the gypsies who clearly know the story well and react without the soldiers' hysteria, and then again when she glosses it in private for Manrico. In Act Four she re-enacts it yet again as she realizes her destiny is also to be burnt alive. And throughout, she clings to her mother's dying words, 'Mi vendica!' (Avenge me!). 'When [Manrico] is dead,' writes Verdi, 'her feeling of revenge becomes gigantic, and she cries in exaltation [to the young Count]: 'Si ... egli era tuo fratello ... Stolto! ... sei vendicata, o madre!' (Yes ... he was your brother ... Fool! ... you are avenged, mother!). But where does that leave the filial love? Azucena's bond with Manrico is not just predictably protective and dependent, but also quasi-incestuous. In Act Three, she sings to her captors: 'Fonder love than I still bear him no mother here on earth could show!' Though she doesn't know it, her glowing music is identical to that which Leonora sang back in Act One when she expressed her erotic love for Manrico. For the audience, the cross-reference is breathtaking.

For the private colloquy between Azucena and Manrico in Act Two, Verdi called for 'free and new forms'. Novelty was his obsession at the time. In an earlier letter to Cammarano (1850), he had written of their proposed *King Lear* 'there is no need to make [it] into the usual kind of drama … rather, we must treat it in a completely new manner'. *Lear* was never written, but we can understand from Azucena's scenes what that new manner might have involved. First, in addition to large closed forms (arias and songs) he developed open dramatic ones. These comprised directed chains of different units, some of which were still small closed forms (say, the ternary A-A^1-B-A), but most of which were enhanced recitative. Second, as we have noted, he used recurrent music in new guises; and third, he shaped entire sections as large affective surges (or 'wave forms'). He uses a surge when, with mounting tension, Azucena tells of tossing her own baby on the fire. 'Quale orror!' (What horror!) cries Manrico at its apex, repeating the words five times, with Azucena writhing to the end. (In Act Two of *La traviata*, Verdi pushed surging further with Violetta's overwhelming 'Amami, Alfredo!' (Love me, Alfredo!))

In the last act, Azucena and Manrico are alone again. They are now in a 'horrid dungeon'. Their finale begins with a similar chain that now leads into a closed form, a tender little triple-time duet in which Manrico comforts his fatigued mother. But within the duet she reacts unexpectedly with her poignant, comatose 'Ai nostri monti' (Let us return to the ancient peace of our mountains). Suddenly, Leonora bursts in to free Manrico. But Manrico is filled with suspicion: what sacrifice has she made to do this, he asks? Yet their fraught duet is overlaid by Azucena's quiet and unexpected repetition of 'Ai nostri monti'. She is oblivious of the young. This invasion of one closed form by a remnant of another again creates a 'completely new' effect, the engaged and the disengaged pushing extremes without going over the edge. Of this scene Verdi wrote to Cammarano: 'Don't make Azucena mad. Exhausted with fatigue, with sorrow, terror and lack of sleep, she is unable to speak rationally. Her senses are overwrought, but she is not mad.'

The majority of critics, however, start, not with Verdi, but with Salvadore Cammarano – who in turn was adapting Antonio García Gutíerrez's play of 1836. From start to finish, Cammarano's superbly focussed libretto pursues a double story-line, one involving the Count, the other the gypsies. 'The four-part structure,' writes Gabriele Baldini '… is emphasized by the fact that each part is divided in two.'[3] There are four principal soloists, and not two, and a parallel action in which the old Count's dying injunction to the young Count to find his abducted sibling reflects the old witch's to Azucena to avenge her. If the old Count's instinct tells him the stolen child is still alive, so too does Manrico's instinct tell him not to kill his brother (the Count di Luna). The parallels are endless. The same critics also point out how so many conventions of Italian opera find their locus classicus in *Il trovatore*: Leonora's aspiring cavatina in Act One and her macabre 'Miserere' aria in Act Four fleshed out with stage music; Count di Luna's melting aria in Act Two; the magnificent ensemble finale at the convent in the same act; the stirring Freedom Chorus for Ferrando and the Count's soldiers in Act Three; and the savage duet between the Count and Leonora in Act Four. These count among the glories of Italian opera, and are indeed 'by the book'.

Yet – crucially – some of the most striking effects are achieved by subverting the same conventions. When in Act One, the young Count di Luna steps forward to apostrophize Leonora, his andante is snatched from him by the haunting, off-stage troubadour-song of Manrico; after Leonora has arrived and mistaken him for Manrico (who soon arrives too), he bursts into what would be the fast, raging conclusion of his aria (the *cabaletta*). But the other two join in, and the resulting trio is significant precisely for frustrating his solo. Similarly in Act Two, when, after their intimate exchange, Manrico asks so poignantly of Azucena, 'E chi son' io, chi dunque?' (And who am I, who then?), we are denied the bewildered, introspective aria that would have opened up new vistas on the evidently troubled Manrico. Instead, the embarrassed Azucena gets him to sing a heroic cantabile explaining how he spared the Count di Luna in battle – a revelation she at once rebukes. After a messenger has brought news that Leonora is retreating into a convent, Manrico calls for a horse to save her. Here one would expect him to lead the fast conclusion of his 'number'. But Azucena is so alarmed at losing her 'son' that she takes the lead, forcing Manrico into resistance before riding off. This time the re-arrangement testifies to the gypsy's frustration.

Yet between Verdi's initial idea of *Il trovatore* and Cammarano's final one there stands a third: a Romeo and Juliet story of two lovers caught in the crossfire of two camps. Realistically, they have nothing in common: 'How could [Manrico] interest a well-bred lady [Leonora]?' asked Verdi tartly.[4] Yet such is the force of the effects of superstition, that the two seem compelled to seek each other out and become its tragic victims. The music, in promoting new forms, old forms, and forms that fuse new and old, rises to the ensuing horrors as never before.

Notes

Source: 'Fear and Loathing in Ancient Aragon: the Music of *Il trovatore*', *Il trovatore* (Giuseppe Verdi), The Royal Opera programme, April 2009, pp. 36-41.

1   Ronald Hutton, *The Triumph of the Moon*, Oxford: Oxford UP, 1999, p. 66.
2   *Letters of Giuseppe Verdi*, trans. and ed. from the *Coppialettere* by Charles Osborne, London: Gollancz, 1971; letter to Salvadore Cammarano (on *Il trovatore*), Busseto, 9 April 1851: pp. 78-81. Cf. Letter to Cammarano on *King Lear*, Busseto, 28 February 1850, pp. 69-73.
3   Gabriele Baldini, *The Story of Giuseppe Verdi. 'Oberto' to 'Un ballo in maschera'*, trans. and ed. Roger Parker, Cambridge: Cambridge UP, 1980, pp. 209-30, and especially p. 213.
4   *Letters of Verdi*, 1971, p. 79.

Sigmund Freud
(Milein Cosman, early 1980s)

Part Six

Psychology

Introduction

My opening definition of opera posited three irreducible elements governed by song: dramatized music, musicalized drama and the transfiguring power of both pulling together. However, there are also staged actions involving characters, spectacle, movement and song that are not, strictly speaking, operatic: sacred representation, masque, intermezzo and school piece (Brechtian Lehrstück*) among them. These use the joint power of music and drama to assert the authority of a religious order, a ruling class, a political stance or whatever. They do not seriously question it. Indeed, in pre-operatic stagings such as the Florentine* intermezzi*, flattery of the Medicis was uninhibited. Of course, there will always be an element of assertion: opera is an expensive medium funded and staged by people with a certain outlook. And if we mean by 'dramatic' that which explores conflicting positions – pre-eminently the conflict of right and right – we face three possibilities:[1] operas that end with a satisfactory resolution – comedy and tragedy with a happy end* (lieto fine)*; those that end without a satisfactory resolution – tragedy with an unhappy end; or those that are in some way inconclusive.[2]*

Opera is conventionally associated with the vices and vicissitudes of the grand passions. This is not wrong. The conflicts it arouses touch on the deepest issues of our being, and music can give them voice with unparalleled effect. For more than a century these issues have become the province of psychoanalysis. (More recently the province has extended to psychiatry, the material terms of which are most usefully thought of as complementary, rather than opposed, to psychology.)[3] Yet although the different schools of psychoanalysis regularly mount new attempts to bring music, and especially operatic music, under their purview – and have tried at least since the 1930s – they have been more successful in addressing drama than music. We may put Shakespeare's Macbeth on the couch, but not the overture to Verdi's Macbeth *(where the passions are already high). What makes a true opera composer is the ability to recognize the deep conflicts, and engage with them musically and dramatically from start to finish. In this, pacing is crucial. It is not enough to write a series of beautiful musical set-pieces around a plausible libretto – the problem, say, with Schubert's operas* Alfonso und Estrella *(1822/54) and* Fierrabras *(1823/97). A sense of theatre is all. In turn, knowledge of psychoanalysis has helped shape libretti, notably Hofmannsthal's for Strauss's* Elektra *(1909), (Marie) Pappenheim's for Schoenberg's* Erwartung *(1924), or Neveux's for Martinů's* Juliette ou* la clé des songes (Juliette or the Key to Dreams) *(1938).* [4] *It is only a rare opera composer who 'does not do psychology'.* [5]

In recent years critics and scholars in the arts have put psychoanalysis under pressure: they claim that its propositions are largely untested, and, comparable insights can be achieved through historical understanding – so why complicate the mix? This is not the place to argue the case for or against. But the scepticism does make it imperative for the aficionados of applied psychology to offer interpretations that are well grounded and clearly argued. For the creator, there is the equivalent dual challenge of balancing outer form with inner process (psychological form). This section identifies situations in opera where there are evidently issues to be addressed.

The first entry began as a talk to the North London Collegiate School for Girls (the invitation came from the pupils). It unpacks just one of Freud's essays in light of instinct theory, and relates its findings to operatic design. In effect, it is an exercise in the interpretation of signs. The second entry traces different kinds of mental disorder – neuroses – in four characters from Wagner's Ring *cycle. Here I interpret neurosis classically, as the unresolved conflict between defence and wish. I also suggest a link to Wagner's creative personality. The third entry stays with Wagner and crosses a phrase from the fifteenth-century ballad on Danheüser (Tannhäuser), 'Maria, mother, pure maid', with the title of a modern psychoanalytic study by Estela V. Welldon, 'Mother, Madonna, Whore'. Welldon's subtitle refers to 'idealization and denigration', and it is Tannhäuser's polarized mental disorder that drives the opera. (Elisabeth may be his saintly, self-sacrificing redeemer, but she too has her own problems: we first meet her coming out of a severe depression.) The fourth entry addresses loss, a key psychological topic in the work of Freud, Klein, Bowlby and countless others. It questions how much credence may be attached to the popular notion that father-daughter relationships were special to Verdi, and concludes that if, in the 'Piave works,' there is any relationship, it involves father, daughter and a dead mother (in early life Verdi himself had lost both a wife and a daughter). Here, the absent figure – a dramatic stereotype – assumes a special significance. The final entry comes out of a meeting of the British Psychoanalytic Society, at which I was joined by various psychoanalysts and therapists. The aim was to probe the character of Rigoletto. The entry is in two parts: the first offers some professional diagnoses, and the second outlines the musical processes Verdi devised to articulate the psychodynamics involved (the technical knowledge required of the reader here is small).*

Modern directors have often seized on the psychological aspects of an opera at the expense of the circumstantial ones. Yet it is the tension between outer duty and inner wish that is the subject of so many works (power, money and sex being at the root of most operatic evils). It is thus essential to project both aspects in any production.

Notes

1   In Mozart's *La clemenza di Tito* (1791) the core conflict lies between Tito's innate benevolence and Sesto's innate fidelity, virtues put to the ultimate test by circumstance. The libretto is adapted from one by Pietro Metastasio.

2   The most extraordinary example of a tragedy with a happy ending is Rameau's *Hippolyte et Aricie* (1733). The librettist Simon-Joseph Pellegrin replaces the grim close of his sources, Euripides's *Hippolytus* and Racine's *Phèdre*, with a dance for the eponymous young lovers to the *air* of a nightingale sung by a shepherdess.

3   A recent 'psychiatric report', and possibly the first, is: John Cordingly, *Disordered Heroes in Opera*, ed. Claire Seymour, London: Plumbago, 2015.

4   I have not included an entry on *Elektra* (1909), although I have written on the piece three times (as listed in the Bibliography). See in particular my 'Hard Acts Hard to Follow' in: *A Hard Act to Follow: the Shadow of the Parent*, ed. Jonathan Burke, London: Karnac, 2018 (forthcoming at the time of writing). The relation of theatre to psychology from Zola, Strindberg, Jarry and Artaud to the present day (with reference to Aristotle, Freud and Lacan) is described in: Fintan Walsh, *Theatre and Therapy*, Houndmills (Basingstoke): Palgrave Macmillan, 2013. My review of Aribert Reimann's *Ein Traumspiel* (1965) [derived from August Strindberg's seminal *A Dream Play* (1902)] appeared in the *Times Literary Supplement*, 3 March 1989, p. 233.

5   These are the words of Harrison Birtwistle. He and I were discussing why, in *The Mask of Orpheus* (1986), Orpheus does not look back (psychologically a supreme 'moment that matters'). I described his stage works as 'dramatic lyrics' rather than 'operas', a description he was happy to 'buy'.

1 *Freud and Opera*

Citations from (in order): Jacques Offenbach: *La Belle Hélène*;
Jacopo Peri: *L'Euridice*; Richard Wagner: *Lohengrin* and *Siegfried*;
Giuseppe Verdi: *Aida*; Pyotr Il'yich Tchaikovsky: *The Queen of Spades*;
Benjamin Britten: *Billy Budd*; Georges Bizet: *Carmen*

Talk to the North London Collegiate School for Girls, Edgware, 25 January 2007

1 *Freud's 'Motive of Casket-choice'*

There is something a bit special in talking about Sigmund Freud here in North London: for it was an Englishman, Ernest Jones, who rescued the 'father of psychoanalysis' from Vienna and brought him here in the dark days of the late 1930s; and for the last months of his life he lived in a house in Maresfield Gardens, which is not so far away – the house is now the Freud Museum. What's more, there has always been an intelligent British interest in Freud. At the end of an essay on 'Psychology and Art Today' written back in 1935, the poet W. H. Auden looked to psychoanalysis for the *understanding* it can bring. Freud, he said, had been 'misappropriated by the irrationalists eager to escape their conscience'; rather, it was to the gentle 'voice of reason' that the man directs us.[1] On the other hand, we are no longer living in the 1930s and much has happened since Auden. The psychoanalytic movement has split into factions – Carl Jung's defection was an early major blow – and even Freudians continue to revise their leader's findings. Indeed, the most outspoken critics of our time have asked bluntly, 'Do we need the unconscious at all?' They take heart from the words of the French scholar Gilles Deleuze, who maintains that

> A schizophrenic out for a walk is a better model than a neurotic lying on the couch.[2]

Jung, in fact, thought there was *no* part for psychoanalysis to play in the arts, beyond addressing the psychopathology of creators, performers and listeners – that is to say, the individual psychic tensions that do not strictly belong to the collective nature of a work of art. And for our part, we have to accept that Freud had very little interest in music: his biographer mentions a handful of operas and no more.[3] Has he really anything to teach us as musicians, we ask? Isn't talking about psychoanalysis and music just a pose, and a rather dated one at that? Seventy years on from Auden, we have a cause to defend rather than advance.

Now, despite all this, I am taking as my starting point a fairly early essay of Freud's written around 1913 to show how his ideas can, in fact, stand the test of time. Freud called the essay *Das Motiv der Kästchenwahl*, which means literally, 'The Motif of the Casket-choice'. In the first English translation, it appeared as 'The Theme of Three Caskets'; I myself would call it, 'Shakespeare and the *Rule of Three*'.[4] A note attached to the essay in the Penguin edition shows that back in 1913 Freud connected the paper 'with his own three daughters'. The reasons for this will become obvious.

In the best psychoanalytic traditions, I must also declare an interest of my own. When the Freud Museum was launched at the Camden Town Hall in 1986, there were a number of talks by eminent Freudians. The one I remember best focussed on this very essay. So my talk today is a celebration and critical *re-enactment* of that event.

In the essay, Freud takes two scenes from Shakespeare: one from a comedy, *The Merchant of Venice*, the other from a tragedy, *King Lear*. In the first

> The fair and wise Portia is bound at her father's bidding to take as her husband only that one of the suitors who chooses the right casket from among the three before him. The three caskets are gold, silver and lead: the right casket is the one that contains her portrait.

The first two suitors choose gold and silver respectively – and fail. The third chooses lead – and wins. He is Portia's adored Bassanio. Caskets, Freud notes, are like 'coffers, boxes, cases, baskets, and so on' in representing women: they all harbour an enclosed space (a womb). So, by 'symbolic substitutions' of the caskets, each suitor is really choosing 'between three women'. In the second

> The old King Lear resolves to divide his kingdom while he is still alive among his three daughters, in proportion to the amount of love that each expresses for him. The two elder ones, Goneril and Regan, exhaust themselves in asseverations and laudations of their love for him; the third, Cordelia, refuses to do so. He should have recognized the unassuming, speechless love of his third daughter and rewarded it, but he does not recognize it. He disowns Cordelia, and divides the kingdom between the other two, to his own and the general ruin.

Once again, a man chooses between three women and determines a fate which it is the course of the drama to reveal.

Let us put these examples together. In the first scene Bassanio *chooses* the third, in the second scene Lear *rejects* the third. In both cases the third is conspicuous for being dull or silent – that is to say, leaden or inarticulate.

What do we make of this? We note that the action occurs in a well-defined context; that this context is a ritual; that the ritual takes various forms, such as choosing or testing; that when it reaches the third in a row there is a change, or *reversal*; that there is *irony* in the choice – dullness may conceal joy, silence may be articulate; that the progression is dramatically crucial; that high emotion (or affect) is engaged; and that the outcome is bound up with a sense of *genre* – whether comedy, tragedy or whatever. Taken together, then, these attributes define what I shall call the *rule of three*. This *rule* is a model that we can rediscover in other contexts than Shakespeare, including those that involve music, above all opera.

Before we go on, though, a word of warning. The model must be distinguished from other significant groups of three in which there is no reversal, no dramatic intent. At the Olympic Games, for example, the winner of a bronze medal merely stands alongside the winners of the gold and silver medals: there is no suggestion of a change of fortune, of a black spot behind the third medal – indeed, the medals could be awarded in any order. In such a case we refer merely to a *rite of three*. Later we shall see how artists 'play' with this distinction between *rule* and *rite*.

Now, Freud gives other examples of the *rule of three*, starting with the shy Cinderella and her brash pair of sisters. We are hardly surprised: fairy-tale, legend and myth are the home of magic and ritual. But with two of the examples he takes us towards music. The first comes from the operetta *La Belle Hélène* (1864) by Jacques Offenbach. Here Paris describes (in passing) how, in the 'Judgement of Paris', he had to give the golden apple to one of three women, Hera, Athena or Aphrodite. He chooses Aphrodite. He sings,

> The third, ah!, the third …
> The third says nothing.
> All the same she has won the prize …

Freud calls this treatment 'modern'. For he points out that Aphrodite's peculiarity is 'dumbness'; that we know from dreams that dumbness is 'a common representation of death'; and that the silent woman thus stands for the Goddess of Death. Paris has not chosen quite what he thinks. We shall return to this point shortly. (In the ancient version of the story, of course, Aphrodite promises Paris the love of the world's most beautiful woman, Helen. Helen, though, is already the wife of Menelaus, and the fulfilment of the promise sets off the Trojan War.)[5]

The second example is indirect. Freud refers to the three Norns, whom we know from the opening of Richard Wagner's *Twilight of the Gods* (*Götterdämmerung*, 1876), the last part of *The Ring of the Nibelungs*, though he never actually mentions Wagner. The Norns, or Fates, derive from three Moerae, who 'were closely related' to the three Graces and the three Horae – the Seasons, of which antiquity knew only spring, summer and winter. On the one hand, the Horae reflect the inexorable workings of time as we see them in Nature. On the other hand, the Moerae, like the Norns, were concerned with 'the ordering of human life' – and stood for 'what was', 'what is' and 'what shall be'. Freud named the three spinners – the Norns – as Clotho, Lachesis and Atropos. Clotho represented the order of things, Lachesis the accidental that interacts with the order, and Atropos, the 'ineluctable', or Death. Thus the third Norn in *Twilight of the Gods* is the deathly Atropos and it is she who makes a fatal and accurate prediction when she sings:

> When the timber blazes
> Brightly in the sacred fire,
> When its embers singe
> The glittering hall with their searing heat,
> The downfall of the immortal gods
> Will dawn for all eternity.[6]

But at this point we sense an objection. In *La Belle Hélène* Paris chose the Goddess of Love. But what had she really to do with Death? In *Twilight of the Gods*, the immortals die, but Brünnhilde, a child of the gods, performs a 'world-redeeming act of love' and leaps into the flames on the back of her horse. Love faces down death. Is there not a contradiction here? Freud's answer would be that in psychoanalysis such extremes are linked. For humans may choose to *deny* Death by asserting its *opposite*, Love. And in asserting the Goddess of Love, they choose a figure touched by the same eternal force as Death. That is to say, humans replace the ineluctable (Death) with its most desirable alternative (Love). Such use of a *pair of opposites* is fundamental to Freudian thought in general, and essential to how we approach dramatic art.[7]

In fact, we already find this duality in the second opera ever written. This was *L'Euridice*, composed by Jacopo Peri in 1600 to a text by Ottavio Rinuccini. The story derives loosely from Ovid's *Metamorphoses* (book 10). The demi-god Orpheus learns that his future bride Euridice has been mortally wounded by a snake. As he cannot accept her death, he vows to descend into the underworld and get her back. As he prepares for the journey, the skies open and Venus comes down on a chariot. She will accompany him on his quest. Once they are in the underworld, Orpheus uses his uncanny gift of song to persuade Pluto to release Euridice. Pluto complies. Orpheus and Euridice return to the land of living and the opera ends with universal joy and wonder. Now this, of course, is a 'fantasy of denial': the impossible has happened, Death itself has been conquered by an exceptional form of speech – fine singing. Moreover, it is a Renaissance conceit: nothing of the kind happens in the classics, and in later operas Orpheus won't always have it that easy. The action, though, neatly constellates Freud's perception of the underlying connection between Love and Death, or, in his terms, between Eros and Thanatos.

Freud also reflects on the *act of choice* itself. In *La Belle Hélène* Paris appeared free to give the golden apple to whichever woman he wanted. But in truth there is *no* free will. 'A choice is made,' writes Freud, 'where in reality there is obedience to a compulsion.' However unwittingly, Paris submitted to ineluctable destiny. He *compulsively* tried to avoid order and conflict by embracing love. In Wagner's *Ring*, too, there was a tension between those who *knew* that the entire action is preordained – the Norns (or Fates) – and those who acted as if they were free to do as they please – above all Siegfried and Brünnhilde. This paradox has been noted by critics, notably by Theodor Adorno.[8] More paradoxically still, even where a figure knows he is doomed, he may still act as if he was free. This is the situation of Wotan in the last act of *Siegfried* (even though Wotan is head of the gods, he is also all-too-human).

All of this is to say, then, that when a character appears to choose freely from a group of three in a drama, a fairy-tale or an opera, he or she is driven unconsciously by the play of the forces of Love and Death and the choice, according to the rule of three, is inevitable. For this reason Freud also argued that whatever or whoever is eventually chosen has something peculiar about them, something abnormal; and this is a point we shall amplify as we turn to opera. For music itself is more adept than words or actions at giving credence to the peculiar and abnormal – or as Freud called it, the 'uncanny'.

2 Wagner's 'Lohengrin'

As I have said already, Freud wrote his essay around 1913. Yet when we look at opera before then, it is hard to believe that creative artists didn't already understand the *rule of three*, or didn't assume the same understanding in their audiences. Let me give a few brief examples from well-known works.

In Wagner's *Lohengrin* (1850), Elsa of Brabant is falsely accused of murdering her brother. The King orders her to defend herself against her accusers. Like many Wagnerian heroines, Elsa is vulnerable and nervous: Thomas Mann saw her as a type given to 'lofty hysteria'.[9] Under pressure, she describes a vision she has had of a saviour knight. Twice trumpeters summon the knight. Twice nothing happens. There is silence. For the third time, Elsa takes the matter into her own hands. She prays. And now, eerily, the knight arrives, drawn in a boat by a swan. There is huge excitement. The knight – Lohengrin – offers to defend Elsa, and in the following combat gains victory. The situation has been utterly reversed. Lohengrin's haunting music is just as Freud would have wished: it has an 'uncanny' orchestral sheen, it floats between two keys with unearthly effect, and its lines glide like the magical swan itself. More still, Lohengrin is invested with the distinctive peculiarity associated with all other 'thirds' in our group of three. He agrees to protect Elsa on the strict condition that she never asks his name. On this issue she must be *silent*. Elsa accepts. She and Lohengrin soon marry. Love alone will defend her against mortal threat. At the same time the knight's forbidden question marks the crack in the system that invites us, in

Freud's words, 'to guess at what lies beneath'. The crack comes to the fore on the wedding night. Elsa complains that her relationship with Lohengrin is one-sided; how can it develop if she has no way of addressing him?, she asks (after all, he can call her 'Elsa'). She becomes insistent. Eventually Lohengrin buckles, the marriage collapses there and then, and after some political turmoil the knight returns to the distant land from which he hailed. Elsa is distraught and dies. The only consolation is that Lohengrin's swan turns into her lost brother, the lawful protector of Brabant. Order is restored; Elsa has not died in vain; Love has conquered.

This working-through of the *rule of three* with its classical inversion of Love and Death is fascinating for the double standard we as audience bring to Elsa. On the one hand she pays heavily for her disobedience: she cannot sustain the *fantasy* of Love she has conjured up. On the other hand, by destroying the fantasy she confronts the *reality* of Death. This action releases her into making, however unwittingly, the ineluctable self-sacrifice necessary to restore order to Brabant – that is to say, into engaging a higher form of love. Where she *fails* in fantasy she *succeeds* in reality. If we are still uncertain where our own judgement stands, *for* Elsa or *against*, it is because art itself asks two things of us. As Auden put it, we need both

> escape-art, for man needs escape as he needs food and deep sleep, and parable-art, that art which shall teach man to unlearn hatred and learn love.[10]

We now add this pair of opposites, escape and parable, to our own understanding of Freud's *rule of three*.

3 Wagner's 'Siegfried', Verdi's 'Aida', Tchaikovsky's 'The Queen of Spades', Britten's 'Billy Budd'

So far, we have seen how in opera the *rule of three* can release startling and uncanny music. It does so time and again because it embodies a platonic 'Idea': that is to say, we may know the *rule* through countless instances, but no one instance will be wholly representative. So I want to devote the rest of this talk to further examples. In doing so, I shall introduce two more issues: how do dramatic characters understand and even exploit the workings of the *rule*? And how does an artist exploit the audience's expectations of the *rule*?

Let us go back to Wagner's *Ring*, this time to the first act of *Siegfried* (1876). Two characters are locked in deadly rivalry: Mime, a sly dwarf, and Wotan, whom we already know as head of the gods. Alone in the forest Mime is raising the young Siegfried until he is strong enough to kill the dragon that guards the gold: whoever wins the gold will rule the world. Unsurprisingly,

Wotan too has his eye on the hoard. Here the conversation takes the form of a ritual. Mime wants to be rid of the god but Wotan insists on a 'wager of wits'. Wotan decrees that both must answer three questions correctly: whoever fails forfeits his head. Mime puts his three questions to Wotan, all of which the god answers easily. Wotan nevertheless notes that Mime has avoided asking any question that really matters to him. Mime, that is to say, has treated the ritual as mere *rite*, though Wotan can understand the *suppression* involved. Next it is Wotan's turn. Mime answers the first two questions easily enough. But then comes the third question. 'Who will forge the sword that will slay the dragon?' asks Wotan. Mime leaps up in terror to suddenly rapid music. He has no idea; he has himself tried and failed repeatedly. Wotan is unsparing: 'That is the question you could and should have asked,' he says to the dwarf, 'in due course I shall have your head.' Wotan leaves. To extraordinary music Mime has a panic-attack: he believes the fearful dragon is actually racing towards him. In this scene, therefore, Wotan has knowingly played the *rule of three* – and won; Mime has *positively* chosen not to play it – and lost.

The next instance shows an opera's authors exploiting the audience's expectations. In the last act of Giuseppe Verdi's *Aida* (1871), a heroic young captain, Radames, is brought before the priests, realistically accused of treason. Twice the High Priest Ramfis calls 'Radames! Radames! Radames!' and delivers the charge. 'Defend yourself!' he cries. Radames remains silent. Ramfis draws the inevitable conclusion: 'He is silent: a traitor!' Cast and audience now draw their breath. What will happen on the third occasion? Can Radames be saved? 'Radames! Radames! Radames!' calls Ramfis, and again accuses him of treachery: 'Defend Yourself!' But still there is no reply. 'He is silent: a traitor!' concludes Ramfis, now for the last time. Everyone – including the audience – is shocked. What seemed to have begun as a *rule of three*, with the hope of a life-saving reversal, has revealed itself as a *rite of three*, with the certainty of death. The music for each of the three calls is in effect the same, only rising a semitone each time as tension mounts. The silent Radames is duly condemned to death and in the final scene is buried alive. When we find that the adoring and loyal Aida has joined him underground in Death, we recognize her as an emissary of Love.

Exactly the opposite happens in Tchaikovsky's *The Queen of Spades* (1890). The Byronic hero Hermann is fascinated by gaming and longs to learn the secret of success at cards famously guarded by an old Countess. He craves untold wealth. This is his opportunity. Using the old woman's ward Lisa as a go-between, he gains access to the Countess's bedroom; yet when the Countess sees Hermann she dies of fright. Later, however, she returns by night as a ghost. She enjoins him to marry Lisa and reveals the secret of success. There are three cards that have to be played in succession: three, seven, ace. Hermann races off to the gambling den. On the way, he meets his beloved Lisa. But Lisa gives up all hope for him and commits suicide. The scholar Richard Taruskin now takes up the story:

> Hermann arrives, makes straight for the gaming table … and places an unheard-of 40,000-ruble bet. It is reluctantly accepted; his 'three' wins as per formula. He doubles; his 'seven' wins. Before staking his last card … Hermann sings a maniacal song whose incipit could serve as the opera's epigraph ('What is our life? A game!'); finally his 'ace' turns out to be the Queen of Spades, which – he is certain – looks back at him sarcastically with the Countess's face. Mad, he stabs himself. [He has lost all, and dies.] [11]

The uncanny Countess thus seeks revenge from beyond the grave for the death of Lisa and acts in effect as the Goddess of Love: it is no surprise to Freudians that the Countess was once known as the Muscovite Venus. In this case, the closing *rule of three* reverses the earlier *rite of three* heard in the incantation of the secret of the three cards as revealed by the dead Countess: three, seven, ace; three seven, ace … It is a *rite* in which Hermann appears to have had unswerving confidence. Yet we understand that in committing himself to *rite* while disregarding the attached condition – of marrying Lisa – he had in fact chosen *rule*. Here, *rite* involves crime, *rule* punishment.

For a modern instance, we turn to Benjamin Britten's grand opera *Billy Budd* (1951). This is based on a story by Herman Melville. Within the action (as well as in the framing Prologue and Epilogue) the characters constantly probe the meaning of the events in which they are caught. Literally and metaphorically, they are all 'at sea' in difficult times: the opera is set on a British man-of-war in the tense years following the French Revolution and rumours of mutiny are rife. In the first act, three men are press-ganged into the crew. As they are forced aboard they are interviewed one at a time by the sadistic master-of-arms, John Claggart, in the presence of three officers. First is Red Whiskers, a butcher. He is of 'little use' and is dispatched to the forepeak. Second is Arthur Jones, a weaver. He too is 'nothing special' and is again dispatched to the forepeak. Now comes the third, Billy Budd, a significantly homeless able seaman. He is uncannily good-looking. Claggart is transfixed: 'A find in a thousand,' he gasps, '… a beauty, a jewel … there are no more like him.' However, when Billy tries to explain his origin, he stammers. This is his Freudian peculiarity of speech. He recovers quickly enough and the interview proceeds. He is posted to the foretop, and 'overcompensates' for his lapse by bursting into an exultant aria 'Billy Budd, king of the birds'. He may stammer and fall silent, but he can really *sing*. Now all of this fulfils the *rule of three* to the letter. And as the opera unfolds it comes as no surprise that, although Billy is an unqualified force for the good, his stammer leads him to strike the master-at-arms who accuses him falsely. John Claggart falls dead. A court martial follows. Billy is found guilty and hung before the assembled crew. This 'beauty', who excites the love of all, has turned out to be an apostle of Death. What is unusual in this version of the *rule* is the knowing comment of the Sailing Master when Billy first stammers: 'There is always some flaw in them, always something.' That is to say, Billy is demythologized at the very moment he is hailed as mythic. It is as if by 1797 the crew had already read their Freud.

4 Bizet's 'Carmen'

My last example is the most fascinating. It comes from *Carmen* (1875) by Georges Bizet, the work held up by Friedrich Nietzsche in his attempt to face down Wagner. Here the treatment is more complex, and demonstrates Auden's claim that in works of art Freudian psychology changes our perception of 'space and time'.[12] To understand the *rule* we now have to put together two passages that form a stark contrast in their setting – their space – and are dramatically widely separated in time.

The first passage comes near the start of Act One. We see a busy square in Seville with a guard-house on the left. When Carmen makes her first appearance she launches at once into her famous Habanera. It distils what she believes to be her outlook on love. There are two verses, of which the first goes like this:

> Love is a rebel bird
> That no-one can tame
> And indeed it's in vain we call to her
> If she's not minded to play our game.
> Nothing persuades her, threat or plea:
> One man speaks well, the other is silent,
> But it's 'the other' whom I prefer,
> He's said nothing, but all the same he pleases me.
> Love, love, love, love!

To this she adds a refrain:

> Love is the child of bohemia
> It has never, never been bound by law,
> If you don't love me, I'll love you,
> But if I love you, take care!

Now, we have learnt from Freud that silent ones, like Cordelia, spell doom; and when Carmen claims to prefer the 'silent other', and warns the chosen to be on guard, we realize that unwittingly she is choosing Death. In the same way, the music for the verses may be outwardly exotic and titillating: but the key of D minor and its sinking chromatic lines tell us that inwardly it may be preoccupied with suffering. The suffering, moreover, is proudly concealed by the D major of the catchy refrain. Unsurprisingly, the refrain extols Love.

Carmen thus claims to be free when in fact she's bound. Her disdain is too good to be true. Indeed, she knows what kind of person she will choose *even before she meets him*: in psychoanalytic terms, she has a readiness (*Bereitschaft*) for a certain kind of 'object choice'. When in due course she ignores the young men who thrust themselves at her, and rather sets eyes on a silent, preoccupied soldier, the die is cast. The music changes tone. A darkly expressive theme emerges in the cellos. It doesn't close but dissolves on an ambiguous diminished harmony. Silence follows. We all hold our breath. Carmen throws a flower at the soldier – his name is Don José – and runs away. She has chosen flirtatiously, yet the music is laden with doom. The other women gather round the soldier and laughingly repeat Carmen's refrain. However, it is Carmen's choice of José that launches the drama, a case of Aristotelian *peripeteia*.

But what has this to do with the *rule of three*? True, Carmen has made a choice, the chosen one is silent, and the music reverses from light to dark. But what of the first two elements in the chain? Where are they? How can the choice of José be a third when there has been no first or second?

In fact, we have to wait until Act Three for an answer. The setting is no longer Seville, but a desolate and rocky spot far from the town. Carmen has persuaded Don José to abandon the army for the gypsy way of life. But she is already tired of him: indeed, she will take a new lover, Escamillo, a priapic toreador. Yet she cannot shake off José and everything he entails. Rather the choice strikes back, as the *rule of three* is now enacted in a famous ensemble for a trio of women. The three women are in effect gypsies who can read fate in their cards. Indeed, their trust in the cards is absolute. Here the vocal casting is crucial. The first two women are bright sopranos – Frasquita and Mercédès; but the third is a husky mezzo-soprano – and this is Carmen. That is to say, Carmen's voice is lower than that of the others; it already has one foot in the shades. Frasquita and Mercédès lay out the cards: three to the left, three to the right, four above and four below. These two have nothing to fear: they know the game well. To playful music they ask in turn, which of their lovers will betray them, which will be true? The cards respond. Mercédès's man will be youthful and ardent, a pirate who perches her on his horse – in other words, a kind of Byronic hero. On the other hand, Frasquita's man will be old and rich: he will soon die and leave her his fortune. Both women rejoice: they will acquire wealth by stealth. (Notice that as the first two elements in this *rule* they form a *contrast-pair*.) They cut the pack again. Now it is Carmen's turn – and she is the third in the chain. As she turns up the cards anxiety grips her: in the orchestra her motif sounds to diminished harmony, first very quiet (*pianissimo*) and then very loudly (*fortissimo*). 'Diamonds! Spades!' she gasps into empty space. There is a portentous silence. Again we hear her motif; and then she interprets the cards. They refer to herself and José. She sings:

> Death! I've understood it well! First for me, then for him – for both of us, death!

Now to Freudians this reversal comes as no surprise: Death, as we have seen, was implicit from the beginning. But how does Carmen react to the recognition that is now forced upon her (Aristotle's *anagnorisis*)? At first, she suffers: there is a great stab in the orchestra (Aristotle's *pathos*). But then, as the music slips into F minor, the key traditionally associated with death, she finds a dignity to match that of any expiring hero. Her *andante* falls into two short waves followed by a long wave, rising from very quiet to very loud – from *pianissimo* to *fortissimo*. There is a studied artlessness to her singing: it is syllabic, unadorned, and for the most part moves by intervals of a step; the rhythm of the accompaniment is inexorable. That is to say, she is utterly passive before Fate. She finds she has *no* freedom after all:

> In vain to try and avoid the bitter reply [of the cards]
> In vain you might shuffle them,
> That will do you no good,
> The cards are sincere and will tell no lies.

After this Carmen turns up card after card: 'Again! Again! Always Death!' she gasps. And she continues to repeat these words throughout the third and last part of the trio, as Frasquita and Mercédès resume their duet oblivious of their companion. The result is music that enshrines the very spirit of the *rule of three*: the two upper voices are bright and cheerful, the third voice – Carmen's – sinks beneath its burden of doom. The effect unites the genres: it is as if comedy and tragedy unfold as one. And, of course, the cards are right: in the last act Carmen and José die exactly as predicted.[13]

There are many other cases of the *rule of three* I should like to consider,[14] along with examples of the *rite of three* – those groups where there is no expectation of reversal.[15] But I must draw to a close. At the start of this talk we learnt how Auden upheld the pursuit of *reason* as the task of psychoanalysis. And it is the reason behind the *rule of three* I have tried to bring to light. For opera is a two-headed beast. With one head it celebrates the mysteries of the grand passions; with the other it analyses their workings forensically. In his day Freud might have been Auden's best companion at the opera; were he still with us, he would certainly be ours.

Notes

Source: 'Sigmund Freud, the "Rule of Three" and Opera', talk to the North London Collegiate School for Girls, Edgware, 25 January 2007. A different version was given as a colloquium at King's College London in March 2009.

1   See: 'Art and Psychology Today' (1935), *The English Auden. Poems, Essays, & Dramatic Writings, 1927-39 by W. H. Auden*, ed. Edward Mendelson, London: Faber and Faber, 1977, pp. 332-42, and especially pp. 341-2. '*Die Stimme der Vernunft ist leise*' ('the voice of reason is gentle') is the inscription on Freud's tombstone in Vienna.

2   Gilles Deleuze and Felix Guattari, *Anti-oedipus* (1972), London: Continuum, 1984, p. 2.

3   See: Peter Gay, *Freud. A Life for Our Time*, London: Dent, 1988, p. 168. Gay writes that Freud 'made a point of proclaiming his ignorance in musical matters and admitted he could not carry a tune. ... But he did enjoy opera, or, rather, some operas. His daughters, searching their memories, could come up with five: Mozart's *Don Giovanni*, *The Marriage of Figaro* and *The Magic Flute*; Bizet's *Carmen*; and Wagner's *Meistersinger*.'

4   Sigmund Freud, 'The Theme of the Three Caskets', *Art and Literature*, The Penguin Freud Library, vol. 14, London: Penguin Books, 1990, pp. 233-47. Since giving this talk I have read the chapter on 'The Rule of Three' in: Christopher Booker, *The Seven Basic Plots. Why We Tell Stories*, London: Continuum, 2004, pp. 229-35. Booker does not mention Freud or Freudian process, but confines himself to folk-tales and literature. From these he draws up four categories: (i) the 'simple' or 'cumulative three' [equivalent to my 'rite of three'] (ii) the 'progressive' or 'ascending three', where each element is stronger than the previous one [in a prize ceremony, say, the order is often 3rd, 2nd, 1st,, though this can easily be reversed into a 'descending three'] (iii) the 'contrasting' or 'double-negative' three, where the first two elements are wrong and only the third is right [the recruiting scene, say, in Act One of Britten's *Billy Budd*)] (iv) the 'dialectical three', where the first two elements are 'wrong' in different ways and only the third is right [as is the case with the trio from *Carmen* described in the last part of this talk]. Booker interestingly contrasts 'the rule of three' as *process* with the 'completion' achieved by groups of two (a man-woman pair, say) or four (two such pairs) – D'Artagnan, say, finally becomes 'the fourth musketeer'. The unification of man and woman is indeed an emblem of stability, the two-ness thus representing an irreducible one-ness. [When we witness the death of a hero, we are sad because such oneness is thwarted; when we witness the death of both hero and heroine, we derive some perverse satisfaction that the two have been united, albeit in extinction.]

5   Rubens's painting of *The Judgement of Paris* (c. 1632-5) hangs in the National Gallery, London. Paris is watched by Hermes, or Mercury, as he chooses between the three women (who are described by their Roman names): Minerva (with her owl and her armour), Juno (with her peacock) and Venus (with Cupid). As Paris makes his choice, the Fury of War appears in the sky as a portent. The immortals may thus be aware of the tragedy the future holds; only the mortal, Paris, seems innocent.

6   *Wagner's Ring of the Nibelung. A Companion*, trans. Stewart Spencer, [London]: Thames and Hudson, 1993, p. 282. The German reads: 'Brennt das Holz heilig brünstig und hell, sengt die Gluth sehrend den glänzenden Saal: der ewigen Götter Ende dämmert ewig da auf.'

7   Cf. J. Laplanche and J.-B. Pontalis, 'Pair of Opposites', *The Language of Psychoanalysis*, London: Karnac Books, 1988, p. 295. The authors assert that a pair of opposites is

irreducible and stands 'at the root of all conflict', representing 'the motor of any dialectic'.

8 Theodor Adorno, *In Search of Wagner* (1952), n.p. [UK]: New Left Books, 1974.

9 Thomas Mann, 'The Sorrows and Grandeur of Richard Wagner' (1933), *Pro and Contra Wagner*, London: Faber and Faber, 1985, pp. 91-148.

10 W. H. Auden, 1935/77, pp. 341-2.

11 Richard Taruskin, '*Queen of Spades, The*', *The New Grove Dictionary of Opera*, ed. Stanley Sadie, London: Macmillan, 1992, Vol. 3, p. 1197.

12 W. H. Auden, 1977, p. 341.

13 The passage is described in: Theodor Adorno, 'Fantasia sopra *Carmen*', *Quasi una fantasia*, trans. Rodney Livingstone, London: Verso 1992/94, pp. 53-64. The work endorses and lays bare 'The Force of Destiny'. Indeed, one remembers a remark of Freud's at the beginning of his essay on Wilhelm Jensen's story 'Gradiva', itself written in 1903: '[I have] ventured, in the face of the reproaches of strict science, to become a partisan of antiquity and superstition.' (Freud, 1985, p. 33.) That is to say, Freud faces up to the fatal instinct, rather than dismisses it. For her part Carmen never seeks to evade death, even when towards the end of the opera she is warned about the presence of Don José. Indeed, she appears to collude in her predicted fate, rather like Riccardo in Verdi's *Un ballo in maschera* (another work fascinating for its handling of the *rule*). In this regard Carmen behaves differently from the two characters in Shakespeare, Bassanio and Lear, who make the choices and decisions that set off the action: she is *chosen*.

14 Other operatic examples of the *rule of three* include: the refusal of Puccini's convent sister Suor Angelica to admit to desire when she is the third of three nuns asked to confess (the other two yearn for the lambing season and succulent fruit): not surprisingly the work ends with her suicide; the roll call of 12 prostitutes from Puccini's *Manon Lescaut*, in which Manon is the third (with the others pushed into the background): when she and her lover board a ship for the New World, the vessel turns out to be a ship of death, the land is arid, and Manon dies there; the three riddles in Puccini's *Turandot* with a closing reversal, this time from death to love; and the three final bequests in Puccini's *Gianni Schicchi* that shock us with their ineluctable ceremony in favour of Schicchi. There is the crucial Pushkin-esque card game with the Devil in Stravinsky's *The Rake's Progress*, with a patterning of the language that itself moves in a *rule of three* (the card game is itself similar to that in Stravinsky's *L'Histoire du soldat*); before that the three lots in the auction scene wittily endorse Freud's perception that the third in the rule may involve a peculiarity of speech (Baba the Turk bursts from silence into song). There are two sets of three men in Berg's *Lulu*, where prostituted love inverts into a remorseless love-death. And in Mozart's *Don Giovanni*, there are the three tunes played at the banquet the Don is invited to attend, when the third turns out to be by Mozart himself – a witty use of the *rule of three*, where Death is merely waiting in the wings. The use of the *rule of three* throughout Wagner's oeuvre is pervasive, as has already been indicated: it is discussed further in the entry on 'Colloquy' in Part Five of this book. Outside opera there are countless other examples of rules and rites: I merely draw attention to their use in three films by Ingmar Bergman, *So Close to Life* (1958), *The Magician* (1958) and *The Virgin Spring* (1960).

15 Notably in Mozart's *Die Zauberflöte* (1791) and Harrison Birtwistle's *The Mask of Orpheus* (1986), where such *rites* are ubiquitous.

2   On Neurotics

Richard Wagner: *Der Ring des Nibelungen*

W. H. Auden once remarked that 'Wagner has to be listened to in a very particular way'.[1] For what the composer offers are 'devastatingly accurate portraits of neurotics, with all the attractions [that] make people become neurotic'; 'his genius was that he often gets you to admire [these] people', whereas in life one couldn't 'really admire Siegfried very much' (because of his 'low IQ');[2] on the other hand, he found that Wagner could get 'too close' to a subject, especially in the first act of *Siegfried* where the relationship of the hero and Mime is downright 'embarrassing'; and in *Die Meistersinger* where the severity of the treatment of Sixtus Beckmesser amounts to a downright artistic mistake. His own favourite part of the *Ring*, he added, was *Die Walküre* – which indeed pushes each of its characters to his or her limit.

Auden's insights, in fact, open the door to a very particular listening to the *Ring*. They remind us that the impulse behind Wagner's drive to push back operatic convention in favour of musico-dramatic process was to probe the psychopathology of eminently human figures caught in a web of mythic enchantment, while continuing to promote a personal aesthetic rooted in German Romanticism. From this point of view, the most significant scene is precisely that between Siegfried and Mime: only the uncanny hero, a demi-god in all but name, can re-forge the shattered fragments of Siegmund's sword (Notung) after the duplicitous dwarf, consumed with delusions of grandeur, has shown he is unable to do it himself. Siegfried sings with an unprecedented cthonic abandon and we are more than happy to suspend our disbelief. Even in the next act, when Siegfried, empowered to understand Mime's lethal intent (psychoanalytically 'to listen to the unspoken'), murders the simpering dwarf, we watch and listen as if to a German fairy-tale. Our disbelief is still suspended: we markedly acquiesce in the extraordinary. Indeed, from the moment the cycle begins, with sonic eddies rising hypnotically from the bottom of the Rhine, it is as if we too are caught in a spell.

1   Sieglinde

'Neurosis' can come in many forms, and each of Wagner's neurotics has their own profile. At its most classical, neurosis can indicate an unresolved psychic conflict between defence and wish, a 'compromise' rooted in childhood. This is pre-eminently the case with Sieglinde. In the first act of *Die Walküre*, we meet a married woman of remarkable intuition, whose feeling for a stranger – who turns out to be her brother Siegmund – races ahead of their wary exchanges. This secret feeling is at first conveyed by the orchestra, which, as elsewhere, is only too happy to share with us what is concealed from the characters on stage. Over the act their mutual passion so burgeons that the curtain has to fall in haste as they begin to consummate their love (and conceive Siegfried). In the second and third acts Sieglinde is racked by guilt over her incestuous adultery (defence); in her sleep she re-enacts the trauma of her burning home and loss of family (childhood);[3] she awakens as her husband Hunding bears down on Siegmund (repetition of the trauma); and on learning that she is pregnant with Siegfried, she proclaims 'O hehrstes Wunder!' (O supreme wonder) with 'utmost emotion' (wish). Since this radiant 'Wunder' motif becomes the cycle's wordless musical epitaph, Sieglinde's 'admirable' neurosis takes us to the core of the work's aesthetic (of this more later).

2   Wotan

Wotan's neurosis, on the other hand, has a powerful narcissistic component that befits an arch-depressive. The narcissism, which reflects his omnipotence as head of the gods and is often displaced through colleagues, is a rich source of musical invention: we listen with delight to the rainbow bridge (*Das Rheingold*) and the fire that defends Brünnhilde (*Die Walküre*), just as we marvel at his invisible deeds of magic in Hunding's hut, in the forest (*Siegfried*) and even in the Gibichungs' hall (the last act of *Götterdämmerung*). Yet the depressive in him builds Valhalla as a fortress against fear: its theme may claim authority from its stately sarabande rhythm but, as the first musical interlude of *Das Rheingold* tells us, derives its contour from the despotic 'ring' motif. Wotan understands, realistically, that even this defence can only crumble. He has paid the giants for building Valhalla with ill-gotten gold, and Alberich's curse on him strikes home: indeed, its musical motif, first heard at the end of *Das Rheingold*, will haunt the cycle like a black spot, surfacing pitilessly to underscore each catastrophe. In his intimate exchange with Brünnhilde in the second act of *Die Walküre*, Wotan unleashes self-hate of extraordinary ferocity as he contemplates his ineluctably bleak future: 'Das Ende!' (The end!), he cries, 'Das Ende!' Even more awesome is his fury when he countermands Brünnhilde's rebellious support for Siegmund: first he destroys his doomed son and then pursues her to music of thunderous violence. As for the dwarves – Alberich, the Nibelungs and, later, Hagen – they are Wotan's shadow-figures, who always show him, to unflinchingly grim music, the dire effects of his 'compromise'. Indeed, the cycle is constructed in sets of parallels between god and dwarf.

However, it is the polarization of Wotan's neurotic extremes in the third act of *Siegfried* that yields two of the work's greatest colloquies. First, Wotan summons the straight-talking, all-wise Erda from her dreams: how can he resolve his inner conflict, he asks, as though appealing to a therapist? She replies tartly that he is not who he thinks he is. Wotan retaliates by foretelling the end of the gods and the redemptive mission of Siegfried and Brünnhilde. Musically, this utopian vision is the most powerful assertion of Wotan's 'alternative reality', to which Erda responds with passive aggression: she returns to sleep in silence. In the very next scene, however, Wotan encounters Siegfried on his way to Brünnhilde. Far from standing aside, he falls back on his old narcissism. Whose magic made your sword?, he asks; who enabled you to understand the latent meanings behind Mime's ditties and the Wood-bird's song? And above all: whose missing eye is in your brow (for Wotan is one-eyed and Siegfried is his grandson)? Siegfried laughs; Wotan threatens him; Siegfried destroys Wotan's spear (the emblem of his outer authority). An exchange that began in light ends in darkness as pride on both sides is stung to the core. Musically, it is a superb demonstration of the art of moving from one extreme to the other – an art central to Wagner's work, as Carl Dahlhaus once observed. Thereafter in *Götterdämmerung* we follow Wotan only vicariously: in the first act as Waltraute describes his profound depression and wish for the return of the ring to the Rhine-daughters (a capitulation); and in the last act, when (as it seems) he exerts dark magic by disturbing the ravens that allow Hagen to murder the distracted Siegfried. When by magic he lifts the hand of the corpse of Siegfried to prevent Hagen from seizing the ring, he finally acquiesces in his own immolation: Brünnhilde steps forward and controls the end-game.[4] Even in death, Wotan's narcissism is unimpaired: musically and visually, his fiery demise is his finest 'show'.

3 Siegfried

Psychologically, Siegfried's 'low IQ' aligns him with the Rhine-daughters and Erda in that they all behave with little or no restraint (only the third Rhine-daughter urges caution). Freudians would view such a lack of a civilizing ('super-ego') function as two-edged: for his part, Siegfried destroys whoever stands in his way, but also, being guileless and resistant to warnings, is easily outwitted and destroyed by Hagen. Yet Siegfried's music is not entirely fresh-faced and forceful. As he gradually learns of the separate deaths of his parents, he is imbued with sadness and a need for revenge. His neurosis is induced, not by experience, but by reflection. Savagely rejecting the claims to parenthood of Mime, he thinks of his dead father while re-forging Notung; as he lies in the forest at noon beneath the tenderly murmuring trees, he laments his lot as a sole orphan; confronting Wotan, he recognizes his father's killer; and when, after removing Brünnhilde's helmet, he meets a woman for the first time, he not only cries 'Mutter!' (Mother!) but also asks, with heart-melting timidity, 'So starb nicht meine Mutter? Schlief die minnige nur?' (So my mother didn't die? The lovely creature only slept?). His subsequent union with Brünnhilde is thus reparation for the loss of both parents as well as an advance in maturity. This is reflected in the overwhelming force of their love music, which is spread over the end of *Siegfried* and, following their first night of love, into the Prologue to *Götterdämmerung*: in artistic terms this necessarily exceeds the rapture of Siegmund and Sieglinde's union, itself an unprecedented riposte to the lovelessness of Sieglinde's marriage to Hunding. Later, in the third act of *Götterdämmerung*, as Siegfried recounts his heroic exploits to Hagen, we hear again his earlier, troubled music: he cannot forget this bit of his emotional past.

4 *Brünnhilde*

By contrast, Brünnhilde has to negotiate two sets of neuroses. Both are inherited from her parents. On the one hand, she is the beneficiary of Wotan's wishes and victim of his fears, a polarity she has to live through with all its attendant thrill and pain. On the other hand, she inherits the fearless integrity of her mother Erda, an integrity she cannot suppress; and although Erda is anything but neurotic (she is the cycle's leading 'eternal'), there is a stark tension between her and Wotan, as we learn from *Das Rheingold* and *Siegfried*. This tension creates the second polarity. Brünnhilde has the resilience to pull through both sets, becoming 'all-wise' through suffering (like Wagner's Parsifal). She is an immortal until the end of *Die Walküre*, and a mortal thereafter, though in the final act of *Götterdämmerung* she seems to reacquire some divinity by communicating with the Rhine-daughters. Her music throughout is remarkable. In the second act of *Die Walküre*, her fervent cries of 'Hojotoho! Heiaha!' launch an entrance aria unlike any other, a forthright representation of Wotan's defences; and when she appears to Siegmund as Wotan's emissary of death, the numinous solemnity of her motifs gradually dissolves into a rebellious whirl as she apprehends Siegmund's selfless devotion to his sister: she cannot be false. Indeed, *Treue* (loyalty) is the cycle's keyword. Wotan upbraids and expels her before her eight Valkyrie sisters in a superb interactive dramatic chorus. But Brünnhilde skilfully renegotiates the expulsion to suit them both. She gets Wotan to agree that only some hero will wake her from the protective flames, yet a motif in the music confirms what they both know and cannot admit, that the hero will be Siegfried. Wotan thus bids her a complex farewell: he grieves at the loss of his wish-child, but is profoundly gratified that, vicariously, she will deliver his wishes. The effect is overwhelming. Awoken in due course by Siegfried, Brünnhilde first extends her musically uncanny greeting to the sun. Then, under erotic pressure, she pours out the 'Siegfried Idyll' song, in which the text urges restraint, but the beguiling music ensures release. She and Siegfried finally unite in, of all things, a revitalized, old-school operatic duet.

Götterdämmerung thrusts Brünnhilde into the very world that has induced Wotan's neurosis: that of greed, treachery and ruthless politics. It sucks in even the relatively ordinary Gibichungs, Gunther and Gutrune. At the end of Act One Siegfried returns to the rock in the disguise of Gunther. Brünnhilde is appalled: 'Verrat!' (Betrayed!) she shrieks, snarling alliteratives at the absent Wotan: 'Ergrimmter, grausamer Gott!' (Angry, cruel god!). But, as an orchestral reminiscence of the 'Siegfried Idyll' song tells us, she can still recognize Siegfried, albeit (as Wagner instructs) unconsciously. Here music serves psychology as never before. Indeed, Brünnhilde's Erda-like intuition will unravel Siegfried. Her pitiful entrance in Act Two as Gunther's 'bride' is prepared by lavish, rollicking music for the Gibichungs, and what follows is an accumulative mad-scene. Raging at Siegfried, she emits breathless cries of 'Betrug!' (Deceived!); she swears mortal vengeance; to a turmoil of musical motifs she ponders the dark magic abroad; she reveals to Hagen how to destroy Siegfried and, in an operatic trio, endorses his destruction on oath, asking Wotan to bear witness. This demand touches the height of irony: for by aligning herself with Hagen's lethal music she acts out Wotan's deepest dread. It is only in Act Three, after she has spoken to the Rhine-daughters, that Brünnhilde becomes her mother's child: answering Waltraute's earlier plea, and closing the Valhalla theme previously left open, she lays Wotan to rest and rides into the flames affirming her recovered love for the dead Siegfried. By allowing the Rhine-daughters to reclaim the ring – and drown Hagen – she also allows a reworking of the cycle's opening music, itself representative of a timeless love. Her 'neurotic journey' is at an end, as indeed is everyone else's.

5 Wagner

Wagner's musical style is often compared with the fluid 'development' sections of Beethoven symphonies, where inter-related themes (leitmotifs) are constantly combined and contrasted for dramatic purpose, with stable 'closed' sections (songs and interludes) in the minority. Although the ubiquitous back-stories allow for symphonic recapitulation, their purpose is always to move the story on. The reworkings of Brünnhilde's awakening music (from *Siegfried*), first by the saturnine Norns (the Fates) and then by the dying Siegfried (in *Götterdämmerung*), are fresher than any new inventions could have been. This is true even at the end. Brünnhilde works herself, Isolde-like, into a self-sacrificial frenzy using Sieglinde's theme of the 'highest wonder'. Yet the theme has changed its meaning from *Die Walküre*: the world is to be redeemed and purged, no longer by a new breed of man, but by the renunciation of the fantasy of such a breed (through the return of the ring).

But both extremes, the 'superman' fantasy and the annihilation, signal neurosis. Faced with the pressures of the modern world, Wagner's stage characters, like other Romantic heroes before them, invariably withdraw (even Hans Sachs renounces and warns). But whether they withdraw in transcendent glory or uncompromising despair is neither here nor there: the extremes co-exist, the outcome is ambiguous. This means that not only are Wagner's characters 'neurotic', but so too, in a sense, is the creative personality of Wagner. Yet in another sense, the health of the *Ring* lies in its consummate achievement as music drama: to the unprejudiced, Wagner's cycle *works* magnificently. As Auden also said, 'the outcome of emotions you get from all good art is joy', even if the art addresses sadness.[5] It follows that the *Ring*, being great art, has the power to bestow great joy.

Notes

Source: 'Listening to *The Ring* with Auden' (Richard Wagner), Longborough Festival Opera, 2013 season programme, pp. 6-9.

1 Transcribed but unpublished radio interview with Hans Keller, BBC Radio Three, 1971.
2 IQ = 'Intelligence quotient: a number representing a person's reasoning ability (measured using problem-solving tests) as compared to the statistical norm or average for their age, taken as 100.' *The New Oxford Dictionary of English*, Oxford: Oxford UP, 1998, p. 949.
3 I have discussed the music of Sieglinde's trauma in: 'Analysis and Psychoanalysis: Wagner's Musical Metaphors', *Companion to Contemporary Musical Thought*, vol. 2, ed. John Paynter *et al*, London: Routledge and Kegan Paul, 1992, pp. 650-91.
4 This is described in Part Four of this book under 'Peroration'.
5 Interview with Hans Keller, BBC Radio Three, 1971.

3 Mother, Madonna, Maid and Whore
Richard Wagner: *Tannhäuser*

In the late-fifteenth-century folk ballad *Das Lied von dem Danheüser*, the most alluring source for Richard Wagner's *Tannhäuser* (1845-75), the wandering knight counters the plea of Venus to stay at her court with a prayer of his own:

> And that I shall not do, Frau Venus,
> I may stay here no longer.
> Maria, mother, pure maid,
> Help me now in my distress![1]

Here, the sacred, Christian myth of the Madonna who is also mother and maid (the Virgin Mary) is invoked to ward off the profane, pagan myth of the ruby-lipped Goddess of Love (Venus) whom the knight now perceives as a devil incarnate – in our terms, a whore. The departing Danheüser, condemned by Venus ever to sing her praises to the young, journeys to Rome to seek pardon from the Pope. But Urban the Fourth fends him off with a nigh impossible condition: only when his dry staff puts out green shoots can the knight hope to win God's grace. Grief-stricken and bewildered, the devout Danheüser returns to Venus. But on the third day after Danheüser's departure the staff burgeons: Danheüser is saved! 'Where is the knight?', cries Urban, 'he must be found!' A search party scours the land – but to no avail. Danheüser is forever bound to the lady he once rejected, ignorant of the miracle of his absolution. Unlike the opera, the ballad offers neither death nor redemption, and certainly no saintly intercession (the opera's Elisabeth was grafted from other sources, notably Ludwig Bechstein's *Die Sagen von Eisenach und der Wartburg, dem Hörseelberg und Reinhardsbrunn* (1835)).

In fact, Wagner took pains to deny he was using his 'large Romantic opera' to advance anything as simple as a morality play. Nor was he trying to emulate Heinrich Heine's laconic 'take' on the ballad (1837) that begins as a cautionary tale:

> Good Christians all, lest Satan you
> With wicked guile ensnare
> I'll tell you now Tannhäuser's tale
> To make your souls beware.[2]

Nor even was he guided by the 'coquettish mysticism and catholic frivolity' of Ludwig Tieck's story, *Der getreue Eckart und der Tannenhäuser* (1799), though he may well have taken Wolfram's compassion for Tannhäuser from

E. T. A. Hoffmann's *Der Kampf der Sänger* (1819). On the contrary, in 'A Communication to My Friends' (1851) he called critics 'absurd' to 'insist on reading into my *Tannhäuser* a specifically Christian and impotently pietistic drift!' Rather, he was fired by a 'loathing' of 'the modern world' and its 'modern art' and sought to unite the 'opposing channels of my being ... into one stream: a longing for the highest form of love.'[3] And he reinforced this in 1852 by claiming that at the end of the full (Dresden) version of the overture 'both dissevered elements, both soul and senses, God and Nature, unite in the atoning kiss of hallowed love.'[4] Transcenders of repugnant modernity, trailblazers of revolutionary art, harbingers of divine love: such were his hero and heroine with their new, Young-German agenda.

But how are we to understand such 'hallowed love' today? Does it do any more than embody the dichotomy Isaiah Berlin describes in *The Roots of Romanticism* (1999) between a self-denying but terrible 'unsatisfied desire to soar into infinity' and 'sheer self-assertion', 'egomania and primitivism'?[5] Certainly, dichotomies are of the essence here as are parallels between the lovers. Tannhäuser – 'Heinrich' – is torn between two women (the voluptuous Venus and the saintly Elisabeth) just as two men compete for Elisabeth (the decent but forlorn Wolfram and the unruly but driven Tannhäuser). The two women project a struggle within the knight-errant while the two men peg out the options for the favourite daughter of the Wartburg (the famous castle at the epicentre of threatened German identity). Both conspicuously lack parents, yet both have an exaggerated need to belong: Tannhäuser is rootless yet also the most dedicated of the Rome pilgrims; Elisabeth sees an exceptionally 'kind father' in her uncle (the Landgrave) yet defies him to the core by pinning her hopes on Tannhäuser. No two are more revered in the Wartburg, where decorous song is valued both for its own sake and for its power to galvanize the body politic, yet no two do more to threaten its artistic and chivalric codes. Indeed, both have numinous gifts – Tannhäuser with his Orphic power of song, Elisabeth with her authority to intercede in Heaven. (Soon after her death, in fact, the historical Elisabeth was canonized.)

Romanticism, concluded Berlin, 'is, in short, unity and multiplicity'. And it is no surprise that in a seminal essay 'On the Most Widely-found Type of Debasement in the Field of Love' (1912), Sigmund Freud, the white-coated heir to Romanticism par excellence, first establishes a dichotomy between the 'sensual' and the 'affectionate' in young men and then unifies it by positing an internalized image of the restraining mother.[6] So when in Act One Tannhäuser abandons Venus to the cry of 'Maria', we have to understand less a progression than a switch from one extreme to the other: the sacred and the profane, the Madonna and the whore, are but two sides of the same coin whose value speaks devotion to a hidden force. Freud writes of such men: 'Where they love they do not desire and where they desire they cannot love.' Freud diagnoses the split as a phase in maturing; Kleinians might see it as a reclaimable 'position'. But the opera couches the guiding image of a restraining, partly maternal force (Elisabeth) in yet another paradox: on the one hand the uncannily empathetic Tannhäuser aspires to redeem the pain he has caused her through a mature union, but on the other hand joins her in a death that has all the appearance of a craven return to the womb – in Wagner's terms, a 'tragic renunciation' of the world. As Berlin might have said, the opera both progresses *and* regresses.

And what of Elisabeth? Is she just a projection of Tannhäuser's? In fact, modern feminist psychology would reject any idea that what goes for Tannhäuser must go, *mutatis mutandis*, for her and insist she has a being of her own. From the start she shows the keenest awareness of the otherness of Tannhäuser; she is a virgin; she is thrilled by the eroticism of his singing; after his initial departure she withdraws from the Wartburg to suffer in solitude (we recognize the hallmarks of depression: eating disorder, hallucination and even self-mutilation); she pays no heed to Wolfram or any other suitor; after the revelations of the Venusberg (a hotbed, surely, of lethal infection) she still defends Tannhäuser against the mortal threatens of the Landgrave; and when Tannhäuser fails to return with the other pilgrims, she wills herself to death to save his soul. What a contrast, though, to Tannhäuser! For he is drawn to Venus and Maria precisely because they are so unreal: to cite Estela Welldon's *Mother, Madonna, Whore* (1988), these opposites inhabit a mythic time where there is no 'biological clock', no awareness of 'menarche, menses or menopause', no death (and hence no meaningful life).[7] This also means that Elisabeth is not symbolically an egregiously 'bad mother' who will pamper Tannhäuser with carnal excess, like Venus; nor is she an exaggeratedly 'good mother' who will inspire collective inhibition and remorse, like 'Maria'. The action, indeed, compels Tannhäuser to recognize Elisabeth for what she is and hence for the psychic integration she offers. In Act One, the selfless Wolfram entreats him to 'Stay for Elisabeth!'; in Act Two, the action brings him face to face with the true scale of her suffering (for Wagner, the nodal-point of the work); in Act Three Wolfram again cries 'Elisabeth' to ward off the predatory Venus; and finally the sight of her bier brings forth Tannhäuser's dying call, 'Blessed Elisabeth, pray for me!' In other words, the inner drama of the opera – its psychological form – traces the convergence of two distinct psychologies, hers as much as his.

The psychologies, moreover, shape the stagecraft as much as the music. In his biography *Mein Leben* (written between 1865 and 1880) Wagner explained how the 'intense degree of passion' in the opening scene between Tannhäuser and Venus was essential to cast a pall over the rest of the drama.[8] So what he devised, after the priapic ardour of the bacchanal and the ensuing heart-melting post-coital languor, was the mounting pressure of Venus's response to Tannhäuser's three-strophe, antithetical lay ('I salute you but beg for release,' he sings): she is bemused, defensively seductive and finally piqued into cosmic fury. In the next scene Wagner counters this with a pristine shepherd's song and a slow pilgrims' chorale that so rouse Tannhäuser that the Landgrave and others need to exert exceptional persuasion to lead him to Elisabeth. The scene's all-male ensembles, indeed, offer the most effective possible antidote to the female aromatics of the Venusberg. In Act Two, Wagner uses the intense passion of the early Tannhäuser and Elisabeth 'love duet' to establish a bridgehead necessary to oppose the Wartburg later in the scene; and he advances the song contest, so weightily introduced by ceremony, chorus and speech, not as a traditional 'concert of arias', but rather as a novel projection of 'an inner spiritual process' within his hero. By gradually having Tannhäuser work back to the Venusberg music and recapitulating part of his lay with such defiance, Wagner not only reveals the effect of Venus's curse on the world but also exposes, ruthlessly, why the Wartburg and its etiolated music could never be for him. For the experience of the Venusberg *has* mattered, and it is just this that so enrages the community. Indeed, the huge concerted ensembles that follow Elisabeth's fiery intervention and lead to Tannhäuser's provisional expulsion pile on pressure of a kind surely unsurpassed in the whole of opera.

More still, in Act Three Wagner asks that, after the return of the pilgrims (their burdens so lifted that they now process in slow waltz-time(!)), the pure Elisabeth should pray with 'all the pangs of the most heartfelt suffering' as perforce she renounces everything that stirs her. Indeed, such is the transfiguring effect of her song – a performance of a kind – that Wolfram, whose main function is now to guide her soul to death, sings a poignant, solitary lay to the evening star. But the main emphasis again lies with Tannhäuser. Wagner has already part-described his traumatic re-enactment of the pilgrimage to Rome in the act's overture and now amplifies it: in a letter to Liszt of 1852 he emphasized how this and others of his operas would stand or fall by the lead singer's ability to command the 'genuine *accent of suffering*'.[9] And by now he has indeed pushed Tannhäuser's sufferings to the limit. All but expelled by the Landgrave, excommunicated by the Pope, he has been doubly impaled on the lethal spear of worldly castrating father-figures. No wonder he is so frantic to return to the Venusberg! Where else is home?

As epigraph to his late essay on 'Religion and Art' (1880) Wagner cited a remark of Schiller's to Goethe: 'In the Christian religion I find an intrinsic disposition to the Highest and Noblest, [yet] its various representations in life strike me as so vapid and repugnant simply because they have missed any expression of the Highest.'[10] It was the task of Art, said Wagner, to recover religion's 'deep and hidden truth through some ideal representation' and to show how through revelation and miracle the 'kingdom of the world' could be transcended; and the only art 'that fully corresponds' with the 'innermost essence' of Christianity, and hence would be capable of achieving such a goal, was 'Music'. At the end of the opera, after the vertiginous trio in which

Wolfram and Venus struggle for Tannhäuser's soul, Elisabeth makes her miraculous intercession from beyond the grave: the Pope's staff burgeons, and the company marvels at a revelation that overrides the worldly offices of Christianity in the name of higher Christian truth (a kind of Utopia). That the broad and stirring events here seem to touch the very ground of our being shows that behind the celebration of 'Maria, mother [and] pure maid' lies a still more vital aim: the penetration of the inner sanctum of Music itself.

Notes

Source: 'Maria, Mother, Pure Maid', Tannhäuser (Richard Wagner), The Royal Opera programme, December 2010, pp. 45-51; reprinted 2016.

1   Richard Wagner, Tannhäuser, ENO/ROH Opera Guide 39, ed. Nicholas John, London: Calder, 1988: see especially the essays by Stewart Spencer ('Tanhausere, Danheüser and Tannhäuser', pp. 17-24) and Timothy McFarland ('Wagner's Most Medieval Opera', pp. 25-32). 'The Tannhäuser Ballad', trans. J. W. Thomas appears on pp. 58-9.
2   'Tannhäuser, eine Legende', Heinrich Heine (Everyman's Poetry), trans. T. J. Reed and David Cram, London: Dent, 1997, pp. 54-61.
3   The Artwork of the Future and Other Works, trans. W. Ashton Ellis (1895), London and Lincoln: Nebraska UP, 1993, pp. 267-392. For 'A Communication to My Friends' (1851) see especially pp. 311-12 and 322-4.
4   Richard Wagner, 'Overture to Tannhäuser' (1852), Richard Wagner's Prose Works, trans. William Ashton Ellis, vol. 1, London: Kegan Paul, Trench, Trübner, 1895, pp. 229-31.
5   Isaiah Berlin, The Roots of Romanticism, London: Chatto and Windus, 1999, pp. 1-20.
6   Sigmund Freud, 'Concerning the Most Universal Debasement in the Erotic Life' (1912), The Penguin Freud Reader, ed. Adam Phillips, London: Penguin, 2006, pp. 402- 13.
7   Estela V. Welldon, Mother, Madonna, Whore: The Idealization and Denigration of Motherhood (1988), New York: Other Press, 2000, pp. 44-62 and 106-28.
8   Richard Wagner, My Life (Mein Leben, written 1865-80, first full publication 1911), trans. Andrew Gray, ed. Mary Whittall, Cambridge: Cambridge UP, 1983, pp. 304-12
9   Wagner is especially interesting about the singing role of Tannhäuser. See: Selected Letters of Richard Wagner, trans. and ed. Stewart Spencer and Barry Millington, London: Dent, 1987, pp. 256-60 (Letter to Liszt, 29 May 1852).
10   Richard Wagner, Religion and Art, trans. W. Ashton Ellis, Lincoln and London: Nebraska UP, 1994, pp. 211-53, especially p. 211.

4 Loss

Francesco Maria Piave (rev. Boito) and Giuseppe Verdi: *Simon Boccanegra*

1 Club Verdi

Walk along a quiet side street of any European city, stop at a black door marked 'Club Verdi', knock twice, and, when the grill opens, murmur deferentially *'padre, figlia'* (father, daughter): at once you will be ushered in. But why deferentially? Because all insiders know that early in life Verdi lost both his sixteen-month-old daughter Virginia (in 1838) and his wife Margherita (in 1840), and that, according to contemporaries, the losses took him to the brink of madness. So, the argument continues, whenever fathers and daughters appear in his operas, we should doff our caps: not only do we behold the composer surreptitiously re-enacting the trauma of those losses but even find him searching out subjects that allow him to do just that. Indeed, when the great archivist Hans Busch asks why in the early 1880s Verdi returned to the 'ill-fated' *Simon Boccanegra* of 1857 (to words by F. M. Piave), he finds his 'answer' in the composer's letters:

> It seems that he was still fascinated by the greatness and tragedy of the hero and by the love between father and daughter, a theme that held very personal meaning for him and that occurs in so many operas.[1]

The letters, though, say nothing of the sort. They never mention the love of father and daughter, and the enthusiasm to revise *Simon*, whipped up by its second librettist Arrigo Boito, is clearly of a different origin.[2] The same goes for other works. With *Rigoletto* (again to words by Piave), Verdi was manifestly inspired by the deformed, Shakespearean figure of Victor Hugo's Triboulet (Rigoletto) rather than the jester's obsession with his daughter Gilda. In *La traviata*, Germont *père*'s attempt to disown his prospective daughter-in law, the courtesan Violetta, hardly signals 'love' any more than does the intolerable political pressure under which the captured Amonasro places his daughter Aida. And anyway, why stop at fathers and daughters? What about fathers and sons – after all, in 1839 Verdi had lost another infant, the boy Icilio? In his operas, surely there is nothing more terrible than Philip II's destruction of his son Don Carlos? For that matter, when it comes to 'very personal meanings', why single out Verdi? What, for example, can match the intensity of Wotan's farewell to his daughter Brünnhilde in Wagner's *Die Walküre* – an encoded farewell to Mathilde Wesendonck? And, for sheer power, is there anything in the annals of opera to cap the lethal shadow cast over his daughter by the murdered Agamemnon in Strauss's *Elektra*? The Club Verdi passwords, it seems, hardly bear scrutiny.

2   The Outer Drama

And yet ... when we sift patiently through the *Boccanegra* documentation and set our findings beside Verdi's music we come to a startling conclusion not so far removed from our starting point. In 1880 the first revisionist task was to improve the work's focus. Verdi and Boito were in agreement that in the 1857 version 'There are none of those characters (always very rare!) that make you say, *"It's sharply delineated!"*'.[3] Nevertheless, it struck Verdi 'that there is something in the roles of Fiesco and Simon that could be used to good advantage' even though they were 'harder to perform than all the others'. Indeed, 'with two good actors for these parts and two good voices for the others [Amelia and Adorno] ... the opera [could] work; otherwise not.'[4] It was not thus the father-daughter relationship Verdi found arresting, but rather that of Amelia's father (Simon) and grandfather (Fiesco). Verdi noted that Simon, the corsair-turned-Doge, was 'an exhausting [baritone] part, like Rigoletto [also a baritone], but a thousand times more difficult. In *Rigoletto* the *part is made*, and with a little voice and feeling one can manage it well. For Boccanegra voice and feeling are not enough.'[5] So what he and Boito developed was a protagonist of such dramatic range and power that the great council chamber scene became (in Verdi's words) 'a grand solo for the Doge with other parts added'. It was no longer the mandatory, balanced central ensemble (*concertato*).

As for the older Fiesco, Verdi hoped for something 'inexorable, prophetic, sepulchral in the voice'; as a bass, he would certainly have to have a good low-note F – a memory perhaps of the assassin Sparafucile's long low 'va' in *Rigoletto*. On the other hand his publisher Giulio Ricordi argued that for the prayer in the prologue and the duet with Simon in the last act, the voice would have to be 'one that blends well, is on pitch, and has a singing quality.'[6] Both tendencies were met. Indeed, they polarize the men's two duets that form the outer pillars of the work: the low notes come in the Prologue as Fiesco bears down on Simon with the ferocity of a Monterone condemning Rigoletto, and the flexible singing emerges in the last act as the contrite Fiesco moves into the same baritone range as Simon's to pour out his grief at the Doge's impending death. What separates and unites them we shall consider in due course.

So what then of Simon's out-of-wedlock daughter, the soprano 'Amelia'? (Her real name, we discover, is significantly the same as her mother's, Maria.) As Verdi intimated, her position in the drama is mainly linked to the fortunes of her *inamorato*, Gabriele Adorno (tenor), and is scrupulously guarded. So much is clear from Act One. Her balmy opening aria reveals a virginal affinity with nature tempered by a realistic anxiety over 'Genoa' and its politics. In the ensuing duet, Adorno – who combines the fiery temperament of an Alfredo (in *La traviata*) with the mellifluous tongue of a Manrico (in *Il trovatore*) – swears to protect her; then Fiesco agrees to protect Adorno; and finally Simon promises to protect Amelia against Paolo, the Iago-like villain who sees in her the same path to advancement that he has already seen in Simon. In other words, *everyone* (bar Paolo) works to ensure the couple remain *intacta*: for in the grand scheme of things only their union can bring health to the cancerous body politic. The need for protection, moreover, quickly becomes apparent. In the following council chamber scene, Adorno enters pursued by a mob after murdering a certain Lorenzino for trying to abduct Amelia; yet the dying Lorenzino had confessed to having been set up by a more powerful figure; Adorno accuses the Doge of being that figure, and in full view of the company tries to stab him; Amelia arrives in time to intervene; she successfully persuades Simon to protect Adorno and redirects his suspicion towards Paolo; the assembly place a curse on the culprit whoever he be; and, in a stupendous *coup de théâtre*, Simon compels the guilt-ridden Paolo to repeat the curse – all this in a scene where the plebeians have cried death to Simon and the patricians.

3 The Inner Drama (the Psychological Form)

So much then for the outer aspects of Verdi's priorities, the pairings of Simon and Fiesco on the one hand and Amelia and Adorno on the other. But to unpick the inner drama – the psychological form – we need to probe the role of Amelia a bit further. Because she is a lone woman in an essentially all-male cast, Verdi and Boito had a musical problem: how could they reinforce her vocal colour without inflating her role – especially as they were cutting back on some of her exit music (the cabalettas)? One solution was to support her entrances with a mixed chorus: this they did in the council chamber as she and the people intrude with full force, and again in the finale as she and the full company grieve over the dying Doge. (Boito justified the popular intrusion by remarking that 'it is a well-known fact that women play a principal role in people's riots; think of the Commune [of 1871] in Paris.')[7] Another solution was to strengthen her character. Although Amelia has to handle Simon like a shy Gilda (in *Rigoletto*), she does so with the force of an Amneris (in *Aida*). In the council chamber scene, indeed, she so mollifies Simon that he can deftly turn the assembly from strife to peace. And in the searing trio that concludes Act Two, as Simon considers clemency towards Adorno after Adorno has appealed to Simon (he has challenged the Doge for his alleged designs on Amelia), she seeks to defend her man by praying to Heaven with utmost intensity. The prayer, crucially, is to her dead mother: it is as if, *in extremis*, she needs the presence of both parents, as if she sings for both herself and the other Maria.

If, then, this trio is a kind of quartet with a missing part, so is the poignant duet between Simon and Amelia in Act One a kind of trio with a missing part. Simon has gradually come to realize that 'Amelia Grimaldi' is none other than his lost daughter, child of his illegitimate union with Fiesco's daughter (Maria): as the melody of sublime rapture unfolds in the orchestra, the parting couple embrace to the words 'padre! figlia!' (father! daughter!). Yet the centrepiece of the duet has focussed on Amelia's dead mother. Amelia knows of her only from a portrait passed on by an old woman who had briefly tended her: 'Mi baciò, mi benedisse, levò al ciel, pregando, i rai ...' ([the woman] kissed me, blessed me, raised her eyes to heaven in prayer). Simon, however, has a matching portrait of his own; and as he listens in mounting excitement to Amelia's story, he calls out his daughter's true name, Maria. It is the dead mother who has sealed their reunion. The situation is similar to that in the no less poignant duet between father and daughter in first act of *Rigoletto*. Rigoletto and Gilda greet each other with joyous cries of 'figlia! padre!' (daughter! father!). But they get to the heart of the matter – why Rigoletto protects Gilda so vehemently – when the daughter prises open her father's overwhelming distress at the loss of her mother. At the opera's close, moreover, it is to the mother in heaven Gilda appeals at her own moment of death.

The dead mother, indeed, returns us to the root of the problem between Fiesco and Simon. Simon originally transgressed the Genoese moral code by having a child by Maria Fiesco out of wedlock. In the Prologue we hear and see the reaction to the death of Maria, whom Fiesco has for long kept under lock and key; in a charged meeting, the aggrieved Fiesco curses the contrite Simon until he hands over the illegitimate child; but, alas, the child is lost – hence Simon's persistent search over the next twenty-five years. In their second, final-act duet, Fiesco reveals himself again, now with the portentous authority of the returning Commendatore from Mozart's *Don Giovanni*: but even though Simon reveals that mercifully the child is found – and hence that the curse can be lifted – Fiesco can only collapse in pity as he reveals that Simon has been fatally poisoned (by Paolo). This triangle, then, of Simon, Fiesco and the departed Maria stands at the work's core. It is one, moreover, that accounts for the parallel ironies in the stagecraft. In the Prologue, Fiesco curses Simon for Maria's death while in gathering excitement the people proclaim Simon as their new Doge; in the last act, Fiesco and Simon successfully resolve their differences while the Genoese 'sea of lights' celebrating the marriage of Adorno and Amelia are extinguished and the Doge moves towards death.

So where does this leave our Club Verdi passwords? If anywhere, as 'padre, madre, figlia' (father, mother, daughter). A special Verdian love of father for daughter gains credence only when it stands in the shadow of a dead mother.

Notes

Source: '*Padre, Madre, Figlia*', *Simon Boccanegra* (Giuseppe Verdi), The Royal Opera programme, June 2010, pp. 41-5; reprinted 2013.

1   *Verdi's Otello and Simon Boccanegra (revised version) in Letters and Documents*, trans. and ed. Hans Busch, 2 vols., Oxford: Clarendon Press, 1988, p. xxxvi.
2   For a discussion of the alternate use of Simon/Simone, see the separate entry on 'A Name' in Part Four of this volume.
3   Busch, 1988, p. 43.
4   *Ibid.*, p. 37.
5   *Ibid.*, p. 28.
6   *Ibid.*, p. 34.
7   *Ibid.*, p. 78.

5   Encapsulated Repression

Francesco Maria Piave (after Hugo) and Giuseppe Verdi: *Rigoletto*

1   The Drama

Towards the end of the first act of his film version (1983) of *Rigoletto* (1851), the director Jean-Pierre Ponnelle introduces a startling image: Rigoletto is drunk.[1] Sprawled on the ground and clutching a bottle, the jester blearily intones the words 'Ah da quel vecchio fui maledetto!' (Ah, I have been damned by that old man!). He sings them to the same accusatory musical figure that the Count of Monterone used against him earlier in the act. Today the crisis of opera (to use Henry Pleasants's term) lies at the door of the director, so the image may hardly seem important. It is, after all, a fleeting one, and its departure from the printed stage directions as found in Martin Chusid and Philip Gossett's excellent new edition follows an all too typical pattern of apparently wilful reversal: according to Verdi and Piave, Rigoletto ought to be preoccupied (*concentrato*) rather than dissipated, and should collide with the courtier Borsa, something he can do only were he upright.[2] Yet it is the rest of the production that makes the image so arresting. For, apart from his constant delight in matching image and music, Ponnelle shows a sophisticated awareness of the critical issues surrounding the work – so much so, indeed, that the departure demands an explanation. As we shall see, the image of the drunkard both celebrates and tries to dispel the unease that audiences may feel at this point. Psychoanalytically, it is a 'compromise formation'.

The overall plot has to be understood in the light of several paradoxes. Rigoletto, a hunchback, is court jester to the promiscuous and irresistible Duke of Mantua (an 'Apollo'). His master has everything he does not have, and Rigoletto views him with deep ambivalence: he derives vicarious satisfaction from the Duke's promiscuity even though he entertains murderous feelings towards him. He spurs on the Duke to constant seduction of courtiers' wives and daughters, although at home, secretly locked away, he keeps a daughter of his own. He mocks the courtiers, but when they hear of Rigoletto's 'woman' and assume her to be his mistress, they avenge themselves by abducting her. He thus reaps the fruits of his scorn. Worse still, when Rigoletto heaps supreme contempt on Monterone, whose daughter has been ravished by the Duke, the old man (as we have noted) damns him with a curse. It is this curse that marks the real beginning of the drama, the start of its inner form.

Let us trace the events following Monterone's malediction. After an encounter with Sparafucile, who offers him his assassin's services, Rigoletto arrives back home. It is a sad place, a house with a walled garden and locks on the gates. His wife is long since dead. His only child, Gilda, has been brought up in a convent from which she has just returned. Although now a young woman, her movements are exceptionally restricted, and she is overseen by a duenna, Giovanna. Gilda nevertheless greets her father affectionately. She quickly senses his distress, but cannot get him to reveal its cause. Bizarrely, he has never told her his name, nor whether he has any friends; instead, to her consternation, he merely pours out grief for his lost wife. He assures Gilda of his dependence on her. He also asks about her day: has she been out? No, she replies. He insists that she must always look after herself. In a significant aside, he adds 'Potrian seguirla, rapirla ancora' (she might be followed, abducted even): the resulting dishonour would make him, the jester, a laughing-stock at court. He sends for Giovanna. Is she absolutely sure that no one followed them to church on Sunday, he asks? Absolutely, she lies. He orders her to keep the gate locked at all times. She will never open the gate, not even to the Duke, she responds, again mendaciously. Least of all to him!, expostulates Rigoletto. After an anxious and protracted farewell, Rigoletto takes leave of Gilda. What happens next confirms his worst fears. As soon as Rigoletto departs, Gilda speculates about the handsome stranger she met at church on Sunday. The stranger suddenly appears: it is the Duke! He has evidently bribed Giovanna to admit him. Giovanna withdraws. Without revealing his true identity, the Duke confesses love to the overwhelmed Gilda. Giovanna returns. She has heard voices in the street and is worried: she begs the Duke to leave, which he does, though not without standing on the ceremony of an elaborate farewell. Gilda is left alone repeating to the night, dotingly, the false name he has given her – Gualtier Maldè, a poor student. From the other side of the wall, the assembled courtiers bend their admiring gaze on Rigoletto's young woman.

It is from this point on that the audience's credulity is tested. Rigoletto returns. He is drawn back for reasons he cannot understand ('Riedo! Perché?'), though, as we know, he is in the grip of Monterone's curse. After bumping into Borsa (it is dark), he establishes the identity of the courtiers. But what is his reaction to finding them on his doorstep? Horror? Accusation? Threats? Abuse? Not at all. When the courtiers propose abducting the wife of the man next door, Count Ceprano, Rigoletto breathes a sigh of relief ('Ahimè respiro') and all too readily agrees to join them in what is a blatant deception. A courtier masks and blindfolds him, and gets him to hold the ladder for the others to climb. Rigoletto, who can now hear and see nothing, becomes an accessory to the very deed he dreads. With vicious glee, the courtiers reach the terrace, enter the house, seize Gilda, and carry her off. During the abduction, she drops a scarf and appeals to her father for help. Rigoletto hears nothing, not even the courtiers' cry of victory. The stage directions take up the story:

> Bringing his hands up to his eyes he impetuously pulls off the
> blindfold and the mask; by the light of the lantern (left behind) he
> recognizes the scarf, sees the door wide open, enters, drags out (the
> frightened) Giovanna, at whom he stares as if transfixed; he tears
> his hair and wishes to cry out but cannot do so.

Finally, with enormous effort, Rigoletto acknowledges that the curse has struck
home. Monterone's fate has become his.

Faced, then, with the embarrassment of Rigoletto's 'gullibility', Ponnelle
must have felt impelled to devise a strategy to overcome the audience's disbelief.
This he does in two ways. First, Rigoletto is made to accept a diminished
responsibility for his actions: drunkenness lowers his guard. Secondly, and
more subtly, this maudlin inebriation appears to bring out his self-contempt.
Throughout the episode, Rigoletto looks at and addresses his own image, a
jester's head on a stick. It is as if he knows that he has returned to be mocked.
Indeed, when the courtiers emerge, he acts out this folly with eagerness. Later,
when Gilda has been abducted, and Rigoletto has torn away his blindfold,
Ponnelle again departs from Verdi and Piave's directions. The camera pulls
back to show Rigoletto caught on the branches beneath the terrace, absurdly
and pathetically waving his stick. Giovanna has already left the house, reward
in hand. There is nobody left to help him. Had he planned things himself,
Rigoletto could not have made himself more of a laughing-stock. His self-
contempt is visible to all.

There are obviously many ways of producing this episode. But Ponnelle's
version has the merit of underscoring what Victor Hugo made explicit in the
preface to *Le Roi s'amuse* (1832), Piave and Verdi's source play. Hugo not only
observed that Triboulet (Rigoletto) was a hunchback and a jester, but also that
he was 'sick'. Of course, the exact nature of the sickness is not spelt out: it is
the work's essential mystery. But recently three psychoanalytically-trained
writers have offered new diagnoses. These differ, but are by no means mutually
exclusive. What they share is a fascination with the very abduction scene that
appears to have embarrassed Ponnelle.

The first diagnosis comes from the late Robert Donington in his posthumous
Opera and its Symbols (1990).[3] Although best known for his Jungian study of
Wagner's *Ring*,[4] Donington was once 'junior assistant' to Donald Winnicott,
who described the art-work in general as a 'transitional object', something that
mediates between the inner self and outer reality. Donington writes:

> …when we learn that Rigoletto keeps his daughter Gilda in such
> close confinement that the courtiers take her for his mistress,
> it occurs to me as quite probable that in his unconscious he
> wishes that she were. Certainly in the outside world we should
> have to regard so close a tie as constituting psychologically an

incestuous situation. But if that is so, it would look as if in holding the ladder bemusedly for Gilda's abduction, some sane part of Rigoletto were colluding inadvertently in seeking for her, and even more importantly for himself, the liberty which the sick part of him denies … Old Monterone's curse could then be seen as constellating outwardly the doubts, the suspicions and the hallucinations with which Rigoletto is now being assailed inwardly; in terms of psychology, a persecutory fantasy; in terms of theatre, a melodramatic masterstroke.

Rigoletto's 'sickness', then, is psychological incest; his complicity with the courtiers is both self-criticism and an attempt to cure himself. Yet it is a cure that fails. When Gilda has been abducted and raped by the Duke, she pleads with her father to forgive the assault, and to leave Mantua. He insists that he must first complete one piece of business: the assassination of his employer. This will be done by Sparafucile. But the murder misfires, and it is Gilda who dies in the Duke's place. Donington writes:

> The stabbing of Gilda may … symbolize vicariously and horribly the sexual penetration which both she and Rigoletto not less urgently than unconsciously desire.

In this way *Rigoletto* prefigures the erotic symbolism that daggers and stabbing were later to assume in Bizet's *Carmen* (1875).

The second diagnosis comes from Barbara Robson, a London-based psychotherapist. Comparing Rigoletto's hunched back with Cyrano de Bergerac's nose, she describes Rigoletto as a 'loser', someone 'struggling to deal with his sense of lack of love – especially Mother's'. It is this mother – Mother Nature – who has given him 'a massive chip on his shoulder', a chip which is literally and metaphorically the hump on his back. This, she argues, has induced in him a 'massive encapsulated repression'. He experiences himself as 'a freak', and deals with his lot by 'clowning denial and scornful bravado':

> Lumbered with such a self-image, and denial of such an image, what happens to sexual development and the hope of love? Wouldn't everything seem too hopeless?

This hopelessness emerges powerfully in the scene with the ladder, as well as at the dénouement. Here Robson predicates her analysis upon the notion of a split identity for Rigoletto's mother, with whose death, she suggests, he has never come to terms: she is, inevitably, a beloved object, but also a hated one. The loved one 'lives still – he seems to insist – in his daughter'. But what of the hated one? A task of the drama is to reveal what happens as the hatred works itself through. Robson comments:

When Rigoletto's sense of being accursed is reinforced by
Monterone, he seems to succumb to his sense of being doomed.
With his persona-mask to the fore, and his awareness blindfolded,
his Own Worst Enemy aspect takes over, setting in motion the
tragic sequence of events which terminates in his murderous
revenge upon the hated Rejecting Mother embodied within the
idealized Beloved Gilda.

Robson's proposition that Rigoletto unconsciously aids and abets the abduction
of Gilda in order to defile her beauty, and thus take revenge upon his own
deformity, offers an important clue to the solution of another problem: why,
in the final act, does Gilda offer herself for sacrifice in place of the Duke who
has ravished her? It seems that she equates herself with the Duke as a victim,
actual or potential, of her father's aggression, and assumes the added burden
of guilt bequeathed to her by Rigoletto's mother.

The third and most elaborate diagnosis comes from Alex Tarnopolsky, a
member of the British Psychoanalytic Society. He begins by defining the figure
of the jester as one who 'compulsively laughs, mocks and attacks'. In this case,
Rigoletto indulges in public mockery because he can afford no private feelings
of deprivation:

He has lost his wife, and any other loss will reactivate his mourning,
with the emergence of guilt and pain. Thus, controlling Gilda is
an attempt to control his own feelings. He also uses mechanisms
of denial, contempt, omnipotence, triumph and projection …
When he mocks Ceprano and Monterone for their loss (of wife
or daughter), he is projecting his loss onto them: he becomes
sneeringly superior and insensitive. Unconsciously he means: 'I
have not lost my wife' – denial – 'it is they who have suffered losses.
I mock at them, rather than show them concern, because that helps
me to control IN THEM any possible pain that I might experience
myself.' The denial extends to ignoring his past. He hides his own
name and his wife's from Gilda: out of sight, out of mind, but also
out of heart. When she asks for more freedom, he panics because
he senses the emergence of his unresolved mourning: every loss
reactivates past losses.

Rigoletto, then, is sick because he has not worked through his mourning. This
is because

In mourning, the most painful feeling to control is guilt.
Unconsciously, guilt relates to the fear of having destroyed or
attacked the loved object, and therefore having contributed to its
death.

But this guilt is something Rigoletto cannot acknowledge; and his 'unconscious conviction' that he has destroyed his wife 'appears in the abduction scene' which Tarnopolsky interprets 'as a dream whose symbolic meaning is "I am co-responsible for the loss (abduction) of my wife (daughter)"'. This dream-image is especially powerful. Rigoletto is blindfold, and the vertiginous series of events, with the fantastic masked figures releasing a muted, but awesome aggression, has indeed the quality of a nightmare. Well might it haunt Rigoletto. But to the meaning of the nightmare, however, the jester is literally and metaphorically blind.

All of these interpretations, then, place the abduction scene, with its extraordinary collusion of father and courtiers, at the centre of their investigation. For Ponnelle, the episode prompts a strategy that bypasses the performing instructions of Piave and Verdi; for Donington, it indicates the unconscious incestuous desire of father for daughter; for Robson it shows the hunchback's revenge upon the hated aspect of his mother through an attack upon the idealized aspect embodied in his daughter Gilda; and for Tarnopolsky, who equates the dead wife with the living daughter, it contains an unconscious admission of the aggression implicit in the guilt normally associated with loss, a guilt that Rigoletto's role as jester necessarily compels him to deny.

Donington, Robson and Tarnopolsky also share a concern for two other mothers apart from Rigoletto's: Gilda's and the Duke's. These are conspicuous in the drama through their absence. Gilda's dead mother (Rigoletto's wife) is inadequately replaced by mother-substitutes (the church and Giovanna) who prove powerless before the Duke. Yet the bond of daughter and mother is far from dead. Gilda's dying words to her father are, 'Up above in Heaven, beside my mother, I shall pray for you through eternity' (Lassù in cielo, vicino alla madre in eterno per voi pregherò).

About the 'exaggerated Duke of Mantua', who 'is such good theatre that we are happy to go along with him', Donington writes:

> [he] is only one of your more preposterous Don Juans persuading himself and others that he is following the most virile of impulses when in actuality he is obeying the least rewarding of compulsions: a mother's boy at bottom, and by no means the fine fellow he thinks he is.

Similarly, Tarnopolsky argues that the 'abusingly loving mother' Donington posits

> heightened [the Duke] to the peaks of her idealization and fostered his belief of possessing an unrivalled seductiveness. In the words of Braunschweig and Fain (1971), they affirm genitality without paternity.

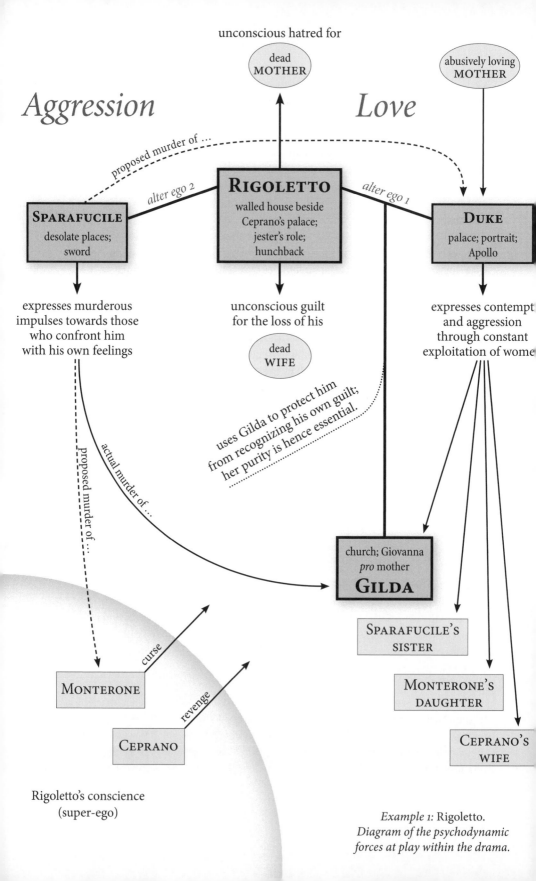

Aggression

Love

unconscious hatred for

dead **MOTHER**

abusively loving **MOTHER**

proposed murder of ...

alter ego 2

RIGOLETTO
walled house beside
Ceprano's palace;
jester's role;
hunchback

alter ego 1

SPARAFUCILE
desolate places;
sword

DUKE
palace; portrait;
Apollo

expresses murderous
impulses towards those
who confront him
with his own feelings

unconscious guilt
for the loss of his

dead **WIFE**

expresses contempt
and aggression
through constant
exploitation of women

uses Gilda to protect him
from recognizing his own guilt;
her purity is hence essential.

proposed murder of ...

actual murder of ...

church; Giovanna
pro mother
GILDA

SPARAFUCILE'S SISTER

curse

MONTERONE

MONTERONE'S DAUGHTER

revenge

CEPRANO

CEPRANO'S WIFE

Rigoletto's conscience
(super-ego)

Example 1: Rigoletto.
*Diagram of the psychodynamic
forces at play within the drama.*

Although, interestingly, we see a portrait of the Duchess, we know nothing about her, or whether she and the Duke have children. The Duke's paternity is never asserted.

The compatibility of these approaches suggests that some meaningful synthesis is possible. This may be expressed in diagrammatic form. Example 1 represents the psycho-dynamic forces at play within the drama. To the left of the diagram are the manifestly aggressive projections, to the right the manifestly loving and erotic ones. (The eroticism is also latently aggressive.) The boxes represent the principal figures in the drama as 'splittings' of Rigoletto, with the assassin (Sparafucile) and the seducer (the Duke) as extreme 'alter egos'. Within the boxes are the places or attributes associated with the protagonists; the absent mothers are encircled. The arrows denote the direction of psychic energy, the function, quality or outcome of which is explained in every case. In the bottom left hand corner a curved line separates the figures of Monterone and Ceprano, who assume a punitive super-ego function. It is the over-determination of the forces described in this diagram that accounts for the incredible behaviour of Rigoletto that Ponnelle 'explains' with the simple yet drastic image of a bottle.

2 The Music

How, though, do these approaches relate to Verdi's musical understanding of the abduction? The question is strictly delimited, since it leaves aside Verdi's own reflections on the opera during its gestation,[5] as well as Tarnopolsky's enquiry into what the choice of subject, and the exceptional musical response it evidently elicited, tells us about Verdi's own psychopathology.[6]

Let us consider the key scheme from the point when the courtiers have assembled outside Rigoletto's house to the end of the first act (scene no. 7). The tonality sinks depressively by a semitone, from the balmy E major of Gilda's aria (no. 6), a 'sharp-side' key traditionally associated with the expression of tenderness under duress, to the raw E♭ minor that accompanies Rigoletto's gasping recognition of the fulfilment of Monterone's curse, a 'flat-side' key traditionally associated with the portentous. The intervening keys that assist in the process of modulation also carry their own associations: A♭ major restores the key of the courtiers from the first scene, and its dominant, E♭ major, is the heroic key to which the courtiers proclaim victory once the abduction is complete.

This overall sinking from E major to E♭ minor connects the abduction scene to the duet between Rigoletto and Gilda earlier in the act (scene no. 4). As a falling minor second, it also provides an example of what the English music theorist Donald Francis Tovey described as an 'inverted Neapolitan' key-relation. In Example 2, Line 1 shows how E major, together with other keys

KEY RELATIONS: Rigoletto's tonal control of his daughter

Example 2: Rigoletto, *Act One, Scene 4. Rigoletto's tonal control of his daughter.*

in which the top note E is prominent (C major and A major), is associated with Gilda's mounting belief that she can find some liberation from her father; reciprocally, E♭ minor, together with other keys in which the top note E♭ is prominent (C minor and A♭ minor), is associated with the mounting fears attendant upon Rigoletto's attempt to control his daughter. That is to say, E is Gilda's 'sounding-note', E♭ Rigoletto's.

Line 2 of the example shows how Verdi also finds musical equivalents for ambivalence. 'Do not recall your lost mother,' Rigoletto orders his daughter, and the music blends the assurance of the command (major) with the pain that the forbidden recollection induces (minor); similarly, in his instruction to Giovanna to guard Gilda well, the assertion of his protective E♭ major turns to the bleak E♭ minor that prefigures the consequences of not protecting her. Other kinds of opposition may also lie between harmony on the one hand, and genre, articulation and instrumentation on the other. At the end of her exquisite E major 'Caro nome' (scene 6), Gilda retires from the terrace doting on the name of Gualtier Maldè (alias the Duke); she basks in the comfort of her reiterated closures and in the innocent, narcissistic pleasure afforded by her trills. In the street below, the courtiers pause before the beauty of the woman they believe to be Rigoletto's mistress; their minor mode inflections – using a fifth-to-flattened sixth motif (B-C) – not only add erotic flavour to the purity of her lines, but more importantly suggest the violence that their presence portends: we also hear a predatory tread of the timpani. Musically, Gilda's aria comes to a close; dramatically, the action remains open.

In the following recitative (*recitativo*), Rigoletto asks himself why he has returned home to the same ominous B-C motif adumbrated by the courtiers.

In turn, the courtiers prepare themselves for the abduction in a surreptitious but bright C major (their music thematically foreshadows the following andante). Rigoletto inflects this C major with a flattened-sixth-to-fifth motif ($A^\flat$-G) as he broods on Monterone's curse. Although once again the mixture of the modes dramatizes the opposition of the characters, the darkness now lies with Rigoletto and not the courtiers.

The abduction plan is stated and executed in a pair of closed forms (*andante assai mosso* and *allegro*). These are delightful exercises in the jocular-macabre, a genre Verdi also explored in *Macbeth* (1847/rev. 1865) and *Un ballo in maschera* (1859). For the courtiers, revenge is as fun as it is ruthless. In the *andante*, all the characters, including Rigoletto, float snatches of dialogue over the orchestra, which now carries the musical argument; hence the oppositions are more complex. The exaggerated courtly dotted rhythms, the airy, insolently regular four-bar phrases, and the smug contrasts between the brazenly welcoming *fortes* and the knowingly secretive *pianissimos* – all these project the confidence of the courtiers' $A^\flat$ major. The venom, on the other hand, lies in the working out of the harmony, which raises major triads on minor scale degrees ($^\flat$VI, $^\flat$III and briefly $^\flat$IV), and allows figures involving chromatic notes derived from them to lie provocatively on the music's surface (especially $C^\flat$-to-$B^\flat$ and $F^\flat$-to-$E^\flat$). The following *allegro* also deploys a *sotto voce scherzando* texture, where the courtiers fleck the conspiratorial hush (*piano*) with moments of unrestrained glee (*forte*), and where the manifestly heroic key of $E^\flat$ major unfolds over the notes of the portentous $E^\flat$ minor pegged out in the bass.

In the last part of the finale, the venom rises to the surface and triumph cedes to disaster: as Gilda struggles and loses her scarf, the high note $A^\flat$ is established within the key of $E^\flat$ major. This moves linearly to G for the courtiers 'Vittoria!' and then depressively falls to $G^\flat$ for Gilda's 'Aiuta!' (Help!). The diminished harmony accompanying this $G^\flat$ is taken up by Rigoletto who struggles to loosen his blindfold: it is as if inwardly he has heard Gilda's cry even though outwardly he is deaf to it. For an agonizing nineteen bars of mounting dynamic tension (*pianissimo* to *fortissimo*), this dissonance is extended by passing consonances in the orchestra; it is resolved into the harsh reality of a full cadence in $E^\flat$ minor, once Rigoletto has interpolated the 'curse' figure, breaking the harmonic rhythm as he reintroduces the note C from the beginning of the finale. The bitterness is reinforced by the falling chromatic scales, which race to a starkly emphatic conclusion.

What is striking throughout is how closely the musical continuity has related the denigration of the idealized object, Gilda, to the disillusionment of Rigoletto. First, it binds together remote tonalities; and second, it creates a network of oppositions in which the destructive elements at first lie buried, and later rise to the surface to confront Rigoletto with the ineluctable consequences of his own actions. And it is vital to see how, from both points of view, the musical processes represent the outcome of associations formed earlier in the act. For, although outwardly the opera is cast into separate 'numbers', inwardly the musical concerns override and unite them. There is certainly no caesura at the point the abduction begins. In an admittedly small way, Ponnelle's bottle is a visual image that diminishes the aural continuity, and hence obscures Verdi's musical grasp of the work's psycho-dynamics. Yet it is this grasp, together with the copious invention, that never ceases to astonish and delight us.

Notes

Source: 'Rigoletto's Bottle: Psychoanalysis and Opera', *New Formations* ('Psychoanalysis and Culture' issue), No. 26, Autumn 1995, London: Lawrence and Wishart, pp. 108-19. The essay was based on a talk given to the British Psychoanalytical Society on 21 June 1991 jointly with the psychoanalyst Alex Tarnopolsky. I am grateful both to him and to Barbara Robson for permission to use their words. I also pay tribute to the encouragement I received from the late Robert Donington.

1   Available on DVD and VHS video-cassette, Decca 071 401-3.
2   Giuseppe Verdi, *Rigoletto*, Milan: Chicago UP and G. Ricordi & Co., 1983; vocal score 1985, trans. Andrew Porter.
3   Robert Donington, *Opera and its Symbols*, London: Yale UP, 1990, pp. 85-90.
4   Robert Donington, *Wagner's 'Ring' and its Symbols*, London: Faber and Faber, 1963.
5   Cf. Julian Budden, *The Operas of Verdi*, vol. 1, London: Cassell, 1973, pp. 475–510.
6   This is addressed in the previous entry on 'Loss'.

Part Seven

Performance

Introduction

In the Poetics, *Aristotle never discusses actors or staging, though he clearly had a command of repertory. Yet performance is the goal of tragedy and comedy, for the cast as much as for writers, and for audiences as much as for critics and theorists. Performance necessarily belongs to time, place and circumstance; it may catch the mood of the moment; it may be discussed but not replicated; and its impact may exceed what is suggested by the text. And although its effect can be captured in illustration or on film, the dangerous living it entails, with its keen management of time, cannot. By analogy, it ought to be the most important part of a book on opera, yet it is the hardest to write. Nevertheless, the effort must be made.*

This part consists of a number of opera reviews, arranged by the date of the works concerned. The composers thus form a progression, from Handel (1735) to Judith Weir (1994). For the most part, the reviews first appeared in the Times Literary Supplement, *and have been selected from a larger body listed in the Bibliography. Each of them focuses on a topic thrown up by the work or its performance. Some of the topics have been aired in previous parts of this book. Others, though, are new: these include ballet, scenery, costumes, memorability, style-height, mechanism and negative virtue. The appraisal of conductors and singers is largely admiring, whereas that of directors is mixed. Modern opera production, of course, is notoriously controversial, yet the philosophy – or 'concept' – behind any staging needs to be understood before it is celebrated or condemned. The reviews adopt no a priori stance. The entries are preceded by a Prologue, a conference report that focuses on two stagings of Handel's* Ariodante – one *'authentic', the other 'modern'. They are followed by an Epilogue, a review of Tom Sutcliffe's chronicle of opera production in modern times. This ends by asserting the importance of the musical score: in opera, we listen with our eyes, watch with our ears and react with our whole being.*

The subject of a review is usually serendipitous: it is in the gift of editors to match contributor to performance, just as it is up to them to bestow titles on what they receive. As the reviews were written, type-set and printed under pressures of time and space, they inevitably contained slips: these slips have been corrected. I have also replaced some words, added a phrase here or there to clarify an argument, invented new titles and added end-notes where necessary.

Prologue: Alternative Rhetorics

George Frideric Handel (anon. after Salvi and Ariosto): *Ariodante*

A Response to the IAMS International Conference on 'Ariodante: Baroque Drama and Handel Opera*', held at King's College London, 17-18 April, 1993.*

The first session of Reinhard Strohm's *Ariodante* conference might make any scholar pause before pronouncing unequivocally on the subject of opera production. Its title, along with its speakers, almost wilfully courted confrontation: '*Ariodante* at Covent Garden, 1735, and at the Coliseum, 1993.' For '1735' were Dene Barnett, author of the conference's seminal document, *The Art of Gesture* (1987) – a fascinating manual – and the omniscient Winton Dean, whose detailed account of the work had yet to appear;[1] for '1993' were Nicholas John, the innovative dramaturg of the English National Opera, Kate Brown, an undogmatic director with some experience of Handel, and David Alden, the director of the 1993 *Ariodante*, whose previous work for ENO on *Un ballo in maschera* and *Oedipus rex* has caused an unprecedented number of learned teeth – including my own – to gnash.[2] Predictably, the confrontation was between revitalized European tradition on the one hand (eighteenth-century theatrical rhetoric, we were told, takes at least four years to learn (!)), and, on the other, a new cosmopolitan music theatre with a strong line in popular psychologism and its roots firmly planted in the personality cult of the modern director and his untutored, spontaneous reactions to the music. Even the shade of Samuel Beckett was invoked to add his imprimatur. Symptomatically, the TV cameras were present to photograph just Alden.

In the context of the suavely-renovated Great Hall of King's College London and a select international audience, it was not hard to take sides with the ancients against the moderns. Barnett won sympathy by declaring himself 'belligerent' to the new ideas, while Dean advocated a production of which Handel 'would have approved'. Dignity seemed to lie on the side of abrogating our late-twentieth-century impulses, with study and revitalization of lost practice as the sure path to virtue. These thoughts, indeed, were reinforced at least twice the next day: first by a passing allusion to Handel's musical rhetoric from Sarah McCleave (KCL) in answer to a paper by Lucia Mencaroni (Rome) – the gavotte-type, she argued, had sinister implications in various operas; and second, by the dignified and thoroughly worthwhile 'workshop performance' of Act Two of *Ariodante* mounted by Ian Caddy at the Royal Academy of Music in light of Barnett's gestural rhetoric. The whole enterprise seemed cast in the same *Werktreu* spirit in which Brahms once claimed he had found his individuality by following Beethoven's every instruction, or, in the field of recent opera production, in which Peter Stein unforgettably revitalized Verdi's *Otello* and *Falstaff* for Welsh National Opera.

But, in fact, would Handel have been 'belligerent' towards, or disapproving of at least some of the radically new versions (it is easy to accept that all the necessary modern adjustments to size of proscenium, depth of stage, lighting, scenic flaps, disposition of instruments and so forth do not represent significant departures from the 'spirit of the original')? Or, to put the matter more provocatively, are composers in general remotely concerned with preservation? Let us shift the matter for a moment from production to composition. The question may come down to the difference of artistic temperament, but it is hard to think of a single composer who, faced with the music of the past, has not wanted to absorb it into his (or her) present. One doesn't have to cite the obvious examples of composers devouring the music of others – Stravinsky and Pergolesi, Schoenberg and Monn, Schumann and Bach, Brahms and most of music history known to him, and so forth; one need think only of composers in relation to their own writings: the history of Verdi's operas is a history of rewritings; Wagner sought to update his Romantic operas into music dramas; Mahler rewrote symphonies for different venues; and Handel himself rewrote his anthems, cantatas, masques, operas and oratorios *ad nauseam* for new occasions. Indeed, one could argue that what is exceptional for a composer is to settle for the immutability of his (or her) work. Composers move with the times: they never stop the clock.

A modern production, then, is a way of acknowledging just this. It says, were the composer still with us, he (or she) would surely have adapted the score to suit our new conditions. And this brings us back to the confrontation aired at the start. In 1985, the director David Pountney revived Michael Tippett's *The Midsummer Marriage* (1955) for ENO. Pountney's typical preoccupation with the demotic, and in particular with the character of the chorus, lent the work a new emphasis. In Act Two, for instance, he turned the ritual dances into a group improvisation, giving each member of the chorus their own 'shadow' – their Jungian dark side – whereas in Tippett's original there had been just one couple, the hunter (a female dancer) and the hunted (Strephon). The result did not please some critics – myself included – who duly leapt to the defence of 'the work'. It was not just that the impact of the interrupted third dance had been diluted, we complained, but that the all-important shock Bella experiences after witnessing the dances, and from which she takes time to recover, was simply not there. Surely this was a case of the director bending a work to his own concept, thereby driving a stake into its heart?

Imagine, then, the astonishment we all felt on learning that, after reading the reviews, Tippett had been in touch with the Coliseum and assured them that they had 'done well'. It was as if, at a stroke, the composer's approval had destroyed a central plank of the responsible critic's enterprise – the defence of masterpieces in the face of upstarts and poseurs. If Tippett sanctioned this, where would a bottom line be drawn? But what Tippett recognized, I suggest, was the alignment of his ideas with the emerging Zeitgeist: multiple shadows and split characters were then a theatrical preoccupation, as was evident from Karlheinz Stockhausen's *Donnerstag aus Licht* (1981) and Harrison Birtwistle's *The Mask of Orpheus* (1986). Indeed, the demotic images thrown up by Pountney's production were not so dissimilar to those Tippett incorporated in his next (and final) opera *New Year* (1989) staged at Glyndebourne, with its exploration of the people in 'Terror Town'. All that had been wrong at ENO was that the music of 1955 hadn't been revised to keep pace with thirty years of development in the art of stagecraft! It wasn't that 1985 had broken step with 1955.

Let us be absolutely clear, then, from this and other similar cases, that to mount an 'authentic' Baroque opera or oratorio performance, with whatever skill, is an antiquarian exercise, *tout court*. Of course, it may be a kind of exercise that revitalizes modern composition: Alexander Goehr's oratorio on *The Death of Moses* (1992) was in part a recreation of a performance by his father (Walter) of Monteverdi's *Vespers* (1610) forty years earlier. It may be more satisfying than what comes after it, especially a production that fails to rise to the range and quality of the challenges set by the implicit or explicit stagecraft of an original (as with Peter Sellars's recent updated, dialogue-free *Zauberflöte* for Glyndebourne that caused a near-riot). It may demand a discipline in every way more admirable than the improvisatory approach of our own times (especially regarding dance and movement). But it cannot be said to have anything to do with the spirit of 'the composer'. There can be no legitimate appeal to the ghost of Handel to sanction antiquarianism: he might recognize Barnett's recovered 'art of gesture' (though his music was not especially 'rhetorical'), he might admire it (as we certainly do), but that does not mean he would sanction it for 1993. He wouldn't. For the creator, the only time that matters is the here and now, the only relationship that counts is between his (or her) music and an audience in tune with the present.

What, rather, is extraordinary is that the inventive and versatile modern designs shown to the conference by Heinz Balthes, the opera designer from Karlsruhe, are there to accompany the music of a man who died in 1759: we have no contemporary genius of Handel's stature to provide the sounds they demand, and we should not be mislead by Balthes's argument that there is a fruitful ('post-modern') tension between, on the one hand, the music of Handel's *Scipione* (1726) and, on the other, the set of the Sheraton Hotel, Kuwait at the time of the Gulf War. The operative word is 'tension', and we can be sure that were Handel with us now, at the ripe old age of three hundred and eight, he wouldn't settle for it for one moment.[3]

So what do we conclude? Merely to say that we must live with *Ariodante* as both Baroque opera and modern drama is to repeat the title of the conference's first session: we are all aware of the chasm between 1735 and 1993. Nor is it helpful to resort to the fashionable argument that works 'reveal themselves through the history of their reception', the stance, say, of Carl Dahlhaus. On the whole, they do not. The production of Alden and the designs of Balthes tell us mainly about our times, just as in the early twentieth century the now-discredited compressed performing versions of Handel by Dr. Oskar Hagen tell us about his.

Now, 'our times' are Janus-faced. Negatively, as far as main-stream repertory is concerned, they impose Ten Commandments for any aspiring opera director:

1   Alter the opera's ending to conform to your Work-concept (which has its own network of symbols).

2   Reduce all scenery to a single set, preferably one that rotates (thereby eroding any distinction between private and public spaces).

3   Devise stage metaphors for the tortuous inner life of the characters (ignoring their outer life as defined by time, place and circumstance).

4   Invent new sub-plots where none previously existed (especially those that hint at dangerous liaisons).

5   Act out any image thrown up by the text (so nothing is left to the audience's imagination).

6   Contradict stage directions wherever you can (even when supported by the music).

7   Invert all pathos – high seriousness – into bathos – low farce (remembering that it is mandatory to trash Wagner).

8   Distract attention from the singer with 'other business' wherever he or she might steal your thunder (and be sure to level the characters by cloaking them in black and white).

9   Deny the sole authority of music whenever it asserts itself by introducing mime (notably in overtures and interludes).

10   Leave the stage littered with detritus (to show that it is your party that is well and truly over).

But – and it is a big 'but' – these do not necessarily form a yardstick for judgement. They may be the rules of a largely perverse stylistic game, yet, taken individually, they can have their effect: there are occasions when an infidelity to the letter can be a higher fidelity to the spirit.[4] For, positively, our times can release a new understanding of the social, political and affective issues an old opera raises by reference to the mass of critical writing, especially on psychology, that reaches back for over a century. Such fresh understanding will manifest itself mainly in the gesture and movement of singers, but also in stagecraft, costume and design. Yet it does not have to imply the radical reconstruction of an original, and the music will set interpretative limits that have to be respected.

However, what links the 'then' and the 'now' is the perennial and mysterious attraction of certain subjects over others. *The New Grove Dictionary of Opera* (1992), for instance, places Handel's *Arianna in Creta* (1734) in a line of Ariadne operas that stretches from Monteverdi (1608), Cambert and Grabu (1674) and Porpora (1714) to Benda (1775), Massenet (1906), Richard Strauss (1912/16), Milhaud (1928) and Martinů (1961), to which we may now add Goehr (1995) and Birtwistle (2008 – *The Minotaur*). But why is there no such line with *Ariodante*, Méhul (1799) apart? Is the subject intrinsically less appealing, and if so why? Or might there still be something in it that could attract both modern directors and composers beyond the academy? The answers might even help to negotiate the chasm that the first session of Strohm's lively conference opened up so unerringly.

Notes

Source: Submitted to the *Newsletter of the Institute for Advanced Music Studies*, King's College London, 1993, but not published. It has been updated to include reference to recent works.

1   See: Winton Dean '*Ariodante*', *Handel's Operas 1726-1741*, Woodbridge: The Boydell Press, 2006, pp. 285-311.
2   My review of Alden's production of *Oedipus rex* appears later in this part.
3   Postscript, 2017: post-modern tension, on the other hand, can have its day – witness the choreographer Jiří Kylián's striking *Six Dances* for the Nederlands Dans Theater (1997), where the dance is modern, the music is by Mozart, and the transitional (new-old) 'prop' is the heavily powdered wig worn by each dancer. In cinema too, the use of old music to comment on the new by exploiting the distance between the then and the now has been widely exploited, sometimes to great effect.
4   No one who has seen it can forget the impact of Patrice Chéreau's production of Wagner's *Ring* at Bayreuth (1980, and subsequently released on DVD): when Wotan lifts the patch on his eye to confirm the 'outer' sacrifice he has made for 'inner' wisdom, Chéreau introduces business so apt that we cannot believe that Wagner would have disapproved. Likewise, the rotating and multiply dividing set for the Café Momus in Act Two of Richard Jones's production of Puccini's *La bohème* at The Royal Opera in September 2017 was nothing but a delight.

1 *Authentic Inauthenticity*

Antoine Gautier de Montdorge (*et al*) and Jean-Philippe Rameau:
Les Fêtes d'Hébé (*opéra-ballet*)

There is no doubt that this week's resurrection of Rameau's *Les Fêtes d'Hébé* has been one of the triumphs of the season. But why should such a neglected piece hold a large and appreciative audience in thrall from start to finish? The work was composed in 1739 and, like Rameau's equally pleasing *Les Indes galantes* of 1735, is cast as an *opéra-ballet*. The genre emerged in the late seventeenth century and, unlike the *tragédie lyrique*, which unfolds conventionally over five acts, merely asks that a few self-contained *entrées* (acts with slender story lines) are strung together around a central theme, and that each *entrée* should contain a *divertissement* (comprising song and dance). Since modern audiences have little direct knowledge of the type, an 'old' work like *Les Fêtes d'Hébé* can strike them with the force of a new one.[1]

Even from this concert performance by Les Arts Florissants under William Christie, it is easy to see how Voltaire could lament that *opéra-ballet* had knocked his own tragedy out of court: *Les Fêtes d'Hébé* contains an extraordinary variety of beautiful little numbers and ostentatiously ignores grandeur. Three *entrées* address themselves to 'the lyric talents' of poetry (Sappho), music (Tyrtaeus) and dance (Eglé, a shepherdess) respectively.[2] Yet ironically the best song occurs in the dance section (the arresting *arietta vive* for Mercury), and the best dance in the music one (the Oracle replies to Iphise in a dumb show, or mimed ballet). In this genre, entertainment, and not instruction, is all.

Similarly, though critics have shown that *Les Fêtes d'Hébé* reintroduces Greek gods and heroes into comedy,[3] this performance prompted the thought that, on the contrary, the inclusion of classical figures is a wittily audacious advance of dandified pastoral. For the gods seemed more human than the humans, and the interaction of the singers provided a rich source of amusement, even in concert. Especially pleasing was the duet-recitative 'Non, je n'aimerai que vous' (No, I shall love only you), described fairly in the programme as 'full of voluptuous ardour', and the ravishing trio preceding the stirring finale to the second *entrée*. Moreover, just as a French librettist wrote in 1718 that graceful airs were fundamental to the enterprise, so too did Rameau's delicately ornamented airs never lose their poise – even in the laments – and his dances were joyfully differentiated.

The piece was enormously popular in its day, but went through umpteen revisions. William Christie's new performing version merely continues the practice: authenticity here would have been inauthentic. He has changed instrumentation, added a charismatic pipe and tabor, and introduced a number of cuts that lend the work an air of unexpected pithiness. Les Arts Florissants, too, showed all the benefits of authenticity's by-now-familiar timbral facelift, most impressively in the strings. Yet it also set uncanny new standards in its ambitious tempi, firm articulation and expressive contrasts: these approached, without crossing, the threshold of exaggeration. Indeed, the players' ability to turn dance-tunes into lithe and buoyant extended melodies should be the envy of all musicians brought up under the modern shadow of 'the large line'.

In a cast that included fine and committed solo performances from Sarah Connolly, Sophie Daneman, Paul Agnew and Thierry Félix, pride of place went to the tenor Jean-Paul Fouchécourt. Through wit and gesture he in particular demonstrated just how pleasing can be the will to please.

Notes

Source: 'Deity Dancing', *Observer* (Review), 22 December 1996, p. 11.

1 The first complete staging of the work in modern times was at Monte Carlo in January 2014.

2 Of the story Graham Sadler writes: 'The gods' cupbearer Hebe (soprano), tiring of Olympus, persuades her attendants to fly with her to the banks of the Seine, there to celebrate those gifts most cherished on the operatic stage – poetry, music and dance. These 'lyric talents' provide the subject matter of the ensuing entrées.' *The New Grove Dictionary of Opera*, vol. 2, ed. Stanley Sadie, London: Macmillan, 1992, p. 175.

3 Graham Sadler also writes: 'The return to stock classical Greek material … may seem retrogressive. In fact, the latter was more in line with current trends, since the vogue for *opéra-ballets* on mythological or legendary subjects had established itself in 1723, with François Colin de Blamont's *Les Fêtes grecques et romaines*.' *Ibid*.

2   *Psychologizing the Gods*
Richard Wagner: *Das Rheingold*

In his programme note to Götz Friedrich's production of the *Ring* cycle, Peter Porter envisages a new millennium when 'the gods' will be close to us and our 'psychoanalytic humours' once again. One wonders how much Friedrich would agree. His *Rheingold*, set in his 'Henry Moore' time-tunnel, undoubtedly has its triumphs: Alberich's gaudy subterranean gold factory, with its television screens fearsomely eyeing the workforce, would have delighted Bernard Shaw. So too would the staging of the mechanical dragon. Wotan's Valhalla offers a comparably ambiguous image: as both stage-picture and magic apparition it has the power to lure the gods – here, a troupe of actors – down the tunnel in a measured, side-stepping dance-of-death. Loge, too, is not only fire-god but also a felt-hatted Wagnerian impresario, by turns peevish, anxious and excitable (Kenneth Riegel turns in a virtuoso performance): he distances himself from the gods by stepping beyond the proscenium to appeal to the audience in a Brechtian act of parabasis. Yet the production can feel oddly dislocated from the music. Why should this be, when in terms of social analysis it often seems so right?

Porter's gods may well hold the answer. Wagner's *Das Rheingold* (1869) shows the beginning, not only of material things, but also of psychological ones. (Ironically, by resisting Wagner Brecht acknowledged just this.) What Alberich and Wotan – and indeed all the characters bar Loge – have to confront is their reaction to the loss of the original, maternal love epitomized by the Rhine-daughters and Freia. The *Ring* as a whole maps out Wotan's fumbling, complex and by the end tragi-triumphant effort to make reparation for a love-for-power sacrifice made even before the cycle begins. Alberich's reaction to loss, on the other hand, precludes reparation: for him, Erda, the earth-mother who speaks to Wotan as his conscience, has nothing to say. For him, she is wilfully 'split off'.

The curious quality of Friedrich's staging is that it too seems to avoid confronting original integrated love *ab initio*. There is no real role for Mother Nature. The Rhine-daughters in their severe monochrome costumes and setting are merely narcissistic and punitive; the waves of the Rhine, simulated by undulating veils lifted from the maidens at the start, suggest not so much water and light as the factitious sheen of synthetic fibres; and the gold they guard is represented as a textbook analysis of its own structural properties in 3-D. And because it is hard to feel nostalgia for any of this when it is lost, the later stages of the evening lose their psychological point: why should

Wotan pay any attention to the Rhine-daughters' plangent call for the return of the gold? There seems no real work for reparation to do (even though the reparation demands a renunciation of the world as Wotan knows it).

The irony is that, of the various parts of the cycle, the 'preliminary evening', *Das Rheingold*, suffers least from this sort of treatment. This may be because so much of it is concerned with exploring the consequences of loss. In this respect, Friedrich's production, supported by Bernard Haitink's alert musical direction, is often impressive. Ekkehard Wlaschiha's Alberich projects terror as he places a curse on the ring; Helga Dernesch's Fricka elegantly tempers moral outrage at the sacrifice of Freia with self-interest as she comes to see in Valhalla a personal benefit; and Alexander Oliver's Mime is unusually affecting when he recalls better days forging trinkets for women. Similarly, the movements and grouping are often eloquent, not least when Anne Gjevang's Erda, dressed in a welcome red, emerges from the depths of the time-tunnel to deliver her warning. Only James Morris's Wotan has yet to achieve the authority needed to persuade us that, alone of the gods, he has the power to win through (in however a complex way). That his power is deeply related to the psychological shortcomings of the production may explain why the evening is not quite as rewarding as it could be.

Source: 'Up Among the Gods', *Times Literary Supplement*, 27 September 1991, p. 21. The *Ring* cycle was given by The Royal Opera. The review is slightly revised.

3 Reclaiming Anti-opera

Maurice Maeterlinck and Claude Debussy: *Pelléas et Mélisande*

When Pierre Boulez was invited to conduct *Pelléas* for The Royal Opera back in 1969, he saw his mission as twofold: to rescue the work's 'dramatic energy' from a tradition of 'safe' understatement, and to restore its 'mythic dimension'.[1] With this new production for the Welsh National Opera, his mission is pursued, if anything, with an even greater zeal. 'Dramatic energy' for Boulez begins with the painstaking preparation of the orchestra, and here the fruits of his labour are apparent at every level: in the 'Musorgskian' detail (the eerily icy chords at 'on a brisé la glace avec des fers rougis'),[2] in the supple handling of affective nuance in the work's various duologues, and in the totally assured shaping of scenes, acts and interludes. Boulez's reclamation for the work of something of Wagner's symphonism (from *Tristan*, Act Two) goes a long way to allaying the traditional charge that *Pelléas* (1902) is no better than a play set to music, a wilfully-restrained 'anti-opera' as Auden described it.

Boulez's other concern, with the 'mythic dimension', also recalls Wagner, though in a necessarily more complex way. In *Pelléas*, mythic timelessness emphasizes how, in the dank, gloomy isolation of a castle (beautifully realized in Karl-Ernst Herrmann's elaborate, partly 'real' and partly fantastic sets), all the main characters stand in the long shadow cast by loss, sickness and death. Boulez focuses principally on the paranoid violence of Golaud, which he understands as a re-enactment of the events that led to the death of his first wife, events not actually recounted in the play. This violence is brought to the fore earlier and more powerfully than in other productions, and has the effect of stressing the special quality of the score: Golaud's horrific sense of psychological imprisonment derives from the fact that Debussy's musical motifs, like Maeterlinck's words, resolutely refuse to explain cause and effect in the way that Wagner's do. Golaud's music may derive from *Parsifal*, but it functions quite differently. It enshrines 'symbolist' mystery.[3]

The work's contrasts are no less powerfully handled. Pelléas (a charismatic Neil Archer) is portrayed as a *fin-de-siècle* aesthete for whom Mélisande (Alison Hagley) offers not only the promise of sexual experience, but also a release from an innocence encircled by the sickness of relatives and friends. The production (by Peter Stein) uses mobile black surrounds and cut-outs with great effect to frame scenes as it charts the lovers' progress: they move from the contained, gilded pleasures of early acquaintance, through shared wonder at an uncannily lit, newly revealed subterranean world, to the final, fear-driven confessions of love, during which Pelléas's extravagant and frantic movements encompass the entire stage. Less convincing is the emergence of Pelléas and Golaud into a rare burst of midday light after their visit to the castle vaults. An enormous stage sun emits a blinding light before which the two half-brothers act as in a shadow-play: the force of this image seems oddly at variance with both the musical delicacy of Pelléas's response to the fragrance of the flowers and Golaud's more ominous warnings about Mélisande's pregnancy.

Yet for all its extraordinary merits, this production is oddly less moving than the more erratic recent staging by the English National Opera. It is not just that Donald Maxwell's fine performance as Golaud is vocally lighter than Willard White's, or that there are features that will surely improve with time – some scenes begin too soon, a lighter flute is needed at the start of Act Three, the live sheep in Act Four is too much of a distraction, and so forth. It is rather as if the tenderness of Arkel's observation, made in the face of Golaud's cruelty, that 'Si j'étais Dieu, j'aurais pitié du coeur des hommes',[4] has not yet found an equivalent in the production. But this is criticism at the highest level; and it can only be hoped that Boulez will return to Cardiff, as some reports have suggested he might, for what could surely be an equally enthralling *Boris Godunov*.

Notes

Source: 'Standing in the Shadow', *Times Literary Supplement*, 27 March 1992, p. 19.

1   Pierre Boulez's essay 'Reflections on *Pelléas et Mélisande*' appears in: Pierre Boulez, *Orientations*, trans. Martin Cooper, London: Faber and Faber, 1986, pp. 306-17. Boulez writes: 'The real difficulty in interpreting *Pelléas* is to avoid both pointlessly *heroic* gestures and rhetorical attitudes on the one hand and timidity and 'safe' understatement on the other.' (p. 315)

2   'One has broken the ice with red-hot irons'.

3   For a discussion of the parallel, see: Robin Holloway, *Debussy and Wagner*, London: Eulenburg Books, 1979.

4   'Were I God, I would have pity on the hearts of men'.

4 *Enduring Ephemera*

F. de Croisset and Cain with Jules Massenet: *Chérubin*

If Debussy had had his way, The Royal Opera wouldn't be staging *Chérubin* at all, let alone in such a flattering production. In his letters he refers to its composer, Massenet, as a 'talent-less mountebank', the kind of French artist who caught the 'melancholy' and 'sentimentality' of the suburbs; and his *Werther* displayed 'an extraordinary talent for satisfying all that is poetically empty and lyrically cheap in the dilettante mind'. Yet Debussy would have known that his and Massenet's materials were not always so different; and he must have taken thought as Massenet served up work after work when so many of his own theatrical projects never came to fruition. In *Monsieur Croche, antidilettante* (posthumously published in 1921), he even expressed envy for Massenet's 'untiring curiosity' about the 'feminine soul', conveyed in music whose harmonies are like 'enlacing arms', and whose 'melodies are the necks we kiss'.

The truth is that, genius or not, Massenet was still a fastidious opera professional. *Chérubin* (1905) may be toothless and far from his best work, but it survives because it aims to please, and no more. In this it succeeds. Its best moments set music and drama in ironic opposition. Chérubin has the peasants perform a reedy *fête pastorale* during which he can assess the local female talent; he and Ricardo fight a duel to the strains of a gavotte played by a stage quartet of violins; and the King's mistress sings her climactic aubade, 'Vive l'amour qui meurt en une nuit' – a deliciously callow paean to her one-night stand with the besotted Chérubin – to the intimate sounds of a mandolin. These moments are all savoured by the production: none could have been penned by Debussy.

And what of the designs in relation to the music? This *Chérubin* crosses skin-deep invocations of Mozart and Beaumarchais with those of Offenbach and Bizet, thereby recreating a narcissistic world in which it is still possible for a seventeen-year-old to philander with the wives of dukes, counts and barons. Antony McDonald's sets and costumes wittily transmute this world into ours, blending Rococo titillations with those of consumer culture: his electric colours are period but surreal, and the white houses of Seville have neon-lit balconies and walls studded with glowing pink shells. In the last act, even the peeling fleur-de-lys wallpaper gives the same lie to instant sexual gratification as does the orchestration: in the closing minutes, Massenet is master enough to raise the work's emotional tone.

Chérubin's greatest source of pleasure, though, lies in its meticulous vocal writing. The title part was originally composed as a trouser-role for Mary

Garden, Debussy's first Mélisande (trouser-roles clearly appealed to her: she famously insisted on singing the tenor lead in the 1910 New York production of Massenet's *Le Jongleur de Notre-Dame*). Here, Chérubin is cast as a mezzo-soprano, with the pure soprano parts left to Chérubin's women. In Tim Albery's production, 'he' is played by Susan Graham, an American singer new to The Royal Opera. She may have little of Garden's Gallic insolence, and her voice may lack Mediterranean menace, yet her strong, bright mezzo has a thrilling ability to cut through ensembles. Her infectious stage presence is most telling when humiliated by the King's mistress: Chérubin's distress effectively marks the beginning of the sentimental education that it is the task of the lad's tutor, the engagingly worldly 'Philosophe', to promote. Similarly, the poor, sad, spurned, devoted Nina, to whom the hero perforce returns, is taken by the vocally charismatic Angela Gheorghiu: her impeccable rendering of Chérubin's poem is the high-point of the first act.

For all its grace, skill and wit, *Chérubin* nevertheless remains an ephemeral piece. It is curious to see such attention lavished upon a squib. In a less self-conscious musical world, there ought to be similar works to take its place. But there aren't. Engraved on the hearts of most contemporary French composers is the name *Pelléas*, not *Manon*. Indeed, it can be argued that the 'anti-dilettantism' of the Wagnerian Debussy has all but stifled the growth of French opera, especially under the post-war championship of Olivier Messiaen, whereas dilettantism, in the expert hands of Poulenc and the neo-classicists, for a time proved more durable. Whatever the case, the revival of *Chérubin* tells a story. The conductor is Mario Bernardi, an effective last-minute replacement for Gennadi Rozhdestvensky.

Source: 'A Suburban Squib', *Times Literary Supplement*, 4 March 1994, p. 18.

5 Credible Magic

Hugo von Hofmannsthal and Richard Strauss: *Die Frau ohne Schatten*

It was an interesting idea to invite David Hockney to design the sets for this new production of *Die Frau ohne Schatten* (1919) since they are able to pull together many features of his other operatic work. Hofmannsthal's story of two couples whose relationship is put to the test – the (apparently) Jungian title refers to the childlessness of each of the two women – obviously recalls Hockney's Glyndebourne *Zauberflöte*, and their trials are enacted in halls with the same fantastic-macabre air as Sarastro's. For the imperial gardens and chambers Hockney draws on the enchanted luminosity he achieved with Stravinsky's *Le Rossignol* (a lovely blend of blues, greens, mauves and silvers) and the final watery landscape exudes something of the vitality of his work on Ravel, Satie and Poulenc.[1] The opera, his images remind us, is a comedy, albeit one with biological roots, as the fertility symbols he weaves into the designs testify. The effect of all this is to create a magical world that, for once, is credible: it seems only too natural that glistening fish fly into a frying pan, a tree of life pulsates with gold, and numinous apparitions come and go. More importantly still, the sets enhance the magic of Strauss's astonishingly refined orchestration and use of offstage sounds: the morbid keening of a falcon and the singing of unborn children are forces that shape the whole drama.[2]

If there is a limitation, though, it lies in the quality of Hockney's contrasts. When, for example, the Empress and the Nurse fly from the enclave of their palace to the land of the pugnacious, deprived and smelly humans, the transition is hardly reflected in the scenery. Although Hockney follows the stage directions faithfully enough, he perhaps takes too much hedonistic pleasure in the shapes and colours of the Dyer's house. Why should the wife of Barak (the Dyer) want to exchange this world of ubiquitous stripes and surreally-cast phials of coloured water for the gaudy universe with which the Nurse tempts her? The effect of this hedonism is to exaggerate just one aspect of Strauss's score: the nostalgia of the songful melodic writing, the conventional basis of the harmony and the fluency of the musical continuity. But its darker, Wagnerian side, which projects the mortal danger of the trials and is, perhaps, its most impressive aspect, is somehow left to go its own way.

Partly for this reason, the evening belongs even more to the musicians than to Hockney. Bernard Haitink's consistently assured conducting is at its most poignant in the great orchestral cantilena of Act One – one of many remarkable purely musical passages – in which the Dyer movingly embraces his childless wife; Jane Henschel's engagingly wicked Nurse surmounts the notorious vocal challenges of her role with mercurial zest; and the elegance and authority of Anna Tomowa-Sintow's Empress secures the heart of the opera in her climactic refusal to accept the shadow of another woman. What, though, of Gwyneth Jones as Barak's wife? In the first act, her singing is so erratic – notes are scooped, the vibrato is overblown and the tone severe – that she seems outclassed by the rest of the company; yet at the end of the second act, her renunciation of the possibility of having children shows how magnificently and accurately she can still rise to the great challenge. In the tortuous duologue of the third act, where the hidden strength of the marriage is revealed for the first time, the sheer force of her stage presence brings out the best from Franz Grundheber's generally pleasing Barak. All this is not just good for The Royal Opera, but also good for the state of opera today.

Notes

Source: 'Richard Strauss, *Die Frau ohne Schatten*', *Times Literary Supplement*, 4 December 1992, p. 19.

1   Examples of Hockney's stage designs appear in: Marco Livingstone, *David Hockney*, London: Thames and Hudson, 1981, new enlarged edition 1996. For an example from *Die Frau*, see p. 265.
2   That Hockney's approach resonates with Hofmannsthal's thought can be seen from the end of the first paragraph of the librettist's prose story of the same name: 'Seven mountains of the moon enclosed the lake that encircled the island with ebony black water. Once more the nurse imagined herself watching the half-grown child as it changed into a bright red fish before her eyes and swam gleaming through the dark flood, or took on the shape of a bird and fluttered between the gloomy branches.' Hugo von Hofmannsthal, *The Woman without a Shadow*, trans. Jean Hollander, Lampeter: Edwin Mellen Press, 1993, p. 1.

6   The Memorable Tune

Sergei Prokofiev (after Gozzi): *The Love for Three Oranges*

According to Prokofiev's biographer, Harlow Robinson, the catchy march tune from *The Love for Three Oranges* (1921) was once used to introduce an American radio show, *The FBI in Peace and War*.[1] The producers clearly knew what they were on to. Although in the opera the march is used just for entrances and exits and the Act Two interlude, it remains the only truly memorable piece in the entire work – and this notwithstanding the multitude of vividly-contrasted little textures Prokofiev deploys throughout, or the orchestral brilliance he demonstrates at every stage. When delicately instrumental, the march is wry, witty and fugitive. At its most brashly assertive, it epitomizes the flamboyant energy of iconoclastic modernity. And even beyond this, it distils the cosmopolitan essence of an opera that began life in 1761 as a kind of *commedia dell'arte* by Gozzi, was then transformed satirically into a Russian fairy-tale at the start of the twentieth century by Meyerhold, before being adroitly adapted for music in 1919 by Prokofiev and subsequently translated out of Russian into French for a first performance in Chicago.

Yet the tune's effect and function in Richard Jones's production (first performed by Opera North in 1988) is rather different. Jones chooses not to recognize that there may be sufficient irony in the music, and, in the handling of rival groups of the stage audience, to allow the psychologically pregnant story of a hypochondriac prince, a witch (Fata Morgana) and a princess trapped in an orange to unfold more or less as it comes. Rather, he extends caricature into every aspect of the production, thereby turning the work into a parochial, partly scatological romp. The harlequin figure, Truffaldino, is dressed as Billy Bunter, the strapping Fata Morgana ostentatiously picks her nose and the demon Farfarello breaks wind at everyone in sight. The general stench at court is made to seem overwhelming, so that members of the chorus wear gas masks throughout, and each member of the audience is equipped with a 'microfragrance card' to allow him or her to savour the odours, fair or foul, that emanate from various parts of the action. Since the stage movements are consistently overdone, never more so than in the preposterously hammy close of Act One, the possibility of suggesting grace, awe and intimacy – never, it is true, Prokofiev's operatic strong point – is largely foregone. In this context, the reprise of the Act Two march tune for the curtain-calls tell its own story: this is a jolly show, *tout court*.

It may say something about the work, however, that it survives such potentially lethal treatment so well. Indeed, the evening is enjoyable, even though on its own terms it remains uneven. The high spirits of the English National Opera, so evident in the company's recent production of Kurt Weill's *Street Scene* (1947), again sweep all before them. Lesley Garrett adds to her unlikely triumph as a bearded Oscar in the Coliseum's confused *Ballo in maschera* an utterly enchanting Ninetta (the princess); Bonaventura Bottone, together with his acrobatic double Paul Miller, exercises a benign charm as Truffaldino; Sue Blane's part-modernist, part-picture-book costumes are vivid and entertaining (more so than the gothic gloom of the sets, which fail to complement the bright colours of the score); and the music is energetically handled by David Atherton. Although there are some good production jokes, including the shooting of the Compère at the footlights before the show begins, there are also unnecessary changes to the stage directions. The libretto calls for a small rat in Act Three to become a big rat in Act Four: reversing this is a failure. Similarly, the giant cook's splendidly-outsize kitchen makes the three oranges look far punier than the text demands.

That these are mainly dramatic points reinforces the sense that *The Love for Three Oranges* is essentially musically enhanced theatre. Indeed, there are only three or four points in the score that are at all redolent of the wilfully uneven pacing of traditional (number-based) opera. Yet though Prokofiev deploys this aesthetic far better than Dargomïzhsky did in *The Stone Guest* of 1872, and would himself go on to have a greater achievement with *The Fiery Angel* of 1923/55, he still handled it less effectively than had Ravel in *L'Heure espagnole* of 1911. What perhaps he owed most to his march tune was its capacity to suggest that his score accomplishes more than it actually does. Who knows, but that may have been its appeal to the FBI.

Notes

Source: 'The Fruitful and the Fruity', *Times Literary Supplement*, 15 December 1989, p. 1391. The opera was staged at the London Coliseum.

1   Harlow Robinson, *Sergei Prokofiev*, London: Robert Hale, 1987.

7 *Production as Reinvention*

F. S. Procházka *et al* (after Čech) and Leoš Janáček: *The Adventures of Mr. Brouček*
Leoš Janáček (after Ostrovsky): *Káťa Kabanová*

1 *The Adventures of Mr. Brouček*

In the extraordinary second scene of Act Two of *The Adventures of Mr. Brouček* (1920) the 'author' Svatopluk Čech unexpectedly steps forward: his story, he complains vehemently, 'is condemned to irony instead of [hailed for its] hymns to valiant soldiers'. The scene offers a striking example of what the director David Pountney calls the work's 'neurotic dramaturgy, never reassuringly linear in the manner of bourgeois drama'. It also marks the point where the intensity of Janáček's music reaches its climax. As Čech's monologue gathers to a head, the music broadens thrillingly from three to four in a bar, the volume increases and the rapidly reiterated orchestral motifs acquire a new urgency. Pountney's production rises movingly to the occasion: an extravagant screen shows film of present-day crowds in the newly-liberated Wenceslas Square destroying the symbols of occupation. Later, when these scenes are replaced by a Hussite battle (returning to 1420), and the tiny coxcombed figure of Brouček is seen behind the screen literally flying from the fight, the point of the comedy, the condemnation of the Czech spirit of the early part of this century, is encapsulated in a brilliant and memorable image.

In fact, the production overflows with such invention. Stefanos Lazaridis's opening nocturnal cityscape, crazily angled like Vlaminck (only more so), with the Sacristan's bed poised precariously at the top of a spiral staircase, provides just the right starting-point for the fantasies of the inebriated, Svejk-like Brouček. These transport him, in the second scene, not to the lunar landscape of the original, but through a series of tableaux illustrating the excesses of our own artists and thinkers. That Pountney has taken the liberty of replacing the ironies of Janáček's times with those of our own is hardly offensive – satire is nothing if not of the moment, and his contemporary images are consistently witty: a Hockney pool that turns out to be a trampoline; a yellow canvas hung with a pair of old boots; a series of waltzes in which the partners flop effetely into each other's arms; crazy operatic surtitles; punk feminists and bridesmaids (the handling of groups is a delight throughout); a black box marked 'melody and form' from which the spirit of music emerges coyly to the censure of the critics; and an amazing equestrian statue made up of welded televisions.

Pountney overcomes what he sees as the work's 'problem' – that its two acts derive from separate stories, albeit both by Čech – with another masterly stroke: in Act Two, he makes the fifteenth-century Hussites and their horses appear as giants, so that Brouček ('little beetle') appears shrunken and a natural butt of the burlesque that is now turned against him. Brouček's garrulously craven monologue contrasts vividly with the pipes and drums, organ and bells of the music for the warriors (and shows to advantage the clarity of Graham Clark's diction). Later, after the battle of Virkov Hill, the act finds its centre with the poignant lament of Kunka for her father, a lament that forms a fitting climax to the third of Vivian Tierney's three well-differentiated roles in the work: as Málinka on Earth and Etherea on the moon, she is also an indefatigable huntress of men. Likewise, Bonaventura Bottone's suave and forceful victory song brings together his three roles as Mazal, Blankytný and Petřik, and gloriously epitomizes Janáček's partiality for high-tessitura male-voice writing.

Indeed, for all that Pountney may deem the opera's 'problematic' central division as 'undoubtedly messy', the fruit of his labours, as well as those of the conductor Charles Mackerras, is to make the whole seem unquestionably, and triumphantly, cogent.

2 Káťa Kabanová

Trevor Nunn's production of *Káťa Kabanová* (1921) – the first at Covent Garden – begins during the orchestral prelude with a religious procession dimly perceived through a diaphanous silver curtain. It ends as the procession returns. The priests now stand revealed as the authority behind an oppressed rural community in Russia, and the source of the wordless 'voices' that have driven Káťa to suicide. They are also survivors of the climactic storm that earlier in this last act has destroyed a rickety chapel swarming with holy men. In all of this, Nunn has changed the original. In the score, the prelude adumbrates the human drama; the 'voices' are those of the River Volga; and the chapel is already ruined by the time Act Three begins. Yet the changes are effective, partly because they address one of the three forces animating the work through their emphasis on the role of God.

But in his treatment of the other two forces – Nature and Science – Nunn is less successful. Towards Nature, the attitude of Janáček and Alexander Ostrovsky (author of the source play of 1859) is strictly ambivalent. To the community, the storm is the awesome manifestation of a retributive God; to the chemist and teacher Kudrjáš, it is energy that may be tamed with a lightning conductor. Significantly, it is also Kudrjáš who finds a source of 'natural' joy in the sight of the Volga. The tragedy of Káťa is that she instinctively shares the oppressive moral values of the community to which she is bound through her marriage to the ineffectual Tichon, yet at the same time aligns herself with the new order through her adulterous relationship with the relatively free Boris.

Before she makes her fatal leap into the river, she too identifies with Nature –
with the beauty of the birds and flowers.

Nunn responds to these oppositions again by altering the original, so that
now there is just one set (by Maria Bjørnson). The Volga is spread out across the
backdrop like a cloudscape, and disgorges a muddy path that crosses a bridge
and spirals down into the bowels of the earth; the colours are predominantly
brown, black and grey; and the impact of the whole is unremittingly bleak.
When, therefore, Kudrjáš sings of the beauty hidden in nature, his words fail
to ring true. Similarly, there is little difference between day and night. Nor
is there any contrasting interior to represent the claustrophobic regime of
Tichon's Oedipally-ensnaring mother, Kabanicha. Nunn's huge metaphor for
psychological imprisonment seems not just overstated, but one-sided. The
capacity of Nature to redeem is denied.

This simplification, moreover, is curiously at odds with other aspects of a
production that is often eloquent in its handling of human relations. The love
scene that closes Act Two is remarkable for the delightful performance of the
subsidiary couple, Kudrjáš and Varvara (Christopher Ventris and Monica
Groop). The couple's furtive pleasure in arranging an illicit tryst complements
the more turbulent, guilt-ridden relationship of Káťa and Boris – much of
which is heard from afar – and they movingly touch the nerve-centre of folk-
song with Varvara's 'I am young and I am fair / Stay with me till day is here'.
Impressive, too, is the range of Elena Prokina's formidably assured, strongly
volatile Káťa: she is capable of exceptional vocal restraint, which she puts to
most poignant use in her parting exchanges with Boris (Keith Olsen): 'I was so
sick with longing for you', she sings.

But the most invigorating aspect of the evening is Bernard Haitink's
handling of the score. His performance eschews the strident edge rightly or
wrongly typical of so much performance of Janáček. Rather, it is wonderfully
sensitive to the music's pervasive, pliant eroticism (rarely can a score have so
transfigured an essentially straightforward play). Every phrase is painstakingly
moulded, and the whole falls into place without apparent effort. Indeed, one
hears the work as if for the first time. Eva Randová makes a welcome return to
The Royal Opera as the mother, with Gwynne Howell as her secret lover Dikoj.
And any suspicion that animals should never appear in opera is scotched by
the perfect decorum of a pair of shire horses: it is they who pull the splendid
wagon that carries away Tichon, freeing his wife to submit, fatally, to Boris's
'conquering will'.

Sources: 'Leoš Janáček: *The Adventures of Mr. Brouček*' (London Coliseum), *Times
Literary Supplement*, 8 January 1993, p. 16; 'Leoš Janáček: *Káťa Kabanová*' (Royal Opera
House), *Times Literary Supplement*, 25 March 1994, p. 17.

8   Aesthetic Inversion

Jean Cocteau (after Sophocles) and Igor Stravinsky: *Oedipus rex*
Béla Balázs (after Perrault) and Béla Bartók: *Duke Bluebeard's Castle*

Whatever has happened to the Furies? In a just society, they would have turned out in force for the first night of *Oedipus rex* (1927-8) and *Duke Bluebeard's Castle* (1918) crying out for retribution against surely one of the most provocative pieces of staging in the history of the English National Opera. However, they chose to stay away: and whereas *Oedipus* was greeted with polite restraint peppered with a few nervous cheers, the sturdy vocal performances in *Bluebeard* by Sally Burgess (Judith) and Gwynne Howell (the Duke) generated some just enthusiasm. But even without the forces of retribution, the burning question remains as to who should bear responsibility for a display as inappropriate as it was vulgar.

The first culprit, the conductor, is perhaps the most unexpected. Not that Mark Elder fails to give his customary all in a taxing musical evening: indeed, he handles Stravinsky's sinuously angular lines with loving care, and in Bartók's breathtakingly orchestrated dramatic tone-poem turns the Coliseum's clattering acoustic to good advantage. But there is no evidence that he has exercised restraint on his American director, David Alden. Alden's narcissistic compulsion to distract attention at key musical moments was already in evidence in his *Ballo in maschera* in 1989: here it runs amok. It is his ideas that must rule the roost, and no-one else's. Both the opening chorus and Oedipus's 'Libera, vos liberabo' are overwhelmed by the slow and precarious descent of a King-Kong-size pair of dentures (the jaws of Fate?), swinging apparently out of control; no sooner has the shepherd launched into his touchingly orchestrated 'Oportebat tacere' than the chorus, whom Stravinsky asks to remain immobile, starts to shuffle from the front to the back of the stage; and the effect of the chorus's jocular-macabre 'mortuary tarantella' is nullified by a visual riddle: what is the round object its members extract bloodily from the fish-tank at the front of the stage (solution: an eye the size of a pumpkin)? Had Elder insisted that the key musical moments should speak for themselves, he would have been led, ineluctably, to Stravinsky's oratorio-based conception of the opera. For the score makes minimal concessions to dramatic action: the relative absence of composed stagecraft is as eloquent here as is its presence in the works of Wagner or Berg. The music is pitched at just one level.

To judge from the programme, though, one cannot say that Stravinsky's conception is in any case valued. The dramaturg, Nicholas John, rightly includes extracts from Stravinsky's writing on *Oedipus*. But why omit the aesthetically most relevant passages? These explain Stravinsky's hatred for *verismo*, his conviction that the work's meaning (like that of Verdi's *Forza del destino*) lies in the 'fatal development', and his lack of interest in psychology ('there is no "childhood of the Prince"'). There is also the distancing choice of a 'dead' language, Latin, for the libretto. Yet it is just these points that Alden inverts: in the final scene, Oedipus makes an unscripted pitiful reappearance to crawl, blind and bloodied across the stage: he, not the chorus, usurps our attention. Sung by Philip Langridge in good voice, Oedipus is played as a regressive wimp who predictably fawns on his mother-wife, while Jocasta (Jean Rigby) turns her destructive aggression on the (epic-style) Speaker, here a tape-recorder – which presumably represents Jean Cocteau's 'infernal machine'. In itself, of course, inversion is not necessarily culpable. As Patrice Chéreau demonstrated with his Bayreuth *Ring*, it can sometimes make a work seem more, and not less, like itself. But the effect of Alden's psycho-sensationalism is to turn Stravinsky into a poor traditional opera-composer: the fatalism, with its roots in the rituals of the Russian Orthodox Church, passes for nothing. Worse still, the sight of red-in-tooth-and-claw *verismo* performed in Latin is ludicrous.

Alden's handling of *Bluebeard* is no better. Interestingly, he restores a spoken prologue (again an 'epic' feature), though substituting an obscure one of his own for the admittedly precious and pleonastic original of Balázs. The legendary setting in the castle vaults, so essential for the work's exploration of the inexplicable force that compels Judith to commit herself to Bluebeard, is abandoned, and the action takes place in a drab, tilted room with just one main door, and not the prescribed, magical seven. And the relationship between the protagonists permutes a set of stereotyped gestures – the clinch, the grovelling on the floor, the figure spread-eagled against a wall – without suggesting organic development.

Yet, what is more disturbing than this litany is that its recitation is unlikely to have any impact: the evening seems frankly predicated on the open defiance of the Furies. If this is indeed so, then it is hardly surprising that they refuse to rise: in art as in life, wilful provocation is best greeted by silence.

Source: 'The Furies Refuse to Rise', *Times Literary Supplement*, 1 February 1991, p. 18. The performance was at the London Coliseum.

9   *Remaking a Hero*

Montagu Slater and Benjamin Britten (after Crabbe): *Peter Grimes*

'He is not the Peter Grimes of Crabbe', was E. M. Forster's slightly dismayed reaction to Britten's opera after its first staging in 1945.[1] The reaction, of course, was predictable: most operas do betray their sources, each medium has its needs. Yet there was more to it than that. Forster had toyed with some operatic version of *Grimes* of his own, a kind of *Lehrstück* that would have stuck more closely to George Crabbe's poem of 1810 than Benjamin Britten's did. Its purpose would have been to demonstrate the ineluctable power of human conscience. Even though Grimes was a congenitally sadistic fisherman

> Whose brute feeling ne'er aspires
> Beyond his own brute desires

(here Crabbe quotes Scott), he would still be driven delirious by the ghost of the pious old father he had brutalized and the two wretched apprentices he had all but murdered. Nor would his conclusion have had the downright middle-class decency of Britten's, whose Grimes commits suicide off-stage, at sea, by request of his closest friend, Balstrode. Rather the ghosts would have risen from the 'treacherous flatness' of the estuary to hurl 'blood and fire' into the doomed tenor's face, 'hell would have opened, and on a mixture of *Don Juan* and *Freischütz* I should have lowered my final curtain.' Bleak, deterministic and unsparing though Forster's *Grimes* might have been, it would have chilled its audience to the marrow.

Is the corollary to Forster's dismay, though, to 'neglect Crabbe' as Desmond Shawe-Taylor once urged?[2] Hardly. For one thing, critics have always puzzled over Britten's hero. He is evidently more than the 'Byronic hero' Forster divined, a visionary hounded to his death by a brutal community, a spokesman for the persecuted minorities of the mid-twentieth century. Not only does he retain a brutality that compromises our extension of sympathy towards him, but legitimate doubt also remains as to whether the 'circumstances' of the first apprentice's death were, in fact, 'accidental'. And for another thing, as the sketches, letters and diaries show, these problems were recognized by Britten, Peter Pears (the first Grimes) and Montagu Slater (the librettist) as they worked together. Pears considered that liberal opinion was ready to accept Grimes as an 'excusable misfit'; Britten, 'sticking close' to Crabbe, found himself wrestling with his hero's pathology – 'no reasons, and not many symptoms', he remarked drily; and Slater incorporated in his text the very phrase 'Grimes is at his exercise' that Crabbe had used to indicate the community's complicity in the tormenting of the apprentices (the opera is as much about the group as about the individual). Although audiences may choose to 'neglect Crabbe', the opera's authors certainly didn't.

The English National Opera's broadly enjoyable new production by Tim Albery suggests fresh attitudes to these issues. Of crucial importance is the treatment of the two principals. Grimes, played by the lithe, febrile and charismatic Philip Langridge, is racily side-lit and consistently set apart from the others – on a boat, at the top of steps, high on a cliff. This confirms what Hans Keller wrote in 1952 about Grimes's psychology: '[He] is the living conflict. His pride, ambition and tenderness fight with his need for love: his self-love battles against his self-hate.' And though Keller added 'he can (sometimes) love [others] as intensely as he can despise them, but he cannot show, let alone prove his tenderness as easily as his wrath', he still left more to be said about the quality of that tenderness.[3] So too did Philip Brett, who recently ascribed Grimes's conflict to the internalization of the negative judgment society imposed on him.[4]

By contrast, his partner Ellen Orford is most forceful when surrounded by the people of the Borough, whose conscience she tries to tap. ('Ellen Orford', in fact, derives from another Crabbe poem, a piece of *verismo* so grisly that it can be safely neglected.) The strength of her presence, indeed, draws attention to how little critics have responded to the introduction (by Pears?) of a woman into the story. Movingly sung by the ever-intelligent Josephine Barstow, she is played not so much as a partner as a mother. She is almost sexless, and chides the Borough like a school matron (she is actually a widow and a schoolmistress, as in Crabbe). Hers is a character, indeed, with few precursors in the history of opera. She extends her protection, not only over the new apprentice, but also, relatedly, over Grimes himself. In a poignant production image at the end of the Prologue, as she soothes him after the trial she and Grimes sit alone at opposite ends of a courtroom bench – sharing an intense musical proximity for all that they are physically apart.

For his part, Grimes describes Ellen's breast as a 'harbour' that 'shelters peace' to music that transforms the kiss-motif from *Otello*: here understanding resides in not neglecting Verdi, the overt sexuality of whose music Britten transforms into a regressive cry for the protection of Grimes's internalized good mother. As always, Britten's debt to Verdi is as wide as it is deep. But the operatic Grimes also has the measure of his own brutality. He seems secretly convinced that he is unworthy of a mother's love and cannot in fact 'turn back the skies and begin again'. Though urged by Balstrode (his conscience) to marry Ellen, he avoids the challenge. Rather, he brutalizes the apprentices, projecting onto them versions of his self out of jealousy of their goodness (it is neither necessary nor appropriate to talk of homo-erotic passions here). When Ellen realizes that Grimes is incorrigible, she withdraws her support. Grimes asks what is left for him. Although the portentous Verdian repeated notes, supported by gruff funereal chords, provide him with a lethal, unspoken answer, he will still pretend in the hut scene at the end of Act Two that he may achieve, or retrieve, a 'woman's care'. But by this stage the audience knows better; and when at the scene's close the new apprentice slips and dies, it is clear that it is only a matter of time before Grimes too will meet his end. Albery closes the act with the affecting image of the fisherman carrying the dead boy across the stage.

Earlier, Ellen summarizes her role when, in the beautiful female quartet, she sings of men that 'they are children when they weep, we are mothers when they strive'. Yet the production emphasizes other forces that Grimes has to confront. These tend to be exaggerated. The grimness of the community is projected by the dour immobility of a large chorus packed on to a shallow stage. As a result of the packing, its singing seems lacklustre. On the other hand, the acutely-drawn vignettes of individual townspeople are well handled – especially the pair of (louche) nieces who are made, appropriately, to smoke, flirt and whine. Exaggerated too is the handling of the décor. The reds and blacks of the elemental scenery respond to the turbulence of the nature music when it storms, but not to its calm when it basks in sunlight. This creates a discontinuity with the affective extremes of the characters, which this music is surely intended to reflect.

The most lasting impression of the evening, however, is a musical one. Despite the winsomeness of Langridge's singing, the vocal lines still seem to exude the taut voluptuousness of Pears's tenor, the 'heavenly voice' that haunted Britten throughout the opera's composition. This is especially true of the challenging high melismas of the monologue in the hut – one of the greatest passages in Britten's operas, and, indeed, in British opera. Whatever else an audience may choose to neglect, this, at least, will always prove a ghost hard to exorcise.

Notes

Source: 'The Living Conflict' (Benjamin Britten: *Peter Grimes*), *Times Literary Supplement*, 26 April 1991, p. 15, and here revised. The opera was staged at the London Coliseum.

1   See: 'George Crabbe and Peter Grimes' (1948) in: E. M. Forster, *Two Cheers for Democracy*, London: Edward Arnold, 1951, pp. 190-1.

2   Desmond Shawe-Taylor, '*Peter Grimes*: A Review of the First Performance' (1945), in: *Benjamin Britten. 'Peter Grimes'*, ed. Philip Brett, Cambridge: Cambridge UP, 1983 (Cambridge Opera Handbooks), pp. 153-8, especially p. 158.

3   Keller's remarks appear in a note for a recording of 1951 included in: Hans Keller, *Britten. Essays, Letters and Opera Guides*, ed. Christopher Wintle and A. M. Garnham, London: Plumbago (2013), p. 319. Keller had also written an extended case-study of

242 CHRISTOPHER WINTLE: WHAT OPERA MEANS

the work's libretto, 'Three Psycho-analytic Notes on *Peter Grimes*' included in: Hans Keller, *Music and Psychology. From Vienna to London, 1939-52*, ed. Christopher Wintle, London: Plumbago, 2003, pp. 121-45.

4   Philip Brett: '*Peter Grimes*: The Growth of a Libretto', in: *The Making of 'Peter Grimes'* (2 vols.), ed. Paul Banks *et al*, Woodbridge: The Boydell Press, 1996, vol. 2, pp. 53-78. For some of my information I am indebted to this volume.

10   Revising Revisions
E. M. Forster, Eric Crozier and Benjamin Britten (after Melville): *Billy Budd*

A musicological question thrown up by The Royal Opera's new production of *Billy Budd* turns out to hold the key to the work. Not long after the first performance in 1951, Britten recast his marathon four-act, three-interval opera into two acts, a division, in fact, he had originally intended. Connecting Acts Three and Four proved simple; doing the same for Acts One and Two entailed a drastic cut. Many factors, the leading singer's convenience and an unfavourable comparison with *HMS Pinafore* among them, were involved. What was lost was Captain Vere's only appearance in Act One – his first climactic address to the ship's company. Scholars have long pressed for its reintroduction. This The Royal Opera has now done, though retaining the connected pair of acts. So what we now have is an address and an awkward continuity between the first two acts, whereas in Britten's revision there was no address and a smooth continuity. A more refined compromise might yet get the best of both worlds.

Inevitably, the restoration reinforces attention on Vere, in Britten's eyes always the most interesting character. Donald Mitchell, a scholar close to the composer, rightly argues that the scenes showing the changing reactions of crew to captain, from adulation to outrage, form the pillars of the story, and that therefore this first address is vital. Others might add that the address completes a network of parallels between Vere and his diabolical Master-at-arms, 'Jemmy-legs' Claggart. In the restored Acts One and Two, for instance, both men sing soliloquies, both men deal privately with fellow sailors, and both are seen handling the assembled crew. Crucially, both also have to confront the destructiveness of their (partly homo-erotic) impulses aroused by the work's hero, the fresh-faced, charismatically sinless Billy Budd. When he has Budd's life in his hands, Vere will find that he too has a Claggart within.

Francesca Zambello's production reacts to all this with mixed success. Much her most powerful image is that of the executed Budd swinging listlessly over the heads of the crew, representing on the one hand an indictment of the Articles of War that sentenced him (Vere gives his consent in bad faith), and, on the other, the macabre outcome of Claggart's demonic obsession. Her most audacious decision is to use a musical interlude to project an arresting but appropriate image of Budd as Saviour crucified on the mast: the redemption from guilt this signifies in part entails a sublimated consummation, that of Vere, who in the manifestly Christian Epilogue sensuously re-enacts Budd's posture.

The casting, however, is less happy. The Vere forged from Melville by E. M. Forster and Eric Crozier is a bookish introvert whose conscience is not merely at odds with authority – Plutarch, Religion and the Articles of War – but is also partly in tune with it. Incongruously, in the framing Prologue and Epilogue, Zambello's Vere is a diminutive destitute from Cardboard City[1] who shuffles and rolls about the stage, and in the main action a knee-slapping hearty who hurls furniture round his cabin. Graham Clark's bright, rounded tenor (recently so effective for Wagner's Mime) lacks the complexity of Peter Pears's voice (Pears was the original Vere), whereas John Tomlinson's characterful bass creates in Claggart a contrast almost too sympathetically fraught: he seems more Wotan than Iago. Neither are fully helped by the conductor Robert Spano, whose impetuous tempi fail to evoke the unsettling mists of time at the opening or dwell on the sadistic sonorities that pervade the work.

However, Zambello ends the restored passage well by having Budd hoisted onto the shoulders of the sailors – higher than Vere – who thus redirect their affection for the Captain onto one of their own number. Rodney Gilfry, like the first Budd (Theodor Uppman) an American, has a lanky, engaging appearance, and a veiled baritone that lends his later solos a pleasing mellowness: this helps avert the potential embarrassment of a figure whose disarming, smiling innocence neither knows evil nor, fatally, can recognize it. As with the rest of the cast, his diction is excellent.

The ensemble singing by the all-male cast is likewise impressive – paradoxically, Britten triumphs by using sea-shanties to establish the sustaining sense of 'home', through which the sailors forge their only admissible bond with the feminine. However, the costumes, cast in a positive and subtle blend of blues and greys offset by more ominous browns, follow the changing spirit of the text rather than its letter. Yet here the letter has the deeper logic. In the finale, as the crew assembles to witness Budd's execution, the music explicitly introduces each of the ranks, with Vere standing motionless. This forbidding display of authority focuses the Captain's crisis of conscience and goads the men. Zambello, however, ignores the musical ranking, and pre-empts the Epilogue by putting Vere prematurely into his old man's rags: the work's two time-frames, the then and the now, coalesce. Had she followed Britten's directions, however, the change of circumstance from beginning to end of the main action would undoubtedly have spoken more forcefully. This at least would seem the proper consequence of restoring Vere's benign address in Act One.

Notes

Source: 'Restitutions and Redemptions', *Times Literary Supplement*, 16 June 1995, p. 23.

1   'Cardboard City' was a gathering-point for down-and-outs who camped in the labyrinth of concrete passages running under the south side of Waterloo Bridge in central London: at night they would lie on cardboard. It was eventually cleared by the authorities.

11 *The Sacred Sublime*

Olivier Messiaen: *Saint François d'Assise*

London's first complete, semi-staged performance of a sacred opera on the life of Saint Francis at the Royal Festival Hall provided an excellent promotional opportunity for a leading couturier. To commemorate the occasion – it was also Olivier Messiaen's eightieth birthday – Yves St Laurent had prepared a sleek black sachet, emblazoned in gold with their logo. This contained not one, but two programme booklets. In their pages, illustrious composers, critics and arts administrators paid tribute to the Grand Old Man of modern music. Nor were the tributes misplaced: Messiaen's rich endowment of talents could happily be dispersed among a hundred lesser composers, and, remarkably, his recent scores show no signs of age.

What, though, of the work itself? First performed in 1983, the strength of its conception and execution is not in doubt. This five-hour opera on the saint 'who most clearly resembles Christ', presented in eight tableaux, is consummately achieved, the *longueurs* of Francis's sermon to the birds notwithstanding. The Mahlerian instrumental and choral forces yield stunningly novel aviatic and celestial sonorities; the harmonic assurance astounds, not least in the ways it rediscovers the common chord; and musical line is handled with a clarity and variety rarely encountered today. Nor can there be any dispute about the choice of this sacred subject, which aligns the ornithological Messiaen with other great composers of our century motivated by the search for grace – Schoenberg, Stravinsky and Britten among them.

What, however, disconcerts is the ruthlessness and single-mindedness of Messiaen's treatment of a purely musical issue: repetition and contrast. As in Wagner, each character is ascribed one or more motifs. But here they are not so much developed symphonically as stated and restated in ever-proliferating juxtapositions. Eventually, contrast is deprived of its dramatic and dialectical connotations: it becomes an all-too-predictable weapon in the composer's narrative armoury. To make a motif seem ever more tender, for example, Messiaen merely flanks it with ever more violent textures. With such a means, tableau after tableau is drawn to an identical climax. All the ideas, however intimate or brash, are presented in their starkest form; there is no meaningful counterpoint, no complex vocal ensemble. Divinely appointed though Messiaen may consider his mission to be, his means of achieving it resemble those of an aesthetic terrorist: his opera is an uncompromising essay in the Burkean 'sublime'. After *Saint François* one yearns for the 'beautiful' little ironies of a Satie or a Debussy.

Yet even such a reaction has to be qualified. Messiaen's skill alone ensures that his most shameless raids on God-shop imagery (the libretto is his) can hold an audience spellbound. The angel's playing of her viol and St Francis's embrace of the leper are undeniably moving. The brazen, César Franck-like joy of the conclusion is irresistible. Indeed, criticism of *Saint François* experiences the same frustration that a Nietzsche or an Adorno must have felt in accusing Wagner of leaving his audience 'supine': the work merely shrugs off disparagement. As if to prove this, the lithe and charismatic young conductor Kent Nagano led an army of performers, including the London Philharmonic Orchestra and Choir, to a memorable triumph. The piece will doubtless form the focal point of festivals and subsidies for generations to come. Yet what a strange emissary of our times it will surely seem!

Source: 'Celestial Sonorities', *Times Literary Supplement*, 23 December 1988, p. 1422.

12 *Mechanical Pastoral*

Tony Harrison and Harrison Birtwistle: *Yan Tan Tethera*

Melanie Klein had no trouble in offering a confident explanation for the young boy's anxieties in Colette and Ravel's *L'Enfant et les sortilèges*:[1] but what would she have made of Tony Harrison and Harrison Birtwistle's curious but impressive *Yan Tan Tethera* (1986)? This one-act opera culminates in the dissolution of a young shepherd's (unconscious) apprehensions of paternity through his wife's incantation of an old charm he has taught her ('Yan Tan Tethera, 1-2-3, Sweet Trinity Keep Us and Our Sheep') – though only after the shepherd has passed seven years of incarceration, through the wiles of 'the Bad'un', in an ancient burial mound in the company of his new-born twin sons. The work's powerfully projected antinomies of life and death, prayer and sorcery are reinforced by other oppositions: of the corrupt South (where the opera is set) and the pure North (the home for which the shepherd yearns); of the shepherd and his dark alter ego (another shepherd who pillages graves, melts the church bell and courts the first shepherd's wife); and of two flocks of sheep (sung by one set of singers), the fretful Wiltshires and the fertile Cheviots (whose differences are further characterized by two sets of masks, one white, one black). In performance the effect of the work is of a unity. Yet it is still sufficiently puzzling as to demand of its audience some special interpretative effort.

Part of the opera's undoubted fascination lies in the skill with which Tony Harrison has tailored his libretto to Birtwistle's needs. In fact, all of the composer's librettists have served him well, though none as elegantly and concisely as this. Birtwistle's long-standing – and Ravel-like – preoccupation with clocks, toys, mechanisms and folklore is reflected in Harrison's description of *Yan Tan Tethera* as a 'Mechanical Pastoral'. The stylized, artificial elements include some of the scenic specifications (only partly reflected in this staging): the pervasive chanting of the shepherd's traditional counting system (from which the work derives its title), a number of reiterated, strongly characterized stage gestures (for example, the shepherd spins round with the various appearances and disappearances of the Bad'un as a piper), and even the use of a thirteen-syllable line for the chorus of thirteen Wiltshires. Yet offsetting this are a number of beautiful set-pieces of different length, notably the pregnant wife's touching aria in which she upbraids the shepherd for his seeming indifference ('You'd wait all night with your ewes while they lamb / But about your own babies you don't give a damn'). To all this Birtwistle has responded with one of his most cogent and taut scores, where the contrasts work together more purposefully than hitherto, where the references to different musical genres are much clearer and where there is a satisfying interaction between the static, repetitive features and the slowly unfolding narrative.

In this production the textural complexity of the score is often sensed more than perceived, since the orchestra is placed at the back of the stage behind a semi-opaque white gauze. The distance between the players and the singers, who move around on an apron that extends well into the auditorium, not only draws attention to the frequent interchange of vocal and instrumental musical material, but also throws the vocal lines into relief. This is particularly the case with Omar Ebrahim, the unkempt, bronzed young shepherd, whose singing with a tart Yorkshire accent is one of the triumphs of the evening. Richard Suart, as the other, more cunning shepherd, provides him with an effective foil; and both Helen Charnock and Philip Doghan as the wife and piper respectively are well cast, though Doghan's dance testifies to the difficulties of expressing simple pleasure on the stage, even when the pleasure is the Bad'un's. The sheep sing their taxing parts with remarkable assurance, and for the most part stand, squat or process around the peripheries of the action in a manner that recalls the staging at the London Coliseum of the last act of Birtwistle's recent *The Mask of Orpheus* by the same director, David Freeman. (It is also unexpectedly redolent of Birtwistle's earlier 'dramatic pastoral', *Down by the Greenwood Side* (1969), to a text by Michael Nyman.) When they crawl into the centre of the stage to participate in the main events, their partly improvised movements reveal the benefits of the company's field trips to a sheep farm. Only their impromptu bleating seems shy.

Notes

Source: 'Mechanical Pastoral', *Times Literary Supplement*, 22 August 1986. Reprinted in: *Tony Harrison*, ed. Neil Astley, Newcastle upon Tyne: Bloodaxe Books, 1991, pp. 314-15. The work was staged by the Opera Factory in the Queen Elizabeth Hall, London.

1   Melanie Klein: 'Infantile Anxiety Situations Reflected in a Work of Art and in the Creative Impulse', *The Selected Melanie Klein*, ed. Juliet Mitchell, London: Peregrine (Penguin), 1986, pp. 84-94.

13 Reinventing the Style Heights
John Birtwhistle and David Blake: *The Plumber's Gift*

Why should an English composer write opera today? The question is David Blake's, and his answer might well strike audiences as disingenuous. Talking recently about his new opera *The Plumber's Gift* (1989), he took pains to show how he had laid aside the grand political preoccupations of his earlier costume drama *Toussaint* for an intimate, psychologically-orientated investigation of love in modern Britain.[1] Hence John Birtwhistle's skilful and literate libretto had crossed a comedy of manners *à la* Congreve with a recreation of the pastoral convention. This convention is used in the second act to reveal the latent, and partly regressive, emotional sympathies between two couples, one young, the other middle-aged. Inevitably Blake cited *Così fan tutte* and *The Midsummer Marriage* as models of opera built around duets. Yet the effect of his work is different. Within the pastoral lies political allegory, and in the closing scenes, politics come to the fore with the confrontation between modern entrepreneurial capitalism on the one hand and the left-wing ideals of the newly-skilled worker (the plumber) on the other. For Blake and Birtwhistle, the quality of love is inextricably bound up with the condition of society.

As a student, Blake worked with the East German composer Hanns Eisler, Brecht's most politically-committed (and sympathetic) collaborator. It comes as no surprise, therefore, that the most successful aspects of the opera lie in the characterization of the different social strata through the commercialized musical types associated with them: Blake reinvents the Renaissance 'style heights' for our time.[2] The work is set in a guest-house by the sea. The anxious but farcical landlady reminisces to old-time popular music on the radio, and the young plumber Colin sings patter-songs and naïve, rhapsodic love-duets with his girlfriend Sylvia. Sylvia's previous relationship with the middle-aged James has refined her sensibilities (shades here of Goethe's *Elective Affinities*), and she listens enthralled to Mahler on television. James and his wife, the dignified Marian, exchange musical allusions (to Purcell) just as they do poetic ones; and the wilfully infantile pastoral brings with it a simplification of the musical idiom. Any composer, of course, who deploys the banal to depict banality, or uses allusion to match allusiveness, lives dangerously. But Blake overcomes the potential hazards by composing all the demotic music and allusions himself – almost too well, in fact, for one longs to hear more of his 'Mahler'. This allows him to retain complete control of harmony and pacing, which in the first act is excellent.

Like Eisler's, though, Blake's own language is not always sustained at the highest level. Certainly, at the end of the first act, the extended malediction of the hotel guests by one of the permanent residents, the morbidly irascible Commander, is effective enough, as is the second-act storm and the calm, hopeful interlude that follows for all six soloists (as in early opera, there is no independent chorus). But other parts of the work are blighted by threadbare musical support for the rather extensive dialogue. The 'plumber's gift' turns out to be a piece of ornamental metalwork that 'contains mouth organ reeds': the cadenza Colin performs on it seems paltry by comparison with, for instance, the sounds Tamino elicits from Mozart's 'magic flute' – these are hardly the Orphic strains to vanquish the forces of Mammon. At the end, Birtwhistle offers Blake the sophisticated challenge of composing a peroration for a Marian who seems to occupy the moral high ground yet deems herself to be the loser through her inability to make the decisions and commitments that the others can. Yet here too, Blake's music seems insufficiently focused or highly wrought to fulfil its complex task.

However, these shortcomings are in some measure redeemed by Lionel Friend's sympathetic musical direction (the cast includes Sally Burgess as an alluring Sylvia), as well as by Richard Jones's assured production and Nigel Lowery's pleasing designs.

Notes

Source: 'The Quality of Love', *Times Literary Supplement*, 9 June 1989, p. 638. The article ended with a supplementary paragraph on *The Garden Venture* at the Donmar Warehouse (1989):

'Proverbial logic suggests that where something is ventured, something will be gained. Yet *The Garden Venture* of sponsoring seven short experimental operas will yield gains only if the composers are determined to learn from it. Most of the pieces embodied some valuable instinct. Jeremy Peyton Jones and Michael Christie chose effective sources (Poe and Rilke respectively); Andrew Poppy showed a willingness to rethink the theatrical experience; Peter Wiegold invented a novel sound palette; Kenneth Chalmers tried to complement rather than mimic the stage action; Priti Paintal laid out her score clearly. Yet the flaws were daunting. Edward Lambert apart, one seriously wondered whether any of these composers had meaningfully listened to opera before: none could invent effective musico-dramatic ideas, deploy an integrated harmonic language or compose memorable set-pieces, and all failed to sustain their time-span, Lambert most culpably. The moral of the venture is simple: only alert, well-grounded composers can write good operas. On current prognosis, these will be in just as short supply tomorrow as they are today.'

1   Blake's colourful three-act *Toussaint* to a Brechtian text by Anthony Ward (1977, though subsequently revised), is set in revolutionary Haiti between 1791 and 1803.
2   Renaissance rhetoric understands three basic 'style heights': the high (grandiloquent), the plain (temperate) and the low (demotic). These represent three levels of society, and in opera demand three styles to match. We can still observe them in, say, Mozart's *Le nozze di Figaro* (1786) and Weber's *Der Freischütz* (1821).

14 Bardolatry

Stephen Oliver (after Shakespeare): *Timon of Athens*

When it comes to modern British opera, Shakespeare, and everything he represents, has something to answer for.[1] Though still young, Stephen Oliver has composed more than forty stage works, and is manifestly fluent, experienced and theatrically gifted.[2] Yet his *Timon of Athens* (1991), the latest in the English National Opera's enterprising series of commissions, shows all the consequences of extending a misplaced piety towards the text. Literary integrity is placed even before musical effectiveness. The irony here is that, although Oliver is claimed to be 'scrupulously respectful of the nuances and cadences of speech', the speech is not exactly Shakespeare's. The play has not only been pruned (as one would expect), but has also been compressed, updated, reordered and quite simply altered. For example, in Timon's embittered fourth-act monologue, Oliver's 'O you wolves, plagues heap their fevers on you', with its awkward repetition of 'you', conflates two lines that in Shakespeare are distinct and well separated:

> O thou wall
> That girdles in those wolves, dive in the earth,
> And fence not Athens

and

> Plagues incident to men,
> Your potent and infectious fevers heap
> On Athens, ripe for stroke.[3]

Given this degree of flexibility, one may well ask, why should there be so much scrupulous respect for speech, and why doesn't Oliver take the bull by the horns and recast the play for music more radically?

Oliver's answer is startlingly one-sided. His singers are not 'canaries' – he seems to have a studied lack of interest in the human voice per se – but 'actors who speak music'. Yet even here there is a fallacy. Oliver's lines are all set in the same easily-won, syllabic declamatory style, unmediated by the demands of generically-inspired musical ideas. They cannot reflect the differences in the characters' diction in the way that Shakespeare's do, since the appropriate tone of voice an actor will bring to his part has to be recreated by the composer through his use of different kinds of musical figure in voice and accompaniment. Nor does Oliver recognize how much more key words and phrases have to be underlined in the opera house than in the theatre. No traditional composer worth their salt, for instance, would have thrown away the key final line of the first part – 'One day he gives us diamonds, next day stones' – in the way he does here. Since the musical lines, moreover, are all delivered at an apparently similar speed, and since they dominate most of the score, their effect is of some monotony.

Timon, however, is not the only modern opera – British or otherwise – to be composed in this way: declamation seems to be the very condition of 'literature opera'. And if the invention of the music supporting the lines was stronger, the decision to cast the opera as an extended threnody for man, of some expressionistic kind, might indeed have proved the most effective way of handling a difficult subject. Timon's vertiginous transformation from a philanthropist to a 'misanthropus' makes him a poor candidate for portraiture or psychologism in the nineteenth-century manner, and the work is altogether too gloomy to admit more modern ironies, its preoccupation with power, money and friendship notwithstanding. At the very least Oliver's choice of this of all Shakespeare's plays is indicative of one of the ways modern opera has come to be redefined.

However, this production does everything it can to enhance Oliver's vision. Monte Jaffe demonstrates again how charismatic his stage presence can be (he was previously Reimann's Lear);[4] the supporting cast is good; Graeme Jenkins seems to conduct with assurance; and the set, which reveals the dank wastes lying beneath the confident stone meeting-places of Athens, provides the evening's most striking image (for all that it compels Jaffe to sing most of the second half waist-deep in water). Nor does the challenge of working with an all-male cast prove too great: the inclusion of two confident treble voices makes a difference out of all proportion to the significance of their roles. But in the last resort, the work falls far short of its intended impact. The long string counterpoints to the vocal lines demand too much compassion, the contrasting musical episodes never quite integrate – a Stravinsky-like ostinato makes the senators appear to call Timon back to Thebes and not Athens – and the overall pacing is not well differentiated. Opera has lost where Bardolatry has won.

Notes

Source: 'Actors, Not Canaries', *Times Literary Supplement*, 24 May 1991, p. 18.

1   Since 1945, the roll-call has included: *A Midsummer Night's Dream* (Benjamin Britten), *Hamlet* (Humphrey Searle), *Timon of Athens* (Stephen Oliver), *The Tempest* (Thomas Adès), *King Lear* (Alexander Goehr's *Promised End*) and *The Winter's Tale* (Ryan Wigglesworth). It is striking that all have avoided Verdi's three Shakespeare settings: *Macbeth*, *Otello* and *Falstaff* (after *The Merry Wives of Windsor*).
2   Stephen Oliver, 1950-92. His *Timon of Athens*, an opera in two acts, received its first performance at the London Coliseum on 17 May 1991.
3   William Shakespeare, *Timon of Athens*, Act Four, scene 1, lines 1-3 and 30-2.
4   Aribert Reimann's *Lear* was widely performed in Europe following its premiere in Munich in 1978. The first to take the title role was Dietrich Fischer-Dieskau.

15 Anti-romantic Romanticism

Judith Weir (after Tieck): *Blond Eckbert*

'Those who go beneath the surface do so at their peril,' warns Oscar Wilde in his preface to *The Picture of Dorian Gray*. His words could apply equally well to 'blond' Eckbert, the subject of Judith Weir's short but pleasing new opera (1994) based on Ludwig Tieck's novella of 1797.[1] Eckbert is a solitary figure who feels impelled to ask his wife Berthe (to whom he is apparently happily married) to unburden herself before his old friend Walther. But when Walther shows that he knows Berthe's bizarre life-story better than she does herself, he inspires such dread that Eckbert shoots him and Berthe dies of shock. Walther, though, returns in the guise of three other characters – Hugo, a peasant and an old woman – to reveal that Eckbert and Berthe share the same father. 'Why have I always imagined this dreadful thing?' cries the delirious Eckbert. Walther, alias the old woman, replies with lethal effect, 'You heard your father say it when you were a child'.

Weir approaches Tieck's tale with precisely those musical means developed earlier in the twentieth century to repudiate its brand of atmospheric Romanticism (its *Stimmung*). The text may be psychologically pregnant – Jungians could describe the Walther-characters as Hermes-like figures guiding a (guilty) soul to its death – yet her score uses none of the 'knowing' thematic mechanisms of music drama. She ignores the rhetoric of the grand passions and in her libretto avoids the contrast between a nature that is perfect and one that is uninhabitable – Berthe relates how, as a girl, she fled into and away from both the woods and an urban community so brutal that it creates the very circumstances that destroy Eckbert. Daringly, and perhaps too daringly, she includes no aria for paradise, and her only crowd-sounds are brief, ritualized and offstage. These are all negative virtues.

Rather, Weir both distances and heightens her portrayal of Eckbert's anguish by treating it as a narrative-within-a-narrative. In this she follows Stravinsky's quasi-'epic' procedure in *Oedipus rex*. A post-Wagnerian Woodbird acts as the chorus – as in Tieck, the 'Waldeinsamkeit' refrain constantly changes; there is little in-built stagecraft; and there is hardly any display of 'dialogue technique' – the characters mostly tell their own story or reflect on their lot. The music unfolds in long, fluid lines, which, as in Britten, are often thinly supported. Through their sensitivity to prosody, they raise themselves easily from discursiveness to lyricism, something that happens all the more as the opera proceeds. Their unfailing elegance, and the consistency of their orchestral unison doublings (a technique joyfully and exceptionally reclaimed from the nineteenth century), contribute to the work's impressive cogency: the opening melismas of the Woodbird sound all of a piece with the closing ones of Eckbert in his awesome death-throes.

The most affecting moments, though, arise from stylistic cross-currents. Late in the work, Eckbert retraces the woodland journey described earlier by Berthe: as the peasant emerges (with great, eccentric, loping strides), the music assumes a modal Scottish gait: the ethnic reference is predictable (Weir is a Scot), but the effect is uncanny and riveting. Similarly, as Berthe haltingly writes her death-bed letter, a subversive and startling Janáček-like motif vividly represents her troubled conscience. Like Janáček, too, are the quietly impassioned, free-standing phrases of the prelude to Act Two, a tone-poem on the death of Walther that includes the work's best music.

That Tim Hopkins's production is only intermittently successful is due partly to the difficulties of a static score, and partly to a defensive need to pre-empt the audience's responses, a fault of much contemporary staging. He invents a stylized body-language for the singers, but inhibits its evolution by sustaining the same level of neurotic intensity throughout. The fantastic, jewel-laying Woodbird is never seen in its dazzling plumage, but from the outset assumes the black pall appropriate to the close. The use of neon lights for 'Strohmian', the dog's name that Berthe forgets but will crucially remember, may be a necessary compensation for its low-keyed musical articulation – generally, Tieck's dog is less well handled than Tieck's bird;[1] but certainly, during Berthe's narrative the dissolution of the (unnecessary) black-and-white film accompaniment into a puppet-show is merely bathetic.

The singing of Nicholas Folwell as Eckbert, Anne-Marie Owens as Berthe and Nerys Jones as the Woodbird is impressively committed, and Christopher Ventris as Walther (*et al*) shows that a smiling tenor can be even more sinister than a scowling bass. Only historians can say whether or not this is the first time a woman conductor, Sian Edwards, has introduced another woman's opera to a big London house.[2]

Notes

Source: 'Blonds Have Less Fun when the Woodbird Sings', *Times Literary Supplement*, 6 May 1994, p. 18. It was staged at the London Coliseum.

1   At the turn of the eighteenth and nineteenth centuries, the genre of novella comprised a concentrated, suspenseful action defined by a magical 'turning-point' that introduced a surprise novelty (*novella*) leading to an unexpected conclusion. 'The Romantics favoured supernatural motifs to convey irrational experience ('Novellen-märchen'), the first example being Ludwig Tieck's *Der blonde Eckbert* (1797).' 'Novelle', *The Oxford Companion to German Literature*, ed. Henry and Mary Garland, Oxford: Clarendon Press (Oxford UP), 1976, pp. 642-3.

2   On 5 January 2012 I wrote in my opera diary: 'Mention of a new opera by Judith Weir, *Miss Fortune* (The Royal Opera, 2011/12), brings back a memory. A little time ago I

was travelling to London from Tunbridge Wells. I had been to see Judith's *Night at the Chinese Opera* (1987) and found myself in the same carriage as her. 'You'll never guess where I got my idea for the third act!' she said (the doomed hero, Chao Lin, meets an Old Dweller up the mountain path). '*La Wally*?' I ventured (Catalani's hero and heroine die in the Tyrol, she singing of an Edelweiss). No. 'Early German cinema?' (Junta, heroine of Leni Riefenstahl's *Das blaue Licht*, is only happy when she stands proudly atop the crags). Again, no. Then, declining to mention Henze's *Elegy for Young Lovers*, in which the young couple die in a blizzard up the Hammerhorn, I threw in the sponge. '*Siegfried*!' she cried – and 'of course' is my rejoinder: how could I have overlooked that rapt ascent by which the hero learns wonder before he learns fear at the sight of Brünnhilde? Still, I consoled myself with the thought that Weir's music had little in common with Wagner's. But then nor did her sharp, disenchanted style in *Blond Eckbert* have much in common with Ludwig Tieck's.'

Epilogue: Production versus Music?

Tom Sutcliffe: *Believing in Opera* (book)

Hans Keller once said, in defence of Shostakovich, that 'the lover understands better than the hater'. It is a dictum Tom Sutcliffe might well appropriate. For his account of modern operatic staging and design is not just a labour of love: it is also a polemic aimed at faint hearts and fogies. In his view, their often vociferous hating fails to understand how in this century generally, and in the post-war years especially, 'intrusive [opera] productions' have promoted a new and authentic theatrical challenge; the museum culture that the 'conservatives' prefer is irrelevant (the point of Wagner was not 'Nordic revivalism'); and their belief that opera is the exclusive province of the librettist, the composer, the Diva or the great conductor is misplaced. On the contrary, he understands opera as a collaborative activity with pride of place going to the director-designer (and -lighter) team. It is they, he believes, who most immediately relate to the audience. Hence, for the past twenty-five years or so, he has scoured Europe and America in pursuit of the new staging; he has meticulously described the work of Brook, Berghaus, (David) Alden, Vick, Neuenfels *et al*, and in the process has gathered a mass of fascinating information. It is clearly a laudable, novel and timely enterprise, the fruit of which adds significantly to our knowledge.

Does such a lover's understanding, though, necessarily carry value? Sutcliffe subtitles his book 'Questions of staging and design', but, in truth, few questions are asked.[1] Indeed, his writing is largely un-philosophical. The general effect is oddly disconcerting. Here, for example, is his description of the Richard Jones-Nigel Lowery production of Handel's *Giulio Cesare* in Munich from 1994: after the initial scenes, 'a towering Tyrannosaurus Rex subsided into a jagged crater at the centre of the stage. Ann Murray as Caesar wore a bald wig and camouflage kilt, khaki shirt, maroon beret and pair of Doc Martens; the head of Pompey was handed over in a Munich supermarket plastic bag. Ptolemy (in a Harpo Marx wig) sported a puce uniform-suit with silver-lamé stripes and played shocking jokes with Pompey's headless corpse, stuffing a large cocktail-flag into its neck – the gory humour of 1990s Hollywood'. Later, with Cleopatra in 'red velvet dress and waitress apron', 'a nuclear rocket climbed out of the crater during [her] closing pleas to the gods at the start of Act Two – and exploded at the start of the naval battle … blowing a collection of (irradiated?) great white sharks out of the crater'. From this account alone, the impact on the audience cannot be assessed any more than the coherence of the staging can be judged. No prose, however vivacious, is a substitute for the dynamics of a live experience.

No one today would argue in principle against transpositions of time and place. Nevertheless, directly or obliquely, Sutcliffe does invite approval, and it is the terms of the invitation that constitute the book's challenge. First, there is the recognition of a relatively closed international group of directors and designers working competitively over a tiny repertoire. Jones's staging was 'even more unexpected' than Willy Decker's 'post-modern German-style' Glasgow production, or Peter Sellars's American version set in the Cairo Hilton with Caesar 'as a Kennedy clone': 'the British', Sutcliffe proclaims, 'came to Munich, were seen, and conquered. Cheers (and a few boos) at curtain call went on for 15 minutes.' Second, there is acquiescence in a US-dominated, media-led fantasy with (in this case) 'burlesqued' images of power and energy. Third, there is admission of a fascination with exotic sex, as Caesar 'slips under an enormous sheet on a leopard-skin settee with Lydia (alias Cleopatra)'; and finally there is delight in the iconography of shopping – although the Doc Martens are trumped in Jones's *Götterdämmerung* by a paper bag that covers Brünnhilde's head to assert her commodity status.

On the night, this may seem 'fun', though hardly of an elevated kind. But, taste apart, to share Sutcliffe's enthusiasm to the full is to accept his word that 'none' of this 'strictly disciplined hyperactivity' departs from the 1723 text of *Giulio Cesare* by Nicola Haym (whose most spectacular stage instruction refers to no more than the appearance of Virtue and the nine Muses on Parnassus) and that every audience will view the 'decorum' of Handelian *opera seria* as 'dead'. In other words, scholarly productions such as those of Andrew Jones in Cambridge which, with sensitivity and learning, attempt to match Handel's music with appropriately stylized gesture and movement, cannot lead to a real theatrical experience. Contemporary relevance is all. Yet – and here is a refreshing contradiction – Sutcliffe is also prepared to praise a production as self-consciously *Werktreu* as Peter Stein's *Falstaff* for WNO, with its virtuoso but far from un-faithful staging of the final choral fugue (for this writer, one of the outright triumphs of modern production).

What is neglected in all this is the relation to music. Opera, by definition, differs from staged drama in being wholly or predominantly sung to the accompaniment of instruments; and operatic music enhances the categories of narrative, character, reason, diction and spectacle proposed by Aristotle – one of Sutcliffe's touchstones. Although the music may contribute symbolically to the drama's social, political and psychological arguments, its main function is to transfigure the drama with 'feeling-tone'. Now, although Sutcliffe cites Cosima Wagner on this question, often asserts his directors' respect for the score, comments perceptively on conductors, and shows a keen awareness of singers, in effect he deals with stage drama independent of music. He seems reluctant to exercise his listening eye. Hence, he avoids the two real challenges in his subject: first, how to discriminate between directors whose work makes us listen as well as, if not better than, the music demands (the best of Patrice Chéreau's Bayreuth *Ring*), and those who positively hinder such listening (Götz Friedrich's London *Lulu*); and second, how to assess the new-old tension when modern images are set against ancient sounds.

Sutcliffe argues at one point – challengingly – that modern composers have failed to provide modern music for modern stagecraft, and, at another – with some truth – that the new movement in staging and design in any case prefers to re-read than to read afresh. Although every such re-reading must indeed be judged by its effect on the night, by its nature the modern stagecraft lives dangerously with regard to the score. Hence the 'voice from the gallery' that cried out in Munich against the Jones-Lowery *Giulio Cesare*, 'Kinder, Kinder',[2] was a legitimate participant in the performance. Sutcliffe's characteristic response – 'Who precisely were the kids?' – may be one-sided. Yet, for good or bad, it is not one that is likely to go away.

Notes

Source: 'Kinder to the *Kinder*', *Times Literary Supplement*, 3 January 1997, p. 20. On: Tom Sutcliffe, *Believing in Opera*, London: Faber and Faber, 1996.

1   The subtitle appeared only in the review proof-copy.
2   'Children, children.'

Bibliography
&
Index

Bibliography

In this full list of writings on opera by Christopher Wintle, ➤ indicates that the entry appears in this volume. Reference to 'Royal Opera House' (ROH) or 'Covent Garden' normally takes the form 'The Royal Opera'. UP = University Press.

1   Essays for Books and Journals

'Wagner – Richard (1813-83)', *Makers of Nineteenth Century Culture (1800-1914)*, ed. Justin Wintle, London: Routledge and Kegan Paul, 1982, pp. 658-61 (biographical and critical essay).

'Issues in Dahlhaus' (on writings by Carl Dahlhaus: *Richard Wagner's Music Dramas* and other writings), *Music Analysis*, vol. 1, No. 3, October 1982, pp. 341-55 (this includes a close musical analysis of a passage from Act One of *Tristan und Isolde*).

'The Numinous in *Götterdämmerung*', *Reading Opera*, ed. Arthur Groos and Roger Parker, Princeton: Princeton UP, 1988, pp. 200-34.

'Analysis and Criticism', *The Wagner Compendium*, ed. Barry Millington, London: Thames and Hudson, 1992, pp. 404-8.

'Analysis and Psychoanalysis: Wagner's Musical Metaphors', *Companion to Contemporary Musical Thought*, vol. 2, ed. John Paynter *et al*, London: Routledge and Kegan Paul, 1992, pp. 650-91 (discussion of selected passages).

'Lefanu, Nicola', *The New Grove Dictionary of Opera* (4 vols.), ed. Stanley Sadie, London: Macmillan, 1992, vol. 2, p. 1122.

'Wotan's Rhetoric of Anguish: Carolyn Abbate, *Unsung Voices*', *Journal of the Royal Musical Association*, vol. 118, Part 1, 1993, pp. 121-43.

➤ 'Rigoletto's Bottle: Psychoanalysis and Opera', *New Formations* ('Psychoanalysis and Culture' issue), No. 26, Autumn 1995, London: Lawrence and Wishart, 1995, pp. 108-19.

'A Fine and Private Place. Christopher Wintle reflects on recent performances of operas by Sir Harrison Birtwistle and Alexander Goehr in London, Glyndebourne and Konstanz', *The Musical Times*, November 1996, pp. 5-8.

'The Psychology of Opera' [edition of three essays by Hans Keller on (i) 'Three Psychoanalytic Notes on [Britten's] *Peter Grimes*' (ii) First Opera Performances in England [including Britten's *The Rape of Lucretia*]' (iii) 'Off and On [Britten's] *The Little Sweep*')] in: Hans Keller, *Music and Psychology. From Vienna to London (1939-52)*, ed. Christopher Wintle, London: Plumbago, 2003, pp. 121-56.

'Tristan à la mode?' (on Richard Wagner's *Tristan und Isolde*), *The Wagner Journal*, March 2010, vol. 4, No. 1, pp. 50-60 (review article).

'"Socrates Knew . . .": Affect (*Besetzung*) in Britten's *Death in Venice*', *Socrates in the Nineteenth and Twentieth Centuries*, ed. Michael Trapp, Aldershot: Ashgate, 2007, pp. 141-66.

'"Suddenly Finding it Really Matters": Psychology, Verdi, and Aristotelian Form', *Open Spaces*, issue 7, Fall 2005, pp. 225-40 (New York: supported financially by the Department of Music, Princeton University, NJ).

'The Dye-line Rehearsal Scores for *Death in Venice*', *Rethinking Britten*, ed. Philip Rupprecht, New York: Oxford UP, 2013, pp. 262-83. [This includes material from 'Socrates Knew ...' (above)]

Edition (with A. M. Garnham) of: Hans Keller, *Britten. Essays, Letters and Opera Guides*, London: Plumbago, 2013.

'Kundry's Baptism, Kundry's Death', *The Wagner Journal*, vol. 8, No. 3, 2014, pp. 4-18.

'Wagner's Spatial Style', *The Wagner Journal*, vol. 9, No. 3, 2015, pp. 4-23.

Edition of: Arnold Whittall, *The Wagner Style. Close Readings and Critical Perspectives*, London: Plumbago, 2015.

'Hard Acts Hard to Follow: Sophocles, Hofmannsthal, Strauss and *Elektra*' in: *The Shadow of the Object*, ed. Jonathan Burke, London: Karnac Books, 2018 (forthcoming).

2   Essays for Opera Guides and Programmes, Talks

▸ 'The Questionable Lightness of Being: Brünnhilde's Peroration to *The Ring*', *Twilight of the Gods* (Richard Wagner), English National Opera/Royal Opera Guide No. 31, ed. Nicholas John, London: John Calder, 1985, pp. 39-48.

'*Elektra* and the "Elektra Complex"' (including the author's 'Thematic Guide'), *Salome/Elektra* (Richard Strauss), English National Opera/Royal Opera Guide No. 37, ed. Nicholas John, London: John Calder, 1988, pp. 73-86.

▸ 'Which Traviata?', *La traviata* (Giuseppe Verdi), English National Opera, 1988 (three unnumbered pages).

▸ 'Towards a New Prologue', *Arianna* (Alexander Goehr/Claudio Monteverdi), The Royal Opera programme, 1995, pp. 29-33.

'Madness in the Method', *Elektra* (Richard Strauss), The Royal Opera, 2003; rev. as 'Music and Psychology: the Modernity of Strauss's *Elektra*', November 2008; reprinted as 'Music and Psychology', The Royal Opera, October 2013, pp. 21-6.

▸ 'The Beginnings of *Das Rheingold*', *Das Rheingold* (Richard Wagner), The Royal Opera programme, 2004, pp. 32-5.

▸ 'The Enlightened Sounds of Fate: the Prelude to *Un ballo in maschera*', *Un ballo in maschera* (Giuseppe Verdi), The Royal Opera programme, 2005, pp. 31-5; reprinted 2009; rev. as 'Verdi and the Jocular Macabre', The Royal Opera programme, 2014-15, pp. 42-7. (First version preferred.)

'Unthinking the Thinkable', *Siegfried* (Richard Wagner), The Royal Opera programme, October 2005, pp. 20-4.

'Fifty Years On: Rewriting the Rules', *The Midsummer Marriage* (Michael Tippett), The Royal Opera programme, October 2005, pp. 15-19.

▸ 'Sigmund Freud, the "Rule of Three" and Opera' (on various operas), talk to the North London Collegiate School for Girls, Edgware, 25 January 2007.

‣ '400 Years of Tempests', *The Tempest* (Thomas Adès), The Royal Opera programme, March 2007, pp. 40-1.

‣ 'Why *Stiffelio* Matters', *Stiffelio* (Giuseppe Verdi), The Royal Opera programme, April 2007, pp. 17-20.

‣ '*Rigoletto*: A Melodrama in Three Styles', *Rigoletto* (Giuseppe Verdi), The Royal Opera programme, July 2007, pp. 29-35; rev. as: '*Rigoletto*: A Melodrama of Two Styles', February 2009, pp. 28-35; reprinted 2010, 2014, 2018.

'Finding the Extremes', *Der Ring des Nibelungen* (Richard Wagner), The Royal Opera programme, October 2007, pp. 81-4; reprinted September 2012.

‣ 'Tragedy of Affliction or Bourgeois Drama?', *La traviata* (Giuseppe Verdi), The Royal Opera programme, January 2008, pp. 32-6; revised 2009; reset May 2010, pp. 27-30; various reprints to July 2017.

‣ 'From *Don Carlos* to *Don Carlo* – and Back', *Don Carlo* (Giuseppe Verdi), The Royal Opera programme June 2008, pp. 14-19; reprinted as: 'Fra *Don Carlos* til *Don Carlo* – og tilbake', *Don Carlo*, Den Norske Opera, trans. into Norwegian by Ole Jan Borgund, September 2008 [unpaginated]; reprinted, The Royal Opera programme, September 2009; rev. May 2013, pp. 12-17; further rev. May 2017, pp. 12-19. Reprinted as liner note for The Royal Opera DVD (EMI), 2010, with translations in German and French.

'Before Wagner and After: the Case of *Ariadne*', *Ariadne auf Naxos* (Richard Strauss), The Royal Opera programme, June 2008, pp. 30-4; reprinted 2014, 2015.

'*Der fliegende Holländer*: from Kernel to Crucible', *Der fliegende Holländer* (Richard Wagner), The Royal Opera programme, February 2009, pp. 25-9; reprinted 2011, 2015.

‣ 'Fear and Loathing in Ancient Aragon: the Music of *Il trovatore*', *Il trovatore* (Giuseppe Verdi), The Royal Opera programme, April 2009, pp. 36-41.

‣ 'A Beguiling Synopsis', *Aida* (Giuseppe Verdi), The Royal Opera programme, May 2010, pp. 13-17; reprinted March 2011, pp. 11-14. Reprinted as 'En Forlokkende Historie', Norwegian National Opera programme, April 2012, pp. 12-18.

'Character and Psychology', *Billy Budd* (Benjamin Britten), talk to Glyndebourne Opera Festival, 16 May 2010.

‣ '*Padre, Madre, Figlia*', *Simon Boccanegra* (Giuseppe Verdi), The Royal Opera programme, June 2010, pp. 41-5 (including ‣ 'A Note on the Title'); reprinted 2013.

‣ 'Maria, Mother, Pure Maid', *Tannhäuser* (Richard Wagner), The Royal Opera programme, December 2010, pp. 45-51 (including ‣ 'A Note on the Edition').

‣ 'Verdi's Endings' (on the last acts of *Rigoletto*, *Simon Boccanegra* and *Otello*), *Plácido Domingo Gala Performance*, The Royal Opera programme, 27 October 2011, pp. 27-33.

‣ 'Wagner's Satyr Play', *Die Meistersinger von Nürnberg* (Richard Wagner), The Royal Opera programme, December 2011, pp. 28-33.

‣ 'Verdi's Boccaccian Comedy', *Falstaff* (Giuseppe Verdi), The Royal Opera programme, 2012, pp. 31-6; reprinted 2015, 2018.

‣ 'Opera in Flux', *Written on Skin* (George Benjamin), The Royal Opera programme, 2013, pp. 25-31; reprinted as liner note for the Opus Arte DVD (2013); reprinted 2017.

▸ *'Rise and Fall of the City of Mahagonny'* (Bertolt Brecht and Kurt Weill), King's Opera programme, Desmond Tutu Bar, King's College London (Strand), March 2013, pp. 7-9; reduced reprint for The Royal Opera *Mahagonny,* digital app, 2015.

▸ 'Listening to *The Ring* with Auden' (Richard Wagner), Longborough Festival Opera, 2013 season programme, pp. 6-9.

▸ 'Happy Were He?' *Gloriana* (Benjamin Britten), The Royal Opera programme, June 2013, pp. 32-8.

▸ 'Wild Dionysiac Poetics', *Capriccio* (Richard Strauss), The Royal Opera programme (concert performances), July 2013, pp. 16-21.

▸ 'Fortunate Untruth', *Les Vêpres siciliennes* (Giuseppe Verdi), The Royal Opera programme, October 2013, pp. 36-41; reprinted 2017.

   (Three Britten-Centenary talks for BBC Radio 3:)
   ▸ 'Sources of Musical Invention', *Death in Venice* (Benjamin Britten), 9 October 2013.
   ▸ 'The Comic in Opera', *Albert Herring* (Benjamin Britten), 23 November 2013.
   ▸ 'Topic, Time and Decorum', *The Rape of Lucretia* (Benjamin Britten), 28 December 2013.

▸ 'Voicing *Parsifal*', *Parsifal* (Richard Wagner), The Royal Opera programme, November 2013, pp. 47-50.

 'A Case for Libretto Glasses', *Die Frau ohne Schatten* (Richard Strauss), The Royal Opera programme, March 2014, pp. 26-32.

▸ 'Play, Intermezzo and Opera', *Ariadne auf Naxos* (Richard Strauss), Insights Talk to The Royal Opera, 12 June 2014.

▸ 'The Tone in the Title', *Der Rosenkavalier* (Richard Strauss), The Royal Opera programme, December 2016, pp. 30-4.

▸ 'En vus ma mort, en vus ma vie', *Tristan und Isolde* (Richard Wagner), Longborough Festival Opera, 2017 season programme, pp. 28-9.

▸ 'The Pre-post-modernism of *The Magic Flute*', *Die Zauberflöte* (Wolfgang Amadeus Mozart), Longborough Festival Opera, 2017 season programme, pp. 58-9.

3   Opera, Opera-book and Conference Reviews

'The Orchestration of Comedy' (André-Ernest-Modeste Grétry: *Zémire et Azor*), *Times Literary Supplement*, 4 April 1980, p. 388.

'After the Tiger' (Alban Berg: *Lulu*), *Times Literary Supplement*, 27 February 1981, p. 226.

'Tolstoy in Translation' (Iain Hamilton: *Anna Karenina*), *Times Literary Supplement*, 5 June 1981, p. 634.

'Music for Words' (Anthony Burgess: *The Blooms of Dublin*), *Times Literary Supplement*, 12 February 1982, p. 160.

'The Comic Archetype' (Edward Cowie: *Commedia*), *Times Literary Supplement*, 5 March 1982, p. 252.

'Time and Space' (radio presentation of Goethe's *Faust*), *Times Literary Supplement*, 9 April 1982, p. 411.

'The Tone of a Tale' (Thea Musgrave, radio opera, *An Occurrence at Owl Creek Bridge*), *Times Literary Supplement*, 1 October 1982, p. 1066.

'For Womanly Times' (Ian McEwan and Michael Berkeley: oratorio, *Or Shall We Die?*), *Times Literary Supplement*, 18 February 1983, p. 156.

'Between Depot and Terminus' (Peter Maxwell Davies: *No. 11 Bus*), *Times Literary Supplement*, 30 March 1984, p. 346.

'Questions of Fidelity' (Michael Tippett: *The Midsummer Marriage*), *Times Literary Supplement*, 31 May 1985, p. 609.

'Entertaining Angels' (Karlheinz Stockhausen: *Donnerstag aus Licht*), *Times Literary Supplement*, 27 September 1985, p. 1064.

'Redeeming Angels' (Ludwig van Beethoven: *Fidelio*), *Times Literary Supplement*, 18 July 1986, p. 788.

> 'Mechanical Pastoral' (Tony Harrison and Harrison Birtwistle: *Yan Tan Tethera*), *Times Literary Supplement*, 22 August 1986, p. 914; reprinted in: *Tony Harrison*, ed. Neil Astley, Newcastle upon Tyne: Bloodaxe Books, 1991, pp. 314-15.

'Wars Without Reasons' (Aulis Sallinen: *The King Goes Forth to France*), *Times Literary Supplement*, 10 April 1987, p. 387.

'Pre-revolutionary Problems' (Craig Raine and Nigel Osborne: *The Electrification of the Soviet Union*), *Times Literary Supplement*, 16 October 1987, p. 1141.

'Centre of Attention' (Giuseppe Verdi: *Falstaff*), *Times Literary Supplement*, 30 September 1988, p. 1072.

'*Carmen*' (Georges Bizet), *The Wykehamist*, No. 1336, November 1988, pp. 15-16

> 'Celestial Sonorities' (Olivier Messiaen: *St. Francis of Assisi*), *Times Literary Supplement*, 23 December 1988, p. 1422.

'Elemental Sound and Fury' (Aribert Reimann: *Lear*), *Times Literary Supplement*, 3 February 1989, p. 111.

'Darkening Dreams' (Aribert Reimann: *Ein Traumspiel*), *Times Literary Supplement*, 3 March 1989, p. 233.

> 'The Quality of Love' (David Blake: *The Plumber's Gift*; The Garden Venture at the Donmar Warehouse), *Times Literary Supplement*, 9 June 1989, p. 638.

> 'The Fruitful and the Fruity' (Sergei Prokofiev: *The Love for Three Oranges*), *Times Literary Supplement*, 15 December 1989, p. 1391.

'A Tale Untold' (Helen Roe and Russell Hoban: *Some Episodes in the History of Miranda and Caliban*), *Times Literary Supplement*, 27 April 1990, p. 447.

'Wunderkind in the Modern Wilderness', (Wolfgang Amadeus Mozart: *Die Zauberflöte*), *Times Literary Supplement*, 1 June 1990, p. 583.

'Subverting the Sphinx' (Mark-Anthony Turnage: *Greek*), *Times Literary Supplement*, 5 October 1990, p. 1086.

'Allegorically Engaged' (Richard Wagner: *Siegfried*), *Times Literary Supplement*, 19 October 1990, p. 1128.

▸ 'The Furies Refuse to Rise' (Igor Stravinsky: *Oedipus rex*; Béla Bartók: *Duke Bluebeard's Castle*), *Times Literary Supplement*, 1 February 1991, p. 18.

▸ 'The Living Conflict' (Benjamin Britten: *Peter Grimes*), *Times Literary Supplement*, 26 April 1991, p. 15.

▸ 'Actors, Not Canaries' (Stephen Oliver: *Timon of Athens*), *Times Literary Supplement*, 24 May 1991, p. 18.

▸ 'Up Among the Gods' (Richard Wagner: *Das Rheingold*), *Times Literary Supplement*, 27 September 1991, p. 21.

▸ 'Standing in the Shadow' (Claude Debussy: *Pelléas et Mélisande*), *Times Literary Supplement*, 27 March 1992, p. 19.

▸ 'Richard Strauss: *Die Frau ohne Schatten*', *Times Literary Supplement*, 4 December 1992, p. 19.

▸ 'Leoš Janáček: *The Adventures of Mr. Brouček*', *Times Literary Supplement*, 8 January 1993, p. 16.

▸ '*Ariodante*: Baroque Opera or Handelian Music-drama? A Personal Response to an IAMS International Conference held at King's College London, 17-18 April 1993.' Unpublished review for the Institute of Advanced Musical Study (King's College London) Newsletter.

▸ 'A Suburban Squib' (Jules Massenet: *Chérubin*), *Times Literary Supplement*, 4 March 1994, p. 18.

▸ 'Leoš Janáček: *Kát'a Kabanová*', *Times Literary Supplement*, 25 March 1994, p. 17.

▸ 'Blonds Have Less Fun when the Woodbird Sings' (Judith Weir: *Blond Eckbert*), *Times Literary Supplement*, 6 May 1994, p. 18.

(*The* Ring *Cycle at The Royal Opera directed by Richard Jones:*)
'From Derision to Poignancy' (Richard Wagner: *Das Rheingold* and *Die Walküre*), *Times Literary Supplement*, 4 November 1994, pp. 20-1.
'Cleaving the Gas Cooker' (Richard Wagner: *Siegfried*), *Times Literary Supplement*, 14 April 1995, p. 18.
'A Gimcrack World' (Richard Wagner: *Götterdämmerung*), *Times Literary Supplement*, 3 November 1995, p. 19.

▸ 'Restitutions and Redemptions' (Benjamin Britten: *Billy Budd*), *Times Literary Supplement*, 16 June 1995, p. 23.

'The Lack of Love' (Richard Wagner: *Tristan und Isolde*), *Times Literary Supplement*, 23 February 1996, p. 19.

'*La traviata*' (Giuseppe Verdi), *Observer*, 15 September 1996, p. 11.

▸ 'Deity Dancing' (Rameau: *Les Fêtes d'Hébé*), *Observer*, 22 December 1996, p. 11.

▸ 'Kinder to the *Kinder*' (on Tom Sutcliffe's *Believing in Opera*), *Times Literary Supplement*, 3 January 1997, p. 20.

'Sexing the Cherub' (Jules Massenet: *Chérubin*), *Observer*, 5 January 1997, p. 11.

Index

When, in the main text, the title of a work appears in both its original language and translation, the original appears here. For reasons of space, singers are not indexed.